Praise for Ted Loder

"A creative and prophetic poet who will not stay i
—Dr. W. Paul Jones, Professor Emeritus, Saint Paul School of Theology

"To read Ted Loder is to hear a different drummer, a different tune . . . his prose is poetry. He hears what we strive so hard to hear: the inner meanings, the truth about ourselves and our relationships."
—Dr. William F. Fore, Executive Director, Communication Commission, National Council of Churches

"One of the prophetic voices of the future."
—Dr. Bob Edgar, President, School of Theology at Claremont; Former member of the United States House of Representatives

"Creative imagination is rare enough in our time, and when it appears under literary and theological discipline in a preacher, it is cause for celebration. Ted Loder brings his phenomenal gifts to ancient biblical stories, and in his lyrical, penetrating retelling of them we confront ourselves."
—Dr. B. Davie Napier, Professor Emeritus, Yale University; President Emeritus, Pacific School of Religion

"Ted breathes life into biblical paperdolls, scrubs them clean of their pious patina, and frees them to tell their stories of holy and profound interconnectedness. Again and again Loder blends holy and human skillfully to show that there is no place where God and humanity don't intertwine."
—*Minneapolis Star Tribune*

"[Loder] liberates the imagination to new experiences of God, grace, and the stuff of life."
—*Sojourners*

"[Loder] puts into words so much of what [we've] longed to say. It is his creativity, blended with penetrating honesty and unexpected humor, that lifts [his writing] out of the ordinary."
—*St. Anthony Messenger*

"[Loder] compels readers to level with themselves about some of the most intimately delicate areas of human life. To read Loder's writing is to look with penetrating honesty into one's own personality, relationship with God, and need for neighbor."
—Dr. William Muehl, Yale Divinity School

"[Loder offers] a gift of evocative images which name the things that we dread, confirm us in hope, and add color to our vision of God."
—Dr. John W. Vannorsdall, Former Chaplain, Yale University; President Emeritus, Lutheran Seminary, Philadelphia

"Loder's [words] are a lantern to illumine the wonders, terrors, and miracles of our passing days."
—Rev. William Sloane Coffin, Pastor Emeritus, Riverside Church, New York

"Loder helps us to stretch our experiences, our emotions, and our imaginations just a little bit more."
—Rev. William H. Gray, III, Senior Pastor, Bright Hope Baptist Church; President/CEO, United Negro College Fund

"I know no one else who so movingly and honestly brings us before God in [words] that touch the personal and the social dimensions of our lives."
—Tex Sample, Robert B. and Kathleen Professor Emeritus of Church and Society, Saint Paul School of Theology

Praise for *Guerrillas of Grace*

"An embarrassingly beautiful collection of prayers."
—Dr. William Muehl, Yale Divinity School

"These prayers liberate the imagination to new experiences of God, grace and the stuff of life."
—*Sojourners*

"Fresh, provocative, outrageous, funny, agonizing . . . always poetic, often prophetic."
—Rev. Robert Raines

"One of the best such collections I have ever read . . . a poet who articulates for us what we long to say."
—Bishop Forrest C. Stith, Bishop of the New York West Area of the United Methodist Church

Praise for *Wrestling the Light*

"If you haven't discovered the literary contributions of this preacher/prophet/poet/storyteller, let this new book be your joy . . . there's more grace in his poems and stories than in all the sweet talk about Jesus in America."
—*Circuit Rider*

"Ted Loder gives expression to our human struggle to meet God in our living and our dying . . . he touches what is most human in himself and invites us to find grace along With him."
—Dr. Herbert R. Reinelt, Professor of Philosophy, University of the Pacific

"A robust book that will enrich anyone who wants an authentic word of faith in today's world . . . catapults us past the surface to the wonder and mystery of God's grace."
—Rev. Dr. Arvin R. Luchs, Conference Council Director, Oregon-Idaho Annual Conference, The United Methodist Church

"A conversation with God that fills the heart, exposes the insecurities, and renews the spirit . . . sheds the usual saccharin certainties and makes God the very bread of life."
—Dr. Carvn McTighe Musil, Feminist Educator, National Fellow, Association of American Colleges

"A breath-taking peep at a grace-filled, high spirited God . . . Loder fans will not be disappointed!"
—*Faith at Work Magazine*

Praise for *The Haunt of Grace*

"*The Haunt of Grace* is up close and personal—about the speaker, and about us. We know we're being grabbed. But I like the full pack of Loder's Hounds of Heaven at my heels: wit, poetry, language, challenge, acute observation, emotion."
—David Ogston, Parish Minister, St. John's Kirk of Perth, Scotland; Author of *White Stone Country*

"Loder's words, frank, compassionate and personal, call to us through the wilderness of modernity; they help us recognize signs of the transcendent and gain our bearings again."
—Dr. Bob Edgar, General Secretary, The National Council of the Churches of Christ in the USA

"Ted Loder has been a beacon for a whole generation . . . he has shown us how to combine creativity and social witness . . . and fired our imaginations. *The Haunt of Grace* reveals the spirit behind this lifelong witness and shares the joy—and heartache—that lie at its generous and ever-hopeful heart."
—J. Barrie Shepherd, Minister Emeritus, The First Presbyterian Church in the City of New York; Author of a dozen books of poetry and meditation

"In our largely secular country, Ted Loder's *The Haunt of Grace* teaches us how to see God's footprints in everyday occurrences and hear God's whispers for social justice and forgiveness in the faces we pass daily. Loder's words illuminate God's mystery and give us courage to surrender to it."'
—Caryn McTighe Musil, Vice President, Diversity, Equity, and Global Initiatives, Association of American Colleges and Universities, Washington, DC

Praise for *Tracks in the Straw*

"[Loder] gives us glimpses of the awesome, startling, and life-changing power of the nativity by presenting this oft-told story from fresh perspectives . . . Congregations will want to read some of these stories aloud in small groups or in the sanctuary."
—*Values & Visions*

"Ted Loder's *Tracks in the Straw* is a read-aloud Christmas storybook from one point of view and a spur to deeper insights from another. In this age of aggressive Christmas commercialism, *Tracks in the Straw* is a refreshing offering and can be appreciated on many different levels of understanding, from children to grandparents. What a Christmas gift to us all!"
—*Pathways*

"The splendid new stories in the revised edition of *Tracks in the Straw* are deep and intriguing, and draw us toward a fresh experience of the nativity through the eyes of unlikely participants in the first Christmas. The new personal prologue and epilogue reveal Ted Loder's keen eye for holy mystery, and I'd buy a new copy just for those! The new arrangement, with readings for each day in Advent, makes this book a read-aloud antidote for the crazy commercialism of the season."
—Marjory Zoet Bankson, President, Faith at Work

"*Tracks in the Straw* is brilliantly and compassionately written. It tells 'the old story differently,' in vivid and engaging ways, powerfully demonstrating the Advent experience in the lives of real people in real situations. It is a MUST-READ for all who long to experience Christmas in a rich, new way. You'll not only want to read the stories this Christmas season but every Christmas to come."
—Mary Scullion, RSM, Co-founder, Project H.O.M.E., Philadelphia

Breathe

Restlessness

into

Me

The Subversive and Inspired Poems and Meditations of

TED LODER

Breathe Restlessness into Me

FORTRESS PRESS
MINNEAPOLIS

BREATHE RESTLESSNESS INTO ME

The Subversive and Inspired Poems and Meditations of Ted Loder

Portions of this book were previously published in the following titles:
Guerrillas of Grace: Prayers for the Battle copyright © 1984, 2004, 2023 Estate of Ted Loder, admin.
Wrestling the Light: Ache and Awe in the Human-Divine Struggle copyright © 1991 Innisfree Press Inc., 2004 Augsburg Fortress.
The Haunt of Grace: Responses to the Mystery of God's Presence copyright © 2002 Estate of Ted Loder, admin.,
Published by Innisfree Press Inc., 2004 Augsburg Fortress.
Tracks in the Straw: Tales Spun from the Manger copyright © 1985,
1997 Innisfree Press Inc., 2005 Augsburg Fortress.

Library of Congress Control Number: 2023943802 (print)

Cover design: Laurie Ingram
Cover image: Watercolor and gouache abstract oval frame of landscape, bird, sky, and moon.
Yuliya Derbisheva/iStock

Print ISBN: 978-1-5064-8886-8
eBook ISBN: 978-1-5064-8887-5

Contents

Guerrillas of Grace: Prayers for the Battle

Wrestling the Light: Ache and Awe in the Human-Divine Struggle

The Haunt of Grace: Responses to the Mystery of God's Presence

Tracks in the Straw: Tales Spun from the Manger

Guerrillas of Grace

PRAYERS FOR THE BATTLE

For Jan . . .
guerrilla of grace,
companion in faith,
gift of joy.

Ground Me in Your Grace

Eternal One,
    Silence
        from whom my words come;
    Questioner
        from whom my questions arise;
    Lover
        of whom all my loves are hints;
    Disturber
        in whom alone I find my rest;
    Mystery
        in whose depths I find healing
            and myself;
enfold me now in your presence;
    restore to me your peace;
        renew me through your power;
            and ground me in your grace.

Probing

Why would anyone call a book of prayers *Guerrillas of Grace*? The two images, "guerrillas" and "grace," seem to be an unlikely, if not contradictory, conjunction. And yet . . . are they really?

Somewhere I read a description of poets as "guerrillas of beauty." I suppose it is fitting that I can't find the article, or even identify it, but the phrase struck me and took captive a piece of my imagination, as if demonstrating the power of the image. Or maybe it would be more accurate to say the phrase *liberated* a piece of my imagination. I began to see "guerrillas of beauty" as applying to the risky and exciting struggles of people attempting to live out their faith in more free and joyful ways in the midst of difficult, resistant, often even oppressive circumstances. I began to understand the phrase as applying well to people who pray and to the prayers they utter.

Yet, as important as I believe beauty is, and as powerful as I have experienced it to be, I think it is even more provocative to call those who pray, and the prayers themselves, "guerrillas of grace."

The notion of guerrillas seems to be rooted in the ancient Judeo-Christian tradition. The Old Testament prophets can easily be conceived of as guerrillas doing battle with the established powers of their day; and their thundering, poetic words and images surely can be read as forms of prayer. Certainly Jesus was the preeminent guerrilla of grace; he confronted repressive institutions and liberated captive minds and hearts with his words and his life. A prime weapon in his effort was prayer, and it is little wonder that he taught his disciples to pray.

The early Christians understood and rallied to Paul's battle cry: "For we are not contending against flesh and blood, but against principalities, against powers, against the world rulers of this present darkness . . . " They, along with Christians across the ages, confirmed the idea that we are guerrillas.

There are two or three characteristics of guerrillas that give particular relevance to the use of that image to describe Christians. By any of our usual measures, guerrillas are a weaker force set against a superior and more organized power, a power that exerts both subtle and blatant pressures to conform. Such pressures are not commonly or quickly perceived or interpreted as oppressive, but frequently something in them is experienced as, at least, vaguely stifling to the spirit.

Guerrillas, then, are engaged in the battle to reclaim some territory, or some part of life, for a higher purpose, a truer cause. To wed guerrilla with grace suggests that the truer cause is God's kingdom. Since the "principalities and powers" are never completely "out there," but also stomp and rumble "within," a significant piece of the life to be reclaimed or liberated is the pray-er themself. In an unavoidable way, the struggle begins—and begins again and again and again—with choosing sides. Choose one side and you're a conformist; choose another and you're a guerrilla!

Doesn't "guerrilla" describe the contemporary church in many third world countries? Christians in those countries have been cut off from typical religious support systems, yet have survived and grown in obviously hostile environments. Wasn't Dr. Martin Luther King Jr.'s civil rights movement in the 1960s a nonviolent guerrilla force, born and nurtured in the Black church? Don't you suppose prayer was a critical part of what those Christians were about?

It is also important to note that guerrillas usually work in groups. In some fashion we never pray alone. We always pray toward someone and with someone—namely, whoever resides within us as teacher, friend, enemy, burden, brother, sister, spirit. However private our prayers may seem, we are still the cloud of witnesses when we pray (just as we are when we think or act). So the prayers in this volume, though framed in personal terms, could easily be used as corporate prayers, and in many instances have been. The point is that both grace and guerrilla are relational terms.

And finally, guerrillas are never quite so desperate as they are confident. They believe they are fighting on the winning side, in spite of any and all appearances to the contrary. We have to be exceedingly careful in even considering this characteristic, for abuses perpetrated by religious arrogance are all too evident and painful. Still, guerrillas are willing to give their lives, if necessary, because they believe the cause for which they struggle, and which struggles in them, will finally prevail. Even so, the prayer is always saying, one way or another, ". . . thy kingdom come."

Yet, prayer is always against the odds set by logic, by scientism, by realism. So, it is always against the odds of our own skepticism and doubt. Even when prayer is inchoate in something that sounds like a curse or a moan or a desperate plea or a spontaneous "whoopee," there is a gut-deep, intuitive refusal to accept the odds or to calculate too closely either the limits of the possible or the sneakiness of grace.

When the prayer is more intentional, the guerrilla raid may at least suspend those odds for a bit longer and open the one who prays to broader dimensions of reality than we have entertained before. Once that happens, there can never again be quite an end of it. Some part of us is taken captive or set free, and that shift changes the world a little. At those moments we also (and rightly) refuse to calculate what might be changed in the world beyond us, what might be gracefully released in it by our prayers.

It may be presumptuous to call oneself, and one's prayers, "guerrillas of grace." Grace is the sole property of God. It distinguishes the quality of God's love from human love. But then, how does grace become operative in the world? What is the process? Admittedly, those are large and complicated questions about which volumes have been and will be written, and which are beyond the scope of this introduction.

Still, one simple answer, and wondrous, is that God's grace operates in the world quite independently of us. Prayer is one way of attempting to focus on grace, to pay attention to it, to praise it. The French mystic Simone Weil is right in saying, "Perfect attention is prayer." Surely it is true that any attempts to be attentive, however imperfect, are also prayers. Imagination is crucial to paying attention, for attention is far more than observation. Imagination involves penetrating something, or being open to being penetrated by something, in order to sense its meaning, its possibilities, its depths, its "story."

Another simple answer, and equally wondrous, is that praying itself is part of the process by which grace becomes operative in the world. The prayer becomes a participating point of the entry and expansion of grace, so that Augustine is also right in saying, "Without God, we cannot; without us, God will not."

In this sense imagination is crucial as a way of prefiguring the shape or course the future may take. Imagination is an indispensable faculty in the process of deciding and acting toward the future. Thus, prayer can be playful because the imagination plays with possibilities, putting them together in different combinations before we begin to enact them. Since children are naturally adept at such play, perhaps that is one reason Jesus said, "Unless you turn and become as children, you will never enter the kingdom of heaven." Since prefiguring is an ongoing process, the imagination is always engaged in adjusting and reformulating. Thus, the future is always being partly created by the imagination of the prayer and the pray-er.

Therefore, since paying attention is one condition of prayer, the occasion of attending is a guerrilla action through which grace takes, or liberates, new ground in the praying person. Yet, through the mysterious dynamics of exchange, prayers and pray-ers themselves are the guerrilla action by which grace helps shape the future: ". . . without us, God will not." Prayer, through the process of imagination, becomes part of the answer to the remainder of the question, "Without us, God will not do *what*?" Prayer, as is faith or hope or love, is always guerrilla action in the world of time on behalf of the eternal.

Personally, my prayers happen in two ways. The first way, I believe, is nearly universal: the urgent, spontaneous outbursts, if not of half-formed words, fragmented and fleeting, then surely of a surge of emotions, sensations of awe or wonder or yearning that suddenly flood in and overflow to connect me, perhaps only in dim awareness, to the springs and rhythms of life and its impenetrable mysteries. I suppose only mystics and poets could, or should, even attempt to communicate these kinds of prayers with others, though these prayers are perhaps the most common. They are intensely personal and the type I most frequently mutter or moan.

The second way my prayers happen is as the more articulated works of my imagination. These are the kind of prayers contained in this book. Imagination is a basic faculty of faith and poetry, indeed, of any creative act. Imagination is surely one quality of God's image in us, just as is the capacity to love. For me, imagination is a way of gathering up the present and the immediate past—the things, persons, experiences to which I have been attentive, or sometimes just dully present—and putting them into images, into language that I hurl toward God and toward the future. Prayer is one way I participate in the ongoing creation. Prayer, through imagination, opens me and (I am presumptuous enough to contend) opens the future to new options, different possibilities. Imagination is a way of reinterpreting the past, re-viewing the present, and previewing the future and the way I can act toward it. Imagination is a way of interrupting the programs for repetition into which I so easily set myself.

I have heard, with only partial understanding but with imagination, that the images of artists and poets often precede and instruct scientific discovery. If that is in any way true, the implications boggle the mind. Could it be that the images of poets and artists (and prayers) not only precede scientific discovery in some instances but that they actually help *create* what the scientist later discovers? Indeed, could prayer be one of the fundamental ways "the universe becomes conscious of itself," to use that intriguing phrase by which some cosmologists explain not only how the universe seems to be unfolding, but why it is unfolding at all? But enough! I have strayed into depths well over my head.

Still, the depths themselves are an essential condition to acknowledge in prayer, at least for me. Depths swirl about the word "mystery," affirming that when we have to do with God, deep mystery is always one of the first conditions that pertain. God always out-distances our thoughts, words, knowledge, creeds, litanies, lives; outdistances them either because God is too simple for us to apprehend, or too complex for us to comprehend, or both.

An illustrative instance of what I am suggesting is the effort to de-sexualize the language and thinking of the church and to apply traditionally "feminine" characteristics to God. Such an effort is accurate and overdue! It opens us to dimensions of God we have missed, and opens to God ways of being with us that have been denied. This experience of opening demonstrates what the richness of the depths of mystery means when referred to God, and how attentively exploring those depths liberates more territory for grace. That we explore those depths, and they us, makes us guerrillas of grace. But the unfathomable quality of mystery reminds us that it is the grace of God that we are exploring.

Mystery means that, in spite of all our efforts, all our insights, discoveries, and experiences, we will never do much more than touch the hem of God's robe. It is enough that such touching brings healing. It is too much, idolatrously too much, to claim more than very little information about the wearer of the robe. And even that little information, we can claim only with enormous humility. However, humility is the twin of trust.

It has been said, referring to the temptation to which biblical literalists often succumb, that we should never confuse the love letter with the lover. We all have our version of such literalism, our dogmaticisms, our exaggerated (if unadmitted) claims of knowledge. Humble acknowledgement of mystery delivers us from the imprisonment of such certainties into the awesome dimensions of possibilities. Trust begins there. So, in some primitive way, does prayer.

Historically, the church has used the term "holy" to refer to what I mean by the word "mystery." My bias for the word mystery is grounded in the awareness that holiness is a term that often has been too well defined and too aggressively applied in too many inquisitions. Jesus gave the mystery a personal name, as did the prophets, but Jesus did not thereby eliminate or domesticate the mystery. The point is, mystery simply reminds us that God is free to be God in ways we have no knowledge of at all.

Since God is free to respond to prayers in surprising, sneaky ways (you may have noticed I like the word "sneaky") that no one can prescribe, we also are free to do new things, pray new ways, imagine new images, find different words. We are never required to be liturgical literalists. We are never restricted merely to repeating the prayers of our tradition, however beautiful and helpful. Nor are there "right" prayers, or "right" ways of praying, or "right" words with which to pray. Guerrillas *extend* grace, not encapsulate it.

So, the second way I pray, articulating from my imagination, involves work! There are people who insist that the only prayers that are valid are those offered spontaneously at the immediate inspiration of the Holy Spirit. Such prayers certainly are valid, but they are also usually more inchoate than inspired or inspiring, and they tend to be repetitious and dull. I believe the Holy Spirit inspires me just as well when I am struggling to think, to attend, to write, to find the appropriate words, symbols, images that will open me, and perhaps those who pray with me, to those new perceptions and possibilities that hint of grace.

Poet John Ciardi states that the poets' morality resides in "never cheapening their choices" of words or images. I concur and think it is almost immoral for a person consistently to cheapen their prayer choices by trying to avoid the cost of paying attention, for attention does have a cost. I think it is almost immoral, and certainly lazy, for anyone not to work carefully and honestly to shape prayers, since ". . . without us, God will not." And probably "God will not" without our best efforts! Who dares to be a sloppy guerrilla? Who deserves one?

So, my attempts to pray, to use my imagination as I pray, involve three factors. The first is to express—through words, images, symbols—what I see, feel, attend to, and experience, but to do so in ways that both sharpen my awareness and perhaps provide me and my companion guerrillas a shift in perception, a slightly different way of seeing, interpreting, and responding to life. In that shift, however slight, I believe my prayers are already being answered. The guerrilla process has begun because the shift involves probing, reaching, playing with different images and options that are changing me. Grace is sneaky!

The second aspect of imaginative praying is to be open to words, thoughts, feelings, visions, and alternatives that bubble up or float down when I am struggling to find a way to be honest and creative and to have some integrity in that prayer process. Sometimes the muse does ride, or better, the Spirit does move. But often the impulse or image that comes seems, at first blush, to be too radical or profane or outrageous to be acceptable or to use. But that may be exactly the time to work at staying open and following the lead, the intuition, the inspiration. Passion, which is surely part of praying just as centering and quietness are, is not always nice or proper! Unfortunately, passion seldom seems to be part of what we have been taught is involved in being religious or praying. Passion touches on one reason I like the prayer included in this volume that adds to the familiar phrase describing God as being the one "from whom no secrets are hid" another phrase: "and none need to be."* Grace is sneaky, not superficial.

The third factor in my praying is to let my prayer carry me. I saw an expression somewhere that asked, "If you aren't carried away, why go?" There is at least some delightful truth in that, except that the rest also needs saying: namely, for the most part, you don't get carried away if you don't hoist your sails to the wind by doing the work of preparation and persistence.

But often, because of our anxieties about control and losing it, when the wind starts to blow, we tend to lower our sails. Once new possibilities start to emerge, once the future gets imaged differently, once the impulse tugs to try an option other than the familiar rut, then the inner and outer argument begins. The limits of what is possible start to get calculated "realistically" again. The ballast of odds becomes heavy. The territory that had begun to be freed by the guerrillas of grace gets retaken by the armies of conformity and caution. Is this true for you, too, or do I refer only to myself?

* *"I Am So Thankful to Be Alive," page 34*

It has taken me a long time and hard struggle even to begin to wrestle effectively with this third factor. Mostly it still pins me without giving me a blessing. I've discovered that it has something to do with expectations. On the one hand, we can expect too much, too fast, and give up praying when it doesn't happen. Jesus, and saints since, have said much about this danger. Yet, on the other hand, we can get frightened and give up praying when different options do emerge and we are nudged toward them. However much we talk about our longing for change in ourselves and the world, the actual prospect of that change, and the cost of it in terms of engaging in battle with the powers of conformity, produces some ambivalence at best. Ambivalence generates resistance. It is hard to get carried away when we're hanging on tightly to the familiar.

I'm discovering that getting carried away doesn't necessarily mean moving at the speed of light or to the gates of heaven (or whatever you envision as a quick escape, or a safe haven from the toil and trouble of change). It may mean being carried away as a stoker on a slow freighter, as it were. For me, the process of being carried away does happen slowly, even painfully, albeit joyfully, an inch a day, another at night, for a lifetime. But I am getting there. Grace is sneaky and persistent!

Being carried away also involves, for me, some intentional participation in the mystery, some attempt to embody the images and exhibit the perceptions of some piece of my prayers. It involves willingly, perhaps foolishly, taking the risk about which we are warned in the old joke, "Be careful what you pray for; you may get it." But, isn't that possibility precisely why prayers are guerrillas of grace?

So you see, I cannot believe that praying doesn't make a difference. If it doesn't, what else could?

For at last I believe life itself is a prayer,
    and the prayers we say shape the lives we live,
just as the lives we live shape the prayers we say;
    and it all shapes the kingdom which expresses itself in and among us,
        and for which we are guerrillas.
I hope these prayers help you to take some new territory,
    to liberate imaginatively some part of your life,
        my sister and brother guerrillas.
            ". . . thy kingdom come . . ."

—Ted Loder

Prayers OF QUIETNESS & LISTENING

Listen to Me Under My Words

O God,
I come to you now
as a child to my Mother,
out of the cold which numbs
into the warm who cares.
Listen to me inside,
under my words
where the shivering is,
in the fears
which freeze my living,
in the angers
which chafe my attending,
in the doubts
which chill my hoping,
in the events
which shrivel my thanking,
in the pretenses
which stiffen my loving.

Listen to me, Lord,
as a Mother,
and hold me warm,
and forgive me.
Soften my experiences
into wisdom,
my pride
into acceptance,
my longing
into trust,
and soften me
into love
and to others
and to you.

Guide Me into an Unclenched Moment

Gentle me,
Holy One,
into an unclenched moment,
    a deep breath,
        a letting go
            of heavy expectancies,
                of shriveling anxieties,
                    of dead certainties,
that, softened by the silence,
    surrounded by the light,
        and open to the mystery,
I may be found by wholeness,
    upheld by the unfathomable,
        entranced by the simple,
            and filled with the joy
                that is you.

Hear Me Quickly, Lord

Hear me quickly, Lord,
for my mind soon wanders to other things
    I am more familiar with
        and more concerned about
            than I am with you.
O Timeless God, for whom I do not have time,
catch me with a sudden stab of beauty
    or pain
        or regret
that will catch me up short for a moment
to look hard enough at myself—
    the unutterable terror
        and hope within me
and, so, to be caught by you.

Words will not do, Lord.
Listen to my tears,
    for I have lost much
        and fear more.
Listen to my sweat,
    for I wake at night
        overwhelmed by darkness and strange dreams.
Listen to my sighs,
    for my longing surges like the sea—
        urgent, mysterious, and beckoning.
Listen to my heart beat,
    for I want to live fully
        and stay death forever.
Listen to my breathing,
    for I gulp after something like holiness.
Listen to my clenched teeth,
    for I gnaw at my grudges
        and forgive myself as reluctantly
            as I forgive others.

Listen to my growling gut,
for I hunger for bread and intimacy.
Listen to my curses,
for I am angry at the way the world
comes down on me sometimes,
and I sometimes on it.
Listen to my cracking knuckles,
for I hold very tightly to myself
and anxiously squeeze myself into others' expectations,
and them into mine,
and then shake my fists at you
for disappointing me.
Listen to my sex,
for I seek fulfillment
through the man-woman differences
and beyond the differences,
a new, common humanity.
Listen to my footfalls,
for I stumble to bring good tidings to someone.
Listen to my groans,
for I ache toward healing.
Listen to my worried weariness,
for my work matters much to me
and needs help.
Listen to my tension,
for I stretch toward accepting who I am
and who I cannot be.
Listen to my wrinkles,
for growing years make each day
singularly precious to me
and bring eternity breathtakingly close.

Listen to my hunched back,
for sometimes I can't bear
the needs and demands of the world anymore
and want to put it down,
give it back to you.
Listen to my laughter,
for there are friends and mercy,
and the day grows longer,
and something urges me to thank.
Listen to my humming,
for sometimes I catch all unaware
the rhythms of creation,
and then music without words
rises in me to meet it,
and there is the joy of romping children
and dancing angels.
Listen to my blinking eyes,
for at certain moments
when sunlight strikes just right,
or stars pierce the darkness just enough,
or clouds roll around just so,
or snow kisses the earth into quietness,
everything is suddenly transparent,
and crows announce the presence of another world,
and dogs bark at it,
and something in me is pure enough
for an instant
to see your kingdom in a glance,
and so to praise you in a gasp—
quick,
then gone,
but it is enough.
Listen to me quickly, Lord.

Calm Me into a Quietness

Now,
O Lord,
calm me into a quietness
that heals
and listens,
and molds my longings
and passions,
my wounds
and wonderings
into a more holy
and human
shape.

I Need to Breathe Deeply

Eternal Friend,
grant me an ease
to breathe deeply of this moment,
  this light,
    this miracle of now.
Beneath the din and fury
  of great movements
    and harsh news
      and urgent crises,
make me attentive still
  to good news,
    to small occasions,
      and the grace of what is possible
        for me to be,
          to do,
            to give,
              to receive,
that I may miss neither my neighbor's gift
  nor my enemy's need.

Precious Lord,
grant me
    a sense of humor
        that adds perspective to compassion,
    gratitude
        that adds persistence to courage,
    quietness of spirit
        that adds irrepressibility to hope,
    openness of mind
        that adds surprise to joy;
that with gladness of heart
I may link arm and aim
with the One who saw signs of your kingdom
    in salt and yeast,
        pearls and seeds,
            travelers and tax collectors,
                sowers and harlots,
                    foreigners and fishermen,
and who opens my eyes with these signs
    and my ears with the summons
        to follow to something more
            of justice and joy.

In the Silence, Name Me

Holy One,
untamed
by the names
I give you,
in the silence
name me,
that I may know
who I am,
hear the truth
you have put into me,
trust the love
you have for me,
which you call me to live out
with my sisters and brothers
in your human family.

Help Me Listen

O Holy One,
I hear and say so many words,
yet yours is the word I need.
Speak now,
and help me listen;
and, if what I hear is silence,
    let it quiet me,
        let it disturb me,
            let it touch my need,
                let it break my pride,
                    let it shrink my certainties,
                        let it enlarge my wonder.

It Would Be Easier to Pray if I Were Clear

O Eternal One, it would be easier for me to pray
 if I were clear
  and of a single mind and a pure heart;
 if I could be done hiding from myself
  and from you, even in my prayers.
But, I am who I am,
 mixture of motives and excuses,
  blur of memories,
   quiver of hopes,
 knot of fear,
  tangle of confusion,
   and restless with love, for love.
I wander somewhere between
 gratitude and grievance,
  wonder and routine,
   high resolve and undone dreams,
    generous impulses and unpaid bills.
Come, find me, Lord.
Be with me exactly as I am.
Help me find me, Lord.
 Help me accept what I am,
  so I can begin to be yours.
Make of me something small enough to snuggle,
 young enough to question,
  simple enough to giggle,
   old enough to forget,
    foolish enough to act for peace;
 skeptical enough to doubt
  the sufficiency of anything but you,
 and attentive enough to listen
  as you call me out of the tomb of my timidity
   into the chancy glory of my possibilities
    and the power of your presence.

Grant Me an Enchantment of Heart

O God of children and clowns,
as well as martyrs and bishops,
somehow you always seem to tumble
a jester or two of light
through the cracks of my proud defense
into the shadows of my sober piety.
Grant me, now, an enchantment of heart
that, for a moment, the calliope of your kingdom
may entice my spirit, laughing,
out of my sulky self-preoccupations
into a childlike delight
in the sounds and silences
that hum of grace;
so I may learn again
that life is never quite as serious as I suppose,
yet more precious than I dare take for granted,
even for a moment;
that I may be released
into the possibilities of the immediate,
and rush,
smudge-souled as I am,
to join the parade of undamned fools
who see the ridiculous in the sublime,
the sublime in the ridiculous;
and so dare to take pratfalls for love,
walk tightropes for justice,
tame lions for peace,
and rejoice to travel light,
knowing there is little I have or need
except my brothers and sisters to love,
you to trust,
and your stars to follow home.

Lead Me Out of My Doubts and Fears

Eternal God,
lead me now
    out of the familiar setting
        of my doubts and fears,
    beyond my pride
        and my need to be secure
into a strange and graceful ease
    with my true proportions
        and with yours;
that in boundless silence
    I may grow
        strong enough to endure
            and flexible enough to share
                your grace.

Give Me Ears to Hear

Lord,
I believe
    my life is touched by you,
        that you want something for me,
            and of me.
Give me ears
    to hear you,
eyes
    to see the tracing of your finger,
and a heart
    quickened by the motions
        of your Spirit.

Prayers OF THANKS & PRAISE

Praise from All Creatures

Praise be to you, O Lord,
who spins shining stars across the wondrous heavens
    and stretches out the seas,
who lifts the dawn into place
    and sets boundaries for night,
who awes the earth with storms
    and gentles it with green,
who gives everything a season
    and breathes life and love into the dust of me.
Praise be to you.

Praise in all things,
    for all things:
the soft slant of sunlight,
    the sweat of battle,
a song in the wilderness,
    the evening breeze,
the deep breath,
    the tended wound,
mercy, quietness, a friend;
for the miracles of the daily,
    the mysteries of the eternal.
Praise be to you.

Praise from all creatures,
    laughers and list-makers,
        wonderers and worriers,
            poets and plodders and prophets,
                the wrinkled, the newborn,
                    the whale, and the worm,
                        from all, and from me.
Praise, praise be to you
for amazing grace.

Bless What Eludes My Grasp

Lord, so many things skitter through my mind,
and I give chase to gather them
and hold them up in a bunch to you,
but they go this way and that
while I go that way and this . . .
So, gather me up instead,
and bless what eludes my grasp but not yours:
trees and bees, fireflies and butterflies,
roses and barbecues, and people . . .
Lord, the people . . . bless the people:
birthday people,
giving birth people,
being born people;
conformed people,
dying people,
dead people;
hostaged people,
banged-up people,
held down people;
leader people,
lonely people,
limping people;
hungry people,
surfeited people,
indifferent people;
first-world people,
second-world people,
third-world people;
one-world people,
your people,
all people.
Bless them, Lord.
Bless what eludes my grasp but not yours.

Praise Be to You for Life

Praise be to you, O Lord, for life
    and for my intense desire to live;
praise be to you for the mystery of love
    and for my intense desire to be a lover;
praise be to you for this day
    and another chance to live and love.

Thank you, Lord,
    for friends who stake their claim in my heart,
    for enemies who disturb my soul and bump my ego,
    for tuba players,
        and storytellers,
            and trapeze troupes.
Thank you, Lord,
    for singers of songs,
    for teachers of songs,
        who help me sing along the way,
    . . . and for listeners.
Thank you, Lord,
    for those who attempt beauty
        rather than curse ugliness,
    for those who take stands
        rather than take polls,
    for those who risk being right
        rather than pandering to be liked,
    for those who do something
        rather than talking about everything.

Lord, grant me grace, then,
and a portion of your spirit
that I may so live
    as to give others cause
        to be thankful for me,
thankful because I have not forgotten
    how to hope,
        how to laugh,
            how to say, "I'm sorry,"
    how to forgive,
        how to bind up wounds,
            how to dream,
    how to cry,
        how to pray,
    how to love when it is hard,
        and how to dare when it is dangerous.
Undamn me, Lord,
that praise may flow more easily from me
    than wants,
thanks more readily
    than complaints.
Praise be to you, Lord, for life;
praise be to you for another chance to live.

I Praise You for What Is Yet to Be

Wondrous Worker of Wonders,
I praise you, not alone for what has been,
or for what is,
but for what is yet to be,
for you are gracious beyond all telling of it.

I praise you
that out of the turbulence of my life
a kingdom is coming,
is being shaped even now
out of my slivers of loving,
my bits of trusting,
my sprigs of hoping,
my tootles of laughing,
my drips of crying,
my smidgens of worshiping;
that out of my songs and struggles,
out of my griefs and triumphs,
I am gathered up and saved,
for you are gracious beyond all telling of it.

I praise you
that you turn me loose
to go with you to the edge of now and maybe,
to welcome the new,
to see my possibilities,
to accept my limits,
and yet begin living to the limit
of passion and compassion
until, released by joy,
I uncurl to other people
and to your kingdom coming,
for you are gracious beyond all telling of it.

Thank You for Each Moment

Lord, thank you for each moment,
for the blue-sky moment,
the softening earth, the freshening wind,
for the sap flowing,
the bird nesting, the yellow bush,
for my full heart,
and the joy rising in me.
Soften me
to receive whatever comes as a gift
and to praise you in it.

Lord, thank you for each moment,
for the twilight moment,
the pause, the good tired,
for the quiet reflection,
the slowing down, the mysterious sunset,
for my contented heart,
and the wisdom growing inside me.
Gentle me
to feel whatever comes as a gift
and to praise you in it.

Lord, thank you for each moment,
for the midnight moment,
the loneliness, the fretful wondering,
for the watchful stars,
the long ache, the sleepless wait,
for my restless heart,
and the hope straining in me.
Focus me
to see whatever comes as a gift
and to praise you in it.

Lord, thank you for each moment,
for the high-noon moment,
the job, the necessary routine,
for the sweaty struggle,
the high-risk challenge, the impulse to change,
for my fierce heart,
and the courage gathering in me.
Ground me
to wrestle with whatever comes as a gift
and to praise you in it.

Lord, thank you for each moment,
for the shared moment,
the listening, the unguarded word,
for the fragile openness,
the ready smile, the accepted difference,
for my passionate heart,
and the trust rooting in me.
Stretch me
to grow with whatever comes as a gift
and to praise you in it.

Lord, thank you for each moment,
for the charged moment,
the confrontation, the accurate demand,
for the hard decision,
the breathless gamble, the unexpected growing,
for my intense heart,
and the truth expanding in me.
Excite me
to be open to whatever comes as a gift
and to praise you in it.

Lord, thank you for each moment,
for the holy moment,
the music, the child's eyes,
for the sunlight,
the touch, the tears,
for the trembling pleasure,
the unutterable beauty, the breathing,
for the life and love and heart in me, aware,
and the wholeness spreading in me.
Touch me
through whatever comes as a gift
that I may be graceful
and praise you in it all.

I Am So Thankful to Be Alive

Persistent Friend, Insistent Enemy,
from whom no secret is hid (and none need to be),
out of the thoughts and feelings which whirl within,
I grope for language to carry to you my secrets
and all the wonders that seize my heart.
Praise be to you
for holding me in the womb of mystery
through all the eons of creation until now,
and raising me to life
in this time and place.

I am so thankful to be alive—
breathing, moving, sensing,
wide-eyed, cock-eared alive—
in this mysterious instant,
at this luminous time,
on this nurturing earth,
this blue pearl of great price
whirling through uncharted space,
attended by vigilant stars;
during these days of chance and battle,
with streaks of hope and holiness on the horizon,
touched by nature's pleading beauty
and friendship's steady hold.

I am so thankful to be alive—
eyes in love with seeing,
ears in love with hearing,
heart in love with attending,
mind in love with connecting;
eager to miss no message of grace
in the ballet of beauty
or in the cramp of struggle
of this incredible gift of life;

attentive to all the clues of love,
daringly and outlandishly
scattered for me through Jesus's life,
overturning habit and hate;
attentive to the dreams he renews,
the wounds he heals,
the promises he nails up
for me to step out on.

I am so thankful to be alive,
thankful for those times
when the rhythms of my life
catch the cadences of your kingdom,
when there is a lightening in me
for a moment,
when the creep of courage
allows me to dare to serve the gifts
you have put in me;
thankful for the neighbors you have put beside me
and the possibilities you have put before me;
thankful for the surge of determination to accept difficulty
not as an excuse for passivity
but as a goad to creativity,
as the door to abundant life,
and the seed of a peace the world cannot take away,
as it takes away so much else.

I am so thankful to be alive,
O Persistent Friend, Insistent Enemy;
hold me always in the womb of mystery,
and raise me again and again, forever,
to life,
and to love,
and to the claims of your kingdom.

O God of Timelessness and Time

O God of timelessness
  and time,
I thank you for my time
and for those things that are yet possible
  and precious in it:
    daybreak and beginning again,
      midnight and the touch of angels,
        the taming of demons in the dance of dreams;
a word of forgiveness,
  and sometimes a song,
for my breathing . . . my life.

Thank you
for the honesty which marks friends
  and makes laughter;
for fierce gentleness
  which dares to speak the truth in love
    and tugs me to join the long march toward peace;
for the sudden gusts of grace
  which rise unexpectedly in my wending from dawn to dawn;
for children unabashed,
  wind rippling a rain puddle,
    a mockingbird in the darkness,
      a colleague and a cup of coffee;
for all the mysteries of loving,
  of my body next to another's body;
for music and silence,
  for wrens and Orion,
    for everything that moves me to tears,
      to touching,
        to dreams,
          to prayers;
for my longing . . . my life.

Thank you
for work
which engages me in an internal debate
between right and reward
and stretches me toward responsibility
to those who pay for my work,
and to those who cannot pay
because they have no work;
for justice
which repairs the devastations of poverty;
for liberty
which extends to the captives of violence;
for healing
which binds up the broken bodied and broken hearted;
for bread broken
for all the hungry of the earth;
for good news
of love which is stronger than death;
and for peace
for all to sit under fig trees and not be afraid;
for my calling . . . my life.

Thank you
for the sharp senses of the timeless stirring in my time,
and your praise in my heart;
for the undeniable awareness, quick as now,
that the need of you is the truth of me,
and your presence with me is the truth of you,
which sets me free
for others,
for joy,
and for you;
for your grace . . . my life . . . forever.

Prayers OF UNBURDENING & CONFESSION

Empty Me

Gracious and Holy One,
creator of all things
and of emptiness,
I come to you
full of much that clutters and distracts,
stifles and burdens me,
and makes me a burden to others.
Empty me now
of gnawing dissatisfactions,
of anxious imaginings,
of fretful preoccupations,
of nagging prejudices,
of old scores to settle,
and of the arrogance of being right.
Empty me
of the ways I unthinkingly think of myself as powerless,
as a victim,
as determined by sex, age, race,
as being less than I am,
or as other than yours.
Empty me
of the disguises and lies
in which I hide myself from other people
and from my responsibility
for my neighbors and for the world.
Hollow out in me a space
in which I will find myself,
find peace and a whole heart,
a forgiving spirit and holiness,
the springs of laughter,
and the will to reach boldly
for abundant life for myself
and the whole human family.

Drive Me Deep to Face Myself

Lord, grant me your peace,
for I have made peace
with what does not give peace,
and I am afraid.
Drive me deep, now,
to face myself so I may see
that what I truly need to fear is
my capacity to deceive
and willingness to be deceived,
my loving of things
and using of people,
my struggle for power
and shrinking of soul,
my addiction to comfort
and sedation of conscience,
my readiness to criticize
and reluctance to create,
my clamor for privilege
and silence at injustice,
my seeking for security
and forsaking the kingdom.
Lord, grant me your peace.
Instill in me such fear of you
as will begin to make me wise,
and such quiet courage
as will enable me to begin to make
hope visible,
forgiving delightful,
loving contagious,
faith liberating,
peacemaking joyful,
and myself open and present
to other people
and your kingdom.

Loosen My Grip

O God, it is hard for me to let go,
most times,
and the squeeze I exert
garbles me and gnarls others.
So, loosen my grip a bit
on the good times,
on the moments of sunlight and starshine and joy,
that the thousand graces they scatter as they pass
may nurture growth in me
rather than turn to brittle memories.

Loosen my grip
on those grudges and grievances
I hold so closely,
that I may risk exposing myself
to the spirit of forgiving and forgiveness
that changes things and resurrects dreams and courage.

Loosen my grip
on my fears
that I may be released a little into humility,
and into an acceptance of my humanity.

Loosen my grip
on myself
that I may experience the freedom of a fool
who knows that to believe
is to see kingdoms, find power, sense glory;
to reach out
is to know myself held;
to laugh at myself
is to be in on the joke of your grace;
to attend to each moment
is to hear the faint melody of eternity;
to dare love
is to smell the wildflowers of heaven.

Loosen my grip
on my ways and words,
on my fears and fretfulness
that letting go
into the depths of silence
and my own uncharted longings,
I may find myself held by you
and linked anew to all life
in this wild and wondrous world
you love so much,
so I may take to heart
that you have taken me to heart.

Release Me from the Dark Fury

O Holy and Haunting Presence
whose spirit moves quietly
    but surely
in the sound and fury of the world
    and of my life,
you know me
    as rushing water knows the rock
        and releases its beauty
            to reflect new light.
Open me
    to the insistent abrasiveness of your grace,
        for I often trivialize love
            by abandoning the struggles
                which accompany its joys
            and rejecting the changes
                which lead to its fulfillments.
Release me
    from the dark fury
        of assuming I am unloved
    when the day calls for sacrifice
        and the night for courage.

Release me
from the ominous fear
of thinking some sin
or failure of mine
can separate me from you
when life demands hard choices,
and the battle, high risks.
Release me
from the dangerous illusions
of independence
when the human family summons me
to the realities and promises
of interdependence
among races, sexes, nations.
Release me
from being possessed
by riches I do not need
and grievances that weary me
when you call me to share
my very self
with neighbors,
and to reflect for the world
the light of the kingdom
within me.

What Can I Believe?

O God, I am so fragile:
    my dreams get broken,
    my relationships get broken,
    my heart gets broken,
    my body gets broken.

What can I believe,
    except that you will not despise a broken heart,
    that old and broken people shall yet dream dreams,
    and that the lame shall leap for joy,
        the blind see,
            the deaf hear.

What can I believe,
    except what Jesus taught:
    that only what is first broken, like bread,
        can be shared;
    that only what is broken
        is open to your entry;
    that old wineskins must be ripped open and replaced
        if the wine of new life is to expand.

So, I believe, Lord;
help my unbelief
    that I may have courage to keep trying
        when I am tired,
    and to keep wanting passionately
        when I am found wanting.

O God, I am so frail:
my life spins like a top,
bounced about by the clumsy hands
of demands beyond my doing,
fanned by furies
at a pace but half a step from hysteria,
so much to do,
my days so few and fast-spent,
and I mostly unable to recall
what I am rushing after.

What can I believe,
except that beyond the limits
of my little prayers and careful creeds,
I am not meant for dust and darkness
but for dancing life and silver starlight.

Help my unbelief
that I may have courage
to dare to love the enemies
I have the integrity to make;
to care for little else
save my brothers and sisters of the human family;
to take time to be truly with them,
take time to see,
take time to speak,
take time to learn with them
before time takes us;
and to fear failure and death less
than the faithlessness
of not embracing love's risks.

God, I am so frantic:
somehow I've lost my gentleness
in a flood of ambition,
lost my sense of wonder
in a maze of videos and computers,
lost my integrity
in a shuffle of commercial disguises,
lost my gratitude
in a swarm of criticisms and complaints,
lost my innocence
in a sea of betrayals and compromises.

What can I believe,
except that the touch of your mercy
will ease the anguish of my memory;
that the tug of your spirit
will empower me to help carry now the burdens
I have loaded on the lives of others;
that the example of Jesus
will inspire me to find again my humanity.

So, I believe, Lord;
help my unbelief
that I may have courage
to cut free from what I have been
and gamble on what I can be,
and on what you
might laughingly do
with trembling me
for your incredible world.

Unlock the Door of My Heart

Jesus said,
"Your sins are forgiven;
rise and walk."
Forgiveness is an unlocked door
to walk through
into a wide-whoopee-open world.
Forgiveness is a seed
to water with new dreams and wild risks
until it bears unexpected fruit.
Forgiveness is an enemy-friend
to be born out of,
a quietness beneath the clamor.
Forgiveness is a flower to smell,
a wind at my back,
a gull to scream with,
a pain to laugh beneath,
a burden that carries me.
It is I
becoming We
becoming Yours.
Forgiveness is a song to sing.
O Lord,
unlock the door of my heart.

There Are Things I Do Care About

Holy One,
most of the time
you don't seem very close or real to me—
only a word, an ought,
a longing, maybe, a hope—
and, for the most part,
I don't care much about you,
and that is the not-so-pretty truth of it.

But there are things I do care about:
myself mostly,
and some people I feel close to—
families, friends, children,
most of all children.
I do care what happens to them.

So, I do care about love,
about being loved,
and about loving
(or trying to);
and I wonder about it,
how to do it,
and what makes me want to do it.

With those close to me,
I care about laughing,
and crying,
and learning,
and talking honestly (a little);
and fighting openly and fairly,
and forgiving (a bit more),
and admitting I want to be forgiven
and need to be (once in awhile).

I care about things,
about getting them
and being gotten by them;
And I do care about money
and all the things I do for it,
and with it,
and what it does to me;
And I care about being a little freer
of all that, somehow,
because I care about being secure
core deep.

I care about my neighbors,
at least some of them,
sometimes;
and about all the things that would make it better,
and perhaps easier
for us to live together;
and the hard decisions and sacrifices
it would take for that to happen.

Which means I do care about justice,
though mostly from a distance,
because I care about what it might require of me;
and then I get testy or silent
but am haunted by it
because something in me
won't let me stop caring about it,
even though I often wish I could.

So, I care about my enemies,
and am tired of being angry
and suspicious so much,
which is such a waste;
and I care about the least—
the hungry
and the sick
and the terrorized
and the exploited of the earth—
because I care about peace
and long for it inside and out,
and am weary of being afraid
for myself and the children.

I care about this tiny fragile blue planet,
this home, this mother earth and all her offspring,
all the creatures who share the mystery of life.
And I really do care about beauty,
about the songs in me,
the poems, the stories;
I care deeply about
the wondrous, puzzling,
aching struggle
that I am;
I care about this joy I feel
flickering sometimes, flaring sometimes,
when I touch hands or eyes
or minds or sexes or souls,
and ache, then, for more.

I care about living—
living more fully,
abundantly—
and about my urgent longing for that;
I care about what makes me restless,
makes me reach
and stretch
and grope for words,
for dreams,
for other people,
and . . .
for you.

Holy One, you,
I do care about you,
sometimes fiercely,
or I wouldn't be stumbling along like this,
trying to pray,
trying to put myself in your way;
I care about you,
and such is my faith,
however faltering it is;
and I trust that, past words
you care about all these things
that I care about,
care about them more,
infinitely more,
than I care about them;
and that you care for me,
even when I am careless
of the things I care about.

There Is Something I Wanted to Tell You

Holy One,
there is something I wanted to tell you,
but there have been errands to run,
    bills to pay,
        arrangements to make,
            meetings to attend,
                friends to entertain,
                    washing to do . . .
and I forget what it is I wanted to say to you,
    and mostly I forget what I'm about,
        or why.
O God,
don't forget me, please,
for the sake of Jesus Christ.

Eternal One,
there is something I wanted to tell you,
but my mind races with worrying and watching,
    with weighing and planning,
        with rutted slights and pothole grievances,
            with leaky dreams and leaky plumbing
                and leaky relationships I keep trying to plug up;
and my attention is preoccupied
    with loneliness,
        with doubt,
            and with things I covet;

and I forget what it is I wanted to say to you,
    and how to say it honestly
        or how to do much of anything.
O God,
don't forget me, please,
for the sake of Jesus Christ.

Almighty One,
there is something I wanted to ask you,
but I stumble along the edge of a nameless rage,
haunted by a hundred floating fears
    of terrorists of all kinds,
        of losing my job,
            of failing,
    of getting sick and old,
        of having loved ones die,
            of dying,
    of having no one love me,
        not even myself,
    and of not being sure who I am
        or that I am worth very much,
            and . . .
I forget what the real question is that I wanted to ask,
    and I forget to listen anyway
        because you seem unreal and far away,
            and I forget what it is I have forgotten.

O God,
don't forget me, please,
for the sake of Jesus Christ.

O Father and Mother in Heaven,
perhaps you've already heard what I wanted to tell you.
What I wanted to ask is
forgive me,
heal me,
increase my courage, please.
Renew in me a little of love and faith,
and a sense of confidence,
and a vision of what it might mean
to live as though you were real,
and I mattered,
and everyone was sister and brother.
What I wanted to ask in my blundering way is
don't give up on me,
don't become too sad about me,
but laugh with me,
and try again with me,
and I will with you, too.
What I wanted to ask is
for peace enough to want and work for more,
for joy enough to share,
and for awareness that is keen enough
to sense your presence
here,
now,
there,
then,
always.

I Remember Now in Silence

Lord,
plunge me deep into a sense of sadness
at the pain of my sisters and brothers
inflicted by war,
prejudice,
injustice,
indifference,
that I may learn again to cry as a child
until my tears baptize me
into a person who touches with care
those I now touch in prayer:
victims of violence,
of greed,
of addictions;
prisoners in ghettos,
in old age,
in sexism;
people with broken bodies,
with broken hearts,
with broken lives,
whom I remember now in silence before you
because I have too often forgotten them
in the shuffle of my fretful busyness.

Prayers FOR COMFORT & REASSURANCE

Sometimes It Just Seems to Be Too Much

Sometimes, Lord,
it just seems to be too much:
too much violence, too much fear;
too much of demands and problems;
too much of broken dreams and broken lives;
too much of war and slums and dying;
too much of greed and squishy fatness
and the sounds of people
devouring each other
and the earth;
too much of stale routines and quarrels,
unpaid bills and dead ends;
too much of words lobbed in to explode
and leaving shredded hearts and lacerated souls;
too much of turned-away backs and yellow silence,
red rage and the bitter taste of ashes in my mouth.
Sometimes the very air seems scorched
by threats and rejection and decay
until there is nothing
but to inhale pain
and exhale confusion.
Too much of darkness, Lord,
too much of cruelty
and selfishness
and indifference . . .

Too much, Lord,
too much,
too bloody,
bruising,
brainwashing much.

Or is it too little,
too little of compassion,
too little of courage,
of daring,
of persistence,
of sacrifice;
too little of music
and laughter
and celebration?

O God,
make of me some nourishment
for these starved times,
some food for my brothers and sisters
who are hungry for gladness and hope,
that, being bread for them,
I may also be fed
and be full.

God . . . Are You There?

God . . . are you there?
I've been taught
and told I ought
to pray.
But the doubt
won't go away;
yet neither
will my longing to be heard.
My soul sighs
too deep for words.
Do you hear me?
God . . . are you there?

Are you where love is?
I don't love well,
or often,
anything
or anyone.
But, when I do,
when I take the risk,
there's a sudden awareness
of all I've missed;
and it's good,
it's singing good.
For a moment
life seems as it should.
But, I forget, so busy soon,
that it was,
or what
or whom.
Help me!
God . . . are you there?

How Shall I Pray?

How shall I pray?
Are tears prayers, Lord?
Are screams prayers,
or groans
or sighs
or curses?
Can trembling hands be lifted to you,
or clenched fists
or the cold sweat that trickles down my back
or the cramps that knot my stomach?
Will you accept my prayers, Lord,
my real prayers,
rooted in the muck and mud and rock of my life,
and not just my pretty, cut-flower, gracefully arranged
bouquet of words?
Will you accept me, Lord,
as I really am,
messed-up mixture of glory and grime?
Lord, help me!
Help me to trust that you do accept me as I am,
that I may be done with self-condemnation
and self-pity,
and accept myself.
Help me to accept you as you are, Lord:
mysterious,
hidden,
strange,
unknowable;
and yet to trust
that your madness is wiser
than my timid, self-seeking sanities,
and that nothing you've ever done
has really been possible,
so I may dare to be a little mad, too.

Gather Me to Be with You

O God, gather me now
to be with you
as you are with me.
Soothe my tiredness;
quiet my fretfulness;
curb my aimlessness;
relieve my compulsiveness;
let me be easy for a moment.

O Lord, release me
from the fears and guilts
which grip me so tightly;
from the expectations and opinions
which I so tightly grip,
that I may be open
to receiving what you give,
to risking something genuinely new,
to learning something refreshingly different.

O God, gather me
to be with you
as you are with me.
Forgive me
for claiming so much for myself
that I leave no room for gratitude;
for confusing exercises in self-importance
with acceptance of self-worth;
for complaining so much of my burdens
that I become a burden;
for competing against others so insidiously
that I stifle celebrating them
and receiving your blessing through their gifts.

O God, gather me
    to be with you
        as you are with me.
Keep me in touch with myself,
    with my needs,
        my anxieties,
            my angers,
                my pains,
                    my corruptions,
that I may claim them as my own
rather than blame them on someone else.

O Lord, deepen my wounds
    into wisdom;
shape my weaknesses
    into compassion;
gentle my envy
    into enjoyment,
        my fear into trust,
            my guilt into honesty,
                my accusing fingers into tickling ones.

O God, gather me
    to be with you
        as you are with me.

I Want So to Belong

O God, I want so to belong;
    teach me to accept.
I want to be close;
    teach me to reach out.
I want a place where I am welcome;
    teach me to open my arms.
I want mercy;
    teach me to forgive.
I want beauty;
    teach me honesty.
I want peace;
    show me the eye of the storm.
I want truth; show me the way to question
    my unquestionable convictions.
I want joy;
    show me the way of deeper commitment.
I want life;
    show me how to die.

Sustain Me in the Coming Then

O God, empty me of angry judgments,
    and aching disappointments,
        and anxious trying,
and breathe into me
    something like quietness
        and confidence,
that the lion and the lamb in me
    may lie down together
        and be led by a trust
as straightforward as a little child.

Catch my pride and doubt off guard
that, at least for the moment,
I may sense your presence
    and your caring,
and be surprised
    by a sudden joy
        rising in me now
to sustain me in the coming then.

I Have So Few Ways to Pray

Lord,
I have so few ways to pray,
    but you have so many ways to answer.
Keep me alert
    to your unpredictable answers,
        to your unexplainable surprises,
and by your grace,
make me one of those surprises,
for the sake of the One
    who taught us the surprises
        of moving mountains,
            healing touches,
                wondrous stories,
                    great banquets,
                        first suppers,
                            broken bread,
                                crosses,
                                    and resurrections.

Remind Me of Your Steady Power

O God,
this is a hard time,
a season of confusion,
a frantic rush
to fill my closets,
my schedule,
and my mind,
only to find myself empty.

Give me hope, Lord,
and remind me
of your steady power
and gracious purposes
that I may live fully.
Renew my faith
that the earth is not destined
for dust and darkness,
but for frolicking life
and deep joy
that, being set free
from my anxiety for the future,
I may take the risks of love
today.

Waken in Me a Gratitude for My Life

O God, complete the work you have begun in me.
Release through me
  a flow of mercy and gentleness that will bring
  water where there is desert,
  healing where there is hurt,
  peace where there is violence,
  beauty where there is ugliness,
  justice where there is brokenness,
  beginnings where there are dead ends.
Waken in me
  gratitude for my life,
  love for every living thing,
  joy in what is human and holy,
  praise for you.
Renew my faith that you are God,
  beyond my grasp
    but within my reach;
  past my knowing
    but within my searching;
  disturber of the assured,
    assurer of the disturbed;
  destroyer of illusions,
    creator of dreams;
  source of silence and music,
    sex and solitude,
      light and darkness,
        death and life.
O Keeper of Promises, composer of grace,
grant me glee in my blood,
    prayer in my heart,
      trust at my core,
        songs for my journey,
          and a sense of your kingdom.

I Teeter on the Brink of Endings

O God of endings,
you promised to be with me always,
even to the end of time.
Move with me now in these occasions of last things,
of shivering vulnerabilities and letting go:
letting go of parents gone,
past gone,
friends going,
old self growing;
letting go of children grown,
needs outgrown,
prejudices ingrown,
illusions overgrown;
letting go of swollen grudges and shrunken loves.
Be with me in my end of things,
my letting go of dead things,
dead ways,
dead words,
dead self I hold so tightly,
defend so blindly,
fear losing so frantically.
I teeter on the brink of endings:
some anticipated, some resisted,
some inevitable, some surprising,
most painful;
and the mystery of them quiets me to awe.
In silence, Lord, I feel now
the curious blend of grief and gladness in me
over the endings that the ticking and whirling of things brings;
and I listen for your leading
to help me faithfully move on through the fear
of my time to let go
so the timeless may take hold of me.

Prayers FOR RESTORATION & RENEWAL

I Am in Need of . . . of What?

Well, God,
I made it through another sweet-sour time,
and here I am,
nibbled,
frazzled,
puzzled,
awed,
and in need of . . . of what?
A chuckle, maybe,
a revolution begun with a belly laugh,
a Bronx cheer in the face of the onslaughts
of disaster and death itself.
Such is my need;
and this is my wonder:
Are you really as humorless,
as grimly serious
as I have made you out to be?
Or do aardvarks and monkeys,
bullfrogs and platypuses,
puppies and porpoises,
and people, perhaps,
reveal the comic side of your grace,
the playful side of your love?
Tickle me into giggling down
the wailing walls
of my endless grievances,
and trip up my waddling pomposities.

Lord of laughter, as of tears,
shake me awake
and teach me to laugh at myself,
at my black-draped solemnity,
over my petty preoccupation with success and failure,
through all the hurt and adversity
until my laughter lures me deep
beneath the terrors without names,
beneath the questions without answers,
beneath the pain without relief;
lures me deep
to the love in me unused,
to the strength unspent,
to the courage untapped,
to the dream unrisked,
to the beauty unexpressed;
all the way down
to the inescapable bottom,
to the awareness that I must get on
with being who I am
as fully as I can,
as unflinchingly as I can,
as accurately as I can,
which is to say,
as gracefully,
as powerfully,
as faithfully
as you have created me to be.

Make Me Simple

O Ingenious God,
I rejoice in your creation,
and pray that your Spirit touch me so deeply
that I will find a sense of self
    which makes me glad to be who I am
        and yet restless
            at being anything less
                than I can become.
Make me simple enough
    not to be confused by disappointments,
clear enough
    not to mistake busyness for freedom,
honest enough
    not to expect truth to be painless,
brave enough
    not to sing all my songs in private,
compassionate enough
    to get in trouble,
humble enough
    to admit trouble and seek help,
joyful enough
    to celebrate all of it,
        myself and others and you
through Jesus Christ our Lord.

Draw Me to Yourself

In this moment
draw me to yourself, Lord,
and make me aware
not so much of what I've given
as of all I have received
and so have yet to share.
Send me forth
in power and gladness,
and with great courage
to live out in the world
what I pray and profess,
that, in sharing,
I may do justice,
make peace,
grow in love,
enjoy myself,
other people,
and your world now,
and you forever.

Help Me Unbury Wonder

O God of the miracles,
of galaxies
and crocuses
and children,
I praise you now
from the soul of the child within me,
shy in my awe,
delighted by my foolishness,
stubborn in my wanting,
persistent in my questioning,
and bold in my asking you
to help me unbury my talents
for wonder
and humor
and gratitude,
so I may invest them eagerly
in the recurring mysteries
of spring and beginnings,
of willows that weep,
and rivers that flow,
and people who grow
in such endlessly amazing
and often painful ways;
that I will be forever linked and loyal
to justice and joy,
simplicity and humanity,
Christ and his kingdom.

Let Wonder Have Its Way with Me

O God, your gracious Spirit
moves over the mysteries of living and dying
and is strangely present to me
in the falling leaves,
the call of the wild geese,
a child's birth,
the light in a friend's eyes,
the sudden lifting of the heart,
and the deep longing which brings me to you now.
Make me aware of your presence
that wonder may have its way with me,
my passion be released,
my confidence renewed in the depths of your holiness
until, for a moment,
my longing for you be fulfilled
and I know I am really free
to share bread and intimacy,
to laugh and exchange mercy,
to be at ease in my struggles,
bold in my loving,
brave in facing down my terror,
hopeful in the rising music of your kingdom,
joyful in my living,
and graceful in my life becoming
a song of praise ever sung to you.

Let Something Essential Happen to Me

O God,
let something essential happen to me,
something more than interesting
or entertaining,
or thoughtful.
O God,
let something essential happen to me,
something awesome,
something real.
Speak to my condition, Lord,
and change me somewhere inside where it matters,
a change that will burn and tremble and heal
and explode me into tears
or laughter
or love that throbs or screams
or keeps a terrible, cleansing silence
and dares the dangerous deeds.
Let something happen in me
which is my real self, God.

O God,
let something essential and passionate happen in me now.
Strip me of my illusions of self-sufficiency,
of my proud sophistications,
of my inflated assumptions of knowledge
and leave me shivering as Adam or Eve
before the miracle of the natural—
the miracle of this earth
that nurtures me as a mother
and delights me as a lover;

the miracle of my body
    that breathes and moves,
        hungers and digests,
            sees and hears;
    that is creased and wrinkled and sexual,
        shrinks in hurt,
            and swells in pleasure;
    that works by the most amazing messages
        of what and when and how
            coded and curled in every cell,
    and that dares to speak the confronting word.

O God,
let something essential and joyful happen in me now,
something like the blooming of hope and faith,
    like a grateful heart,
        like a surge of awareness
            of how precious each moment is,
that now, not next time,
now is the occasion
    to take off my shoes,
        to see every bush afire,
            to leap and whirl with neighbor,
                to gulp the air as sweet wine
until I've drunk enough
    to dare to speak the tender word:
        "Thank you";
            "I love you";
            "You're beautiful";
                "Let's live forever beginning now";
                    and "I'm a fool for Christ's sake."

Gentle My Desperation

Come, Lord Jesus,
touch me
  with love, life-giving as light,
to quiet my anger a little
  and gentle my desperation,
to soften my fears some
  and soothe the knots of my cynicism,
to wipe away the tears from my eyes
  and ease the pains in my body and soul,
to reconcile me to myself
  and then to the people around me,
    and then nation to nation,
that none shall learn war anymore,
  but turn to feed the hungry, house the homeless,
    and care compassionately for the least of our brothers and sisters.
Reshape me in your wholeness
to be a healing person, Lord.

Come, Lord Jesus,
expand me
  by your power, life-generating as the sea,
to accept
  and use my power,
to do something I believe in
  and be something more of who I mean to be
    and can be,
to inspire me to dream and move,
  sweat and sing,
    fail and laugh,
      cuss and create,
to link my passion with courage,
  my hope with discipline,
    my love with persistence,

to enable me to learn from difficulties,
grow in adversities,
gain wisdom from defeats,
perspective from disappointments,
gracefulness from crises,
and find joy in simply living it all fully.
Release me through your power
to be a powerful person, Lord.

Come, Lord Jesus,
startle me
with your presence, life-sustaining as air,
to open my heart
to praise you,
to open my mind
to attend you,
to open my spirit
to worship you,
to open me
to live my life
as authentically and boldly as you lived yours.

Come, Lord Jesus,
be with me
in my longing;
come, stay with me
in my needing;
come, go with me
in my doing;
come, struggle with me
in my searching;
come, rejoice with me
in my loving.

Keep Me in Touch with My Dreams

O Lord,
in the turbulence
    and the loneliness
        of my living from day to day
            and night to night,
keep me in touch with my roots,
    so I will remember where I came from
        and with whom;
keep me in touch with my feelings,
    so I will be more aware of who I really am
        and what it costs;
keep me in touch with my mind,
    so I will know who I am not
        and what that means;
and keep me in touch with my dreams,
    so I will grow toward where I want to go
        and for whom.

O Lord,
deliver me
    from the arrogance of assuming
        I know enough to judge others;
deliver me
    from the timidity of presuming
        I don't know enough to help others;
deliver me
    from the illusion of claiming I have changed enough
        when I have only risked little,
that, so liberated,
    I will make some of the days to come different.

O Lord,
I ask not to be delivered
from the tensions that wind me tight,
but I do ask for a sense of direction in which to move once wound,
a sense of humor about my disappointments,
a sense of respect for the elegant puzzlement of being human,
and a sense of gladness for your kingdom
which comes in spite of my fretful pulling and tugging.

O Lord,
nurture in me
the song of a lover,
the vision of a poet,
the questions of a child,
the boldness of a prophet,
the courage of a disciple.

O Lord,
it is said you created people
because you love stories.
Be with me as I live out my story.

Quicken in Me a Sense of Humor

O God of gifts,
quicken in me a sense of humor
    bright enough to help me find my way
        in these tarnished times,
    fruitful enough to be made the wine of hope
        to warm the hearts of those I live with.
Make me glad to be one of a kind,
    yet one with a kind,
        called not to be more like others
            but more of myself,
                a guerrilla of grace,
                    that, in daring to be authentic,
                        I may become more of a human-kind.

So, O God of gifts,
liberate me to share,
    without apology or arrogance,
        not only the gifts I have
            but the gift I am.

Set Me Free

Lord of wondrous patience,
the earth has risen again,
emerging
from a darkness
in a way it has never quite been before;
whirling
to a fresh time,
an unused space;
alive
with trembling possibilities,
and I with it!
Such staggering grace!
Please,
nurture me in newness;
set me free from the tyrannies
of habit
and complaining
and blaming;
shake from me the dusty melancholy
of too much success and comfort,
pride and pretense,
that, as if on the first day of creation,
I may begin to see
the miracle of life and humanity;
to hear
the hum of grace
unfolding to meet all my needs,
unexpectedly and surprisingly,
and urging me to go on in faith
to whatever is next in love.

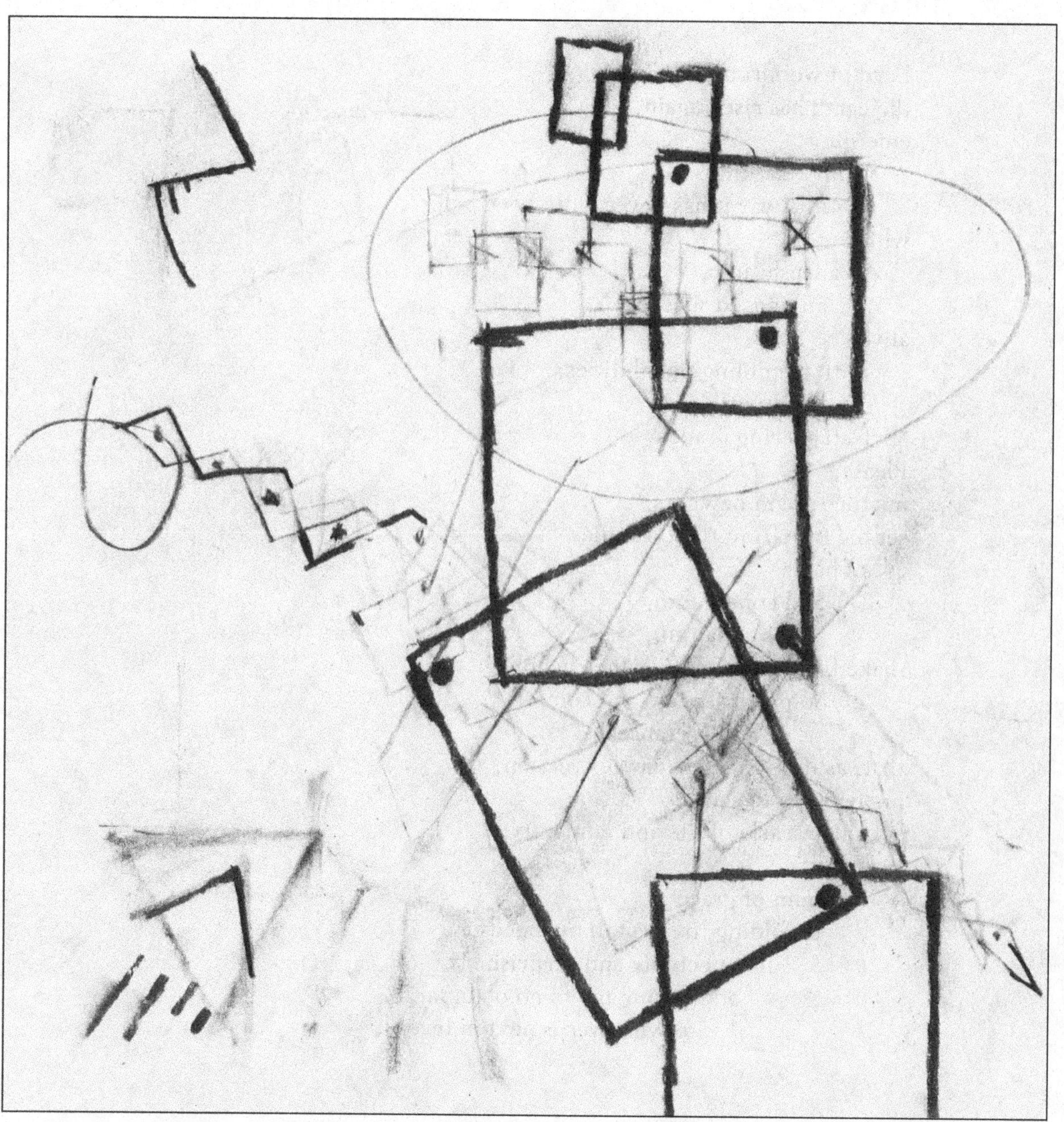

Prayers
OF COMMITMENT & CHANGE

Pry Me Off Dead Center

O persistent God,
deliver me from assuming your mercy is gentle.
Pressure me that I may grow more human,
    not through the lessening of my struggles
    but through an expansion of them
    that will undamn me
    and unbury my gifts.
Deepen my hurt
    until I learn to share it
    and myself
    openly,
    and my needs honestly.
Sharpen my fears
    until I name them
    and release the power I have locked in them
    and they in me.
Accentuate my confusion
    until I shed those grandiose expectations
    that divert me from the small, glad gifts
    of the now and the here and the me.
Expose my shame where it shivers,
    crouched behind the curtains of propriety,
    until I can laugh at last
    through my common frailties and failures,
    laugh my way toward becoming whole.

Deliver me
    from just going through the motions
    and wasting everything I have
    which is today,
        a chance,
            a choice,
                my creativity,
                    your call.

O persistent God,
let how much it all matters
pry me off dead center
so if I am moved inside
    to tears
        or sighs
            or screams
                or smiles
                    or dreams,
they will be real
and I will be in touch with who I am
and who you are
and who my sisters and brothers are.

Help Me to Believe in Beginnings

God of history and of my heart,
so much has happened to me during these whirlwind days:
    I've known death and birth;
    I've been brave and scared;
    I've hurt, I've helped;
    I've been honest, I've lied;
    I've destroyed, I've created;
    I've been with people, I've been lonely;
    I've been loyal, I've betrayed;
    I've decided, I've waffled;
    I've laughed, and I've cried.
You know my frail heart and my frayed history—
and now another day begins.

O God, help me to believe in beginnings
and in my beginning again,
no matter how often I've failed before.

Help me to make beginnings:
    to begin going out of my weary mind into fresh dreams,
        daring to make my own bold tracks in the land of now;
    to begin forgiving
        that I may experience mercy;
    to begin questioning the unquestionable
        that I may know truth;
    to begin disciplining
        that I may create beauty;
    to begin sacrificing
        that I may accomplish justice;
    to begin risking
        that I may make peace;
    to begin loving
        that I may realize joy.

Help me to be a beginning for others,
    to be a singer to the songless,
    a storyteller to the aimless,
    a befriender of the friendless;
to become a beginning of hope for the despairing,
    of assurance for the doubting,
    of reconciliation for the divided;
to become a beginning of freedom for the oppressed,
    of comfort for the sorrowing,
    of friendship for the forgotten;
to become a beginning of beauty for the forlorn,
    of sweetness for the soured,
    of gentleness for the angry,
    of wholeness for the broken,
    of peace for the frightened and violent of the earth.

Help me to believe in beginnings,
    to make a beginning,
        to be a beginning,
so that I may not just grow old
    but grow new
each day of this wild, amazing life
    you call me to live
        with the passion of Jesus Christ.

Breathe Restlessness into Me

Thank you for all I forget are gifts,
    not rights.
Forgive me for all the grievances
    I remember too well.
Save me from the self-pity,
    the self-seeking,
        the fat-heartedness
        which is true poverty.
Guide me, if I'm willing
    (drive me if I'm not),
        into the hard ways of sacrifice
            which are just and loving.
Make me wide-eyed for beauty,
    and for my neighbor's need and goodness;
wide-willed for peacemaking,
    and for the confronting power
        with the call to compassion;
wide-hearted for love
    and for the unloved,
        who are the hardest to touch
            and need it the most.

Dull the envy in me which criticizes
    and complains life into a thousand ugly bits.
Keep me honest and tender enough to heal,
    tough enough to be healed of my hypocrisies.
Match my appetite for privilege
    with the stomach for commitment.
Teach me the great cost of paying attention
    that, naked to the dazzle of your back as you pass,
        I may know I am always on holy ground.
Breathe into me the restlessness and courage
    to make something new,
        something saving,
            and something true
that I may understand what it is to rejoice.

Teach Me Your Ways

Teach me your ways, Lord,
that I may be open to the same Spirit
who moved over the face of the waters
in the first day of creation
and moves also over the chaos of this time
to fashion a day like this,
a world like ours,
a life like mine,
a kingdom like leaven in bread,
like a treasure
buried in the fields of the daily I plow;
and make me aware of the miracles of life,
of warm and cold,
of starkness and order,
of screaming wind and impenetrable silences,
and of the unfathomable mystery of amazing grace in which I am kept.

Teach me your ways, Lord,
that I may praise you
for all the surprising, ingenious ways you bless me,
and for all the wondrous gifts you give me
through artists who introduce me to the beauty of holiness,
who usher me into awesome worlds in which I begin to live anew
in a fullness of pain and joy not possible before.

Teach me your ways, Lord,
that I may accept my own talent openly,
nurture it hopefully,
develop it faithfully,
and give it freely.

Teach me your ways, Lord,
that I may love the kindness of the prophets
and practice it toward the hungry of the world,
the poor and sick and oppressed
that I may learn the healing humility
which responsibly tends the earth and all creatures therein.

Teach me your ways, Lord,
that I may be swept up in worship with the saints,
which surges in wonder, gratitude, and obedience,
and shapes my life into an irrepressible YES to you,
to all my sisters and brothers,
and to the presence of the kingdom among us,
until the ancient vision of mothers burns in me
with a fire to light the world
and warm its heart,
through Jesus Christ,
the singer of passionate songs,
the teller of powerful stories,
the artist of daring ways.

I Claim Your Power to Create

O Ingenious One,
it is not only creation
 but creativity that awes me.
It is a wondrous, fearsome thing
 that you share your power to create.

O Mysterious One,
I shrink from your power,
yet I claim it;
 and it is mine by your genius
  or madness,
 this power to speak
  and have light burst upon a mind or darkness descend upon a heart;
 this power to make music
  to which souls dance or armies march;
 this power to mold and paint and carve
  and so spin out the stars by which I plot my course to heaven or to hell;
 this power to hear and touch and taste
  the love and truth by which life itself is birthed and built,
   or the hate and lies by which it shrivels and dies.

O Daring One,
it is an awesome power you've shared;
and I rejoice in the artists
 who dare to use their gift to create the beauty
  which casts this world into a more whole and holy dimension,
 who dare to breathe visions and vibrations into dullness,
  as you breathed life into dust.

O Gracious One,
it is an awesome power you've shared;
and I honor your power
not only in pianist, poet, and painter
but in those whose encouragement ignites my heart,
whose laughter lights up a room,
whose touch fills a void,
whose integrity inspires my will,
whose commitment builds a church,
whose compassion builds a community,
whose demands stretch my soul,
and whose love makes my day;
and I honor your power in those artists
of kitchen and office and shop,
of courtroom and classroom and sickroom;
in those crazy people
who somehow know the world is always unfinished,
and who happily risk pushing and shoving
and tugging and pounding
and making love to it
until it and all of us
come out in more glorious shape.

O Ingenious One,
it is not only creation
but creativity that awes me.
It is a wondrous, fearsome thing
that you share your power to create.

Turn Your Spirit Loose

O God, turn your Spirit loose now,
and me with it,
that I may go to where the edge is
to face with you the shape of my mortality:
the inescapable struggle and loneliness and pain
which remind me
that I am less than god after all,
that you have made me with hard limits,
limits to my strength,
my knowledge,
my days.
Facing those limits, Lord,
grant me grace
to live to the limit
of being unflinchingly alive,
irrepressibly alive,
fully alive,
of experiencing
every fragile,
miraculous,
bloody,
juicy,
aching,
beautiful ounce
of being a human being;
of doing my duty
and a little more;
of loving the people around me,
my friends and my enemies;
of humbling myself to take others seriously
and delightedly;
of applying my heart to the wisdom of simplicity,
the freedom of honesty.

O God, turn your Spirit loose here,
and me with it,
that I may go to where the silence is
to face with you the utter mystery
of questions without answers,
pain without balm,
sorrow without comfort,
and fears without relief,
which hound my days
and haunt my sleep.

Facing the mystery, Lord,
grant me grace
to wrestle with it
until I name the fears
and force them to set me free,
to move on with whatever limp I'm left with;
to wrestle with it
until the pain teaches me
and I befriend it,
until the silence subdues me
into an awareness that it is holy
and I am healed by it;
to wrestle with it
until I go deeper in it
to gratitude
for all the shapes of wholeness
and of hope that bless me.

O God,
turn your Spirit loose now,
and me with it,
that I may go to where the darkness is
to face with you the terrible uncertainty of tomorrow:
of what will happen,
what might happen,
what could happen,
to me
and to my children
and to my friends,
to my job,
to my relationships,
to my country;
all that I cannot see, but fantasize,
that I would prevent, but cannot,
and so must accept as possibilities.
Facing the uncertainty, Lord,
grant me grace
to look at it directly and openly and truly,
to laugh at it with crazy faith
in the crazy promise
that nothing can separate me from your love;
to laugh for the joy of it,
the joy of those saving surprises
that also stir in the darkness.
And, so, I trust,
despite the dark uncertainty of tomorrow,
in the light of my todays,
in the cross,
and in a kingdom coming,
and, so, I move on and pray on
with Jesus, my friend and redeemer.

Bring More of What I Dream

O God,
who out of nothing
  brought everything that is,
out of what I am
  bring more of what I dream
    but haven't dared;
direct my power and passion
  to creating life
    where there is death,
  to putting flesh of action
    on bare-boned intentions,
  to lighting fires
    against the midnight of indifference,
  to throwing bridges of care
    across canyons of loneliness;
so I can look on creation,
  together with you,
    and, behold,
      call it very good;
through Jesus Christ my Lord.

I Tremble on the Edge of a Maybe

O God of beginnings,
as your Spirit moved
over the face of the deep
on the first day of creation,
move with me now
in my time of beginnings,
when the air is rain-washed,
the bloom is on the bush,
and the world seems fresh
and full of possibilities,
and I feel ready and full.

I tremble on the edge of a maybe,
a first time,
a new thing,
a tentative start,
and the wonder of it lays its finger on my lips.

In silence, Lord,
I share now my eagerness
and my uneasiness
about this something different
I would be or do;
and I listen for your leading
to help me separate the light
from the darkness
in the change I seek to shape
and which is shaping me.

Go with Me in a New Exodus

O God of fire and freedom,
deliver me from my bondage
    to what can be counted
and go with me in a new exodus
    toward what counts,
but can only be measured
    in bread shared
        and swords become plowshares;
    in bodies healed
        and minds liberated;
    in songs sung
        and justice done;
    in laughter in the night
        and joy in the morning;
    in love through all seasons
        and great gladness of heart;
    in all people coming together
        and a kingdom coming in glory;
    in your name being praised
        and my becoming an alleluia,
through Jesus the Christ.

Prayers FOR SEASONS & HOLIDAYS

I Hold My Life Up to You Now

Patient God,
the clock struck midnight
and I partied with a strange sadness in my heart,
confusion in my mind.
Now, I ask you
to gather me,
for I realize
the storms of time have scattered me,
the furies of the year past have driven me,
many sorrows have scarred me,
many accomplishments have disappointed me,
much activity has wearied me,
and fear has spooked me
into a hundred hiding places,
one of which is pretended gaiety.
I am sick of a string of "have-a-nice-day's".
What I want is passionate days,
wondrous days,
dangerous days,
blessed days,
surprising days.
What I want is you!

New Year's Day

Patient God,
this day teeters on the edge of waiting,
    and things seem to slip away from me,
        as though everything were only memory
            and memory is capricious.
Help me not to let my life slip away from me.
O God, I hold up my life to you now,
    as much as I can,
        as high as I can,
            in this mysterious reach called prayer.
Come close, lest I wobble and fall short.
It is not days or years I seek from you,
    not infinity and enormity
        but small things and moments and awareness,
            awareness that you are in what I am
                and in what I have been indifferent to.
It is not new time
    but new eyes,
        new heart I seek,
            and you.

New Year's Day

Patient God,
in this teetering time,
this time in the balance,
this time of waiting,
make me aware of moments,
moments of song,
moments of bread and friends,
moments of jokes
(some of them on me),
which, for a moment, deflate my pomposities;
moments of sleep and warm beds,
moments of children laughing and parents bending,
moments of sunsets and sparrows outspunking winter,
moments when broken things get mended
with glue or guts or mercy or imagination;
moments when splinters shine and rocks shrink,
moments when I know myself blest,
not because I am so awfully important
but because you are so awesomely God,
no less of the year to come
as of all the years past;
no less of this moment
than of all my moments;
no less of those who forget you
as of those who remember,
as I do now,
in this teetering time.

O Patient God,
make something new in me,
in this year,
for you.

New Year's Day

Catch Me in My Scurrying

Catch me in my anxious scurrying, Lord,
and hold me in this Lenten season:
hold my feet to the fire of your grace
and make me attentive to my mortality
that I may begin to die now
to those things that keep me
from living with you
and with my neighbors on this earth;
to grudges and indifference,
to certainties that smother possibilities,
to my fascination with false securities,
to my addiction to sweatless dreams,
to my arrogant insistence on how it has to be;
to my corrosive fear of dying someday,
which eats away the wonder of living this day,
and the adventure of losing my life
in order to find it in you.

Catch me in my aimless scurrying, Lord,
and hold me in this Lenten season:
hold my heart to the beat of your grace
and create in me a resting place,
a kneeling place,
a tiptoe place

where I can recover from the disease of my grandiosities,
which fill my mind and calendar with busy self-importance,
that I may become vulnerable enough
to dare intimacy with the familiar,
to listen cup-eared for your summons,
and to watch squint-eyed for your crooked finger
in the crying of a child,
in the hunger of the street people,
in the fear of the contagion of terrorism in all people,
in the rage of those oppressed because of sex or race,
in the smoldering resentments of exploited third-world nations,
in the sullen apathy of the poor and ghetto-strangled people,
in my lonely doubt and limping ambivalence;
and somehow,
during this season of sacrifice,
enable me to sacrifice time
and possessions
and securities,
to do something . . .
something about what I see,
something to turn the water of my words
into the wine of will and risk,
into the bread of blood and blisters,
into the blessedness of deed,
of a cross picked up,
a savior followed.

Catch me in my mindless scurrying, Lord,
and hold me in this Lenten season:
hold my spirit to the beacon of your grace
    and grant me light enough to walk boldly,
        to feel passionately,
            to love aggressively;
grant me peace enough to want more,
    to work for more,
        and to submit to nothing less,
            and to fear only you . . .
                only you!
Bequeath me not becalmed seas,
    slack sails, and premature benedictions
        but breathe into me a torment,
            storm enough to make within myself
                and from myself,
                    something . . .
something new,
    something saving,
        something true,
a gladness of heart,
    a pitch for a song in the storm,
        a word of praise lived,
            a gratitude shared,
                a cross dared,
                    a joy received.

Be with Me in My Unfolding

It is spring, Lord,
and the land is coming up green again,
unfolding
outside my well-drawn boundaries
and urgent schedules.
And there is the mystery
and the smile of it.
The willows are dripping honey color into the rivers,
and the mother birds are busy in manger nests,
and I am learning again that "for everything there is a season
and a time for every matter under heaven."
O Lord, you have sketched the lines of spring.
Be with me in my unfolding.

It is spring, Lord,
and my blood runs warm with the song of the sap,
longing
for a beauty I would become.
And there is the mystery
and the smile of it.
The buds are swelling on the bush,
the sun is beginning to coax the color
from where it's been curled against the cold,
the air is sweet to the nostrils;
even the city seems to be rubbing its eyes
from a long sleep;

and there is a promise in the season
I know no name for
except life.
O Lord, you have sketched the lines of spring.
Be with me in my longing.

It is spring, Lord,
and something stirs in me,
reaching, stretching,
groping for words,
peeking through my defenses,
beckoning in my laughter,
riding on past my fears,
pulsing in my music.
And there is the mystery
and the smile of it.
Be with me in my reaching
so I will touch or be touched,
this time,
by a grace, a warmth, a light,
to unfold my life to a new beginning,
a fresh budding,
a spring within as well as around me.
O Lord, you have sketched the lines of spring.
Be with me in my reaching.

Shock Me with Terrible Goodness

Holy One,
shock and save me with the terrible goodness of this Friday,
and drive me deep into my longing for your kingdom,
until I seek it first—
    yet not first for myself
but for the hungry
    and the sick
        and the poor of your children,
for prisoners of conscience around the world,
for those I have wasted
    with my racism
        and sexism
            and ageism
                and nationalism
                    and religionism,
for those around this Mother Earth and in this city
who, this Friday, know far more of terror than of goodness;
that, in my seeking first the kingdom,
    for them as well as for myself,
        all these things may be mine as well:
things like a coat and courage,
    and something like comfort,
        a few lilies in the field,
            the sight of birds soaring on the wind,
                a song in the night,
                    and gladness of heart,
the sense of your presence,
    and the realization of your promise
        that nothing in life or death
            will be able to separate me or those I love,
                from your love
                    in the crucified one who is our Lord,
                        and in whose name and Spirit I pray.

Good Friday

I Praise You for This Resurrection Madness

Lord of such amazing surprises
as put a catch in my breath
and wings on my heart,
I praise you for this joy,
too great for words
but not for tears and songs and sharing;
for this mercy
that blots out my betrayals
and bids me begin again,
to limp on,
to hop-skip-and-jump on,
to mend what is broken in and around me,
and to forgive the breakers;

for this YES
to life and laughter,
to love and lovers,
and to my unwinding self;
for this kingdom
unleashed in me and I in it forever,
and no dead ends to growing,
to choices,
to chances,
to calls to be just;
no dead ends to living,
to making peace,
to dreaming dreams,
to being glad of heart;
for this resurrection madness,
which is wiser than I
and in which I see
how great you are,
how full of grace.
Alleluia!

Easter

Touch Me with Truth That Burns Like Fire

Lord,
send the gift of your Spirit
to fill this place
and myself
and the world.
Touch me
with truth
that burns like fire,
with beauty
that moves me like the wind;
and set me free, Lord,
free to try new ways of living;
free to forgive myself and others;
free to love and laugh and sing;
free to lay aside my burden of security;
free to join the battle for justice and peace;
free to see and listen and wonder again
at the gracious mystery of things and persons;
free to be,
to give,
to receive,
to rejoice as a child of your Spirit.

And, Lord,
teach me how to dance,
to turn around
and come down where I want to be,
in the arms and heart of your people
and in you,
that I may praise and enjoy you forever.

Pentecost

Let Me Live Grace-fully

Thank you, Lord,
for this season
    of sun and slow motion,
        of games and porch sitting,
            of picnics and light green fireflies
                on heavy purple evenings;
and praise for slight breezes.
It's good, God,
as the first long days of your creation.

Let this season be for me
    a time of gathering together the pieces
        into which my busyness has broken me.
O God, enable me now
    to grow wise through reflection,
        peaceful through the song of the cricket,
            recreated through the laughter of play.

Most of all, Lord,
let me live easily and grace-fully for a spell,
    so that I may see other souls deeply,
        share in a silence unhurried,
            listen to the sound of sunlight and shadows,
                explore barefoot the land of forgotten dreams and shy hopes,
                    and find the right words to tell another who I am.

Summer

Waken in Me a Sense of Joy

O extravagant God,
in this ripening, red-tinged autumn,
waken in me a sense of joy
    in just being alive,
joy for nothing in general
    except everything in particular;
joy in sun and rain
    mating with earth to birth a harvest;
joy in soft light
    through shyly disrobing trees;
joy in the acolyte moon
    setting halos around processing clouds;
joy in the beating of a thousand wings
    mysteriously knowing which way is warm;
joy in wagging tails and kids' smiles
    and in this spunky old city;
joy in the taste of bread and wine,
    the smell of dawn,
        a touch,
            a song,
                a presence;
joy in having what I cannot live without—
    other people to hold and cry and laugh with;
joy in love,
    in you;
and that all at first and last
    is grace.

My Words Can't Carry All the Praise

Glorious God,
how curious
and what a confession
that we should set aside one day a year
and call it Thanksgiving.
I smile at the presumption,
and hope you smile, too.
But the truth is,
Holy Friend,
that my words can't carry all the praise
I want them to,
or that they should,
no matter how many trips they make.

So this day,
all is praise and thanks
for all my days.
I breathe and it is your breath that fills me.
I look and it is your light by which I see.
I move and it is your energy moving in me.
I listen and even the stones speak of you.
I touch and you are between finger and skin.
I think and the thoughts are but sparks
from the fire of your truth.
I love and the throb is your presence.
I laugh and it is the rustle of your passing.
I weep and your Spirit broods over me.
I long and it is the tug of your kingdom.

Thanksgiving

I praise you, Glorious One,
for what has been, and is, and will ever be:
for galaxy upon galaxy, mass and energy,
earth and air, sun and night,
sea and shore, mountain and valley,
root and branch, male and female,
creature upon creature in a thousand ingenious ways,
two-legged, hundred-legged, smooth, furry, and feathery,
bullfrogs and platypuses, peacocks and preachers,
and the giggle of it—
and turkeys (especially, this day, the roasted kind, not the flops)—
and families gathered, and the thanking;
the brave, lonely one, and the asking;
the growling, hungry ones, and the sharing.

I praise you, Glorious One,
for this color-splashed, memory-haunted,
hope-filled, justice-seeking,
love-grown country
and the labors that birthed it,
the dreams that nurtured it,
the riches that sometimes misguide it,
the sacrifices that await it,
the destiny that summons it
to become a blessing to the whole human family!

O Glorious One,
for this curious day,
for the impulses that have designated it,
for the gifts that grace it,
for the gladness that accompanies it,
for my life,
for those through whom I came to be,
for friends through whom I hear and see
greater worlds than otherwise I would,
for all the doors of words and music and worship
through which I pass to larger worlds,
and for the One who brought a kingdom to me,
I pause to praise and thank you
with this one more trip of words
which leaves too much uncarried,
but not unfelt,
unlived,
unloved.
Thank you!

Thanksgiving

Grant Me Your Sense of Timing

O God of all seasons and senses,
grant me your sense of timing
to submit gracefully
and rejoice quietly
in the turn of the seasons.

In this season of short days and long nights,
of gray and white and cold,
teach me the lessons of waiting:
of the snow joining the mystery
of the hunkered-down seeds
growing in their sleep
watched over by gnarled-limbed, grandparent trees
resting from autumn's staggering energy;
of the silent, whirling earth
circling to race back home to the sun.
O God, grant me your sense of timing.

In this season of short days and long nights,
of gray and white and cold,
teach me the lessons of endings:
children growing, friends leaving,

jobs concluding,
stages finishing,
grieving over,
grudges over,
blaming over,
excuses over.
O God, grant me your sense of timing.

In this season of short days and long nights,
of gray and white and cold,
teach me the lessons of beginnings:
that such waitings and endings
may be a starting place,
a planting of seeds
which bring to birth
what is ready to be born—
something right and just and different,
a new song,
a deeper relationship,
a fuller love—
in the fullness of your time.
O God, grant me your sense of timing.

Winter

I Am Silent . . . and Expectant

How silently,
how silently
the wondrous gift is given.

I would be silent now,
Lord,
and expectant . . .
    that I may receive
        the gift I need,
            so I may become
                the gifts others need.

Advent

Let the Star of Morning Rise

Lord God,
in the deepest night
there rises the star of morning,
    of birth,
        the herald of a new day you are making,
a day of great joy dawning
    in yet faint shafts
        of light and love.

I hear whispers of peace in the stillness,
fresh breezes of promise
    stirring,
winter sparrows
    chirping of life,
a baby's cry
    of need
        and hope—
            Christmas!

In the darkness I see the light
    and find in it comfort,
        confidence,
            cause for celebration,
for the darkness cannot overcome it;
and I rejoice to nourish it
    in myself,
        in other people,
            in the world
for the sake of him
    in whom it was born
        and shines forever,
            even Jesus the Christ.

Christmas

Title Index

Wrestling the Light

ACHE AND AWE IN THE HUMAN-DIVINE STRUGGLE

For Adam,
A beautiful man
Whose sensitivity, courage, and love
Have made music of his life, for our lives.

Focusing

A Preface

Grace is probably the most central and crucial word in the vocabulary of the Christian faith. Yet, even to say quite simply that grace refers to the way, or ways, God restores us estranged creatures to Him/Herself opens the gates to deep and, I believe, irresolvable mysteries.

From the biblical witness on, our Judeo-Christian history is the history of trying to understand not only the "why" and "what" of grace, but especially the "how" of it. As grace is a gift, the expression of God's initiative toward us, the why and what of it have to do with God's freedom to be God with and for us as He/She chooses. That domain is one we glimpse, at best, only "in a mirror dimly."

But the how of grace is the intersection of the ache and awe in the human-divine struggle. The how has to do with the ways grace might come to us, shape us, restore us. The how, then, involves our discernment and experience of life's meaning, our response to this proclaimed gift. That discernment and response is the essence of the religious life, the life of the spirit, the life of faith personally, relationally, and corporately.

Though no less mysterious than the why and what of grace, the how of it becomes more immediate and urgent for us. Theologians have written innumerable volumes about the how of grace, making distinctions between such modes as actual grace, prevenient grace, sufficient grace, efficacious grace. Such distinctions can be useful and clarifying if they help us to discern the fingerprints of grace on our lives.

But this analytic process also has the effect of diminishing the dynamic quality of life, reducing the mystery to definitive categories and, worst of all in my view, making religion or faith just another area of life, and a much too narrow and specific one at that. The how of grace slips into being the "how to" of grace, and thus the particular domain of institutional religion.

Consequently, we tend to miss the more inclusive, subtle, sneaky, supposedly non-religious ways grace could be, and I trust is, operating in our lives. And we usually don't consider our responses to those non-traditional experiences of grace—or "coincidence" or meaning—as having any religious or spiritual significance, if in fact we actually take time to reflect on our responses much at all. As a result we continue in our sense of estrangement, on which I think we do reflect if only in the middle of sleepless nights or on occasions when, for some reason, we cannot escape into busyness.

So it doesn't occur to us that God's grace is always operating to restore us to Her/Himself if we haven't had any commonly defined "religious" type experience. Therefore, our estrangement, or deprivation, includes a kind of prayerless, worshipless, joyless, one-dimensional life in which there is little trust and much anxiety.

Consistently, I come back to the telling of stories as the most congruent way to touch on at least some of the many levels of our ordinary lives in which grace works, perhaps primarily in simply sustaining us in life and giving us choices day by day, choices that convey possibilities for us to do and be something at least somewhat new and different; to move bit by incremental bit toward that freedom, peace, wholeness that salvation implies and these narratives explore.

So *Wrestling the Light* is a book of stories and prayers in which I try to express something of the way I discern grace operating in common, unreligious but, to me, quite amazing and wondrous ways to restore people to God, even though the characters in the stories might not put it that way themselves. If these characters would describe what happens as being restored, or partially restored, to themselves and to others, then surely they have begun to experience the mystery of grace, and of God, beyond tidy labels. If the experiences portrayed in this book help us discern some suggestive and significant possibilities of the mysterious how of grace in our own lives, it will be enough.

Each of these stories, in quite different form, was originally shared with my congregation in the "sermon" portion of a worship service and were, and are, reflections on particular experiences as well as products of my imagination—imagination being, I contend, a critical aspect, a dancing partner of faith. It is my hope that the stories reflect glimmers of the light with which they wrestle—light being something of a metaphor for grace in this book, and wrestling in all its sweaty, twisting, grunting, sensuous, lively, sometimes painful, often humorous and underlying fun-glad-joyful qualities being, for me, a response of faith.

The prayers in *Wrestling the Light* are intensely personal, and they appear here for the first time. These are a new form of prayer for me, something of a departure from the style usually associated with praying. Yet, I think they are rooted in the tradition of the psalms in that they are reflecting before God as a person might reflect on his/her life experience in the presence of a trusted friend. In a sense, they might be called narrative prayers. The intent is to explore and deepen a relationship with God within the stuff of life experience. As in a story, the struggle is to find meaning coming out of experience in the act of praying rather than being injected into it as a result of the prayer. That distinction may be slight and subtle, but it seems accurate and helpful to me.

In the same sense, the stories in *Wrestling the Light* are prayers in some profound way, even though the language and style are very different from those usually used in praying. But to wrestle with, and for, the light, for some meaning in life, is always a way of being in the presence of God, whether consciously or not. And to me, being in the presence of God, rather than the degree to which a person may be conscious of God at any given moment, is what defines the heart of prayer. Of course, the more intense a person's consciousness, the deeper the experience probably will be, as witness *The Revelation To John* in the Bible and the writings of the mystical saints. Yet consciousness alone does not determine the availability of an experience of God's presence, any more than eyesight, whether keen or not, determines the existence of whatever is seen. Grace is always a gift.

In another sense, the prayers in *Wrestling the Light* are attempts to be poetic because I think poetry, in its respect for and use of words and images, is a powerful, often stunningly revealing way to express our human experiences and longings. Poets who do not intend their work to be prayers, and would rightly disavow that they are, still can have their poems read as prayers because they are honest, provocative, and they disclose profound truths in ways that move my soul. Those poems open me to God's presence in undeniable ways.

So to write prayers in a way that intends something of poetry is to try to echo that experience in a reverse but intentional way. Even as the psalms cannot be read only as poetry, however poetic they are, I share these writings not primarily as poetry but as prayers, as ways of wrestling to find meaning, to discern grace operating in life, as a means of participating with God in some small way in creating some bit of new order out of my chaos, in pointing to some shreds of light in the darkness.

A very fresh experience sums up the point of this Preface. Two weeks ago I visited a young, not traditionally religious, close friend who was dying. I sat on one side of his hospital bed and a woman friend of his stood on the other side of the bed. We talked quietly. But every so often my friend would ask, "Who is here?" The woman and I would say our names, and my friend would reply, "I know that. I mean, at the foot of the bed, down there. Who is that?" The woman and I both would assure my friend that it was no one, that she and I were the only ones in the room with him. My friend was not persuaded and kept asking. We kept telling him it was no one. The next day my friend died. Were we right in telling my friend there was no one at the foot of the bed? On the face of it, and by any measurable, verifiable standard, we were. He was medicated. He was undergoing profound neural, chemical changes in his body. He was experiencing great emotional turbulence. Any of that might reasonably explain his vision of an unknown someone at the foot of his bed.

And yet, reason can be just another form of idolatry. I think now we sadly, arrogantly over-stepped our place and power in telling my friend there was no one there. He sensed a presence. Could it not have been an angel, his guardian angel, the angel of death, of grace, there with him? Could it not have been God going about the mysterious, gracious work of restoring my friend—and the two of us on either side of the bed—to Him/Herself, overcoming what estranges us, separates us from God and from each other? The answer, the trusting answer, is "Yes, it could," though it be only a whisper, or awed silence, then a story, or poem, or prayer. The answer of faith is, "Yes, for that is surely how the grace of God comes, as strange glimmers of light into the dark, deep, holy, yet common places of our fearful, hopeful, very daily wrestling.'

I am grateful for those who have wrestled this book into being with me, most of whom must remain anonymous, except these: Adam Geiger, to whom it is dedicated; Lura Jane Geiger, whose faith sustains many and me; Marcia Broucek, whose skill and support as an editor and friend have been invaluable; Ed Kerns, whose vision and talent as an artist and whose kinship in life constantly opens new dimensions to me; my staff colleagues and the people of the First United Methodist Church of Germantown, who share the journey; Mark, David, Karen, Thomas, who are wondrous light to me and whose wrestling with me is a great, saving gift; Christopher, Jonathan, Jeffrey, Nadya, who not only help me to see but to see miracles; and Jan, who is grace upon grace to me.

Theodore W. Loder
Philadelphia, Pennsylvania
September, 1991

Tumbled in Your Shimmering Wake

At that snap of grace,
finger of mystery against finger of purpose,
when first you struck the light,
scattering fire as far as forever,
O Hurler of these shining spheres,
did you know
that across these whirling eons
light would set us against our own darkness?
Did you know
that this insistent pelting
would break our hearts with longing,
that its nurturing, patient power
would pull our souls, like sap
through sea of time,
through root of cell,
through fin and claw
and thumb and tongue,
'til life woke wondering self-aware
and stammered out its prayers to you,
as now I do?
Surely you knew
that light would set my dreams climbing like vines
up the shafts of chance, surprise, and promise;
would draw my eyes to distant suns and pilgrims near,
and lump my throat at beauty I can scarcely bear!

You are its source;
of course, you knew
that light is what life's wrapped around,
what wraps itself in life,
so truth alone can stand its glare,

and love is its appeal,
while justice done displays its hues
and seivants, its intent, like Christ,
and the lilies of the field.

O God,
whose cloak is light,
I'm tumbled in your shimmering wake,
its scarcely weight breaks my heart again,
and I cry and laugh after balance,
gasping to catch my longing, and my breath,
imagining enough to sense the unquenchable in me,
trusting enough to claim you put it there,
beachhead of eternal light against the darkness.

So, wrestled, pinned, branded, set free,
I rise to pray my story, tell my prayer,
a thousand, thousand tiny sparks
and I am one,
a bit of burning dust
of gratitude exacting,
of light turning to praise.

RELATIONSHIPS

A Night Light Against the Darkness

O God,
I am tentative before you,
confused in my clutter of misplaced dreams,
abandoned hopes,
tattered faith;
shriveled by the cramp of busy-ness,
the leak of disappointment,
the grind of cynicism.
From this mock of shadows, this nightmare of botch,
I turn to you,
this prayer a night light
against the darkness.
There is strange assurance in the turning,
as if at the approaching of a long-lost friend.
In my brokenness glimmers an awareness
that only what is broken,
like bread, and hearts, can be shared;
that love is hard, tougher than nails,
humbling as mystery, true to life.
O Broken God,
I would endure this love,
swear and weep to welcome it.
So come, Lord, into my brokenness.
Resurrect the cluttered pieces of me
into a stronger, somewhat whole
and make me brave
to dream anew,
to hope the kingdom in,
to share the bit of truth I am
toward some sweeter, saving end,
to love us creature fools hard,
yet with a merciful, knowing heart.

Grace, then, to fear not the shadows,
but to heed the ripples of light forever breaking in,
bidding me rise and follow
toward brothers, sisters,
the promised day,
and you.

I Do Not Know Myself Yet

Holy One, I would pray
not because you do not know me already,
but because I do not know myself yet,
and seek myself with you.
Shed the light of your grace upon me
and go with me into the dark, untended,
shameful, scary corners of my life.
Ease the frantic, swollen pride
by which I claim too much for my efforts,
credit too little those of others,
and stifle gratitude to them, and you,
Soften my callous belittlement of others
by words that blame,
or collusions that exclude,
and so demean and divide us all.
Straighten me out of the crippling illusion
that my burdens are heavier
than those of others.
Liberate me to share my struggles honestly
so I may embrace the miracle of my humanity
and drink, in exultation,
the wine of others' gifts.
Visit with me my nightmare fears
to dredge them up to light, O God;
and help me give the furies names,
to tame their wild, hypnotic power,
and start to heal my waiting soul
and those I wounded at the furies' prod.
Undamn the juices of my passion,
unbury the riches of my talent,
that in the flow and wield of them,
in my daring and my doing,
a light will break

and I will see my life is far more than it seems,
and trust enough to learn by heart
  the truth of me you know so well,
    and to give by choice
      the gift it is you ask of me.

Unbutton My Proud Bluffs

O God of ferocious tenderness and disarming insistence,
    unbutton my proud bluffs,
        put your ear to my heart,
            listen to what I long for,
                and touch me with healing and with hope.

For I've been seduced to exhaustion
    by the siren hype of others' demands,
        but I responded to them in kind.
I've been impaled on spiky sulks
    when their needs weren't met,
        but I responded to them in kind.
I've been shriveled to bitterness
    by their blame for things gone sour,
        but I responded to them in kind.
I've been scorned to isolation
    when their arrogance forged bias into creed,
        but I responded to them in kind.
In rage and resentment I have closed down hard
    on others, and on myself—
        hearing not, forgiving not, risking not,
            turning no other cheek,
                walking no second mile,
                    loving no enemy.

The darkness of doubt is upon me,
    doubt of my worth,
        my power,
            my possibilities,
                my connection with others,
                    my kinship with you.

O God, separate once more the light from the darkness.

Make light of me,
dispelling my gloomy grudges and guilty fears,
transforming my dreary self-preoccupations
into flicker of giggles, filament of trust,
a kind of radiant confidence in more-than-me you.

Make light in me,
reviving my pulseless impulse
to mount one small revolution of trust,
and so to lift a little light,
span some gap,
pick some deadlock,
tip some scale toward justice.

Make light through me,
igniting a dawn of reunion and peace,
a dazzle of laughter,
a glow of peace,
a splendor of joy,
a great, spangly resurrection of love.

Scorched Aware

O God,
I look,
and find you looking back
in the eyes of lover, child,
enemy, friend, stranger,
in the image in the mirror.
I can scarcely hold watch or long bear
that light in eyes,
that peering of the soul,
your secret hidden in us like a glowing coal—
a haunting, frightening, fascinating
brand of Eden,
burning bush,
empty-tomb holiness.

I look,
and am scorched aware of
how fragile
and how precious
is everything I love,
everything I am, have, do, give.

I look,
and you look back,
and in the lurch and tumble of your fire,
I glimpse again
your power to work miracles
by turning the few loaves and fishes
of my gifts, and me,
into food for some other lonely ones;
your power to ignite to flame
my look, my stretch toward you
and so to inspire to life
other wide-eyed seekers such as I.

In the light of such miracles, O God,
    let there be community,
        the welding of love and courage
            in me, and as far as I can see.

Grant me nerve to dare the wonder,
    willingness to hold watch,
        to walk in the light—
            that fierce, tender, terrible beauty,
                of your looking, your beckoning—
    that ever being burned to death,
        and life,
            by your gaze,
    I may be saved, and sent again, and spent
        in the sacred seek
            toward those I can never be with wholly,
                nor yet be whole without.

The Kettle of the Day

O God
never quite grasped,
yet always at the tip
of my tongue, my mind, my heart,
while it's still dark
I hear the dawn—
winged chatter,
feathered singing,
black, grumpy caws,
clatter of the early train—
and yawning up, I put on
the kettle of the day.

Pink and blue slowly spreads, heaven to earth,
ineffable, inseparable, mysterious as male/female,
timeless probe into my quick time,
transcendence in disguise,
disturbing, welcome reminder
of what I never quite remember,
or ever quite forget,
this wonder at the tip of me,

I stammer my praise, my "O-God-I'm-glad,"
for those I love and who love me,
though who knows the why,
except mercy and grace,
and the willingness to do love's long labors
toward love's deep rewards;
for the sheer delight of this sexual self,
in the sharing with a beloved sexual other;

for laughter, music, family rough and tumbling
    to truly find each other,
        and mercifully find our way home;
for rain on the roof,
    wine and apples,
        sentinel trees;
for hard lessons learned,
    dreams blistered into beginnings,
        and the terrible, lonely freedom of deciding;
for honest, artful words
    that unwind my too tight, tidy mind
        and entwine it to my heart;
for mistakes corrected, weaknesses owned,
    changes made, failures become teachers;
for those who show me the narrow, saving difference
    between cleverness and integrity,
        success and joy;
for the traces of wisdom
    the years have left in me;
for old friends, good stories,
    nothing to do, sitting still,
        listening, watching, thinking, praying, sleeping;
for work to go back to,
    for the sweat for bread;
for peace,
    and for justice,
        which is love with its sleeves rolled up;
for this stubbornly fertile,
    painfully abused,
        incredibly beautiful, beloved mother earth;

for this fumbling, frangible human world,
still bathed in light,
cradled in heaven;
and this for Christ's sake longing at the tip of me,
and at my core,
for what only you could make me long for.

I remember but this meager much
and offer you my thankful prayer.

So Magnificent . . . So Flawed

O God, I am torn.
Do I rant or praise?
This world is so magnificent,
so flawed,
and I cannot divert
my gaze,
or heart,
from either.

So I rage,
shudder out my fear,
cry my compassion
at birth defects;
at kids therapied bald-headed
playing out their short days,
while parents watch, helplessly;
at twisted limbs,
spastic bodies,
blind eyes,
vacant minds;
at AIDS,
like war, thinning a generation,
stealing too much talent away,
mocking youth and us,
malevolent as a drought;
at so many plagues, so many blights,
such endless, frenzied feeding,
germ on cell,
glitch on gene,
species on species;
and at this ugly coil of violence
lurking in my shadows,
striking to wreak its havoc.

I despair.

Damnit God,
why these terrible, hellish,
insidious, all-too-perfect imperfections?
Has it gotten out of hand?
Has it fallen too far?
Have I?
I really cannot bear it!
Can you?
Is this what the cross is about?
I half-trust it is, and yet . . .
I rage and lift the whole to you.
Which means I praise, as well,
for beauty past all telling of it,
which no one in the least deserves;
for the urge of love that stirred the earth
and folded in the dust of us,
and raised us up and set us free,
yet pounds within our veins;
for all that summons from my heart,
for the songs it strangely knows,
for those heights my words don't reach,
but hurl them up, I do—
like courage, truth, and ecstasy,
and the hardest one, trust.
Yes, both rage and praise,
the bag is mixed in me as in the world,
and to deny one is to cancel the other.
So, as an act of trust,
and trustworthiness,
I take these steps,
first limp, then leap,
toward lonely, loving you

and learn to live
    as best I can,
        with all there is
            in this wondrous, puzzling world
        and with myself, as well,
            and, gracefully, with you.

The Bullies Who Follow Me Home

O artful Weaver of the oft-violated,
    yet finally inviolable web of human ties,
        these common, sticky, holy connections
            that define each, and link all,
I bring my friends home with me to you
    only to find the bullies, leeches, ciphers,
        follow me as well,
    those I would leave behind but cannot
        because they are so much a part of me,
            and I of them, at last,
So here they are, I cannot keep them out;
    the fools I laugh at,
        and treat less well than I would
            if I weren't so easily embarrassed;
    the obnoxiously sure who grind at me,
        but perhaps could not
            if I were less insecurely certain, too;
    the colleagues I work with,
        yet of whom I'd be less wary
            if friendship meant as much as power and status;
    the enemies,
        those become now faceless names and nameless faces,
            all those who enrage and frighten me,
                yet might not if I listened more
                    and needed less to win, be right and blameless.
And I bring, as well,
    the lonely and lost,
        the battered and broken,
            the oppressed and addicted,

the sick and grief-stricken.
Here they all are with me,
on my conscience,
in my heart,
as I must be in yours,
please God.
So, by grace,
would I pray us
home.

The Narrow Way of Trust

Lord, give me courage
to confront myself honestly,
shuck the pretense, strip to the real;
to act justly with those close to me,
advocate justice for those at some remove;
to work to heal what is injured in my life
and celebrate the wondrous rest.
O God, lead me in the narrow way of trust
for wide is the way of distrust,
painful the destruction it twists to.
Lighten the baggage I load on myself and others
when I behave as though I were surer of my choices
than I am, or can ever be.
Ease my anxiety about being wrong or exposed as a fool,
for I am always at least a little of both
and all the more when I deny I am either.
Deepen my trust
that together we can unravel the snarls of my life,
the knots I tie myself into,
that, so relieved, I might help untie
the knots I tie others into.
Then go with me into awe or ache so deep
I am forced to sort out what matters,
and to be buoyed by it,
in this illusion-flooded world,
Empower me
to be a bold participant,
rather than a timid saint in waiting,
in the difficult ordinariness of now;
to exercise the authority of honesty,
rather than to defer to power,
or deceive to get it;

to influence someone for justice,
    rather than impress anyone for gain;
and, by grace, to find treasures
        of joy, of friendship, of peace
            hidden in the fields of the daily
                you give me to plow.

A Chance

It had been an ugly day. Kevin Warner lay in bed, one fist under his pillow, the other pressed against the acid burning in his chest. He felt bereft and wished, as he often did, that he could pray toward some kind of ease. He tried to find a word to begin the effort again. He managed "God," "maybe," and "help" before he found himself distracted by the pattern of the street light on the bedroom walls. For a few moments he stared at the patterns. Then he lost interest.

"Damn it," he hissed through clenched teeth, "goddamn bad days hang on like pit bulls. Takes half the night to pry them off. But good days slip away like trout you can't catch, a flash of silver and they're gone. Where the hell's the justice in that? Or the mercy?" A passing car sent a flash flood of light across the wall. "Hope I die fast, of a heart attack or something, not some bitchin' thing that goes on for frigging ever."

He rolled over, trying to relieve the ache in his back. He thought of the therapist he'd seen for a few sessions—at his first wife's insistence. He'd been angry when the guy had suggested that the problem might be in *him,* from his past, not so much in his first wife's behavior, or in whatever was going on around him; that maybe what was wrong wasn't some malicious vims invading from someone else's sneeze, but something in himself, some perverse blindness or deafness or something. Why him? Why his fault? The hell with that. He'd tossed the idea out as being too introspective, too self-preoccupied, no solution to the situation he found himself in. Plus, the idea that his first wife was somehow getting off scot-free made him angry. He'd always thought of problems as being like equations involving an X: an unknown but objective factor that had to be identified in order for there to be a solution.

But maybe the shrink had been right, and he'd been too stupid to see that he was the X, or too proud to admit that he was. Anyway, back then he'd resisted the whole idea of therapy. And after the divorce happened, and his life improved, it didn't seem to matter. Yet recently it began to occur to him that maybe there was some buried guilt around the divorce or something that was making him feel so angry, so defeated, so humiliated now. Whatever was going on, self-doubt nagged at him. He worried about his health, his abilities, his attractiveness. What was the matter?

He realized that he was sweating. He sat up and looked at the clock radio. One o'clock in the damn morning. His stepdaughter, Jody, wasn't in yet. "Jesus," he thought, "she's just eighteen, and she acts like she's twenty-five, for God's sake." He'd come to think of stepchildren as land mines in the terrain of remarriage. You had to be so damn careful where you stepped if you wanted to keep things from exploding. Claire, his wife, had told him that Jody would be home from the party around midnight. "Okay, it's one o'clock," he muttered, "Where is she? And why isn't Claire upset, awake, worrying?"

Anger began a slow burn in him, but then fear partially doused it. He checked off the possibilities. Maybe Jody had an accident with the car. Maybe some guy was talking her into having sex, and she'd end up pregnant or get AIDS. Maybe she was doing drugs—coke or crack or ice or whatever. Drugs petrified him. If there were drugs at the party, who knows what would happen to Jody. "Kids just go along," he growled under his breath, running a hand through his hair and noticing that it felt thinner than ever. That realization broke the spell. "Come on," he told himself, "get hold of yourself. Why do you always think the worst? Jody's probably fine. Besides, it's really up to Claire, and she's not worrying."

He looked over at Claire. She was breathing in a slow, even cadence. Her hair spilled over her cheek and across her pillow, hair dark as mystery itself, the few silver strands only enhancing it. Women were always mysterious to him, alluring yet a little frightening. He thought of his mother: Her practiced grace and religious demeanor had been both irresistible and manipulative, while she herself had remained emotionally inaccessible. Her expectations of him, as well as the rules of their relationship, had never been openly discussed, only vaguely alluded to and casually assumed. The assumptions had then been either verified or broken by his behavior. Her corresponding responses of pride or hurt, echoed by his father, had felt dangerous and confusing to him. He'd tended to withdraw into anger and anxiety—and loneliness.

Now he studied Claire. Sleep seemed to accentuate her beauty. A sudden sexual urge roused in him, an urgent desire to take her, hard, quick, not make love but just be crudely physical, primitive, release his tension, meet a need. Then, as quickly as it had come, the urge cooled in his guilty awareness of how impersonal and exploitative, almost violent, his urge was. That frightened him. Did he want to hurt Claire somehow? He didn't think so, but that the question had even occurred to him was disturbing.

He and Claire had been married eight years, had been friends but not lovers for several years before that. Whatever the reasons for their first marriages—the hunger for sex or security, or simply acting out their families' scripts—they'd been painful mistakes for everyone. The divorces had intensified and made public the frustration, emptiness, and fruitless conflicts that had taken on such stupefying weight over the years. He was sorry for all of it, but deeply grateful to be with Claire now. With Claire, the conflicts were not fruitless.

Yet, looking at her, Kevin was aware that it had been a long time since he'd really noticed how beautiful she was or really even seen her at all. A longing stirred in him, a nostalgia. They had gone through so much in order to be together. He was shocked to realize how many months it had been since he'd felt close to her or confided in her. It was as if everything between them had become perfunctory, functional; they were just keeping things running smoothly for the kids as well as themselves and their careers.

Claire's daughter, Jody, lived with them all the time except for some holidays and a month in the summer when she was with Claire's first husband Newton, and his wife, both of whom traveled much of the time in their jobs. Kevin's seventeen-year-old son, Nate, and his thirteen-year-old daughter, LuAnn, alternated months between living with him and Claire and his first wife, Betsy. There were rough spots, land mines, but no major disasters. Claire's career as an interior designer was going very well; his in advertising was less exciting but okay. They paid the bills, met their social obligations. "Obligations," he thought, "good God, what a way to think of them. What's happening to us?"

He stood up and rubbed his neck. He recalled the chill he sometimes felt when he saw older couples in restaurants, eating their dinners in joyless silence, drowning in their lonely privacies, bound only by resignation to the repetition of the years, too weary or scared to risk anything different. He'd vowed that would never happen to him. But was it beginning? Even to him and Claire? Did it happen inevitably, to everyone—people just slipping into relational black holes? He shuddered.

He reached for his watch on the night table, padded over to the window, and checked the time by the street light. One fifteen. Where the hell was Jody? Surely she knew they'd be worried. Didn't kids think about anyone but themselves? Claire always defended Jody whenever he criticized her. Those exchanges always seemed to escalate into arguments about which of them was guilty of what or jealous of whom. Then they'd reach a limit of what either could bear and settle into a kind of workable trauce for the time being. What was his anger really about? After the arguments, he felt isolated and lonely, as he did now.

He went out into the hallway and downstairs to the kitchen. He poured himself a glass of milk and sat down at the kitchen table. The milk tasted faintly sour. He emptied it out in the sink, washed out the glass, put in some ice, sloshed on some bourbon, thought about his heartburn and shrugged. He took his drink into the living room, sat down in the darkness, and took a long swallow. He slouched down in the chair, stretched his legs out, and idly noticed that the street light patterns reflected mostly on the living room floor rather than on the walls, as they did in the bedroom.

That struck him as profound somehow, something he should write a poem about. He groped for a word, an idea to start, but couldn't. He took another swallow of bourbon. Maybe the drink would help him to sort out all the thoughts that were chasing their tails around in his brain.

He found himself staring at the street light patterns on the floor, sipping his drink. After a few moments, he pulled his legs in and leaned forward. *"Soft light,"* he began composing his poem, "no, *insistent light. Insistent, unassuming light . . . pulling back* . . . that's too strong . . . *tugging, brushing,* ahh, *brushing back the . . . the curtain . . . the veil of night* . . . yes . . . *brushing back the veil of night to* . . . to what? *To show* . . . no, *to reveal the . . . the tantalizing sight of* . . . of what? Oh, Christ, I'm getting maudlin."

It had begun while he was waiting for the seven forty-five train that morning. Roland Brooks, a young black who'd joined his advertising agency, Knapp, Kline, Powell and Row, as a copywriter a couple of years ago came up to him on the platform as he was checking the sports page.

"Hey, Kevin," Roland's off-handed greeting was transparent disguise of his intentional approach.

"Hey, man," he replied, sticking out his hand for their ritual brothers' handshake. Roland ignored it. Kevin felt angry but careful. "What's happenin'? Never saw you riding the train before," Kevin continued.

"Yeah, usually car pool it. Cheaper. But today my pool didn't work out. Too many complications." Roland's smile was enigmatic.

He decided to ignore Roland's barb. "Well TGIF, right? How's it going otherwise?"

"Passable," Roland answered. "By the way, congratulations on landing the Brenman assignment. Juicy job."

"Yeah, thanks." He felt wary, waiting for Roland's other shoe to drop.

Roland tilted his head back slightly and the words came rushing out, rehearsed, urgent, just slightly louder than a whisper. "Look, Kevin, I'm proud, so this is hard to ask; but I want to work on the Brenman assignment with you. I've got some good ideas. You could ask Ollie to make me your assistant on the project. It would break the stereotype of me at Knapp, Kline and give me a chance. Professionally." Roland smiled.

Roland's request caught him completely off guard. His reply was louder than it had to be. "What are you talking about, man? I can't just go to Ollie and ask for something like that. I mean, why? You gotta be kidding."

"I'm not kidding," Roland answered. "I'm asking you because you're the guy who's always talkin' the brothers' talk and shakin' the brothers' handshake. Okay, let's see if you can walk the brothers' walk, as they say. Just ask Ollie to assign me to the project."

His stomach tightened and his upper lip began sweating. "What is this, a test, Roland? Why would Ollie listen to me? What would I be selling, a black copywriter who wants a shot? Won't wash, man. He'd think I'd gone over the edge."

Roland's words came through gritted teeth, "And there we have it, don't we? All you really know about me is that I'm a black guy working at Knapp, Kline as a lowly copywriter, someone you can show off your brothers' handshake with to prove how liberal and open you are. That's it, right?"

He glanced away. "Damnit, Roland, get off my back. What am I supposed to know about you? What did you ever tell me? Now you're asking me for an enormous favor just because you're black?"

Roland bore in. "No. I want the job because I'd be good at it, and you could use me. I want the job because I didn't get it because I'm black."

"What the hell are you talking about, Roland?" He kept wishing the train would come.

Roland turned, spit, sighed and said softly, "What you don't know about me is that I know something about the advertising business. Studied it in college. Worked at it before this job. What you don't know about me is that I have both the talent and the guts to risk putting a proposal together for the Brenman deal, that I'd worked after hours on my own to do it. You just know that I should be grateful to be one of the copywriters. Well, I'm not. So I made a damn good presentation to Ollie and the committee. But they wouldn't even let me make my proposal to Brenman as an option. You had the assignment all the way. And that is how the world works, as if you didn't know."

He felt defensive. "Hey man, I'm sorry it happened that way. But you gotta know Ollie's turned me down a few times, too. And hell, I've been with the firm a few years."

"And you're white," Roland nodded, the flicker of a smile shaded with anger crossing his face.

Suddenly Kevin grabbed Roland's arm and his words bristled. "I think talent was the major factor in my getting the assignment, Roland, whether you like it or not."

"Let go of my arm, please!" Roland said with menacing evenness. After a facesaving moment of staring at Roland, Kevin let go. Roland continued, "Talent? Yes, but is that ever enough? This is your chance to become a partner, isn't it? Could lose it just as easy, though. I can help you. Believe me. If you've got the guts to let me."

Kevin heard the train approaching behind him. He didn't know what to say.

Roland put a hand on his arm and, just loud enough for him to hear over the hiss of the train's brakes and the rush of the commuters for the cars, said very precisely, "Look, I won't be in today. But I'll see you at the office Monday. Please, think about what I said."

Kevin had watched nonplused as Roland walked up the stairs, out of the station. Finally, he had turned to get on the train himself, just as it was pulling out of the station.

The train had been crowded and he'd had to stand all the way. When he got to the office, he'd had one of those dull, all-day headaches.

With a start, Kevin realized that he had lost track of how long he'd been staring at the patterns on the living room floor. Quickly he stood, swished the bourbon and ice around in his glass, took a swallow, and walked to the window. One forty-two a.m. Saturday morning and still no sign of Jody. Maybe he should call the home where the party was. No, even if he knew where the hell it was, that would only embarrass Jody. Or maybe it would just embarrass him. He'd have to check with Claire first, anyway. Maybe he ought to check with the police, discreetly, without creating a fuss. But how the hell could he be discreet with the cops? What would he say?

He shrugged, put down his glass, and decided to check on the other kids. He went upstairs, running his hand over the banister, the feel of the wood like an old friend, comforting. He stood for a moment looking at his thirteen-year-old, LuAnn. The blanket was half off, dragging on the floor, exposing the awkwardly beautiful neck and shoulder, and long, lazily curved back and swelling hip of his sleeping daughter. He retrieved the blanket, tucked it around her.

She opened her eyes. "Oh, it's you, Daddy."

He whispered, "Who did you think it was, honey?" He meant to be tender but sounded gruff. He wanted to say something more, but she had already gone back to her interrupted dreams.

He leaned on the post at the foot of the bed and watched her, his love for her filling in the silence. He recalled how excited she'd been about a dance last weekend. She was going on her first date with some young boy she described as "awesome." But the date had turned sour, and she'd cried as she told him and Claire how her date was a "dweeb" who'd "totally bagged her" for his "butt-breath, buddies" and how males were "shmeg-brained roadkill" she'd never have anything to do with again.

He'd listened sympathetically but realized how helpless he was to protect her from her youthful vulnerability that would inevitably lead to her disillusionment, her growing-up discovery that pain and defeat were as much a part of life as delight. He pondered the curious mix of wisdom and bitterness that the discovery would generate in her and wondered which portion would be the greater. So much of her life would depend on whether wisdom won out over bitterness. He wondered what he had done, or might yet do, to tilt the scale one way or the other. He wondered which was the weightier in him. His eyes teared, and he turned away and left the room.

He walked slowly down the hall to Nate's room. Nate slept like he did everything else: full steam, totally immersed—feet sticking out one side of the bed, one arm wrapped around a pillow, the other dropped off the edge, oddly bent against the floor. He slept oblivious in a sea of pants, socks, shirts, sweaters, jockey shorts, T-shirts, sneakers, soccer shoes, uniforms, and school books, all cast-off, wadded, crumbled, stuffed in all directions by this seventeen-year-old hurricane who, no matter which way he was thrown, or threw himself, always seemed to land on his feet.

Kevin shook his head, leaned over, picked up a couple of unidentifiable pieces of clothing from the floor, and banged his head on an open bureau drawer, which, in reflex of rage, he slammed shut.

Nate lifted his head, muttered, "Hey, wh'zup, man?" and collapsed back on his pillow.

Kevin rubbed his throbbing head and in a whisper as close to a shout as he could manage, he answered, "Damnit, Nate, when are you going to clean up this room, for God's sake?"

Nate's head jerked up again, as though it were yanked by some giant puppeteer, and he mumbled, "Clean? Oh yeah, soon . . . not now. Can't see. T'morrow f'sure. You c'n help me t'morrow, okay?" Before Nate's head hit the pillow, he was asleep again.

In the dim light Kevin checked his own head for blood and stood looking at his blissful son. He'd just been summarily dismissed, but he felt like laughing. He remembered how disgusted he used to be when his own father would say, ad nauseum, that it all went by too fast. But his father had been right. There was little Nate stretched out, big-footed, bass-voiced, smelling slightly of after shave. Nate had been only nine years old when the divorce took place and the bi-monthly shifts between homes had begun. Kevin wondered now if he'd been so wrapped up in Claire, and his career, that he hadn't been as attentive to Nate as he should have.

He wondered if it would have been better for Nate, and for LuAnn, if their mother and he hadn't divorced. Even the thought sent a shiver through him. It would have been worse, much worse, he was sure. But that didn't mean the divorce hadn't caused some damage to them, either. But what? How much? Didn't his own happiness with Claire compensate for at least some of the damage? He had never talked with Nate about much of it. His own father had never talked to him about such matters, either. His parents had always acted as though everything was fine between them, even when he knew it wasn't. The pretense of that was depressing to him. Maybe he should talk to Nate. What would he say? What would he ask? The idea was appealing, and frightening, too. He pulled the sheet over Nate's feet and left the room.

He made his way back downstairs, feeling very old. One fifty-eight a.m. and no Jody. He sat down in the upholstered rocker Claire had gotten him for his fortieth birthday six years ago as sort of a joke. They'd laughed about it then. Now, he felt like he belonged in it. But he wondered where he really *did* belong. What had happened over the years?

Who'd bought him, used him, shaped him? No, that wasn't it. Whom had he *let* buy, use, shape him—and for what? So far, what did his life add up to? What did he really want? Questions, questions, suddenly all these questions. He put his head back, and his mind sniffed back to the meeting he'd had that afternoon with Ollie.

Ollie Row, world-class scum bag, President of Knapp, Kline, Powell and Row because he happened to be the son of one of the founders. Ollie was old money, private school, Ivy League, and only four years older than he. Ollie's charm attracted customers but repelled people who worked very long for him and corroded whatever creative gifts he might once have had. The standard line of office black humor was the comment that someone had "caught the charm," which meant any variation from being conned to conning.

Still, Knapp, Kline was a good advertising agency, and Kevin had worked to be one of its top account execs and its expert in major media ads. But he wasn't a partner and it ate at him. More than once he'd felt twinges of envy toward Ollie, even though he knew that Ollie had become less a man than a commercial for whatever the good life was at the moment, a person for whom truth was reduced to what could fit into a catchy slogan, and for whom human beings were, or ideally should become, consumers of sweet smells, bright colors, sleek cars that would actually transform their lives. The trouble was that Ollie expected everyone who worked for him to hold the same view. But for Kevin, at the end of the day, it all seemed to boil down to the fact that Ollie was successful, he wasn't.

Ollie had called just before lunch. "Kevin, I know you're probably very busy, but I'd appreciate it if you could arrange to see me at two this afternoon. I need your advice about the Poley account."

He'd told Ollie he'd be there, took some aspirin, and left the office for a walk. Why the Poley account? What did Ollie want?

At two, he'd gone in to see Ollie. Ollie had turned on the charm and, after a few minutes of chatter, Kevin had been thoroughly uncomfortable and on guard. What was Ollie after? Then it came.

"I presented the layout to the Poley people," Ollie said. "They liked what I'd done. They signed the contract and gave us the go ahead. They want to have it on the networks and to the mag people by early next month."

He felt angry. "Well, congratulations on what *you've* done, Ollie? Funny, but I thought it was what *we'd* done. I even thought I heard talk about a bonus for some of us."

"Oh, Kevin, Kevin. Why are you so touchy? Of course, a lot of us worked on it, you most of all. In-house, we know where the credit belongs, and a bonus, too, on the slim chance there'll be one. But you know how clients are. Clients like dealing with me because I'm President. My name's the firm name. So I presented it that way. Surely you'd agree that what matters is that the deal gets done. Right?"

He felt he'd been had. "So what you wanted to talk to me about was my not getting any bonus. Is that it?" He started to get up.

Ollie held up his hand, smiling. "No, no. I knew that wouldn't matter much to you after I gave you the Brenman assignment."

He was on the edge of his chair, looking at the carpet, not trusting himself to look at Ollie. "*Gave* me? I thought I earned the Brenman assignment."

Ollie looked grieved. "Of course you did. That goes without saying. Why are you so testy, Kevin? Relax. I expect you to do very well with the Brenman job. You got the job because so much rides on it. For all of us. Now are we on the same page?"

The man was damned clever. With an easy smile and quick feint, Ollie had wiped out his bonus, pointed out his indebtedness, and turned up the screws on the Brenman job. Kevin slumped back in his chair. "Same page, Ollie. So what did you want to talk to me about?"

Ollie stood and walked to his conference table. "I really want to consult with you on the Poley account since you'll be working it out from this point. I want to tell you of a change I made in the approach. Come to an understanding. Here, look," Ollie motioned him over, and reluctantly he moved to Ollie's side of the table as Ollie began talking and pointing to the layouts.

"The theme's going to be 'If Love touches you, you can touch anyone.' I'm excited about it. It's simple and just suggestive enough. We'll run it with pictures of beautiful women, handsome men adoring them, different locations, you know. Overlay it with a bottle of the Love perfume, or show the bottle somewhere in the picture. At the bottom of the page, or the end of the spot, we add the words 'Love by Poley.' Like it?"

Kevin stared at the layouts. What was there about Ollie that made him feel his manhood had been snipped off before he'd realized it? "Ollie," he said at last, "that theme. Don't you think its just a little excessive?" He glanced at Ollie.

Ollie looked smug. "It's your line, Kevin. You dropped it and all I did was pick it up again. I'm surprised you don't like it."

Kevin massaged his eyes with his thumb and fingers, "Ollie, I dropped the line because I came up with it in a brainstorming session without really thinking about it. After we'd run it by once or twice, I realized it makes love out to be a commodity you get at a department store."

Ollie frowned and said softly, "Kevin, that's advertising and you know it. It's a business. It's more than that, it's politics, it's education, it's religion. It gets people to buy your product, and that's what makes the world go around. If wearing this perfume makes a woman feel better about herself, it's done its job."

Kevin turned to face Ollie. "But you have to admit it's manipulative. Ollie. It manipulates by twisting around one of the most . . .

honored words we have. It's like saying, 'Love works if you work it right.' Some lonely waitress out in Keokuk is going to save up her tips for a month and buy a bottle of 'Love' hoping, even against her better judgment, that a few well-placed splashes of it will enable her to touch the 'anyone' of her dreams, wrap him up, and live happily ever after. But it isn't so. Sooner or later she'll find that out. What about that waitress, Ollie? She's the reason I dropped that line."

Ollie looked disappointed. "Kevin, Kevin, nothing much is going to help that waitress, and 'Love,' even if it comes in a bottle, isn't going to hurt her much either. What are these sudden doubts you're having? How can I be confident you're up 10 the Brenman job with these kinds of reservations? Maybe you've just had a bad day. I'll chalk it up to that. So, let's just say I liked your theme for the Poley deal, and they bought it. So take the layouts and work your magic. If you have a problem, let me know."

Kevin wanted to say "No," but he was afraid. Ollie was warning him about the Brenman account. He could lose it, maybe even lose his job. He knew the world was full of bright guys on his heels—guys like Roland. Besides, maybe Ollie was right, maybe there wasn't really a good reason not to do what the client decides they want done. Maybe his own anger, or envy, or whatever, was clouding his judgment. So, he said, quietly, "It has been a bad day, Ollie. You know I'll do it, and you know I'll handle the Brenman job well." The idea of asking Ollie about making Roland his assistant on the Brenman job flitted across his mind, but he knew the timing was lousy. He also realized he'd ask Ollie later about Roland joining him to work on the Brenman project.

"I'll get things rolling." He turned for the door.

Ollie interrupted his exit. "Kevin, I really do appreciate what you do. You are magic with layout. And a superb copywriter."

Kevin scarcely was able to push the words through the rage that constricted his throat. "Copywriter, Ollie? Christ! Is that all I am to you? A *copywriter*?"

Ollie was smiling, but it obviously was a put down, a rapier thrust. "Kevin, I'm just saying you write like Yeats, for heaven's sake. We all write copy here. Take it as the compliment I meant."

He couldn't get Ollie in focus. He gulped and said, hoarsely, "Sure, Ollie, sure. Thanks." His own smile was a sickly imitation of Ollie's. He turned and left Ollie's office. "Copywriter?" he muttered all the way back to his office.

For the rest of the afternoon, he had sulked in his office, wasting time, which had made him feel even worse.

Even now, some twelve hours later, Kevin could feel the anger still churning. He rocked slightly in the shadowy living room and began talking aloud to himself, "Why do I give a damn? It all seems so . . . phony . . . Ollie, me . . . everything . . . Maybe all you can do is cover up . . . color up . . . the ugliness and . . . compromise . . . love's just . . . an illusion . . . a good sell. 'If love touches you . . .' What the hell . . . write . . . a poem about it . . . someday. Copywriter . . . copy . . ."

His head snapped forward. He must have dozed. A car door was slamming. Jody! He looked at his watch. Quarter after two. He got up, walked into the kitchen, and switched on the low counter lights just as Jody came in.

Jody looked startled. "Kevie, what are you doing up?"

"Where did you think I'd be with you out this late? Where the hell have you been!" It was the same tone his father had used on him as a boy. He flinched at the sound of it.

"At the party." Jody leaned against the counter, a wary defiance on her face.

"You were supposed to be home at midnight," he growled. "Why weren't you?"

Jody smiled tentatively. "You want an honest answer or a diplomatic one?"

He didn't dare return her smile or he'd lose his advantage. "You're two hours and fifteen minutes late and in no position to make jokes."

Jody's smile disappeared. "Okay, Kevie, here's the straight answer, but I don't think you're going to like it. I didn't come home because I didn't want to. None of the other kids were leaving, and I wanted to stay. Does that satisfy you?"

He tried to control his temper. "Why didn't you call? Didn't we deserve a call? Didn't you know we'd worry?"

Jody met his eyes and said with an effort that up-pitched her voice, "I knew if I called, you'd just make me come home, I think I'm old enough to make my own decisions about some things. I'm a responsible person."

His anger boiled over and he yelled, "Old enough to decide what? To break your word? To ignore other people? To make them sick with worry? Who the hell is ever old enough to do that?"

"I didn't mean that," Jody yelled back, tears rolling down her cheeks. "I meant I'm old enough to be responsible for some of my own decisions."

"Christ," he snorted. He felt dizzy. He pulled out a chair and sat down at the table. At the quiet core of his anger was the nagging suspicion that there might be some truth to what Jody was saying, and he felt an oddly unexpected pride as she stood there challenging him. He'd never stood up to his own father, who had always made him feel so wrong that he'd ended up not even liking himself. He didn't stand up to Ollie. To anyone. Even to Claire. Maybe he was on the way to ending up like those silent old people in restaurants. "God help me," he thought, tracing the flow pattern on the tablecloth in the soft light.

He looked at Jody, standing there, waiting for his reply. Tears came to his eyes and he looked down at his hands. What the hell was that line he'd learned in Sunday School, something about the sins of the fathers passing on to the children unto the third and fourth generations? Damn if those old Jews didn't know what they were talking about. But how could he stop it? Why couldn't good stuff go from fathers to children? Or even better, from children to fathers? Crazy.

"Look, Jody," he began tensely, unaware that Claire had heard them yelling and was standing in the doorway, "the point is, I was afraid something had happened to you."

"Okay, I'm sorry. I should have called you," Jody blurted out. "You're right about that. But I didn't want to come home and don't see why I should have to. There's no school tomorrow. Why should I have to be home at twelve?"

"That's what the yelling's about?" Claire asked softly.

Claire's voice startled him. He jerked around. "Damn, you scared me. I didn't realize you'd . . ." He waved his hand uncertainly. "Sorry about the yelling. Jody just came in and, yeah, that's what it was about," he answered. He looked back at Jody. "I don't know, Jody, maybe you shouldn't have had to be in by twelve. But why didn't you talk about it *before* you left? You never talk about anything with me." He sat heavily,

"I don't know. You're not home much, for one thing." Jody was lining the toe of her shoe on a crack between the kitchen floor tiles. "And I didn't think you'd want to listen." She raised her eyes to him. "And it's always so one way. You never talk about yourself, what's going on with you. You just want *me* to talk, or you just want to tell me stuff you're afraid about for me. What about *you*, Kevie?"

"I wish you wouldn't call me that," he said, surprising himself. "It sounds like the name of that bird that can't fly." He could see that Jody was startled by his request.

"I've always called you that," she protested. "I'll stop if you want. What should I call you?"

"Try 'Kevin.' Okay? And I talk about things I'm afraid of for you because I care about you. Things happen to kids. You might get hurt."

"I'm not exactly a kid anymore," Jody replied levelly. "And I know about things."

He stood up and leaned against the other end of the counter, not lacing her. "Jody, knowing about things and not getting hurt by them aren't the same. You're young. Maybe your judgment isn't always as good as you think. About drinking. Or driving. About drugs. That things kill you. And sex. There's AIDS out there, and herpes and who knows what. Damn right, I'm afraid for you."

"And how many times have you said all this to me? Don't you think I'm responsible? Can't you trust me?" Jody's tone was exasperated.

"How do I know?" he countered, raising his voice. "Coming in late like this doesn't help much."

"Okay," she conceded, "I said I was sorry. How many times do I have to say that? Or prove myself to you? Really, haven't I earned your trust by now? Forget tonight. No, don't forget it. At least I've been honest with you about it. And I've never come home drunk, or driven when I drink. Sure, I drink a little. Beer mostly. But I think I'm just as responsible as you about drinking. And believe me, I don't do drugs. I'm not stupid. I am trustworthy. But there's one thing you should know: I'm not a virgin anymore. You might as well know that."

"Oh, Jesus," he uttered, sinking down onto the chair. "Don't tell me."

Jody rushed on. "But I am telling you. And I'm telling you I'm still responsible. I'm on the pill. I don't sleep with just anyone. I know you're scared and so am I. And I'll tell you what I'm scared of. Sure, AIDS is part of it. But I'm even more scared about being so scared that I miss my life. I don't want to live like I'm in one of those plastic bubbles kids have to stay in when they can't risk being exposed to any diseases. So, yes, I think about 'things,' Kevin. Long and hard. There, I've talked. Your turn."

He felt angry and frightened. He looked at Claire. She was calm. "You knew all this?" he asked. "About the sex and . . . everything?"

Claire nodded. "Yes."

"You never said anything to me," he protested.

"We haven't talked much lately," she said, putting a hand on his shoulder. "Besides, Jody and I agreed that it was her place to tell you. Now she has. I think that's good. But, Jody, it's not all right for you to come in this late. Kevin's right. You should have talked to us about it before."

"I know, Mom." Jody sounded contrite and tired. "Can we just go to bed now, please?"

He was still trying to grasp what was happening. "Jody, I'm . . . you said it was my turn to talk, but I'm not sure what to say. I love you, and I. . . I'm still scared about AIDS, for one thing. The pill doesn't help with that. And . . ." his voice trailed off.

Jody walked over to him, put her hand over Claire's hand on his shoulder. "Kevin, the sex has been with one guy. Scott. You met him. I know we're young, but we're careful. We think we love each other, but . . . I don't know if you can understand this but somehow the sex thing got in the way of our finding out more about our love because sex kind of dominated everything until we could get it out of the way and see what else there was between us. Mom said it was like that for her and Dad, so they got married. But look at the disaster that was. Scott and I didn't want that. So we did it this way. Can you understand? It just seems the most . . . moral, the . . . best option for us right now. Okay?"

"I don't know," he sighed, his hands massaging his brow. "Maybe it is." He thought about him and Betsy getting married so young, mainly for sex. "Maybe."

There was silence for a moment. Then Claire said, "It's late. Bedtime." She and Jody hugged briefly and Jody left, touching his arm on the way past. Claire watched her, then turned to him and asked softly, "Coming?"

"In a minute," he answered. "Go ahead. I'll be right there." He listened to her climb the stairs. He pushed himself up slowly, walked to the switch, and turned the light off. Leaning against the sink, he stared out the window. After a moment he realized he was staring at something in the yard. He squinted, saw it was a plastic ball from one of the neighbors' kids. The street light made the ball look like a little UFO, one part in the shadow, the other reflecting the street light. The illusion it created made his yard, his world look strangely unfamiliar. Who was the alien? Was it him? Was it the world? He turned away from the window. "Lord have mercy," he muttered, shuffling across the floor. He felt overwhelmingly tired. Using the banister, he pulled himself up the stairs.

When he reached the top, he turned toward Jody's room, approached, and knocked on the door.

"Yes?" Jody responded.

He pushed open the door and stepped in, hand still on the knob. He smiled tentatively. "Jody . . . I'd like to ask you something."

Jody was sitting on the edge of her bed with the headphones of her stereo over her ears. She took them off. "Sure."

He felt embarrassed. "What are you listening to?" he asked.

"Streisand," she answered. "Old tape. Don't know why I dug it out. Felt like something, you know, different, I guess."

"I like her, too," he said. He gazed around the room. "Look, I'm not sure about . . . . what just happened. But, I think you said something about having earned my trust. You think trust has to be earned, right?"

Jody nodded, "Yeah."

"Well," he went on, "I agree but . . . how do we do that? I mean, how do I do that? With you?"

Jody crossed her legs, put one arm back on the bed and leaned into it. "I guess we could start by being honest. I mean, about what's really going on, you know. You telling me straight what you're actually thinking or feeling, about being scared or happy, stuff like that . . . that would make me feel closer to you, trust you. You never do that, so it's like you don't trust me, and then I don't do it 'cause it's like I learned not to trust you, either. See, in the past when I've told you stuff about me—a little, anyway—you've always given me advice, which makes me mad and makes me feel I'm wrong for being the way I am. I wish I knew how it is for you. I need that. I mean, from a man, too." There were tears in her eyes. "You know?"

He leaned against the wall. "That's different from what I learned to do," he said, his voice breaking slightly, "or how it was for me growing up. Maybe I can learn. I'd like to be close. I'd like to trust . . . and be trusted."

He felt a tear roll down his cheek, and he felt that he should stop. But he didn't. "I learned to put the face on things I thought my parents wanted. And my friends, my boss.

My parents made me feel guilty about sex, afraid. I still am, sometimes, I don't know much about trust. For me, there were strict rights and wrongs. Still are, I guess, I hid my wrongs. So when you talk about sex, I get . . . anxious. I'm not sure I'm entirely off the wall about it, but maybe I am, some. I guess I am. I hope we can, maybe, change things."

Jody stood as if she were going to come to him but then seemed to change her mind. She just stayed there with an open expression on her face and looked directly into his eyes. Very softly she said, "We've got a chance, Kevin. We really do." Their eyes held, and there was an ease in their smiles. Then she whispered, "Thanks. Would you turn the light out now? I've really had it for today."

He switched off the light and backed out, aware of the faint beat of the music and the small lights on the stereo dial, like the night lights he remembered leaving on in his kids' rooms when they were small.

The tears continued down his cheeks as he padded down the hall to his own room. The lamp on the night table was on, and Claire was awake. He began to laugh, a very easy, small laugh. Without a word he turned off the light, laid down, leaning on one arm, putting the other over Claire.

Then it broke through him, the sound and the shaking, though whether laughter or sobbing he wasn't sure, only that it was all right. "O God, we've got a chance," he managed to gasp, "I've . . . got a chance." His head came down on the pillow, his body trembling with the small, quiet tremors of a storm as it passed. "You . . . me . . . O God . . . a . . . chance . . . tomorrow." And then he was asleep, with a smile trickling lopsidedly off his face onto the pillow.

Claire turned and looked at him for a moment. "Yes, tomorrow," she whispered, kissing his forehead lightly. A small smile eased across her lips before she closed her eyes. She hadn't noticed the flicker of the street light on Kevin's foot where it splayed from the sheet at the corner of the bed.

The Rustle of Angels

God of thunderous silence,
deliver me from words
that gush, but slake no thirst,
that charm, but scour no truth,
that seduce, but conceive no intimacy;
hush me to quietness
to hear the rustle of angels
in the unaffected laughter and tears of others,
and myself;
and be stunned to awe
by others' simply inexplicable being-there-ness,
their bodies, breathing, eye-lit-mystic beauty,
and by mine.
Ease me, Unhurried One,
into the depths of accurate listening
that, beneath the babble,
I may attend to
the pleading in others' eyes,
the longing in their smiles,
the loneliness in their slump,
the fears in their curses,
the courage in their squint,
the wisdom in their scars,
the joy in their timid loves,
the faithfulness in their beginning yet again;

that on the whispered, groaning, stammering edge
of so much hope and need and grace
    I may begin to wrestle to
        some limp of understanding,
        some tilt of trust,
        some murmur of gratitude,
            for this not-so-minor miracle,
                for this merely beloved all
                    of yours
                        we are.

INTEGRITY

Authentic Scandal

O God of power,
    unleashed to throb
        in flaming suns and roaring seas,
            in honest words and valiant hearts,
now would I strip off
    the tired camouflage of my pretensions
        so freedom might become more than a word to me,
            integrity more than a limp ideal.
It breaks through to Legion me,
    like lightning through the clouds,
        not only that you are God
            but the kind of God you are.
"Jealous" is the word:
    seething, stubborn, pursuing Lover,
        turning things upside down,
            kicking them over,
                striking them open—
                    and me with them;
    gagging me
        on my drooling envy
            of the spangled, flaunting idols
                of status, stock-options, command;
    palsying my snug arrogance,
        which clings to half-truth
            as if it were the whole,
                and sees new truth a threat;
    snickering at my proud juggling
        of some precious good
            into an ultimate one;

groaning at my easy collusion
in converting charm into a commandment,
niceness into an article of faith,
avoidance into an exercise of love,
flattery into the essence of support,
prudence as the way of wisdom,
and playing faith for a reward;
tripping up my sauntering conscience
with the terrifying reminder
that Christ was hardest on hypocrites.

O God,
my illusions have dissembled me,
cowarded me from being into seeming.
Shake me now free of lies
with enough trust
and cock-hearted courage
and laughing love
as will dare, at least sometimes,
to walk your promise,
run your freedom,
wing your joy,
and so become one of this world's
whole-hearted, authentic scandals.

Roused by the Prowl of Grace

My need is great as hope,
    my longing, fierce as wonder,
and I stumble toward you,
    drawn by the light of your promise,
        roused by the prowl of your grace
            in the far country haunt of my soul.
Rush to embrace this prodigal me, O God.
    Listen to my still-not-trusting babble
        and help me accept my way home to you.
Save me from the shadowy, stifling folds
    of timidity,
        duplicity,
            fear,
and give me a stunning glimpse
    of some light-splattered possibility
        to race my blood
            and lump my throat.
Deliver me
    from avoidance
        of life's struggles,
    from denial
        of its pleasures,
    and from the illusion
        that they're separable.
Awe me into awareness
    that I am one of the wonderment
        of only human muddling beings,
    a mix of treachery, reverence, mercy,
        of grab, gift, gender, want, and whim
            of love, meanness, confusing views
                which roil around me, and within,

so as I would no more deny
the holy bafflement of me,
so would I deny no one their place
in my heart, or yours,
or in the just community
or the covenant of grace,
Deepen me, then, in wisdom that defies
the conspiracy of privilege,
the trap of dogmatic closure,
the lure of biases that enslave,
and distinguishes joy from success,
treasure from wealth,
meaning from busy-ness,
love from possession,
peace from comfort.
Release me from my victim's cramp
to the discipline of freedom,
the passion of bold choice,
the dare of creativity,
the courage of an honest voice,
and to the faithful, dicey pressing on,
through a way I can't quite see,
toward the home I never reach,
and the whole I'll only be
with you,
who, even now,
is pressing home to me.

Deliver Me From the Choke

God,
your language is silence:
the hum of worlds
and mysteries,
and spirit;
mine is words:
the cast I throw,
the reel I make
to tell and to retrieve
what meaning as I can.
For a moment,
suffer my language, Lord,
and suffer me;
mercy me out of the snarls
I have made of it,
and it of me,
by my smug pretension
that I have cast far
or reeled much in
from the vasty deeps
of time and spirit,
nature or humanity.
Deliver me from the choke
of my exaggerations,
twisted arguments,
shaded rhetoric,
tilted accusations,
empty flatteries,
cheap excuses,
pompous explanations,
hollow mercies,

complexity hocused
into clever simplicities,
while meaning slips away,
trifling you
and shrinking me.
In the moment,
guide me, Lord,
to the discovery of my own authentic voice:
the glad will to speak
small, sustaining truths
like numbered hairs,
noticed sparrows,
leavened bread
little children,
the "our" of you in Jesus' prayer,
that awed by the gift of words
to reveal and heal,
I be committed anew to
their poetic use,
prophetic power,
priestly care,
accurate cast,
respectful reel.
Through all moments,
teach me, Lord,
your language:
that slow deciphering
to confidence and quietness of mind,
the silence, stars, and seas,
the signing of mute mountains,
the hint of seeds, breathing of wind,
the primal thrust/receive of mate,

fused wonder in the womb,
glad puzzlements of born,
strange rhythms in my living,
intimations in the passing on;
this bearing in, and down, and up,
this for Christ's sake of everything,
and bloody nothing, too.
mysteriously uniting me
inseparably to you;
this all of grace,
for which I make
this wordless kneel of praise.

Teetered on a Ridge

O God,
    elusive Presence,
        insistent Other,
draw me to the border
    where hard, large truth
        escapes soft, small certainty—
            certainly my own—
        and grows in the between of risky encounter:
                honest speaking,
                brave listening,
                painful struggle
                hard-scrabble sifting,
            in that scary, sweaty swing
                toward those sacred others;
and I, being caught, seen,
    spun, stripped clean,
        am teetered on a ridge to see
            a different, saving view
                I hadn't dared to see before
        where I will slowly learn
            the balance of liberating trust
        and find my authentic way,
            between loyalty
                and flexibility,
            commitment
                and openness,
            witness
                and self-righteousness,
            courage
                and self-advancement,
            quietness
                and cowardice.

Grant me not only to tiptoe that edge
but to live it,
to be it—
a glad, welcoming lurch
toward the day of justice,
toward the fleet bright wings of joy,
the radiant call of beauty,
the sear of mercy,
a blaze of love,
a kingdom coming,
an elusively Present,
insistently Other,
saving grace
of you.

Fierceness Churning Like a Sea

O God, in this search of prayer
I discover something fierce in me
that will not be ignored,
and I take it as your stirring
before my strain to ask.
It aches, this fierceness.
It screams past words, past plan,
rising as a world to dare,
in the contractions of rebirth,
in the laughter of adore,
to touch, to shape,
to find myself within,
and to find
a place to reach,
a time to stand,
a God to worship wildly
with everything at hand,
the muck and marvel of it all,
the whole whatever-might-be of me.

It is your stir,
I claim it so.
What else ever could it be?
This fierceness churning like a sea,
flooding my eyes with longing,
ebbing salty down my cheeks,
a kind of amniotic fluid
a burning out and in,
a crying, urgent, holy demand,
by you of me—thus me of you—
to stop my slide to style,
my slink to approval,
my slither of hypocrisy,

and to surprise the day
with this fierceness,
this urge to wholeness,
this passion for integrity,
this no longer deniable insistence
that my life not be a forgery.
O God, transform this fierceness into courage
to say what I mean,
because it will put me at risk
of the rigors of freedom:
being disliked for my honesty
rather than liked for my deceits,
but enabling others to count on my word,
as I count on yours,
for light and life;
to mean what I say,
because it will shame me
into turning dean away
from the small purposes
and comfortable lies
on which I have wasted my energies;
to pioneer my way with you,
in this brave heave of love
toward a stranger self than I have been
within this world you're making new;
and so to be an heir of yours,
claiming this foolish vocation
of announcing Christ's returning
and living for my own.

One Difficult Condition

O God of unfathomable grace,
    you seem to have no conditions
        for being with me
    yet one difficult condition
        for my being with you:
    the giving up
        of my compulsion to perfection,
            this whipping of myself
                into anxious, disappointed bits and pieces,
                    a stubble of complaints, criticisms,
                        rejections, ingratitudes;
            this proud taking more upon myself
                than I can bear,
                    or than makes me bearable,
                and scatters my life into
                    sighs, excuses, poses, tears,
                        perfectly reasonable
                            despair.

Grace, then,
    for my giving up,
        which is what faith comes down to;
    for getting this fractured self
        cemented, sealed, sighted together
            with whatever glue
                of spit and mud,
                    mercy and blood
            you have at hand,
                and heart,

to condition me to be with you,
to limp and love,
sing, scream, and pray,
through this quite imperfect world,
still quite awesome and enough;
to finding my quite mysterious way
to life, and peace, and joy,
my bearing cross,
my empty tomb.

Murky Depths

O God of my murky depths and glorious heights,
here I am:
all my ambivalence and awe,
my churning questions,
and unslaked thirst for you,
my awkward grope,
ecstatic soar,
trudging doubt,
and brief lighted-hearted confidence

Accept it all
and enable me to accept the whole
of my preposterous, puny, perverse,
confusing, graceful, gifted self.
Assure me that it is all right,
and only right at all,
to be who I am,
to struggle my struggles,
dance my music,
embrace my triumphs;
to suffer on my own terms,
not those of demanding others
I falsely try to please,
mistaking their favor for yours,
and to simply turn glad, past whine or boast,
in becoming who I am.
Forgive me out of
my faithless presumptions
that what you ask of me is pretense, not truth,
innocence, not integrity,
certainty, not fidelity;

and forgive me into
a deep-breathing trust
that dares to press beyond the calculated shallows
to the kingdom-haunted depths
of the terribly real me,
and this terribly real world,
toward a terribly real you.

How Sweet the Sound

The more forgetful Deacon Crump became, the more angry Alice Crump became—though only a few would have guessed it. It seemed to Alice that Deacon was escaping, if not from her then at least from whatever she had to stay and endure while he wandered away from their remembered world. But the angrier Alice got, the sweeter she got, until you never heard even the slightest cross word from her. Actually, that development was just the predictable extension of the way she'd been all her life. There were some, mostly at St. James Church, who called her a saint. There were others, mostly at the VFW, who called her a martyr, often prefacing the term with an unprintable obscenity.

In any case, as things got worse, Alice simply worked harder to do what she said she'd done all her life, which was "to take care of my Deacon." Although a few discussed it privately, Alice never asked herself—at least not that anyone heard—why she'd done that all her life, or why things were working out so badly for Deacon and her now, or what she got out of taking care of him either way.

But the real mystery was that the sweeter Alice got, the more rapidly Deacon's forgetfulness advanced. But not many asked why about that either, least of all Alice. People just thought that Deacon's condition was a shame, and the only question they asked was whether he suffered from Alzheimer's disease, which some, with a shudder of apprehension for themselves, were sure he did. Others simply said Deacon was "getting senile."

"Deacon" is what people called him; nearly everyone had forgotten that his real name was Daniel. Deacon was an honorary title bestowed by usage. It went back to about the time he and Alice moved into their house thirty-five years ago, and Alice began attending St. James Church about a block away. Daniel went along occasionally but preferred staying home and reading about one of his favorite subjects—astronomy (his other hobby being skeet shooting, a rather unlikely pursuit for a city dweller, but one he managed to enjoy once in a while).

But his first love was astronomy. He was awed by the pictures of nebulae and galaxies. He was fascinated yet puzzled by the Big Bang theory scientists proposed for the beginning of creation. The closest he could come to picturing it was that it must have been a gigantic version of those tiny glowing dots hurled skyward by Roman candles that suddenly burst into incredible patterns of color during fireworks displays.

"Can you imagine it," he'd mutter to himself as much as to Alice preparing lunch, "everything in the universe exploding out of something as small as a single atom?"

Alice would continue mixing the tuna fish, smile demurely, and reply, "Why, yes. It's like the Bible, Daniel. God said 'Let there be light,' and light exploded like that. And then came land and water and stars, the creation."

Daniel would chide her. "Alice, show me where it says anything about explosions in the Bible. I'll bet the word isn't even there. It doesn't say that the universe began with an explosion, now does it? Or that everything came from a single, little thing like an atom?"

With a prickly little shrug Alice would yield, giving certain words an ambiguous inflection. "Well, no, it doesn't *exactly* say that. You're right, Daniel. I'm sure the exact word isn't in the Bible. I just meant that probably it was something like an explosion when God spoke. But you're right. After all, it is difficult to imagine how an explosion could crease anything."

Daniel would reply with a muted exasperation, "That's not what I meant, Alice. I mean . . . oh, it's not important." Then he'd walk around the kitchen straightening up something or other until a more harmless topic occurred to him to bring up. It was a ritual in which only the subject matter varied over the years. They lived a childless and orderly life, confined on four sides by a bridge club, a bi-monthly potluck group, a travel dub, and, eventually, St. James.

For after Alice became involved in St. James, Daniel was approached in his yard one spring by the Rector, looking dapper in his tan beret. The Rector asked Daniel if he'd help take care of the church grounds because he and Alice lived so close. Daniel found himself imagining the Rector's head as a cup of cappuccino sitting on the saucer of his clerical collar, and Daniel grinned as the earnest man concluded, "Each of us is part of the body of Christ, you know, so each of us needs to contribute toward keeping that body in excellent condition."

Daniel wasn't sure just what that meant, but before he could ask, the Rector had taken Daniel's smile as assent and begun to thank him profusely. He didn't disabuse the Rector, since he liked working in the yard and really didn't mind helping out by being whatever part of the body of Christ it was that fertilized and mowed the church lawn and trimmed its bushes.

But as one Rector followed another, one thing led to another over the years, and Daniel got increasingly involved at St. James. He was asked repeatedly and never declined doing more and more: ushering, financial drives, Men's Club, Property Committee, Sunday School Treasurer, and Church Treasurer. He was even invited to be on the Music Committee because, he suspected, he didn't know much about church music and so could be the organist's "Yes" man.

Somewhere in the process of his being grafted onto "the Body," people began calling him "Deacon." No one was sure who called him that first, but in a short time everyone was calling him "Deacon." It became not only his name but his demeanor; increasingly deferential, cheerfully doing thankless tasks, his bouts of absent-mindedness being interpreted as pious detachment.

Even Alice came to call him Deacon, though she sometimes said it with an inflection that left uncertainty as to whether she intended it as a term of pride or denigration. Often, as they sat in the living room in the evening, she would look up from her paper and say, "Deacon, would you just listen to this."

He would wince at her interruption of his ball game on TV and look over at her. She would smile and proceed to read to him some item from the paper and remark, "Isn't that incredible?" using the same inflection on "incredible" as she did on "Deacon."

Her ambiguity of tone delivered him, for he felt safe in simply answering. "Yes, it is," since he was indifferent to whatever her point was and wanted only to return to his ball game, which his apparent agreement allowed him to do.

Deacon's forgetfulness grew more troublesome as the time drew near for his retirement as Comptroller of Steins, the glorified title he'd been given as office manager and accountant for the largest automobile dealership in the city. He would forget to process the paper work of some car sales. Twice he forgot to write the pay checks. He would go to St. James two or three additional times each week to do some job he'd already done. He would repeat himself, ask the same question again almost as soon as it had been answered. In exasperation someone observed, "Deacon's become like a child trying to get attention." But Deacon stubbornly refused to admit he had a problem.

One Saturday, when he was looking up the word "deactivate," which he'd read in the newspaper but thought had been misused, quite by chance he came upon the word everyone called him. It surprised him, and he began to read what the dictionary said about it. *Deacon,* he discovered, means either a second level of clergy below that of a full priest or minister, or some elected or appointed person with specific duties in the church. That definition would have been acceptable to him, but it didn't stop there. As a verb, *deacon* means to pack fruit or vegetables with only the best side showing. It also means to falsify something or doctor it up. He was surprised to find that one of the old definitions of *deacon* was to castrate a pig or some other animal. Deacon felt like a fool. He slammed the dictionary with such force that Alice jumped.

"Deacon," she exclaimed, "what's the matter, dear?"

"Nothing," he growled as he stormed out of the house, determined to walk around the block in the other direction from St. James. It was the first time he actually got lost. An hour or so after he'd left the house, Alice drove around looking for him. After another hour, she had just about decided to call the police when she spotted Deacon following a group of teenagers into a video arcade some distance from their house. She persuaded him to come home with her, but it was only the first of the episodes that accelerated the tension between them and made Alice anxious about what she would do about Deacon.

Increasingly, Deacon became too much for Alice. He'd ask her, "Where're you going?"

"To the grocery store," she'd answer. "You stay here and read the paper like a good Deacon, and I'll bring you your favorite candy bars."

Before she'd gotten her coat on, he'd ask, "Where're you going?"

"To the store, Deacon dear. You do remember, don't you?" Then she'd go to the kitchen for her shopping list and purse.

By the time she'd got to the front door, he'd ask again, "Where are you going?"

She'd smile and say, "Oh, Deacon, I know you remember. Just relax and I'll be right back."

When she'd get back, his first question was always, "Where've you been?"

She'd sigh and give him a candy bar and tell him, "I went to the store to get you this."

One day when she got back, he was gone. She found him walking in the middle of the street in his underwear shorts, his winter overshoes, his skeet shooting jacket and hat, his shotgun over his arm, his head cocked toward the trees as if searching for birds. Another time, she got home to find him standing idly sipping a cup of tea in the middle of the kitchen while holding in his other hand the smoldering belt of his bathrobe, which she assumed had caught fire from having dangled in the burner of the stove.

When she reported these events to The Reverend T. Randolph Warren, current Rector of St. James, she was quite distraught. "Oh, Randolph, it is truly miraculous that I've happened to arrive home just in time," she exclaimed. "The good Lord must be watching out for Deacon and me. Or maybe, confused as he is, Deacon has some uncanny sense of when I'm coming home. Oh, I don't know. But what if I don't get there in time next time? I just don't know what to do, Randolph."

The Rector gave Alice the name of a practical nurse he knew, an older Irish woman who lived in the parish. Alice interviewed her and found her hourly rate was very reasonable because, as she put it, "I have a calling to serve like this." Alice nodded approvingly and, after offering her a somewhat smaller hourly rate to start, hired her on the spot. Her name was Margaret, "Maggie, for short," she said.

Shortly after Maggie came to work, Deacon's condition took on a peculiar smell that was as hard to identify as it was to miss. At first, when Alice's friends visited, they'd ask her in hushed, sympathetic voices if Deacon had become incontinent. Alice assured them he hadn't, but she didn't know what the smell was either. To mask the smell, Alice started using large amounts of her favorite lavender aerosol. After a while,

Alice smelled strongly of lavender wherever she went, and on several occasions at church, her friends inquired about her new perfume, to Alice's consternation.

Indeed, Deacon's condition, and Maggie's availability, moved Alice to spend more and more time at St. James. Women there continued to touch her on the arm while smiling knowingly, thus conveying an assumed solidarity. Occasionally, they would express a mixture of encouragement and appreciation, such as "You are a model of bravery, Alice"; or "Alice, dear, you're such an inspiration to us."

The Reverend T. Randolph Warren assured her she was doing everything she could "to take care of her Deacon," that God would give her strength, and that she must keep a positive outlook. He always spoke as though he were standing in St. James' carved, elevated pulpit and often intoned to her, "You remember, of course, that St. Paul himself had a thorn in his flesh that he prayed God to remove. But God, in his wisdom, let it remain as a reminder to Paul of his need for humility and forbearance."

As Reverend Warren spoke, Alice found herself wondering what the "T" in his name stood for—perhaps Thomas, she thought, or Timothy maybe, or Theodore or . . . Turkey. She gasped. How did that ever occur to her? "God forgive me," she thought to herself, blushing visibly.

Reverend Warren paused. "Are you all right, Alice?" he inquired solicitously.

She nodded and quickly replied, "Of gobble . . . OF COURSE," she nearly shouted. "I mean, of course, I'm all right. Forgive me, I get so confused sometimes. It's just that it doesn't seem possible that my Deacon is so sinful . . . SENILE. Oh dear. I get so flustered. What I'm trying to say is that Deacon being so senile must mean I've failed somehow."

"No," the Reverend replied. "You mustn't think that. 'Whatsoever things are lovely, whatsoever things are of good report, think on these things.' That's St. Paul's counsel to us, remember? That's what you must do, Alice. God will give you strength to keep everything under control. Don't you worry."

"Thank you, Reverend," she said, "thank you. You are so kind and understanding."

Usually, Deacon Daniel got along fairly well with Maggie, who was quite flexible in her schedule, willing to come early or stay late if needed. But occasionally Deacon would refuse to eat, or get dressed in the morning, or take a shower with Maggie lingering outside the open bathroom door to supervise. Apparently he decided that Maggie's taking that liberty gave him the right to "keep putting his hand where he shouldn't," as Maggie kept reporting it to Alice in a mildly reproving voice usually followed by a chuckle of understanding and wave of dismissal.

And there was the continual problem of getting Deacon to stay in the house and not wander around the neighborhood or go over to St. James. One Sunday morning, when Maggie was there for her agreed-upon two-hour shift, Deacon did manage to slip out while Maggie was watching mass on TV, scuttle over to St. James and, before anyone noticed him, disrupt the eleven o'clock service by loudly singing the wrong hymn during the hymn before the sermon. Fortunately, Deacon was fully dressed that morning, actually in a suit and tie, but the disruption made The Reverend T. Randolph Warren so obviously nonplused that he faltered several times in delivering his otherwise forgettable homily.

But for the most part, Maggie could get Deacon to do what she wanted by telling him that it was what Mrs. Crump wanted him to do. "Mrs. Crump wants you to be nice and do this," she'd say about his eating his vegetables at lunch, or "Mrs. Crump wants you to be nice and not do that," she'd say about his crude belching several times after he had eaten his vegetables. Hearing that, Deacon would shrug, sag a little, and comply.

One afternoon a member of Alice's bridge club commented that Deacon seemed depressed. Alice looked at Maggie, who was sharing desert with the group, and said, "Yes, it is sad. Maggie and I have to struggle sometimes to restrain Deacon from doing things he shouldn't. When we do, he does seem out of sorts for a time, and the only thing that makes it bearable is knowing that what we do is for Deacon's own good." Alice spoke with utter conviction and the members of her bridge club quickly concurred, each adding that she was sure she couldn't manage half so well if she had to face what Alice did. So, under the circumstances, things went along tolerably for Alice and Deacon.

Then one weekend it happened. Weekends were especially difficult for Alice because she was alone in taking care of Deacon, except for Maggie's short Sunday morning shift that allowed Alice to go to church. Occasionally Alice made an arrangement for Maggie to help on a Saturday, but it had to be for a special reason because Maggie spent weekends with her daughter and her family. So usually Alice was completely ready for weekends, having shopped for all of her Deacon's favorite foods and planned all the activities they could do to keep him occupied.

But this particular weekend happened to be Deacon's birthday. Alice had arranged for Maggie to come for an hour late on Saturday morning so she could take care of a few errands in preparation for a party for Deacon to which she'd invited her bridge club and potluck group, most of whom had reluctantly agreed to come. Maggie had made it clear she had to leave promptly at noon in order to attend her grandson's first communion. So when Maggie arrived, Alice had already persuaded Deacon to lie down in bed and rest for a while. Maggie was pleased that everything was calm and that Alice's only instructions were to leave the house open in order to air it out a little.

Alice left feeling confident that Deacon would be fine for the half hour or so she'd be gone. She would go to DeLeone's for fresh flowers and some bayberry candles, to Walker's for party favors and, most important, to Super Mart for the special cake mix they'd been out of earlier in the week. A thirty-minute jaunt, she'd calculated, forty-five at the most.

Everything would have worked out except that each errand took a few minutes longer than she had thought it would. When she left the Super Mart for home, it was already noon. So Alice was driving too fast when she swerved to miss a kid on a bike, hit the curb, blew a tire, and scraped her fender on the pole of a No Parking sign, bending it slightly askew.

By the time she'd gotten everything taken care of with the police, and Triple A had come to fix the tire, over two hours had passed. She'd tried several times to call home but had gotten no answer. None of her neighbors answered their phones either. She was frantic, and when she finally did pull into her garage, she was crying. "Oh please, Lord," she pleaded under her breath as she rushed to the house, "please let everything be all right."

As soon as she opened the door, she shouted, "Deacon! Deacon! Where are you?" She heard only the ominous silence of an empty place and then the ugly roar of a gunshot. She screamed and whirled toward the sound. It seemed to have come from the direction of the church. "Oh, God, nooo!" she moaned, sinking to her knees, hands over her face, imagining bloody disasters in which Deacon was victim or perpetrator.

Then, in a spasm of denial, she whispered, "Maybe it's not him. Oh dear God. don't let it be him." She lurched to her feet and groped her way to the dingy furnace room in the farthest corner of the basement where Deacon kept his shotgun in a little closet near the oil tank. As she reached for the string to pull on the overhead light bulb, she kicked something on the floor. In the swinging light she saw it was an old fondue set amidst discarded Sterno cans and candy bar wrappers. She knelt to examine the fondue pan. It was caked with layers of burned chocolate. The wrappers were from Deacon's favorite candy bars. She'd given them to him and he'd burned them. That was the smell no one could identify. It had wafted up through the heating ducts.

She glanced at Deacon's gun closet and saw that the door was open. "Damnit," she sputtered, pushing herself up, kicking the fondue pan, "damnit, damnit, damnit." She took the stairs two at a time and headed for the church at a trot.

Rounding the corner, she could see through an opening in the trees someone in the high open cupola just where the slate steeple began the sharp ascent to its proudly placed cross. The person was waving what looked like it might have been a shotgun and yelling at someone on the ground below. She realized it was Deacon. Then she saw the crowd and the police cars with flashing lights and the police themselves, dozens of them, lined up, keeping people away. She knew the whole thing was going to be a terrible scandal. What in God's name was Deacon doing up there?

"Son of a bitch, damnit to hell," she gasped, slowing to a walk, surprised by the realization that she was swearing and it felt good. A man at the edge of the crowd turned and started toward her. She recognized Eddie, the church custodian.

"Eddie," she shouted as he approached, "what's going on?"

"It's okay, Miz Crump," Eddie answered, "he ain't shootin' at nobody. It's just that nobody's figured how to get 'im to come down yet."

"What's he doing up there anyway?" she asked, squinting toward Deacon.

Eddie started laughing.

"Eddie, it's nothing to laugh about," she insisted. "He's got a gun. The police are everywhere. Someone will get hurt. Tell me what happened."

Eddie tried to put a sober mask on his face, but it kept slipping away. "Well, Miz Crump, it seems what happened is that the electronic bell thing . . . the, ah . . ."

"Carillon," she interrupted impatiently. "What about it?"

"Yeah, car'lon. Anyhow, it comes on automatic, you know, and the music comes through them speakers up in the tower where Deacon is. Some of the neighbors—you'd know 'em if I could remember their names—tol' the police the car'lon got stuck or something around noon and kept playin' the same thing over and over and over. Nobody was around to turn it off since I was down at the hardware store and then eatin' lunch—over to Ida's Luncheonette, you know Ida's—and the Reverend was off to a funeral, and I don't know where you was. Anyhow, I was just walkin' back when I heard the thing playin' that hymn, you know, 'Amazin' Grace,' only it wasn't playing the whole thing, just this one part over and over again. I knew that wasn't right so I was goin' to check it out soons I got back, but then I heard this shotgun blast and then a couple more. Well, the car'lon stopped all right. What Deacon done was blowed off them speakers we had bolted up there in the cupola." Eddie was laughing again.

"Eddie, stop it. It's not funny," Alice shouted. "It's embarrassing. Dangerous. We've got to get him down." She started toward the crowd.

"Wait, Miz Crump," Eddie implored, "I ain't told you the whole story yet." She stopped and he went on. "Soons I heard that gun, I run to the church and I hear Deacon yellin', 'How sweet the sound, how sweet the sound, how sweet the sound . . . you make me sick, you make me sick, you make me sick.' Then I seen him lean over the edge up there and make like he's throwin' up, makin' awful throw-up sounds, you know, and then yellin' out, 'I'm drownin', we're all drownin' in crap, in a sea of crap, sweet crappy crap, godawful syrup.' Then he raises up that gun and blasts off a couple more shots and starts laughin' like he's havin' hisself a real good time. Anyhow, the neighbors come runnin' from ever which way, and ol' Deacon waves to 'em and yells, 'Hey, I stopped that pukin', sicken' sound, didn't I? Drive you nuts, doesn't it? How sweet the sound, how sweet the sound, my ass. My ass, with the non-deacon bad side showin.' I ain't got no idea what he meant by that, but then he mooned 'em, Miz Crump. From right up there, he mooned 'em."

"He didn't!" Alice stared at Eddie in disbelief.

Eddie chortled, "Yes ma'am, he did. He's been standin' up there in his underwear firin' off a blast every once in a while, and wavin' at people and laughin' and tellin' the police to get the Mayor down here 'cause he's got a few things to tell him and . . ."

"Why don't they get him down?" Her tone was urgent. "We've got to get him down. It's humiliating."

Eddie looked at her and shook his head. "Well, they been tryin', Miz Crump. Police sent me to get you, but you wasn't home. So the police captain—he's the one in the white shirt with that bullhorn—he's been talkin' to Deacon, but it doesn't do no good." Eddie started to laugh again.

"Damnit, Eddie, stop it. This is damn serious."

Eddie caught the snarl in Alice's words and that, and the swearing, shocked him. "Yes ma'am. What I mean is . . . well, it didn't do no good, that's all."

"Why not? Deacon can he handled easily enough." She was breathing hard.

"Don't seem so, at least in this case," Eddie answered. "You see, the captain there, he got the name of that lady what helps you with Deacon, got it from the Reverend, and he radios his headquarters to call her, which they done. They call hack and tell the captain what she said, and then he talks to Deacon on the bullhorn. He keeps sayin', 'Deacon, Miz Crump wants you to be nice and come down now. And . . ." Eddie hesitated.

"And what?" Alice shouted.

Eddie looked down at his feet and tried to fight back a smile. "And he—Deacon up there—he, ah . . . well he just yelled out plain as sin, 'You tell Miz Crump she's full of crap. To hell with her.' You can ask anyone if he didn't say that, Miz Crump." He turned away giggling.

Alice took a deep breath and growled, "He did, huh? Why that little, spineless, pea-headed jerk. How did he get up there?" She started toward the crowd.

Eddie followed her, still giggling. "He got a ladder from the church basement. He knows where we keep 'em. Don't you do nothin' stupid now, Miz Crump."

As she pushed through the crowd toward the police, Alice noticed the ladder leaning on the shadow side of the tower. Then a voice boomed through the bullhorn. "Deacon, this is Reverend Warren," the voice announced.

"In the name of God, please come down. You are bringing disgrace on yourself and your good wife and this church."

Deacon laughed and sang back at the top of his lungs, "'Terrible disgrace, how sour the sound, that saved a wretch like me.' How about that, Reverend? Hey, tell me something. I always wanted to know what that 'T.' in your name stands for."

In spite of herself, Alice smiled. And she realized that Deacon's voice sounded very clear and commanding. She reached the police captain just as Reverend Warren stammered his answer. "Well, it . . . it's just an initial. It doesn't stand for anything. I mean, no name or anything.

Deacon Daniel bellowed, "You mean your parents just gave you an initial as part of your name?"

"It wasn't my parents," Reverend Warren yelled, "the initial was . . . it came later." He meekly handed the bullhorn back to the captain.

An incredulous Deacon shouted back, "You mean you just added the T. yourself? Why? Don't tell me. It was for the high-class sound of it. So no one would even think to call you Randy! Never even think of you as being as earthy as Randy. High class, my ass, Reverend T. Randy, Randy, Randy." The blast of a shotgun filled the air.

Deacon whooped and went on. "And you know what, Reverend T.? You're a deacon, just like me. You know what a deacon is? A fruit wrapped with only the best side showing or maybe a castrated animal. You can look it up, if you want to, Reverend T. old buddy. What d'ya say, shall we give it up? I'll be plain old Danny and you be plain old Randy." Deacon was laughing.

Then he yelled down, "By the way, Reverend T., when you get this thing fixed, why don't you play something besides that sentimental crap once in a while? Broaden out a bit, get religion unstuck. Mix in a little Beethoven or Stevie Wonder every so often. People might love it. At least we could give 'em that, since St. James has been too gutless to do anything else for the city."

Alice started across the churchyard. A cop with a riot helmet on his head caught her and pulled her back. "Where the hell do you think you're going, lady?"

"I'm his wife," she shouted. "Let me go."

He ushered her roughly to the captain. "Here's the guy's wife, sir," he said.

The Captain looked at her wearily, then spoke softly. "Wife? I don't know where you've been or why nobody was watching your husband, and right now, I don't much care." His voice began to rise. "But I want to make one thing clear, lady. Your crazy, goddamn husband is a terrorist, far as I'm concerned. He doesn't get his ass off that tower in about two minutes, we'll shoot it off. You understand? I ain't about to let some fuzzball maniac stay up there shooting a gun until he kills somebody, That clear? Now. you've got two minutes. Here, talk to him." He handed her the bullhorn.

"Just don't shoot him," she demanded, taking the bullhorn. "How does this thing work?"

"Hold it like this. Press this button and talk," he instructed her.

"Okay, but not from here," she insisted, walking quickly out on the churchyard toward the tower.

No one stopped her. "You got two minutes," the Captain called after her.

"Deacon!" Her voice sounded like a roar to her.

"Go to hell, Alice!" Deacon's voice sounded amplified, too. Then he fired the gun in warning.

She kept walking toward the tower. The Captain ordered her to come back. She ignored him. She heard him yell, "Get her, boys!"

She whirled and pointed the bullhorn toward them and yelled, "Stay away from me or you'll regret it. Touch me, I'll sue your asses. And I have witnesses."

The cops retreated. She heard Eddie shout, "You tell 'em, Miz Crump." The crowd cheered.

She turned back toward the tower and started walking. "Go to hell yourself, Daniel Crump." More cheers! She felt excited.

In rapid succession Daniel fired off three or four shots in the air. "Stay away from me, you witch," he screamed at her.

"That's the damn problem," she screamed back. "I've stayed too damn far away from you for too damn long, you . . . you . . . eunuch."

His eyes looked wild and he sputtered, "You . . . you . . . castrating witch. WITCH."

She was at the bottom of the ladder looking up at him. That face she'd known so well suddenly looked like a stranger's to her. She dropped the bullhorn and screamed, "No one gets castrated who doesn't want to be, EUNUCH!"

Glaring down at her, he shouted, "No one's a eunuch who isn't seduced by the syrup. BITCH!"

For nearly a minute, with the crowd responding with hisses and cheers like a Greek chorus, they hurled insults at each other.

"Bitch!"

"Eunuch!"

"Bitch!"

The excitement of it was contagious between them. Both were surprised by the curious pleasure and power of their feelings.

Finally Alice broke the cadence. "Where have you been, you damned phony? You aren't senile, you bastard!" She began to climb the ladder.

He scoffed, "Who said I was?"

"You acted like it. Doctor Hawkins said so," she replied, pulling herself upward.

"What did Hawkins know? Was he in my head? Hell no!" Daniel countered.

She scowled and climbed higher. "Then, why? Why the hell did you do that to me?"

"Do what to you? What do you mean, where have I been? I've been suffocating under all that damned frosting you spread over everything until I couldn't breathe. Drove me crazy. I've been crazy, that's where I've been."

With each rung she climbed, she shrieked higher, "Don't blame me for your being a damned coward. You always withdrew, walked away. You weren't crazy. You were a coward. Did it ever occur to you that maybe I'd have put on much less frosting if you'd been more cake?" Spit was flying from her mouth.

He howled in derision, "Where was the room for the cake under all that frosting?"

She reached the top of the ladder, threw her leg over the ledge, tearing her skirt open as she did. They stood glaring at each other. Then tears began streaming down Daniel's cheeks. "Oh, no," his voice gravelly but determined. "Noooo. This is too easy, blaming each other. You know what? I think we got sucked into a black hole back there somewhere. A damned black hole called nice or orderly or religious or something. A big black hole nothing could escape from, no not-nice things, no bad feelings, whatever they might be—except passion and anger and conflict and being different were among them. Nothing could escape that black hole. Not playful, not crazy, not light, not even love. That's what happened. It all disappeared in the black hole of "nice." *We* disappeared in the black hole of nice. That's where I've been. Hell, that's where we've all been, near as I can tell."

He wiped his eyes and nose with the back of his hand and leaned on the ledge. "You know what else? I don't know if I can, or if I have enough time, but I'd like to try to escape from that black hole. I was lying there listening to that song, 'Amazing Grace, how sweet the sound . . .' for the damn umpteenth time when all of a sudden it hit me. Why the hell is grace always supposed to be a sweet sound? Hell, why not it's like an explosion, like a Big Bang, right? I couldn't wait to get my damn gun and get over here."

"You're crazy, Deacon. Damn crazy."

"Maybe it's about time."

They stood eyeball to eyeball. The wind up there ruffled her gray hair and smelled fresh. She smiled first. "You look pretty sexy in your underwear, Daniel."

He smiled back. "You look pretty sexy yourself with your dress torn like that."

They started laughing, and the laughter rolled down across the churchyard. She took the gun from him. "How do you work this thing?" she asked. "Oh, never mind." She pulled the trigger. It was an automatic shotgun and recoiled like a bucking horse. Her first shot blew the rainspout off the tower, her second went through the window of the church office, the third took out the windshield of Reverend T.'s Grand Prix, and the fourth blew the top off the Rickenbacker Memorial flagpole, sending both the American and Christian flags crashing to the ground. The gun clicked. It was empty. Alice and Deacon Daniel were in hysterics.

Then the first shots from the police ricocheted off the tower. They ducked, Alice tore the sleeve off her blouse, and they tied it to the shotgun and waved it to the police. They stood and, following instructions over a second bullhorn, threw the gun over, and climbed down the ladder. The crowd cheered.

At the bottom, as the police ran toward them, Deacon said to Alice, "We've got a long way to go."

"So let's go on with it," Alice replied.

That night, after having been fingerprinted, booked for disturbing the peace, released on $500 bail each, and cheered as heroes outside the police station by a large crowd of people who'd seen them on TV, Alice and Deacon Daniel Crump had a birthday party. The invited guests came not sure what to expect and, since everyone was a little tired, left early still not sure what to expect.

But the cake was different. Alice and Daniel had made it together, and it had four layers, full of nuts, raisins and spices with a very thin but lovely chocolate-orange frosting. And on top there was just one candle that, in the dark room, seemed quite bright enough. And, it should be noted, all through the party Daniel remained in his underwear and Alice's dress was still quite revealingly torn.

While they were eating the cake, the sound of Stevie Wonder's song "Isn't She Lovely" suddenly filled the night air. When they went to the door, they saw a Grand Prix with its windshield missing, a speaker mounted precariously on the top, and a sign taped to the side saying, "Eddie and Randy wish the former Deacon a Happy Birthday, and Danny and Alice a good life, for Christ's sake."

It was indeed a Big Bang. No one could be sure what kind of universe would follow or how far it would expand.

Crazed into Holy Awareness

Come, Lord Jesus,
confront me as a prophet:
disturb my indifference,
expose my practiced phoniness,
shatter my brittle certainties,
deflate my arrogant sophistries,
and craze me into a holy awareness
of my common humanity
and so of my bony, bloody need
to love mercy,
do justly,
and walk humbly with you
— and with myself,
trusting that whatever things it may be too late for,
prayer is not one of them,
nor a chance,
nor change,
nor passion,
nor laughter,
nor starting yet again
to risk a way to be together,
nor a wild, far-sighted claim
that this human stuff of yours
is stronger still than fail or time,
graced to share a kingdom
and spirited for joy.

CHANGES

An Accurate Reticence

O God, you who wait to be gracious,
you who never flaunt yourself,
what is this tormenting need
to put myself always on display,
to give too much of self away,
to meet every request as if each was a just demand,
or Christ never left the crowds
to withdraw into the wilderness;
as if there is no essential difference
between others' response and yours,
between what I get from them and what I need;
as if I had no right to anything
that was just mine and yours,
a secret that sustains and not a show?
My ambition drains me,
this compulsion to prove a truth, a grace
I do not deeply hold myself,
or let myself be held by.
O God of such unfathomable depths as can alone assure,
draw me down to an accurate reticence,
a waiting resonant with yours,
a self to be chosen, as you do,
and plumbed, with you,
a privacy of faith,
a holding at the core,
a human-divine meeting,
a holy ground
to stand on,
and to withstand
the seduction of a stage,
the temptation of applause.

Calm me to depths I can endure,
learn trust, and abide assured
with abiding,
deeply present,
constant,
sufficient
hidden you.

Something Plain as Bread

Ingenious One,
please hear me out,
so I can hear myself out
in this chant of complaint,
this confession of praise.
God knows—
don't you?—
I've said all this before,
prayed it essentially this way,
perhaps using a few new words I learn,
but only to recite the same needs,
quick gratitudes, solicitations,
propositions, tired guilts,
despairs, disguised instructions,
timid hopes, embarrassed adorations.

It's as if I'm only what I always was,
perhaps with a few different ways I mimic,
but only to make the same responses
I was conditioned to make before I knew why,
yet keep making, fall back upon when pushed,
even though I thought I now knew why not
after all the sacraments of therapy and church,
small failures, successes, long-suffering friends.

I get tired of this me, this more-than-one I am,
of this warring family
of grandparents, parents,
brothers, sisters,
uncles, aunts, cousins,

all those who, though within your providence,
yet infused into my bones
the absolute of right and wrong,
as if their values were at last
no less than yours;
of these insidious comparisons
I was taught to make,
and make still,
to my distress and insufficiency;
of the curse, yet blessing,
of this inheritance I bear,
my tangled legacy of strengths and weaknesses
for which I would be grateful
and want so to forgive.

But I seem stuck in this constant repetition
of being human
when I presume I should be more.
I get stupid with self-pity,
sunk in discouragement.
God, it's all so familiar, isn't it?

And yet . . . who knows why, except you,
something happens,
more often than I realize I believe,
something plain as bread,
clear as wine and lightning,
taken for granted as salt,
a bird song,
a well-worn book,
lilacs;

presumed as mother love,
the laughter of a child,
a lover's touch,
Mozart,
Michelangelo,
Yeats;

all shudders, shifts,
bursts like a shaft of light
into my eyes, my nerve, my heart,
tingles my fingers,
raises my neck hair,
turns my head,
opens my ears,
even now,
to this awesomely unfamiliar,
strange familiar life I'm given back again;
to this enough
I'm slowly becoming;
to these critical, small changes
I've been wounded, weakened,
willed, and wondered into,
and cannot truly disregard;
to all this holy saving going on.

So Ingenious One,
what I want at last to say
is thanks
for the Christly, christening way
you hear me out,
so I can hear myself
anew.

Seraphim in Disguise

O God,
everywhere present, but nowhere obvious,
here I am where I always seem to be:
betwixt cold fronts and crocuses,
dreams and disappointments,
failures and summons,
flaws and gifts,
growing up and growing old;
betwixt isolation and intimacy,
weariness and renewal,
despair and hope,
confidence and fear,
life and death.

O God,
you must know how hard it is
to be in this between
where nothing is certain,
everything's in flux,
this relentless churning
from something I can't quite grasp
to something I can't quite see,
and it's all up for grabs,
and—please God—
for grace.
Mercy out of me
this tumorous sense of fault,
this dead-weight of doubt
that I am not two-sparrows' worth,
and no concern of yours.

Deepen into me
the liberating assurance
that I am where you are with me,
stretched between the kingdom in our midst
and the slow fullness of its coming.

Muster my courage
to let go of the clutch of grievances
that keep rendering me vaguely the same,
to become vulnerable to surprise—by being one—
taking some outrageous, specific dare of love.
Strengthen my trust
that you are in the turbulence
to intensify my struggles,
and to render me, as well,
sociable to joy, subject to your grace.
Keen my awareness
that uncertainty is my dance with you,
crises, seraphim in disguise,
rumpling the air with choice and change,
tonging the coals of another chance,
proclaiming betwixt as holy,
cleansing my soul for gratitude,
freeing me, when sent, to go for you,
a little less afraid,
a little more at ease.

This Earthly Hitch Toward Glory

O God,
who winks quarks and quasars
and braids Saturn's rings,
intrigue me out of my shame
at making mistakes:
fear of the worst I could do or be
keeps me from risking my best.

Remind me, again,
Spinner of galaxies, possibilities,
and my inquisitive, quivering spirit,
that what joins me to you
is less the devout repetition
of the tried and safely true,
than the creative dare,
the imaginative lurch,
the reworking of the expected
toward an unexpected new:
at risk of making errors, yes,
but faith, and love, and merry, too.

O God, confirm me in my power,
as I would confirm you in yours,
for I would claim my power without apology.
I would be trusting done with this smoldering deference,
this chafing humility, ingrown virginity,
quite-too-virtuous denial of strength,
and just claim this power you gave to me,
along with all these visions, impulses, hopes, promptings
that make me laugh, cry, long
to create the hell out of life—
and to heaven with my blunders;

to make my half-believing self
somewhat more believing
and believable.

O God, make me brave, then,
to use my power to create something original,
worth the breath and blood and sweat and joy:
mind over the matter of feared defeats,
spirit over the specter of tragic error;
to employ imagination in the squint to see;
to trust that grace mutates mistakes into surprise,
like the fall turned into the wondrous history
of your lover's quarrel with the world and me;
that what we lost in Eden was our innocence,
not our power or our freedom or your image in us;
that your mercy comes as another chance
I can dare to take.

So would I boldly add my power with your lover's quarrel
and stand hard for justice,
reach far for beauty,
walk long for peace,
be a worthy adversary of whatever
demeans and trivializes this humanity;
thus changing self as well,
become more fully one of this wondrous, wounded all
I would go with on this earthly hitch toward glory,
this graceful twist of history
you've promised to make with me.

Before I Waste Away

O God,
I've been out here too long
in this wasting competition,
this shuffle of disguises,
this diversion of words,
this commerce of fear,
somehow hoping not to be found
unless I could be found innocent,
or discovered for accomplishments.

Now I laugh at my damned absurdity,
laughter, I think,
your tag of grace,
my small burst of wisdom,
and some trust.
It is, as well, a prayer to change,
not for the better, but for you,
and for a self I ache to be
before I simply waste away.

So I would take something, away from words,
and listen with it a while:
not all fear is bad,
and I would learn from mine.

It's you I've been avoiding,
and yet seeking, too,
in all my busy chittering,
frantic performing,
frittering tasks,
fearing intimacy I desire
even in my prayers—
a towering babble

telling you less than you know,
reciting this shopping list
of impressive petitions
for self-improvement,
as if they were the way
to you,
when, if I took the risk of listening,
I might hear, even now,
the fearful invitation
to the fearful novelty
of shucking the anxiety of unassignments,
of daring to ask for less,
and simply taking rest,
in you.

God,
I would no more listen to
all the self-appointed prophets
who tell me who not to listen to
lest I keep missing you,
missing angels in disguise—
rejects, bums, clowns, dreamers—
who make much more than sense;
and all the more keep missing
the promptings of my mind,
the churning of my passions,
this holy glowing intuition
that I carry my destination within—
your image traced upon my soul
branding me as your own,
claiming me for
the not easy,
only rewarding
revolution of love.

The Downsweep of Your Wing

O God of storms as well as stillness,
 of questions on which all answers snag,
  of forbidding holiness as well as exciting horizons,
 when, as always and as now,
  I don't have enough
   inspiration,
    wisdom,
     imagination,
      will,
       or faith
  to do what seems to lay its claim on me,
   or to work the change that seems required,
 have mercy on me
  and cover me with grace
   that I may accept,
    however I can,
     these limits of finitude I face,
      these mortal limits that I am.
Then, grant me to fix upon,
 even with wavering eye
  and wandering mind,
   the glimmer of hope
    without which all is darkness,
 that you, less limited than I,
  will find a way to me,
   bestow some gift I cannot name,
    might not choose,
     probably miss as such—

but will persist in its pursuit,
name me,
miss not my need
or my heart—
though perhaps break both—
and will work the change
I may not quite believe,
yet will give me peace enough
to roll the dice of days again,
as even now I am about to do.

I take the gamble, O gambling God,
at the behest of some urge
I could resist, but won't,
perhaps to feel—
ah, that's the pull—
the sensual surprise of all my senses
that what lays its too much claim on me
is really just your claim of me,
the downsweep of your wing,
your pressing back on pressing me
through the integrity of this world—
its stubborn, haunting beauty,
its resistance to my plans,
which breaks my pride,
its curious loves, perplexing faults,
the home it is I cannot find—
all of this, and so much more,
this bearing down of real weight,
yet tracing, all the while,
the living weight of me,.

ratifying my existence to me,
strangely rending me more willing
for the thresh of prayer,
yet, I surmise,
more strangely still,
readying me, still quite unknowing,
for the giddy updraft of grace.

Is this your prayer
for me to hear?

O God, I'm listening.

Sweet, Mother-Loving Jesus

She was lying in the tub ruminating aloud when the sucking sound of the drain got loud enough to distract her. Enraged at the interruption, she pitched forward, reviling the drain gods, "Just one damn, mother-loving time—is that asking too much?" Her sudden movement created a turbulence of whirlpools and tidal waves, sloshing water over the edge of the tub. As she groped for the wash cloth she'd packed around the drain, she yelled louder, "Sweet, mother-loving Jesus!" She threw the wash cloth against the wall where it sopped up a small patch of paint flakes and flopped to the floor. Freed of that impediment, the water flowed more rapidly down the drain. "Crap," she muttered, and lay back wearily, sending more water splashing from the tub. "Doesn't matter, Norton," she sighed, "nothing matters." She closed her eyes and spit in the air. "No mother-loving, damn thing," she emphasized in the way of someone used to talking to herself or to her long departed husband.

Hannah Holgate's life was reduced to one room and a bath, with a kitchenette on the wall between the hallway door and the bathroom door, in a deteriorating apartment house with which she had a grudging affinity, physically and financially. The lever for operating the drain in the tub had corroded and couldn't be closed tightly, so the water leaked out faster than more water could be added by the balky water heater. A body couldn't soak anything to a comfort or a conclusion.

Resigned to that inevitability, she got out and toweled herself off carefully. She grieved over the spots and folds and creases that must have come slowly upon her body and yet somehow seemed to have arrived with the same shocking suddenness as a late October cold rain quickly turning riotous autumn to somber gray. Hannah appraised herself in the mirror. There was no denying it, but the wonder was that she didn't feel at all as her body looked. Inside, under all the sags, wrinkles, spidery veins, and strangely translucent skin, she felt there was a young woman living as Jonah in the belly of an aged whale.

She assumed a sideways pose. "Hannah Holgate," she whispered to her image, "you ravishing beauty, you turner of heads, you irresistible femme . . ." she turned the other way, "fatale." She dropped the pose and snorted at herself in the mirror, "Right! Fatal's what I got all right. Hannah, if you were to fall over in a forest, would a tree hear? Face it, honey . . . it wouldn't."

She chuckled, held her head back, pulled the skin of her face tightly, and began applying eye shadow while she talked. "Norton, do you suppose my skin's puckering because I've turned bitter? Or maybe I'm just bitter because my skin's puckering." She paused to run lipstick over her lips, purse them together, and then blot them lightly on some toilet paper before concluding: "Either way, it's just too damn bad, isn't it, Norton?"

She shrugged, wrapped the towel around her, flicked off the light switch, and paused in the dark. "The question is, if I'm old, why ain't I wise? The answer is, if I ain't wise, I must not be old." She chuckled, then shrugged. "Or maybe the truth is that all that stuff about the old being wise is a mother-loving myth, Norton. But if that's so, we oughtn't tell anyone or they'll take us off Social Security and Medicare and let us starve, like those people sleeping out there on the sidewalks." She shook her head. "Or maybe I am just crazy, like people say."

She walked into her room, which strained somewhat unsuccessfully to hold the chairs, sofas, end tables, and accumulated bric-a-brac of her sixty-seven years. The twilight softened the shrugging confusion of it and hid places where the water-stained, rambling rose wallpaper had bubbled loose and years of use had scratched and scrunched all the furniture. Around the room she'd hung the familiar pictures that had filled the walls wherever she'd lived for the last fifty years.

Between the pictures, she'd more recently hung, or actually scotch taped, a variety of posters that had caught her fancy, pictures of mountains or meadows of flowers or animals on which were pithy aphorisms, such as, "All we need is an ear to listen, an eye to behold, a heart to feel"; or "A friend comes in when everyone else goes out"; or "Love cultivates, not dominates"; or "None of us is as smart as all of us." She'd liked those posters and simple slogans. They seemed quite religious to her, easily digestible little morsels to feed her soul. Lately though, she'd tired of them as she had of the cheap TV dinners she ate with less and less frequency.

She went to the window, pushed aside a dirty soup bowl on the sill, cranked the window open a crack, leaned on her elbows, and looked out. Far down the street, which ran west to the river, the sky was a smear of indigo and orange running down to crimson, one of those conflagrations that seem to pronounce judgment and give the impression of great fires raging below. It had been raining earlier, and the spring evening felt sodden. The drip of water from the protrusions of the building seemed strangely ominous.

Shivering, Hannah turned from the window, shouting to audibly complete the shiver and to warn whatever furies rode the oncoming night: "Damnit all anyway!" The ensuing silence seemed arrogant. She pressed her hands to her temples. What was it she was supposed to be doing? Was she going out? To a meeting? To a lecture at the Y? Was Norton coming home? For a minute, she couldn't focus. No, it wasn't Norton; he was dead. What was it then? She got things more and more confused these days. Panic nibbled at her edges.

She turned back to the window. She still felt strong physically, and that reassured her. The light from Hahn's, the bargain drug store at the corner, glistened on the wet pavement. She could hear the druggist pulling down the protective grill over the front of the store in preparation for closing. Down from Hahn's was Luc's Convenience Mart, open all night, that was run by a Vietnamese family; then a Deli, a discount appliance store with one display window boarded up, Bryant's cleaners, The Bull's Eye bar, Jack's Pit Barbecued Ribs, McNally's bar, and so on down the block. It was a hip pocket of the city.

Hannah often fantasized about the Hahns and Lucs and Bryants and Jack as she gazed from her window, imagining what their lives were like. But who were they, really? Were they survivors or mutations? In a city, or anywhere, who were the predators, who the prey? Or perhaps a neighborhood is a symbiotic system with changing hosts and parasites. Still, what would happen to these people? Who cared what happened to them? Who had looked out this very same window fifty years ago, or ten years ago, or five? What had they seen? Did it matter? She felt the tears and blinked them back. A man walked his dog through the puddle of drug store light and waited while the dog sniffed and lifted on a hydrant. A bus lurched around the corner and squealed to a stop. Someone got off.

Across the street was the park. In the daytime it was benign; in the night time, malignant. Children played there in the light, demons in the dark. Or so it seemed. She had heard of the terrible things that happened there: drug deals, gang fights, orgies, murders, rapes. There were even stories of people who had gone in there and never been seen again. Even now as she watched, the park appeared to crouch there like some prehistoric beast, its dark heart impenetrable, its tree limbs seeming to twist grotesquely to conceal obscene, nameless terrors, the returned nightmares of childhood. Sound, light, safety, civilization stopped at the edge of the park, reinforcing her assumption that evil must be silent and invisible. "That park scares me to death, Norton."

She put her fingers to her face and felt again the years layered and grooved there. Something in her knew it wasn't just death that the park embodied to her. It was abandonment, utter loneliness. And fear, fear of the abyss, something unimaginable, bottomless, nameless. If you could name things, they had meaning. If you could name something, it would have a certain order, a tincture of hope. Meaninglessness was what the park threatened. Chaos! Senselessness! That was the word the newspapers often used about things—senseless killings, senseless destruction, senseless violence. Senseless, senseless! That was the terror of the park. It was an abyss! You had to bang on tight to keep from slipping into it.

On the far side of the park, and seeming quite far removed from it, she saw the dark outline of the spire of Christ Church, one of the most well known in the city. She'd been there many times. "It's beautiful, Norton," she sighed softly, "so peaceful—the windows, the music, the prayers. Even from here, you can see it's beautiful. Look!" She cocked her head as if to point, then added plaintively, "But there's that park between." Her brow furrowed. Why was the park there, rubbing its back against her building, its head against that beautiful church? What was the connection? Or was there any? Suddenly she felt an urgency, a confusion. What was she trying to get hold of? She rubbed her eyes. Whatever it was had slipped away. Why did she get so confused sometimes? Why was her brain so balky? "Damn mother-loving everything anyway, Norton!" she fumed.

She padded away from the window, switched on the light, sat on the chrome-plastic stool at the kitchenette counter, and picked up the envelope leaning against the toaster. The address was in familiar hand-writing. "Mrs. Hannah Holgate, 15725 Park Drive, Apt. 324." And in the corner that fearful return address: "Susan Holgate, Central State Hospital . . ." It had come three days ago. She pulled out the letter, unfolded it carefully, and read yet again:

Dear Mother,

I'm in the hospital again. To say the least, I'm discouraged. And scared. Everything seems so damned hard, so impossible. Three breakdowns in four years. Guinness Book of Records, right? I keep telling myself I'm really making progress, getting better, that this is a learning experience. But I'm sick of plastic optimism.

You always told me life was a continuous learning experience, a building process, each change bringing us a bit closer to fulfillment. Be positive, you said. Everything will work out. I hate to tell you, Mom, but that's a lot of bull. My life keeps falling apart. So tell me why. What's the truth?

I ask Chaplain Charlie here, and all he can say is that I have to trust God's love, that all this is for my good and I have to make it work for me. Can you believe that? What in Christ's holy name is that supposed to mean? I keep asking C. C., and he just keeps smiling and says we'll keep working on my problems and some day I'll understand. When he said that this morning, I screamed at him, "We? We'll *keep working? How the hell are you working on it? You going to sleep with me tonight? Maybe that would help." Then I laughed like a fiend. He just patted my arm and left, smiling. Condescending bastard!*

Christ, I'd like to crack his sanctimonious pose. Hell of it is, he probably doesn't even know it's a pose! Every morning at 8 or so, C.C. wheels in in his nice little Honda and does his nice little job and around 5:00 he heads back to his nice little house and nice little family he's always talking about and reads his nice little books. And he's the expert! Me? I lie on my cot and listen to the babble of this damn place and get crazier. It's unbelievable.

Well, I wish I could send some good news to you. I guess I'll just have to try again to get my life back together. But I feel panicky. I feel like I've just got to get out of here, one way or another.

Think of me, Mom.

Susan.

Hannah felt defeated. "One way or another," she echoed. Once, Susan had overdosed on sleeping pills and almost died. "Is that what she means, Norton?" she shouted over her shoulder before dropping the letter on the counter. She put her head down. "O dear God," she whispered, "dear God . . ." What was it she wanted to say? "Damn you!" she said through clenched teeth. Yes, that was it. "Damn you, help her! Help her! Help me!"

She stood and paced, thinking about the phone call she'd gotten late that afternoon from Doctor Somebody or other. "I have a call for Hannah Holgate from Doctor Whoever-it-was," the operator said. "Is this Hannah Holgate?"

Then the doctor's voice came on, sounding so detached and professional, saying things she couldn't quite grasp through her slippery fear: "We thought you should know . . . daughter . . . unauthorized departure yesterday . . . notified the authorities . . . quite sick . . . unpredictable behavior . . . be sure to let us know."

It wasn't until he'd hung up that her question focused. She yelled into the dead phone: "Let you know what? What? I thought you were supposed to know!" That's when she'd run the water for her bath. Now she wondered why. What was it she thought she'd do? What was she supposed to do?

"Get dressed, Hannah," she said so loudly it startled her. "Yes, get dressed, it'll come to you." She lurched toward the closet and collided with a chair. The towel dropped off. Tears welled up again. She sank into the offending chair. "Sweet, mother-loving Jesus, help me. Please."

"What Susan says *is* true, isn't it Norton?" she said, beginning to cry. She had believed that life was about continuous progress toward better things, that a positive attitude helped solve temporary setbacks, that a better world was possible because people were basically good. She'd held onto that even when Norton had died after nine hellish months of constant care following a stroke and Susan had been in mental hospitals a couple of times. And God was sort of . . . well, love. Kind of a cross between a Disney Prince Charming and a Clint Eastwood type dealing with the bad guys. Yes, that actually just about described it. She smiled quaveringly at the image. Or maybe these days, judging from what she picked up in the news, God was more a cross between Snow White and Gloria Steinem,

Suddenly the unexamined triviality of it overwhelmed her, and she began to sob. "Oh God, I love Susan. What can I do?" What Susan said seemed true, that believing everything would work out was a lot of bull. The world really wasn't any better after all these years. She'd voted once for Norman Thomas, had been for the New Deal, the Fair Deal, all those deals, advocated population control, marched for civil rights and against wars—and if anything, the world had just as many problems as before that were, if anything, more dangerous ones. So who was the enemy? Where was the enemy?

"I'm not going to think about it anymore, Norton," she insisted. "I have to get dressed and go now." She walked naked to her tiny closet, quickly chose from her meager collection and got dressed quickly: hose with only one run in each, scuffed patent-leather shoes with the low heels, red dress, rust jacket. The only neck scarf she could find was turquoise. She tied it in place.

Then on an impulse, she got down on her hands and knees and reached unsuccessfully toward the back of the closet. A stuffed chair blocked the door from opening fully. She pushed the chair with her legs. The door just cleared. She reached in and got out an inlaid jewelry box. She opened it and took out a huge medallion. Her grandmother had given it to her mother, who had given it to her. Her mother had died politely disappointed in her for some unspoken reason she had never understood but still had tried to rectify, even after her mother's death.

But Hannah had never worn the medallion. For one thing, it was so large and heavy. It had a wide, sculpted metal frame encircling an enameled replica of Michelangelo's earthy, lusty painting of the Holy Family. It must have weighed at least a pound, counting the heavy chain. She slipped it over her head and stood. It swung awkwardly, giving her a slight off-balance feeling as she walked. She paused, feeling dizzy. "Never mind, Norton," she declared with a wave of her hand, "it's time."

She left the apartment house uncertain where she was going or what she was looking for. She started walking. The dizziness increased, things began to blur. She walked faster. Sounds echoed in her head: Susan's colicky cry when she was a baby; the rattle of Norton's breathing after his stroke; the bath water gurgling down the leaky drain; that distant voice on the phone: "unauthorized departure . . . unpredictable behavior." She was sure the incessant, distracting ringing in her ears came from the park.

The ringing turned louder, the ringing of a cash register. She heard the buzzing of talk, glass clanking, dim music from somewhere; a blue and red neon sign was floating through smoke. She realized she was in a bar. A hand was stroking her, here, there. The face's breath was sour. Its lips were moving. She tilted her head trying to locus. The lips were saying, "Come on, babe. Drink up and we'll just get on out of here."

She shook her head trying to clear it. "Who are you?" she pleaded.

"Hey," the face leered at her, seeming to speak from under water, "that don't make no difference, now does it? Just say I'm a buyer, you're a seller." The hands began moving over her again.

She felt sick. How did she get here? "Wait," she stammered, "I've got to . . . to . . . get some air."

"Sure thing, baby," face nodded knowingly, "me, too. Come on, let's get some . . . air." The face winked, floated up; the hand took her arm.

"Oh, please, no," she whispered, then more loudly, "Please. I'm no . . . no seller." The grip tightened on her arm, a hand fondled her. "Please don't," she shouted, "Sweet, mother-loving Jesus. Stop it!"

She tried to push the hand away. Jesus? She struggled to remember . . . prostitutes . . . could she be one? . . . they used the park to . . . to do business. She did know that, but . . . Jesus? . . .

Mary Magdalene his friend because . . . because prostitutes . . . prostitutes . . . what? "What?" She began to cry. "Because he . . . they . . . prostitutes know something about . . . about the park. Yes, what they knew was . . . was . . ."

The hand was under her skirt, fumbling at her garter belt. She swung wildly, hitting the face. "Stop it," she shouted struggling to her feet. "Leave me alone." She started to move away.

The hand grabbed at her dress. "Hold on, bitch," the face growled. The fabric tore.

She stumbled, caught herself. "Lemme go," she screamed.

"Damn whore," the face bellowed, "who'd'ya think ya are, hittin' me?" The hand shoved her hard.

She fell, exposed. She tried to cover herself, to get up, but she slipped down again. There was whistling, jeering, laughing all around her. She rolled to her hands and knees, pushed herself up, stumbled toward the Exit sign shining over the door. Hands pinched, pawed her.

Then she was outside running, crying. "Help me! Sweet, mother-loving Jesus, help me," she sobbed, dodging cars, people, gasping for air, stopping to lean against a wall. "Norton? Norton?" she called, "Where am I supposed to be? Norton?" She bit her knuckle to stifle a scream when she recognized the wall as the wall around the park. Sheet lightning flickered across the sky.

Frantically, she ran back across the street. Cars honked at her. She reached the other side, slowed to catch her breath. At the corner, a street preacher was beseeching pedestrians. Two or three had stopped in disbelief, others walked on laughing and shaking their heads. She paused, mid-sidewalk, gaping. The preacher was wearing only boxer shorts and sneakers, catcher's shin-guards and chest-protector, and a bicycle helmet. She started to chuckle. He looked like a kid at play but was yelling and carrying on like someone demented. On one arm he had fastened a metal garbage lid, and in the other hand he waved a bayonet.

“Go on, laugh,” he shouted, “I don’t mind being a fool for Christ. But you,” he pointed at them with his bayonet, “the Bible says you will be damned fools if you don’t take for yourselves the whole armor of God, the breastplate of righteousness, the helmet of salvation”—with each reference he touched the articles on his body with his bayonet—“the shield of faith, the sword of the Spirit”—holding his bayonet aloft—“otherwise, St. Paul tells us, otherwise the powers of darkness and wickedness will be too strong for you”—emphasizing the words with the stage whisper and knowing wink of an informer—“the fiery darts of the devil will be too much to quench.” As if in the mockery of a comic opera, sheet lightning flashed, and a few drops of rain began to fall.

Advancing toward him, Hannah screeched, “What in the name of sweet, mother-loving Jesus are you talking about, you maniac?”

The sight of her coming at him startled him. “I’m not a maniac,” he protested, “I’m an ambassador for Christ.” The words seem to restore his zeal. He began to roar, “You are the maniac if you do not listen. I’m talking about principalities and powers, the hosts of wick-ed-ness!” He lifted and shook his arms in punctuation.

She arrived in front of him, grabbed each side of his chest protector, and pulled him toward her, speaking in an intense rumble, “What are these hosts? Where are they? Have you ever seen them? Where are they? Where?”

She began to cry and shake him. The preacher tried to hold her off without dropping his shield. They both tripped over the curb and fell in a tangled heap. She wrestled free. Faces in the crowd that had gathered were blurred, laughing. She sat, screaming at them, crying, “Please, tell me where I’m supposed to be? Where? I don’t know . . . don’t know what I was doing back there, in that bar.” She pointed wildly. “And Susan . . . Susan’s . . . unauthorized but . . . where? Where? Tell me if you know!” No one answered. The rain shower suddenly came harder.

She struggled to her feet, wiping her tears, her leaking nose, on the back of her hands. “And y-y-you,” she wheeled suddenly, pointing at the stunned preacher and shuddering to the end of her crying, “you d-d-don’t really know a d-d-damn, a mu-mu-mother-lah-lah-loving th-thing. You just t-t-talk. And, and, and strut around like a, a mu-mu-monkey and pass the hat to bu-buy booze. You’re no am-ambassador, for G-God’s sake. You’re just a se-seller, hoping for bu-buyers, like them,” her arm swept toward the crowd. “It’s all, it’s all . . . prostitution.”

Suddenly she knew where she had to go. She turned, lurched back across the street toward the park. One heel had broken off. She kicked off both shoes and left them in the street. The preacher shouted after her, “Hey, who do you think you are?” She didn’t pause. She’d heard that question before. “Hey, lady, wait a minute. God is not mocked. Come back!”

She was in the shadows at the edge of the park before she stopped to catch her breath. The rain shower had ended, but over her gasping she could hear the rain still dripping off the trees. An occasional sheet of lightning rippled the sky. Spring smells of decay and fecundity mixed in the heavy air. She'd entered the park on the sidewalk by one of the streets that taxis and cars used to cut across town. Now she left the street on a pedestrian path and leaned against a tree. She felt suddenly and overwhelmingly alone, entirely alone, beyond the help of protection of law and order, of words or reason, of kinship or friendship, even of her Eastwood-Steinem God. She'd decided on this course, this baiting of the beast, as a purging, a daring, a searching, but she was as frightened as she was determined, "What is it I'm looking for, Norton?" she whispered, "sweet, mother-loving Jesus, tell me."

She took a deep breath and listened. Nothing. But it was even less than nothing. It was the nothing she'd heard on the telephone when it rang and there was no reply to her hello, no sound, and she'd listened for a moment to the silent listener, and then checked the locks on all the doors. She shivered and began to walk. She heard a sound behind her and picked up her pace, not looking back. Lightning skittered across the sky. In the distance she thought she saw someone walking toward her on the path.

She squinted intently at the small probe of light from the one still-working lamp along the pathway twenty or thirty yards ahead. At the edge of the light someone was walking. A familiar, pigeon-toed sway. Tall. A skirt. In the mist and dim light she couldn't tell. Was it really someone or was it just her imagination?

She heard the noise behind her again. She heard herself whimpering, "Oh sweet, mother-loving Jesus. Please!" It was so dark, so threatening. She was jogging now, as fast as she could. She tried to think. It was urgent. The point . . . about Jesus and . . . and prostitutes and . . . the park? What was it? What?

"Norton," she shouted, as if he'd help her think of it. All she heard in response was someone behind her running, yelling something. Ahead she saw sudden movement in the shadows, heard scuffling, a muffled cry. She had seen somebody.

"Be sure to let us know," the voice had said.

"Let you know what?" she screamed now into the darkness. Then she stopped. She knew.

"Susan?" she called, as a mother calls a child home from play, expecting an answer. It was ominously quiet. She ran toward where she'd seen the scuffling. "Susan! Susan!" she shouted. An arc of lightning etched things in sharp relief. In that second she spotted bushes moving off to the side. Then she heard the sound of struggle. She tore toward the sound, wet branches slapping at her. She pushed through to an open space. Someone grabbed her. "Help!" she screamed, "Sweet . . ."

A hand covered her mouth. "Shut the hell up, whore. You know you askin' for it, comin' in the park alone like this. So you gonna get it. Probably even like it, tell the truth. Know I'm gonna." The hand ripped at her dress, tearing it half open.

She bit and kicked at the same time. A fist hit her hard on the ear. She fell and rolled quickly to her knees. Almost reflexively she pulled the medallion over her head and gripped the chain tightly in her fist. Lightning flashed once, twice. In that instant she saw a man in front of her, unzipping his pants. Beyond him in the clearing she could see Susan's face past the shoulder of another half-naked man kneeling over her, pinning her against the base of a tree with a knife against her throat.

"Susan," she shouted, "Susan."

As the darkness returned to swallow everything, she heard the choked question, "Mom?"

"It's me, Susan," she shouted, trying to sound reassuring. Then she squeezed her eyes shut in terror and gasped, "Sweet, mother-loving Jesus, have mercy." She opened her eyes. They adjusted quickly to the darkness. "Don't hurt her," she pleaded, "Let her go, I'll stay. I'll do anything."

"Well, ain't this somethin', Lefty?" drooled the man in front of her. "Extra thrill, them being mother and daughter, ain't it?" Holding up his pants with one hand, the man cackled and stepped toward her.

"Rape," she screamed, "Help! Rape!" She was on her feet, swinging the medallion. It hit the man's head with a thud. He staggered, slipped down.

She kept swinging and screaming. Then she became aware of another voice bellowing, "The Lord of hosts, the Lord of hosts." She recognized the street preacher. She saw him kick at the man holding Susan. The man fell away, kicked back, and the preacher fell. They began wrestling awkwardly in the mud. Susan staggered to her feet, pulling her skirt down.

"Run, Susan, run!" she screamed. She saw the man plunge his knife into the preacher. "Run," she screamed again, taking a step toward Susan.

But the man who'd stabbed the preacher jumped up and grabbed Susan. As they struggled, the preacher tried to grab the man's legs. By the time Hannah saw the man she'd hit with her medallion lurch to his feet beside her, it was too late. His punch knocked her off her feet.

She landed in a twisted, awkward position, her mouth full of blood and mud. She pushed herself to a sitting position and started swinging her weapon. It was hitting something. There was a groan. She climbed to her feet, slipping uncertainly. Someone kicked her in the stomach. As she fell, she swung her medallion one last time, as if she was splitting a log with an ax. Then she was on her hand and knees, retching. Then as the darkness opened under her, she thought, "It can't hurt me now. I can still see. There's enough light."

Then she was floating. She was a little girl on a swing, pushed higher and higher, invited to jump. She did. The sun was bright in her eyes. Beautiful birds sang around her, but their song was strangely raucous. Everything felt warm and soft. She landed in a cloud of flowers, all different colors. Bees were buzzing, sniffing, talking. She could understand them.

"Careful," they said. And "easy." And "broken." And "lucky . . . alive."

She opened her eyes. Flashing lights seemed to be everywhere. She was strapped to something soft. There was a cool hand on her forehead. Then a pinpoint of light flashed in one eye, then the other. A man's voice assured her, "You're going to be okay. Just take it easy. We're going to the hospital in a minute. You'll be okay," How did they know? "Norton?" she croaked, "how did . . . She coughed up mucous and blood.

"Take it easy." The voice became a man with a mustache leaning over her, wiping her lips.

Another voice hovering at the edge of her vision asked, "Norton's the guy in the shorts and chest protector?"

She tried to answer but it was too complicated. She nodded. The pain was sharp and she winced.

The voice went on. "Easy. Norton's seriously hurt, but his chest protector may have saved his life. Knife wound didn't reach his heart. He managed to stagger out to the street and a squad car happened to spot him. Otherwise . . ."

The voice trailed off. She followed the sound of it to a woman standing at her shoulder, wearing a yellow baseball cap, holding a bag with a tube running down to her. She could feel the needle in her arm.

Another voice from somewhere: "Ground bein' slippery didn't hurt nothin' either. Gave the broads better odds 'gainst those punks."

Another voice: "Did ya' see th' medics hadda pry that damn medal outta her hand? Cut th' scum up good with it. Probably hav'ta go to emergency afta we book 'em."

She turned her eyes back to the mustache face. "Susan?" she whispered through puffed lips.

"The other woman?" mustache man asked gently.

She nodded, holding her breath, suddenly teary.

"She said she's your daughter." The mustache man smiled

Hannah let out her breath at the smile. "Yes," her voice was hoarse, her smile weak in return.

"She's been pretty badly hurt, but I think she's going to be okay," the mustache man assured her. "They're with her now. You're both lucky."

"Sweet . . ." she started to whisper, but then she felt herself being lifted, rolled into place. She realized it was an ambulance. The man and woman with the yellow cap were there, too. Someone else was on the other side of the small enclosure. It was very bright. A door closed. They were moving. A siren sounded far away.

A strange man in a green pajama-type shirt with dark stains on it bent over her and showed her the medallion. There was blood on it. "I hear this is yours," he said, "Maybe you'd feel better if you held it." He put it in her hand.

She nodded and closed her fingers around it. She wanted to ask how he knew it was hers, but the man went right on.

"The police may want it back sometime, I can tell you it did a lot of damage," he confided, winking approvingly.

She tried to clear her throat. She whispered, her eyes filling with tears. "Damage?" What was it? What wasn't it? She felt very confused.

"Yes. I was the first to check the guys who assaulted you," green shirt man nodded, wrapping something on her arm, pumping it tight. "The scalp of one was split open. You must have done that. The calf muscle of the other was badly cut. I'm not sure how you managed that."

"Preacher," she croaked, but the green shirt man was paying attention to something else.

"But that medal probably saved your life," he concluded, unwrapping the thing on her arm, patting her easily on her shoulder. He said something to the mustache man and turned back to the other side of the ambulance.

Assuring her that he'd try not to hurt her, the mustache man inserted a new needle near where the other had been and taped it in place.

Slowly, Hannah's eyes followed the green shirt to the other side. She'd been wanting to look over there since they'd loaded her into the ambulance, but she hadn't quite been able to bring herself to it. She was afraid of what she might see. Yet she hoped.

Her eyes met Susan's staring back, unblinking. Her first thought was that Susan was dead. Then she realized the eyes were glazed, as a child's, with utter weariness and pain, yet were quite alive, focusing on her across the narrow aisle. Her daughter's hair was matted with blood, her check swollen and badly scraped, blood caked at the corner of her mouth. But her eyes were fully open.

"Susan," she rasped. She strained to remember what it was she wanted to say, to find the words. "I . . . I don't know why your life keeps . . . why it keeps falling apart. I just don't . . . know. Forgive me, honey."

Tears filled Susan's eyes, pooled at the bridge of her nose, overflowed. Her words came slowly, weighted by pain, soft with wonder, "Mom . . . it's . . . okay . . . you were . . . there . . . for me . . . a tiger . . ."

"You for me, too," Hannah whispered. "Thing is . . . I'm not sure why . . . why it came together like that, either. It's . . . strange, honey." She was surprised at saying that, but having said them, the words made sense. Maybe that was what she'd been trying to get hold of about Mary Magdalene. But it was too hard to think about now.

"Yeah . . ." Susan gasped, a small smile fluttering through her pain. Before she could go on, she coughed.

"You better take it easy," the mustache man cautioned.

The green shirt man, checking Susan's pulse, glanced up and said, "Might be more important they talk," he said.

Susan struggled to get the words out. "Yeah . . . strange . . ." She grimaced. "God . . . maybe?"

Hannah looked in Susan's eyes, waiting, wondering. "Could be," she whispered, "sweet, mother-loving Jesus . . . it could definitely be . . . yes."

Susan's eyes closed. Hannah felt frightened, but the green shirt man didn't change expression. He kept holding Susan's hand. The mustache man leaned up and wiped off Hannah's brow.

"Susan?" she called hoarsely. "Susan."

Slowly Susan opened her eyes, and her effort to smile succeeded in only one corner of her mouth. Her eyes closed, then opened again.

"You can't . . . give up, honey," Hannah insisted, her voice cracking. "This time I'll . . . I'll be with you. Hear?"

Ever so slightly, Susan nodded her head.

Hannah opened her hand and turned her medallion so Susan could see it. With great effort Susan's eyes went to the medallion, then questioningly back to her mother's face.

"Goes back . . . to your great-grandmother," Hannah said softly, as if beginning bedtime story. "Now . . . it's yours."

She lifted it toward Susan, but it was too heavy and slipped from her fingers. Only the chain around her thumb saved it from falling. She looked at the mustache man. "Please," she whispered.

The mustache man took the medallion and gently put it in Susan's hand. Susan closed her fingers to hold it, then closed her eyes.

Weariness and a kind of peace overtook Hannah. She closed her eyes too, watched the little galaxies of light whirl in that darkness, and asked almost inaudibly, "Does where we're going have a tub with a drain that doesn't leak?"

No Once and for All

O Holy One,
    I am distressed at how slowly,
        if at all, I am being made new.
    How long must I put up with me,
        or how long must you?
    I wonder into sighing
        and grope for a longer view.

O Eternal One,
    free me of this double curse
    of always wondering how I'm doing
    while I'm doing all things else,
        as if the how were your measure,
        not the measures that I've learned
            from a thousand other teachers
            I'm more afraid to disappoint
            than myself . . . or you.

When everything seems to change but me,
    ease my peevish self-punishments
    that proudly lack all sense of you,
    and throw around me the mantle of your mercy,
        that I may be more honest and more gentle
        with my deluded, grasping self
            when I, a simply beloved creature,
            fall short of the godly ideals
            to which, like the first Adam, I aspire.

Then soften me into your patience
as again, and yet again, and always one more time,
I must go on to wrestle these old demons of mine—
rage and fear and envy, dis-ease and self-deception—
which I never really overcome once and for all;
and, as a blessing, a disjointing of my demands,
remind me there is no once and for all
in this earthly pilgrimage I'm on,
that I may limp to a more graceful rhythm.

Scale my eyes to see afresh,
gladden my spirit to embrace
the small yet critical, slow yet cumulative changes
I have nurtured, and been renewed by, over my seasons,
and open my head to understand, my heart to trust
that my willingness to struggle makes me wondrous,
my flailing reach toward you is yet your gift to me,
and the one thing I can brave to do better than anyone
is to keep seeking, faithfully, my truest self with you.

MORTALITY

Daring the Embarrassments

Holy Spirit,
I am weary of the scurry
of many words and much doing,
worn thin by the scour
of time's relentless passing,
warped by claims and expectations
I take on but cannot meet,
lay out but cannot collect.
Holy Spirit,
this mortal thus unmade
turns now to you to be remade.
Shush me to a stillness
in which I can abide,
unthreatened, for a time,
and let the wave of your grace
roll, break, spread
on the shore of my soul,
until there is healing in me,
healing through me;
until I catch the eternal note
on the far side of silence,
signaling me to live
by daring the embarrassments
of reworking what's reworkable
with trust, and love, and mercy,
until some rusted, twisted crux of me
unlocks, releases, opens like a tomb,
responding to my knock and your command—
as I sense happening even now—

and I slip at last into accurate place,
into the strangely familiar
wilderness landscape of my soul,
my exodus to freedom
out of fear to courage,
out of despair to hope,
out of self-pity to creativity,
out of faithless resistance to mortality—
this fearful, distracting kicking
at shadows lapping at my feet—
to shifting my eyes from downward glance
toward stars outshining darkest night,
streams within the wilderness,
wondrous pilgrims on the way,
the promised land,
the cruciform bridge,
and you.

Fall in the Soul

You have made for everything a season
and yet, O God,
when leaves turn and flowers fade
I'm reminded again
it's always autumn in the soul,
or perhaps "fall"
is the better term,
that end of innocence,
that primal whispered warning
coming with self-consciousness—
that second consciousness
of fleeting time,
quite finite talent,

O God, it's always fall in my soul;
first the burst of glorious color,
then paring winds of discontent,
the rains of guilt and dread,
and, as in autumn on beloved earth,
I turn up the collar of my coat,
my well-worn, half-belief,
and this thin, groping prayer,
against the sunset chill,
the passing, passing, passing
of all I long for not to pass.

Oh, the longing, Lord,
this longing that remains,
this longing that I am.
Will nothing quiet it
in this beautiful, terrible world?

There's this strange nostalgia,
this something I can't quite remember,
muffled as I am
in things I do not need,
this fabled and flawed searching
with a candle
for the sun.

What is it I cannot live without?
What is it I cannot die without?
What, but you?

Come, Lord, into the fall of me.
I pray for grace to deal with
what finally cannot be dealt with,
and so must be faced in every season
I am made for, and yet made in,
glorious burst
and wind, rain, chill—
the shadows in my heart,
the ambiguity of my works,
the struggles of my conscience,
the ambivalence of my desires,
the duplicities of my choices,
the limits of my perceptions,
the vacillations of my will,
the finitude of my powers,
and always the crinkling of the leaves,
the creep of spidery wrinkles,
the setting of the sun;
yet, in the longing that I am
is a promised, tender-mercied, graceful spring
past every fall.

O God, grant me the grateful, sore compassion
to take nothing for granted
in this not-to-be-taken-for-granted time,
fragile as I'm learning that I am,
and much less in control,
vulnerable to any-moment, why-not-me
crashes, viruses, clots, lumps, losse . . .
and great leaps of originality;
to take nothing any-season-ever for granted:
neither beauty nor ugliness,
friends nor enemies,
joy nor pain,
music nor moans,
laughter nor tears,
life nor death,
nor love,
nor love,
nor love,
nor this urgent longing that I am;
for it is you I long for
in all this longing,
you I seek the more
in praying for a sore compassion,
you I cannot live
or die without,
you who, I pray, indwell
in this fall of me
to deal with what
cannot be dealt with,
save with you.

O God, breathe life
    and fire and faith
        into this crumbling clay of me,
    for by the mystery of you,
        the cross, the empty tomb,
    is all, can all become,
        even autumn and this fall,
            grace upon grace upon grace,
                and I an act of praise.

Kept by Enthusiasms

O God,
how awesome
is this spirit-driven creation,
this sensuous connection
of my body with the earth
and other creatures like myself—
and yet not quite;
so I would begin
by some mysterious plan
to learn a little
what it means
to be a lover,
and a beloved—
the cross also being
a spirit-driven,
bodily thing.
So I am grateful
for this body,
my mortal definition in time and space
for the joys it knows,
amidst the pains,
and I accept, reluctantly,
the wear of time on it
and its oh-so-reluctant betrayal of me,
growing slower on the inclines.

So I pray to you,
who pronounced creation good,
to pour out your spirit on me
that I may keep, and be kept by,
my enthusiasms—
enthusiasm meaning,
I once learned,

being taken from behind
  by god, overwhelmed,
    wrestled down, up, on.

So take me, God,
  I'm slower now,
    easier to catch,
      and needy.
  Renew me in the face of the forces of cynicism
    and too much religiosity
      that would drain me of life's juices,
  that even now I may grasp
    that more things are possible for me,
      yea probable,
        than the councils of security
          or the cautions of age
            would bid me believe, or try,
  and having grasped,
    be grasped by them.

Take me, God,
  frontwise, sideways, from behind,
    that I may dare to stand for my convictions,
      remove a small plug to let justice' waters roll,
    speak boldly for my visions and of mercy, too,
      though others scoff,
    and live as Christ lived,
      daring others to love or reject me
        for who I am
      rather than pandering to be liked, accepted
        for what I am not
          but pretend to be.

Take me, God,
anyway you will,
keeping me young in your spirit,
and aware of what young truly is:
eager, curious, dauntless,
willing to explore, to struggle,
to be foolish as the world goes,
foolish, caring, trusting, open,
and brave,
mortality not being for cowards
and courage being contagious
(unless the inoculation of security
has taken overly)
since I caught a small dose from others,
and one or two who follow
might catch a bit of it from me.

Take me, God,
that while yet in this body,
this sensuous connection
with the earth
and other creatures,
I may learn the more
to be a lover,
and a beloved,
to do love's labor
stronger than time—
the cross being
a bodily thing
though spirit-driven;

and learn as well
to stretch toward resurrection,
as I did toward birth,
by pushing trustingly against
the limitations.

Take me, God,
and grant me grace
to watch for you
in winter's skies as well as spring's,
in empty places as well as full,
in grandmothers' hands as well as children's,
and in mystery perhaps to see
you in the eye
of this one watching,
enthusiastically.

Unearthly Longings

O God of history,
you created me
as you created each of this human clan,
a creature of time and space
which I cannot escape,
but with intimations of transcendence
which I cannot achieve,
and I am awash with longing
as of moon and sun and starlight.

Come now
to confirm these terrible,
wonderful, unearthly longings
as the light of you in me.

O God of the human generations,
all that struggled from ice age until now,
looking for everything on earth,
and yet for more,
and so God of me,
and of all my times
of sighs and aches, glories, triumphs,
defeats, and interminable in-betweens,
of all the painful work and painful waiting,
the wondrous having and the awful losing;
move with me now in my season of struggle,
as in other seasons your spirit moved
to give prophecies to children,
visions to the young,
dreams to old men and women,

and to all that struggled from ice age until now,
looking for everything on earth,
and yet for more—
as have I in my short life,
and do the more intently now.

O God,
this time and space I cannot escape,
this mortality I'm stuck in
constrains in many relentless ways:
in fading inspiration,
waning energy,
shortening expectations,
troubled sleep,
leaving me with the caution of experience,
questions without answers,
yet worthy duties to be done,
and fidelity the only way past
the circuitries of intellect,
the shifting sands of knowledge.

O God,
I want to scream this prayer,
curse out my frustration,
for my passion has not wrinkled away,
nor has this light of you,
this unearthly, terrible,
seething longing,
been doused;
and so, you surely know,
my screams, my curses,
like the melody of songs,
would be praises stripped of nice words.

O God,
move with me now,
abide with me in my urgenting need
when the petals of spring wither,
when summer ends before what's planned,
when autumn sends chill winds to scout.
and I am caught, cold sweat found out,
hanging on for dear life
to the whipping end of it;
so much started,
so little done,
so many promises made,
so few delivered on,
so many loves unspoken,
so many wrongs ignored,
so much gratitude unspoken,
so much mercy long withheld,
and now I'm scrunched up behind the tasks,
with time shriveling up ahead.

O God,
grant me strength to bear these burdens
but first,
spiritual sight to glimpse the more
you set my heart on from the start;
grant me energy for my duties,
an ingenious way through some dead ends,
but first,
spiritual sight to glimpse the more
you set my heart on from the start.

O God,
    help me to separate the essential from the trivial
        in these however many remaining days
            I would shape and which shape me,
    that in the separating
        I may glimpse the more,
            the kingdom
            you set my heart on from the start.

O God,
    I come driven to you
        by what I cannot escape
            and what I cannot achieve,
        by what I am,
            yet what I'm not,
    wanting passionately now to live for joy,
        not with regret or for some gain;
    to gladly be this creature you created,
        to accept my years,
            my mortal limits,
                and my yet amazing gifts;
    and so to commit back to you
        all of who I am,
            and all of who I'm not,
                then all the rest I'll never know,
                    to find my rest in you.

Abide with me,
O God.

El Beans Greco

There was a fury in her climbing, the edge of screech in her breathless muttering. "Sane? . . . Jezzus H . . . gimme a break! . . . What the . . . crap is sane? . . . Who in God's . . . half-acre . . . knows? . . . That zipper-assed . . . button-brain? . . . Gotta be . . . kidding . . . Scorches my buns . . . I ever gave . . . a fart's worth . . . of energy . . . trying to be . . . something . . . who the hell even . . . knows . . . for sure . . . what it . . . is! . . . Unfor . . . damn . . . giveable . . . waste!" She slipped, caught herself, and kept climbing. The rocks bruised her feet. The scrubby bushes scratched her. She stopped and yelled at them. At the rocks: "SPOILED IDIOTS! I'VE HAD ENOUGH OF YOUR DAMN TANTRUMS. KNOCK IT OFF!" At the bushes: "WHO DO YOU THINK YOU ARE, THE CRÈME DE LA CRÈME? YOU'RE JUST OVERGROWN WEEDS, SO GET YOUR ACT TOGETHER OR I'LL TURN YOU INTO SO MUCH . . . MULCH."

Completely winded by her outburst, she plopped down on a large rock. When she'd finally caught her breath, she resumed her conversation with the landscape: "Sorry if I disturb you, but God knows you have time enough to do nothing. Besides, I just have to . . . to . . ." She didn't know how to say it.

Suddenly she stood, turned toward the mountain top and exposed a long, red, still fresh scar where her left breast had been. She screamed, "FIRST YOU ALLOWED THIS, AND THEN I ALLOWED IT TO INTIMIDATE ME. I TOOK IT AS PUNISHMENT, AND I WAS TOO DAMNED GRATEFUL JUST TO HAVE SURVIVED IT. THAT WAS WRONG." Tears flooded down her face. "Wrong, wrong, wrong." Her voice choked into squeals and snorts of rage, grief, shame. Shortly words began to come in short bursts: "TAKE . . . TH'OTHERONE . . . TOO . . . IFTHAT'S . . . TH'WAY . . . ITHAST'BE . . . BU'THATISN'T . . . GONNASTOPME . . . ANYMORE . . . I'MCOMIN' . . . AFTERYOU . . . LIKEBEFORE."

The gravel shifted under her foot, and she fell awkwardly to her knees. She felt a quick rush of embarrassment, as she had when Sam Pratt had lectured her in front of the children. She tossed her head defiantly, sat heavily and, ignoring her skinned knees, growled, "Hell with retirement. Shove it, Pratt."

She picked up a stone, began rubbing it, giving it orders. "Listen up! You just tell your friends not to get in my way from here on. It's hard enough to be climbing way up here where it's so damn steep and cold without them making it harder for me." She spit on the stone and rubbed harder to bring out its hidden colors. "Besides, I've got to keep going and my feet hurt like hell already. So you tell 'em, hear?" She tossed the stone over her shoulder as far as she could. "By the way, tell 'em I love 'em, too."

She chuckled, got to her feet, rebuttoned her sweater, blew her nose as she'd learned to as a kid from the men building the street in front of her house: leaning over, finger against one nostril, exhaling mightily through the other nostril, letting the stuff fly to the ground; repeating on the other nostril, ending with a wipe on the sleeve. Bowing with a flourish to her surroundings, she said, "Thank you very much. Glad you liked it."

If anyone had seen or overheard her, they would have unquestionably doubted her sanity. Their doubt would not have surprised her. Intuitively, she knew that it was as a test of their doubt—and of her own—that she was climbing Mt. Adams in mid-afternoon so early in the spring. She was after the One people gave the name God to, or whatever other name struck them for the insistent mystery of things. It was time for a showdown. Was she insane? Was the world? Was God? She hitched up her bra strap and grunted more or less toward the mountain top, "Okay, here I come! Get ready!" And with a lurch she started to climb again.

* * *

They'd been looking for her for a half hour or more. A teacher who disappears on a school outing is quickly missed, especially if she's the oldest teacher in the school, just had an altercation with the principal, and stalked off in tears. At first the teachers assumed she'd gone to be alone in one of the little stone restrooms of the state park where they'd brought the youngsters for a scientific field trip and first-of-the-season picnic. When that proved wrong, they assumed she'd gone for a walk nearby. While they waited for her return, they gathered in little groups to gossip about what had happened, careful to not let the students overhear, their attempted protection only intensifying the young peoples' nibbling anxiety.

Miss Marshall, fifth grade Basic Science teacher, seemed to be the most vocal, if not the best informed, of one circle. "Everyone knows she's . . . well, eccentric is putting it mildly. Crazy is more like it. Like from another planet. My God, we've had to deal with it for years."

"That's a little harsh," observed Lisa Springer, who taught Social Studies. "Kirby's got spirit. Good for morale. Except she's seemed pretty down since her mastectomy. I worry about her."

"All the more reason for her to put it to rest," insisted Leah Marshall. "Feeling sorry for her doesn't change anything, really. How many times have we tried to tell her, as gently as we could, that it was time to give it up, retire, rock the grandchildren? But, no, not her. And now this. It's too much. Something just has to be done."

Some of the other teachers nodded, less in agreement than in encouragement, wanting diversion, curious about which tidbits of information floating about were most enticing. Leah Marshall indulged them. "Can you imagine, just when we're starting serious, scientific sex education, she has the gall to tell the children that ants mate inside daffodils at night, that she actually has observed the phenomena many times."

"Observed the phenomena? Get real! Whatever she said, I'm sure she didn't put it that way." It was Joe Straus, who taught computers and delighted in needling Leah Marshall.

Leah Marshall's tone became combative. "Well, *I* put that way! For God's sake, think of the damage it could do to the school if it got out that one of our teachers was spreading that kind of garbage around."

"Oh, I don't know. I bet X-rated biology would be a big hit." Other teachers laughed at Joe Straus' humor.

Leah Marshall didn't join the laughter. "Oh great, make a joke of it. That's really professional. But if you give a damn about education, as I perhaps have wrongly assumed we all do, then you can't ignore that kind of thing. And before you blow it off so lightly, just remember that Sam Pratt thought he had to check it out when he heard the kids talking about it. In fact, some of them wanted to stay here after dark so they could watch the ants, well, 'do it,' as they put it."

Joe Straus smiled and winked. "Maybe if we stayed after dark, they could watch more than the ants 'do it.' What do you say, Leah?" This time the rest of the group laughed even louder.

"Miss Marshall?" The laughter stopped abruptly. While they'd been talking, one of the children had approached unnoticed and was standing at the edge of their gathering. Joe Straus hunched his shoulders up to his ears and muttered, "Damn."

"Why, Thelma, what do you want?" Leah Marshall's smile was too bright, her voice too sweet.

"Nothing, really, Miss Marshall. I . . . I mean, we were just wondering. Ants could mate inside daffodils, couldn't they?"

In a voice icily indignant, Leah Marshall set about to nip this bud of ignorance. "No, they couldn't, Thelma," she instructed, matter-of-factly. "Ants are a highly organized species. Each member of the colony has very specialized functions. Some ants lay eggs, in pre-arranged places in the colony. Other ants fertilize the eggs, and the eggs turn into larvae which . . ."

"Miss Kirby told us all that," Thelma interrupted, "but she said that sometimes some ants get tired of that and go off to start something different. She said they're the ones who 'do it' . . . I mean, mate, in daffodils. That could be true, couldn't it?"

"Maybe it could be, Thelma." It was Joe Straus, kneeling to put his arm around the girl whose lip had begun to tremble,

"Maybe it could." Leah Marshall snorted and turned away.

* * *

In another small group Sam Pratt's explanations were trying to grind away the rough edges of what had happened. "You know I have tried to be patient. Helen Kirby should have retired three years ago, but I kept her on."

"Come on, Sam," the music teacher, Elaine Fisher, countered, "she *could* have retired, not *should* have. Our contract says Administration can't force teachers to retire early."

Sam bristled. "I don't happen to agree with everything in that contract."

"That's your prerogative," Elaine Fisher replied. "Hers was not to retire. So cut the condescending crap about being so patient."

"Whether you know it or not, I have been very patient, Elaine," Sam snarled through clenched teeth. "To say that Helen Kirby has been less than cooperative is an understatement. For at least the past two years she has challenged every procedural change, every decision I've made."

Elaine Fisher chuckled. *"Every* decision, Sam? Surely you decided how many pencils to buy, who the new secretary would be, when to go to the john without Kirby challenging it." The other teachers smiled.

Sam ignored the comment. "The fact is that I . . . well, I just made the best of things. In fact, I did keep her on, even though it cost me a lot of aggravation. In all fairness, surely you've noticed how strange she's been acting, more so all the time?" The teachers diverted their eyes, resigning themselves to Sam Pratt's need to talk because they were almost as afraid as he was.

Sam raced on, trying to stay in control. "In any case, today was just inexcusable. When I overheard Johnny Toffer telling his friends what she'd said about ants 'doing it' in daffodils, I thought I should ask him about it. Then I marched them off to confront Helen Kirby and believe it or not all she could say was, 'Sam, have you ever looked inside a daffodil in the middle of the night? How do you know what's going on in there?'"

"That did it. Wouldn't even admit it was an ill-advised joke. Humiliated me in front of the children. It was absolutely unprofessional behavior for a teacher, and I considered it my duty to deal with it on the spot or the children would have lost all respect for authority. You can see that under the circumstances, I didn't have any choice."

Again, the teachers diverted their eyes. O.D. McKeel, director of physical education, said softly, "You do remember she's had major surgery not too long ago, don't you?"

"I'm her principal, not her chaplain," Sam answered before turning and walking away.

Elaine Fisher noticed a clump of daffodils by the pump house and wondered if they were a wild variety or if someone had planted them there. She also wondered where Helen Kirby was.

* * *

Some of the sixth grade class were having their own conference. "Look, if you saw her go that way, you gotta tell 'em, dorkhead." Nick Alveres was turning his fear into aggressive insistence.

Betty Schuster was dubious. "But if I tell and she went some other way, or if she just comes back, I'll be totally embarrassed, grossed out."

"Tell 'em!" Nick was firm. No one disagreed.

So Betty went to Mr. Pratt. "Mr. Pratt, somebody said they saw Miss Kirby going up that trail marked 'Summit.' We went to find her, but we couldn't."

The knot in Sam Pratt's stomach twisted up to his face. Sweat beaded on his upper lip. "Damnit!" he gasped. "Come on," he shouted to the others, turning and running up the trail, calling, "Helen! Helen Kirby!" Joe Straus, Elaine Fisher, and O.D. McKeel followed.

Within fifteen minutes they came back. "We have to call the State Police," Joe Straus announced. "No sense kidding ourselves that it's just a school matter anymore." Sam Pratt looked as if he was in shock. Some of the smaller children began to cry. The wind seemed to stir in apprehension. Everyone looked through the trees toward the summit, bleached to a remove by the afternoon light, inscrutable to their inquiring eyes.

* * *

She leaned against the big rock, the sun in her eyes, and squinted. The wind sniffed and teased her hair, as a cat teases before pouncing. She faced the mountain top and yelled, between gasps, "OKAY, YOU . . . YOU MISCREATOR . . . HOW D'YA . . . LIKE THAT WORD? . . . MISCREATOR! . . . SO YOU MADE THE WHOLE . . . THING . . . HOORAY FOR YOU . . . BUT YOU . . . MESSED UP . . . I KNOW YOU'RE THERE . . . I CAN SEE YOU . . . COME DOWN . . . CLOSER WHERE . . . WE CAN . . . SETTLE A . . . FEW THINGS . . ."

She coughed, gasped, breathed deeply for a minute. Then, almost to herself, she added softly, "And don't tell me you can't come down here. I've seen you all my life, hide-and-seeking around every damn corner I ever got into, every damn body I ever ran into, the near dying ones same as the just born ones. Even in this bitching thing." Her fingers kneaded the still unfamiliar vacancy on her left chest as if trying to coax the remaining flap into rising again. "You're nervy, all right. Hide and seek until most people give up seeking, almost like that's what you had in mind all the time. Well, you're not getting away with it with me."

She wiped her hand across her mouth. Her throat was so dry. She scooted around to the shadow side of the rock, got a hand full of snow, and began munching on it. Slowly, she worked her way back to the sunny side, and bellowed again: "THIS IS BEANS . . .

YOU HEAR? . . . BEANS KIRBY . . . YOU'RE THE . . . one's RESPONSIBLE for . . . me having . . . that NICKNAME . . . SO LISTEN up . . . I'm TIRED of . . . TRYing to . . . live between . . . the lines." Her already hoarse voice had sunk to almost a whisper. She began remembering. The shadows moved quietly, steadily up the mountain.

* * *

The state police and the park rangers responded professionally, dividing the area into sections, marking maps, passing out equipment, beginning the search. More wood was gathered and fires were started in the picnic area. Two officers with a radio kept track of the search parties as they reported in, marking red Xs on a map laid out on a picnic table.

Parents were notified, and many came to pick up their children, but most children insisted they wouldn't leave until Miss Kirby was found. So the parents joined the vigil along with most of the teachers. Only a few children and teachers went back in a school bus. Typically, the teachers organized the fire tending, coffee making, and distribution of the food that kept appearing.

Such is penance: vague guilt seeking relief in concrete sound and movement. People talked, small talk trying to fill the craters of uncertainty and stave off the silences in which fear often breeds. Birds twittered noisily in the woods. Sam Pratt wondered if there had been so many of them before

* * *

It seemed as if "Beans" had always been her name. When she was a child, people laughed when she reported that she'd seen something they hadn't. On one such occasion, in those days of milder language, someone had said, "Ah, you're full of beans." The name had stuck, provoking more laughter. At first, she'd cried and asked, "What are you laughing at?" When no acceptable answer had been forthcoming, that question had become the core of her argument with God. Was she so different? Was she crazy?

In fourth grade her teacher had said to her mother, "Mrs. Kline, I think Helen may have problems with, well, her . . . vision. We suggest you have her checked."

Dutifully, her mother had taken her to the doctor where she had read the whole chart down to the last line of tiny letters, at which point the doctor had reassured her mother, "Well, that's excellent. Helen's eyes seem to be fine, Mrs. Kline."

Helen had protested, "But, Dr. Parke, there are things on the chart you didn't point to."

The doctor had frowned. "There are?" he asked. "Tell me about them, Helen." His tone and her mother's worried look had made her hesitate. Even now, across all the years, she could still feel that moment, could still see every detail in that office and smell the ominous silence.

Finally, she'd gone on. "Well, down in the corner it says, 'American Optical Co.' And all around the edges are white birds, only they have butterfly wings and wrinkled faces like grandmother's, and on their backs are children except they have shiny blue skin and eyes all orangy like the sun going down and . . ."

"Helen, stop that!" Her mother was shaking her.

Helen had been stunned. She had thought maybe they'd like what she could see. Instead, her mother had begun to cry, and the doctor had made her follow a little light around with her eyes, and after while he had suggested that her mother take her to another doctor.

In a few days they had gone to another doctor, and he'd asked her all kinds of questions and made her put different shaped blocks in different shaped holes and draw pictures. Finally, the doctor had asked quietly, "Helen, do you ever think you see things other people don't see?"

Strangely, she'd wanted desperately to talk about that with someone she could trust, but there didn't seem to be anyone like that in her life. So now when the doctor had asked the question, she knew how she'd better answer it.

"No," she'd insisted, "I only really see what everyone else sees. Sometimes I . . . imagine things . . . for fun, is all."

Her mother had smiled, the doctor had nodded and said, "I thought so. But you're much too grown up for that now. It's time to stop it. I know you will, for everyone's sake." He had turned to her mother. "Helen's fine, Mrs. Kline. As an only child she just has an active imagination she'll soon outgrow. No need to worry." That settled it for everyone.

Everyone except her. What she'd learned was that there were lines—top, sides, bottom—and that was it. It was dangerous to see or talk of anything existing outside those lines. People laughed, frowned, threatened, shook you if you did. They accused you of being full of . . . beans.

She opened her eyes and blinked away the memory. Above her, the mountain seemed to have become a gigantic flame silently sucking into itself the violet sky in which soared a great bird whose wings were dazzlingly white.

"Oh, God," she whispered, "if you don't break our hearts one way, you break them another. It's just too beautiful." Hoarsely she shouted, "IT'S NOT FAIR, YOU NUDNICK. COME AND MEET ME NOW." The bird and the violet slowly circled down.

* * *

Juanita Gomez had named her first son, Greco, after the Spanish painter El Greco, whose paintings she'd so admired when she went with her high school class to the museum, gone with Hector afterward, and ended up pregnant. Now Greco was himself just fourteen, finishing eighth grade, the oldest of eight, forced to make his own way in school and on the streets as well as into the puzzlement of a deepening voice, darkening mustache, and hazards of manhood.

Without understanding why, or asking if he could, Greco had begun hanging around Beans. She, in turn, had become attached to him, encouraging his interest in drawing, for which he showed talent, "as you should with a name like Greco," she'd say. When he had visited Beans in the hospital after her surgery, he had sensed that it had to do with more than just the loss of a breast, which seemed quite frightening enough to his young, erotic fascination with female anatomy. What more it had to do with, he struggled unsuccessfully to piece together from Beans' moody silences and his own churning emotions.

He would sit by her hospital bed for long stretches, sketching the ward, the nurses, the other patients, but mostly Beans lying in various positions on the bed. Invariably the left side of his sketches of her body were tentative, vague, one or two charcoal strokes scarcely touching the section of grainy white that he left as its own indecipherable message. Beans would look at his sketches, smile softly, and say nothing. The ache and the longing in him to understand what was happening to her, and to him, grew sharper even after she'd been discharged and resumed teaching again.

When a search party of park rangers set off in what he was sure was the right direction, Greco followed them. He grew quickly impatient with their progress. After all, he'd heard someone say that time was critical, Miss Kirby's age being what it was. Finally, running toward the slowly advancing party, he yelled, "She isn't lost. She went straight to the top. She always told me the mountain top is where God . . ." He stopped. "Look, just get your asses to the top, and maybe you'll find her before . . ." He stopped again.

The rangers had turned so quickly when he yelled that they almost lost their footing. Irritated, one of them spoke brusquely, "Damnit, who are you and what are you doing here?"

"Doesn't matter. I'm just telling you, you gotta get to the top quick or it'll be too late. You don't, I swear I'll bring a load down on your asses. Sue your asses off. Go on! Hustle!" His voice cracked. "Please?"

They stared at him, disbelieving, hostile. Finally, the one who had spoken earlier said, "Jake, why don't you and Ed go on up? The rest of us will keep the search going here." He studied Greco for a moment and then spoke with disarming softness, "Now, you get back down to the park with the other kids, or I'll have to report you for impeding law officers in the line of duty." In answer, Greco turned and ran up the trail past Jake and Ed. Behind him he heard the ranger call out, "Okay, stay with him, you guys."

Quick tears blurred Greco's vision, and the antiseptic smell of the mountain giddied him. He stumbled, caught himself. "Please, God, help me. I've got to get to her." Squinting toward the sky, he glimpsed a white blur out of which seemed to come a long finger, beckoning him on. He tried to wipe the tears from his eyes. Was it a sign from God? Or was it only a bird, or the slant of light from the sinking sun?

* * *

The nip of cold and darkness herded people closer to the fire where they sipped their coffee, spoke to each other as if to themselves, plucked at the frayed ends of their anxiety, mentioned the need for prayers they seemed to hope others knew better than they how to make. The children's prayers were in the wideness of their eyes and silences. They loved Beans.

Now a few of the adults were realizing that they loved her, too. On the boundary of shadow and firelight, they felt, rather than thought, something about themselves that they otherwise denied, yet somehow needed to have affirmed. Beans had been that affirmation. In her they had seen, if only dimly and as provocation for guilty ridicule, a possibility for themselves of a passion, a mating of dream and daring, spirit and claw, battle cry and love song, that, without their having to risk their consent, might be magically unleashed to force them out of the choke of their rutted definitions into a kind of ecstasy.

But the gravity of pay checks and social convention had been too strong. They'd followed society's proper lectionaries and prayed religion's well-worn prayer books while Bean had at it with God, or whatever was the mystery or the glory that made some people go mad. Secretly, they'd loved her for that. Secretly, they'd vowed that someday they'd get around to having at it, too. Meanwhile, she kept the possibility alive for them. Now the looming danger of her situation had pushed them a stumble closer to getting around to it. That added to their discomfort, which they relieved with talk.

Bits of conversation floated upward with sparks from the fire:

"Did you know she'd been married once?"
"I guess I did. Her husband die?"
"No. It ended. She never said why. Only that it broke her heart."
"Thought she lived with a woman."
"Did for a long time. Artist friend. Had a studio together"
"Think she's a lesbian?" "I don't know."
"She always said it was love that mattered, not a lot of stupid rules."
"Sounds too easy. Too self serving."
"Not the way she went at it."
"Or the way she insisted God goes at it."
"The way she went at it didn't seem to get her much, did it?"
"Depends on what you mean by much, I guess."

"Anyway, who knows how God goes at anything?"

"Or if God goes at anything."

"I don't know."

"Maybe lovers know. A little."

"You mean safe-sex lovers, of course."

"Come on. I mean . . . oh, you know what I mean, for Christ's sake."

"Ido?" "Yes, you do!"

"Beans was always saying that love is all of a piece.

Said teaching can be making love."

"You think her mastectomy changed her?"

"Made her a little quieter is all." "I mean about love." "No."

"You should have heard her teach the kids about wild flowers today."

"Yeah?"

"Made a game of it. She'd give the Latin name for a flower and have them guess what color marker to draw it with on their pads."

"Really?"

"Yeah! She'd say, 'Ranunculus.' Kids had to figure out yellow, for buttercup. 'Lobelia cardinalis.' Red, for cardinal flower. Then she said, 'Podophyllum. Most mysterious color of all.' Kids were stumped for a minute. Beans started laughing and said, 'Come on, you know. White, for May apple.' Kids howled, 'No fair. That's no color, Miss Kirby.' Beans howled back, 'It's every color. That's why it's so mysterious, dummies.' Kids laughed. One of 'em started chanting, 'Po-do-phyl-lum, po-do-phyl-lum.' The others joined right in; 'po-do-phyl-lum, po-do-phyl-lum.' It was great."

"Probably be something they'll never forget, all right."

"Do you think she's right about love?"

"Guess she might be close."

"I know Beans touched something in me all my years of therapy didn't." "You think she's all right? I mean, she's not off the deep end or anything?"

No one answered. They sat quietly and watched the sparks from the fire ascend to become the evening star.

* * *

Beans Kirby leaned one hand against a rock, head cocked, and studied the mountain, tinted shades of violet against the deepening purple of the sky. She shifted her gaze to where, 1500 light years away, a faint Orion bestrided the heavens. Orion was there, in space, yet it swirled inside her brain; there, fifteen hundred light years away, but here, where she stood looking; here, in her, even when she closed her eyes; then, yet now. How could time be visible, sensual? But it was. It was real as a lover, in her eyes, on her skin, in her body.

Her sight felt, listened, touched. In the scarlet edges of the setting sun, she could see the green ray throb from it for a second or two. She could see the wind, vibrations of particles in the air even when no leaf betrayed its presence. She could see the longings of people though they did not speak of them even to themselves. Was the gift her eyes, or what they saw? What was real? Who was sane? What were human beings anyway?

She turned and lay back against the rock, hard as a pew. She smiled and recalled when she was young, going to church, where she'd heard the wonderful stories of those six-winged, flaming-faced seraphim who screamed terrible, holy, wild things. But no one ever screamed terrible or wild things of agony or ecstasy in church except the evangelists who came through and seemed to do it on cue like the rock singers the kids liked so much these days. And church had never let silence get heavy enough to stagger anyone into anything very deep, or awesome, or joyful either. Church was all lines, too: pews, candles, hymns, creeds, plastic cups of juice, even the Bible readings. It was a bore.

She laughed and shouted, "HEY, I KNOW YOU'RE THERE. YOU CAN'T HIDE IN THE DARK OR THE SILENCE. YOU DON'T LEAVE ME ALONE SO I . . ." her voice cracked, " . . . won't . . . let you . . . alone." She sucked in air, went on. "I'M not . . . AFRAID . . . I DON'T . . . believe . . . death . . . is the . . . bottom . . . LINE . . . I SPit . . . at it." She hawked, spit, began to cough, and dropped on her side. When the coughing eased, she whispered, "Go ahead, fight dirty, but I warn you I'm one of those meshuggenehs who won't let go 'til you give me a blessing."

She rolled over on her back and looked into the deepening darkness. Around the lower edge of the sky was a much lighter rim of purple, and at the very center of the overhead dome was an eerie light, as though someone had poked a hole to let in the radiance of some far off sun.

"All right," she whispered, "I know how to be quiet about terrible, wondrous things. But before it's too late, I DEMAND YOU . . . or ONE OF YOUR BUMbling assistants," she started coughing again, ". . . tell . . . me . . . whose lines . . . who drew . . . them . . . in the first place?"

Paroxysms of coughing ripped through her, echoing in a hundred hidden caverns, clefts, and fissures of the mountain, which seemed to transpose it into laughter. The stars watched silently, but a thousand feet further up the mountain, a white-winged bird raised its head from a bit of carrion and lifted majestically into the descending night. Below, a field mouse dove for its hole.

* * *

"Tell me why the stars do shine . . ." One of the parents was leading the children in camp songs. Some of the search parties had straggled back into the picnic grounds. Earlier optimism became only half-believed, and assurances were frequently repeated: "Someone will find her . . . Don't worry."

Then the silence was filled with even more silent prayers, and the sound of little creatures scampering in the woods, and whatever causes dry branches to break, and the indecipherable messages of the wind.

* * *

"Damnit, get a move on. Hustle!" Greco was driven by a terrible urgency. He would have left the rangers behind except they had the essential flashlights

"How do you know we didn't go right past her in the dark?," Ed panted.

"I just know," Greco yelled. "Come on. Enough of your damn resting every two minutes." He turned and started toward the top.

Jake groaned. "Tough keeping up with this kid. Gotta remember to thank Scotty for this assignment." He and Ed got to their feet and went after Greco.

Greco looked back to see if they were coming, then glanced up. Something was moving in the dark sky. It was the white blur again. Was it an angel? If so, was it of life or of death? The blur soared off like a glider. Do birds fly at night? Greco wondered. Was it a bat of some kind? Had the others seen it? "Come on, hurry," he called over his shoulder.

Suddenly from the distance came the sound of something like laughter. The three men froze. "What the hell was that?" Jake shouted.

* * *

Her coughing had stopped. She shuddered, gasped. A searing pain ripped through her chest, the weight of it surprising her, pinning her to the ground for what seemed an eternity. Finally, she managed to rasp through clenched teeth, "So this . . . is how you . . . honor . . . my promise . . . to be quiet? . . . Take away . . . the cough . . . give pain." It took enormous effort to roll on her side, pull her knees into a fetal position. The pain eased.

Slowly, she uncurled. "This is . . . how . . . you come?" she panted. "Well, it's not . . . so bad . . . the pain." Carefully, she rolled onto her back and tried to use her sleeve to wipe the sweat from her face. The pain flared, subsided again when she lowered her arm. "Neither is . . the quiet . . . ness," she said after a moment.

Overhead the stars began to spin. She felt herself spinning with them, it was a pleasant, floating, peaceful feeling. She closed her eyes, smiling, panting. Her lips began to move, the sound they shaped was almost too soft to hear. "Ah . . . the lines . . . aren't . . . what we think . . . are they?" Quietness cradled her. As in a dream, she began to hum fragments of a tune, a hymn, bits of words out of distant memory, "mmmm . . . 'more light' mmm . . . 'and' mm . . . 'truth' . . . mmm 'to break' . . . mmm 'forth' . . . mm 'from' mmmm . . ." The humming ceased for a long moment. Again her lips barely moved. "Always . . . more." Gradually her breathing slowed and she seemed to sleep.

Suddenly her eyes opened as if someone had startled her awake. Somehow she managed to push herself to her knees where she began to hum and sway, extending her hands as if holding out the corners of a gown, an apron, her eyes staring off to a distant time, another place. She spoke surprisingly loudly, clearly, as if to someone at whom she smiled, "Yes, I . . . always dared . . . to see . . . far as . . . I, you . . . able . . . me . . . to . . ."

She swayed now, on the mountain, in her kitchen, on her lover's bed, on her knees with children, with a partner at a dance, catching in her outstretched filmy garment shards of starlight, galaxies of time, scents of creation itself—mud, stone, silence, sea, word and relationship, love and pain, choice and failure, joy and . . . beyond. Then the wonder of it burst inside, gently drifting through her like an afterglow.

"Well . . . hello . . . again," she whispered into the translucent darkness. "I . . . been . . . expectuugh . . ." A bubble in her throat turned her words to a gurgle, " . . . 'ove'ou." She pitched forward and turned slowly face up. A flake of snow crystallized on her forehead, first of thousands that began to fall—white, trembling, peaceful.

* * *

Greco willed himself to find her before the snow forced the rangers to call off the search, as they were already threatening to do. Just as Jake yelled to him, "Hey kid, it's hopeless; we gotta go back," he spotted her, ran, gathered her in his arms, brushed the snow from her face.

"Beans," he implored, "Beans." He'd never called her that.

She opened her eyes for a flicker, smiled, whispered, "Pretty . . . fresh . . . Greco." Her chuckle came out a weak cough. Her breathing was labored.

"Come on, Beans, you're gonna make it," Greco almost shouted at her.

As if fighting sleep, she tried to open her eyes but they refused to stay open. Greco pressed his cheek against hers. She whispered, "You . . . painter . . El . . . Greco's . . . right . . . Proportions . . . are . . . different . . . n' . . . we . . . think . . . Don't . . . forget . . . okay?"

Greco's tears were warm between their cheeks. "Won't ever forget, Beans. Promise." He rocked her gently. "O God," he whispered, "O God, God, God!" When at last he loosened his embrace to look at her, the flashlights of the rangers who stood quietly behind him turned her snow-laced hair into a glowing corona. This time it was Greco's lips moved almost silently, "Podophyllum."

* * *

They took her down in a canvas body bag as off a battlefield: down past the wild daffodils; down past the watchful, tearful eyes in the picnic area; down past the children who, one after another, reached out to touch her still form. Past blind guilt or bitterness or sorrow, they saw with primitive intuition the terrible, wonderful way things do mate, come together, create life in staggering, awesome dimensions, unnoticed and uncelebrated except by the mad, the imaginative, the faithful.

Down she came from the mountain heights from which covenants, visions, mysterious powers had come through the ages, streaming life and renewed struggle in their wake. Down she came, feet first, the head of her shroud carried by Greco who, oblivious to whoever might overhear, kept up his dialogue with her: "I never understood what it was before, but you never really lost it after all, did you? All you lost was your, you know, . . . breast. Okay, bad enough, but not as bad as if you actually lost what mattered. That, you just misplaced for a while, right? I can dig that. Actually, if you hadn't, maybe I wouldn't have, you know, come to see it a little for myself. Like one artist to another, you might say. El Beans Greco, like you said. I suppose it'll drive some people crazy, huh? Including me, right? Yeah, right."

He started to laugh, but it turned to a lump in his throat. His eyes teared up. There was a jolt on the bag that almost caused one of his hands to lose its grip. Clearing his throat, he said with a kind of fierce tenderness, "Hey, watch it. Watch it down there."

Rehearsals for the Eternal

O Lord,
your word creates;
my words stumble after,
resonant, echoing, reflecting,
sharing small bits of power;
but finally they're too frail
to climb the sunlit heights
of my own resplendent life,
or walk its more barren plateaus,
or plumb its ugly, shadowed depths,
or even accurately form your name,
though I must use them, just the same,
to try,
as you have created me to do.

So hear me, "I will be what I will be,"
Lord, Jehovah, Yahweh, Elohim,
Christ, Father, Mother, Holy Spirit,
Alpha, Omega, One, God beyond God,
hear these words that stumble after
and would help me be with you.

This life your word has given me
is such a strange, yet common gift,
so fraught with twists and storms,
betrayals, mercies, inspirations,
revelations, hidden leaven
raising the daily to given bread.
There is pain in it, sometimes,
oft loneliness, riddles and enigmas,
wounds endured, inflicted
beyond the screaming of them,
and terrors I can't name,

yes, and glories, too,
seen, heard, felt,
borne, beyond all telling—
save by praise
my frail words cannot raise to heaven,
but fills a comer
of my heart.

O God,
by your word you take away,
as if you're creating by corrosion,
by the astringent acid of grace,
shrinking slowly, sometimes, always painfully,
those too believable illusions,
which are temptations in disguise,
that I could be more than I am—
mortal being not enough—
by virtue of hard work,
that ultimate of ethics
by which even you are measured,
and usually found wanting,
by the way,
since I, among the we,
want more mountains moved
and mysteries solved.
Surely power for such marvels must be gained religiously
by the exercise of discipline,
the zeal of right believing,
poetic prayer,
arguing like a prophet,
a hunter's love, a schemer's hope,
the faith of sound investors,
the thousand ways to work at immortality

except . . .
slowly, in time, with age,
illusions atrophy, dissolve,
and the hard lesson is learned:
mortal limits are not breached
by mortal assaults, ethical or not.
My words are not all that's too frail,
O Thou beyond my names,
yet I'm more resonant for all of that,
and old enough to pray for grace
and aching now to praise,
trusting that you'll hear my words,
having stripped my illusions away.

O God,
I think of Christ
and am made glad
for this strange gift of life
so strangely shared;
glad for what can be broken,
unbreakable would be less,
broken but not destroyed—
Jesus' life stories are
the stories of my life;
glad for your demonstrated promise
of a love that follows after
no matter where I run,
finally to death itself;
glad for your summons to do justly,
to love mercy—seeing how I need it—
to walk humbly with you
and with this motley crew of brother, sister marvels,
and to find joy in the walking, however far it goes;

glad that what gets broken can be put together again,
made new, some way,
by sharp eyes, and brave, daring hands.
Help me, now and then, to measure myself
not by my fears or failures,
however large,
but by my faith and hope and love,
however small,
that I may truly live this mortal gift
and be a source of life
for those I carry in my heart,
and, by your grace,
and naked to your presence,
all my struggles, all my joys,
will be daily rehearsals for the eternal,
lessons in what it means
to be human,
finite,
and yours.

RESURRECTION MOMENTS

Solitary Unconfinement

O God,
in the darkness of night,
grievance,
worry,
and regret,
as I lay wrinkled with the sheets,
alternating sweat and shiver,
sighing my life away, again,
despairing of even your existence,
despondent over death's foul drool,
sensing its snuffle in my every breath,
an alert sounded in the closing vault of me,
signal that the darkness was incomplete,
strewn, as usual, with the lint of light
caught here and there
on ceiling, wall, corner of bed,
flicked away by unseen hand of wind,
or brush of cloud, or whirl of earth,
but insistently strewn back again,
widening the pupils of my eyes,
unbidden by me,
yet preparing them to learn,
to watchful welcome.
Strange revelation,
oft repeated, too often missed,
spill of even more mysterious ones,
but a kind of resurrection just the same,
if taken as such,
which I am.

My spirit opened, opens even now,
 the shreds of light the keys,
  and memory stirs from its vast store
   occasions, encounters, gifts
    which give life, bless it, keep it;
 and from my solitary unconfinement of prayer,
  gratitude emerges to return to you
   by sieve of words, the quickening of my spirit.

O God,
 I would remember on ahead
  the splendors lacing my daily round,
  parables at every common hand,
  essential things:
   the green-gold-stark turning of the seasons;
   parents who, as best they can, give life;
   children who, trusting it, enlarge it;
   mocking birds (I know of one) somehow taught to sing
    the first four resounding notes of Beethoven's fifth;
   the smell of rain, the sensuous wetness of the trees;
   fierce-tender fathers, nursing mothers, Mother earth;
   poets, like prophets, bringing truth to bloody birth;
   friends who press past the confusing swing of my moods
    to confront and bless the struggles of my self;
   this lover here beside me linking fidelity to grace;
   that large otherness of things and life and you
    that keeps me, somehow, sometimes painfully,
    from being devoured in a frenzy of fancied virtues
    or proudly drowned in an intellectual tidal pool;

moments of surprise, more than meager memory serves,
when the cadences of my life
catch your rhythms
and the spilt radiances of grace
license a curious seeing in the dark
and turn my time to the slow, eternal setting
of terror to peace,
truth to music,
mercy to laughter,
hope to feast,
love to recreation,
me to resurrection.

Whetting of Attention

O God,
creator of life and death,
there is something terrible,
inviolable, holy
not about death so much
as the limits it sets,
confronts us with,
insists upon us
so we cannot miss them
because they do not miss us,
and you who sets them
like cherubim
with flaming swords
at the gates of Eden.

You are the Limiter,
the over against,
more than,
not me,
You—
never owing anything,
always giving something,
forever promising everything,
delivering resurrection,
which is the miracle
of every life, of mine.

So death comes,
one way or another,
and we gather around
the mystery
which is life.

O Limit Setter,
that's death's gift, isn't it?—
to gather us,
to gather me
with a kind of whetting of attention,
awareness honed on fear and praise.

Death comes,
limits press,
horizons compress
to gather us,
to gather me
now, in the now, for the now,
focusing,
summoning me
to end the compromising of my compromises,
to take time before time takes me,
to realize what matters,
to grasp what I might be gathered for,
to look into an other's eyes,
to hold something close, put nothing off,
to make the choice, make it again,
to be a truth,
to be a mere marvel of a human being,
to dance a yes,
to slow the rush;
to be gathered up in strength,
to press on to that awesome passing on,
that "whatever" this mere marvel human being
must pass in and out and through
on the way from this limit of me
to that larger one of there and wherever
but never further, save by you;

by those rites of passage,
passing rights,
births, baptisms, graduations,
weddings, funerals, worship—
yes, worship most of all,
to the life that I would get to,
am called to but . . .
must somehow die to reach.

Dying to something is the only way
to get to anything that matters a lily's worth—
dying to fear, guilt, pride, ambition,
to pride of place which is no place,
to a thousand vanities and martyrdom—
and that's the unanxious love of it,
isn't it, you setter of the limits
we gather around to be raised beyond,
raised out of that pursuit of Eden,
that garden I am limited out of,
to pass on toward a promised land,
a garden east of Eden, a new Jerusalem.

So gather me now, O God,
from the hundred hiding places
my fear has spooked me into,
that I might be free to live
as one possessed
by something larger than myself,
by you, not limited by my limits,
to live as one aware that the grace I seek
is always seeking me,
and all, including death itself,
is grace gathering us to your self.

Only the Light of You

O Christ,
my friend is dying
of something there's no cure for—
mortality, of course—
except his has more immediately
terminal complications
than mine . . . as far as I know.
My friend's death is untimely
which, I suppose, is really
death's only way to be.
So it came to you,
so it will come to me.
I'm sad, afraid, feeling helpless.

O Christ,
how many more times
must I stand by beds, graves,
in rooms of grief,
loneliness,
outraged defeat,
shriveling fear,
anquished guilt
for not having loved well?
What can I do?
I have loved no better,
am no better lover,
surely know no more,
than those I stand with,
or would stand for.
Good Lord, you know mortality,
this dusty way I am,
has its complications.
What is there to do?

I'm no doctor,
no genius of research,
no skilled technician,
just a friend,
a mortal friend.
All I can do is pray—
all there is to do, at last,
probably at first as well,
if any of us really knew.

O Christ,
I'm ashamed at my relief
that I'll survive my friend;
I have no "greater love than this,"
none close to half as great as yours,
and that's my confession, to begin with.

But then . . .
there might be those for whom I'd die
because I love,
if dying would give them life,
so that's my hope and second confession.

Mortality is a heavy load, O Lord.
All I can do is pray out my tears, my faith.

O Christ,
I pray for my friend;
for healing, yes,
but is that the miracle?
After all, how long would that be for?
I ask a deeper healing for him (and me),
which is for you to be with him

in some clear way he'll know
(even though I'll know less clearly),
and so for peace,
a readiness, an easy death,
the fulfillment of your promise
of no more pain nor tears nor night
but only the light of you.
The strange thing is, O Lord,
my friend has grown brave, these days,
and free, and more alive, somehow;
every time I leave,
he says, with a wan smile,
"If I don't see you here,
I'll see you there."

I pray this not so you will know,
but so I might.
It is a kind of dimmer view,
a curious intimation,
an even stranger complication
of this mortality.
Gratitude seems a poor mix with grief
but there it is.

O Christ,
I pray for me,
and in the praying ask
for courage, and for grace,
to wait no longer but to seize
what always waits for me—
life not death,
this friend, and the others,
a hand to clasp, a need to meet, and to have met,

a word to speak, to hear, a tear to shed,
a stand to take here and now, and for a then,
bread to eat, wine to share, a mortal fool to be,
and this decision to make,
    as now I do, and will again,
to give you what you want,
    which is accepting you
        in being who I am,
    and trusting you will raise in me
        what you will, at last,
            and will so in my friend.

O Christ,
    I entrust us to you.
        Please, let me die of nothing less
            than love, and giddy liveliness.

No Verifiable Fingerprints

O God,
you touch everything, but lightly,
leaving no verifiable fingerprints.
In how many thousand quite unlikely, routine times,
like a lucky changing of my mind
and familiar, curious spaces,
like the sacred meeting place of eyes,
and ways of usual, odd coincidence,
like the crucial key of shared insight
(at once preserving my freedom and your lavish mystery),
do you bear me as a father,
guide me as a mother,
captivate me as a child,
challenge me as a friend,
confront me as an enemy,
ignore me as holiness having its own terms,
which are not mine until this mortal's fears turn wiser . . .
as now they slowly do?

O Elusive, Ingenious One,
my dullness, doubt, even my death
does not prevent you from being God,
from touching everything lightly, even me,
from ruffling my spirit like a quick breeze ruffles water,
leaving me aroused and watchful now,
waiting at the edge of love,
praying hard for your return.

Come, Lord,
for the easy sonnets of the day,
the well-honed phrase, the well-learned prayer
rattle empty as night falls
and turn to mock my earlier charade.
Your touch, and time, has shivered me to readiness,
a mortal's quiet willingness,
a listening, a gratitude,
a quaking reliance on your promise of life
in the haunting, risen Christ.

And yet, O God,
this weight upon my heart, this stone,
is too great for me to move alone.
Come, roll it away:
this crush of fear,
this smother of self-preoccupation,
this ponderous ego,
this bloated arbiter of right,
this bejeweled scepter of doubt;
and raise me up in mercy,
raise me up
higher than the drag of past,
higher than all present feeling,
to trust that you
will never give me up
because of what my death
would mean, not just to me,
but even more to you—
a child's death
to a Mother,
to a Father.

O trustworthy Friend,
raise me up to trust like that,
to love like that;
and, perhaps a little past
this dark glass of mortality
in which I but dimly see,
to glimpse, by bold imagination,
a hallowed face, or fiery back,
the making new a thing or two,
a possible new me;
and so, by grace, to come to life,
and come to dare,
and come to hope
your future in.

O God, for Christ's sake,
touch me, even lightly,
once again and . . .
it will be enough.

Caught Up and Crazed

Awesome God,
be with me in this now that slips away,
yet stretches toward forever,
as you promised to be when you began
the tolling out of time,
for I can scarcely bear, and not alone,
the mystery of my being.

I raised again from sleep this morn,
or better, I was raised
by some swish of light,
some stir of who knows what,
returned from that eerie float,
half-remembering that no place.

I'm raised besotted with fragments,
hauntings, strange hints, longings,
buds of blessings, curious pieces—
this unfinished puzzle that I am,
undone work of you, cosmic puzzle maker;
raised as out of that chaos I was made from
on that first of your mornings,
that beginning-out-of-nothing
when the stars started their hum
and there were shouts of joy,
which I, yes, fearfully half-remember.

So raise me, again,
with the quake of your passing train, and time's,
from the stupor of inattention,
dull repetition,
my bleating as a victim,
my quick, cowardly capitulation
to the bluffing of supposed fate;

and hold me for a timeless time
in such deep holiness and peace
that I may know that you are God,
and find trust within my soul—
trust being the only thing
it truly knows, or needs to,
to make the dare of life and prayer;
love and hope,
mercy and praise,
a dazzle of alertness
all come after.

Fill me with your spirit, O wondrous God,
until I am unburdened, unhinged, undamned,
caught up and crazed by something
like glory, power, a tumult of marvels,
and I will never be the same
for being now with you.
Raise me to string this day
on the thread of grace and courage,
to write it with such bloody truth
as will withstand the lies;

to live it boldly, hold it precious,
  do it justice, love it gently;
and then to let it gladly go,
  to be carried somewhere to forever
    o'er the horizon into the night,
      onto storms and stars and sun,
        returning thus to you who gave it;
and in it learn—
  oh courage, God, to learn—
    this way of life fulfilled,
      this release of awe and peace,
        this trace of the unutterable,
          this resurrection rouse,
            this risk of ecstasy.

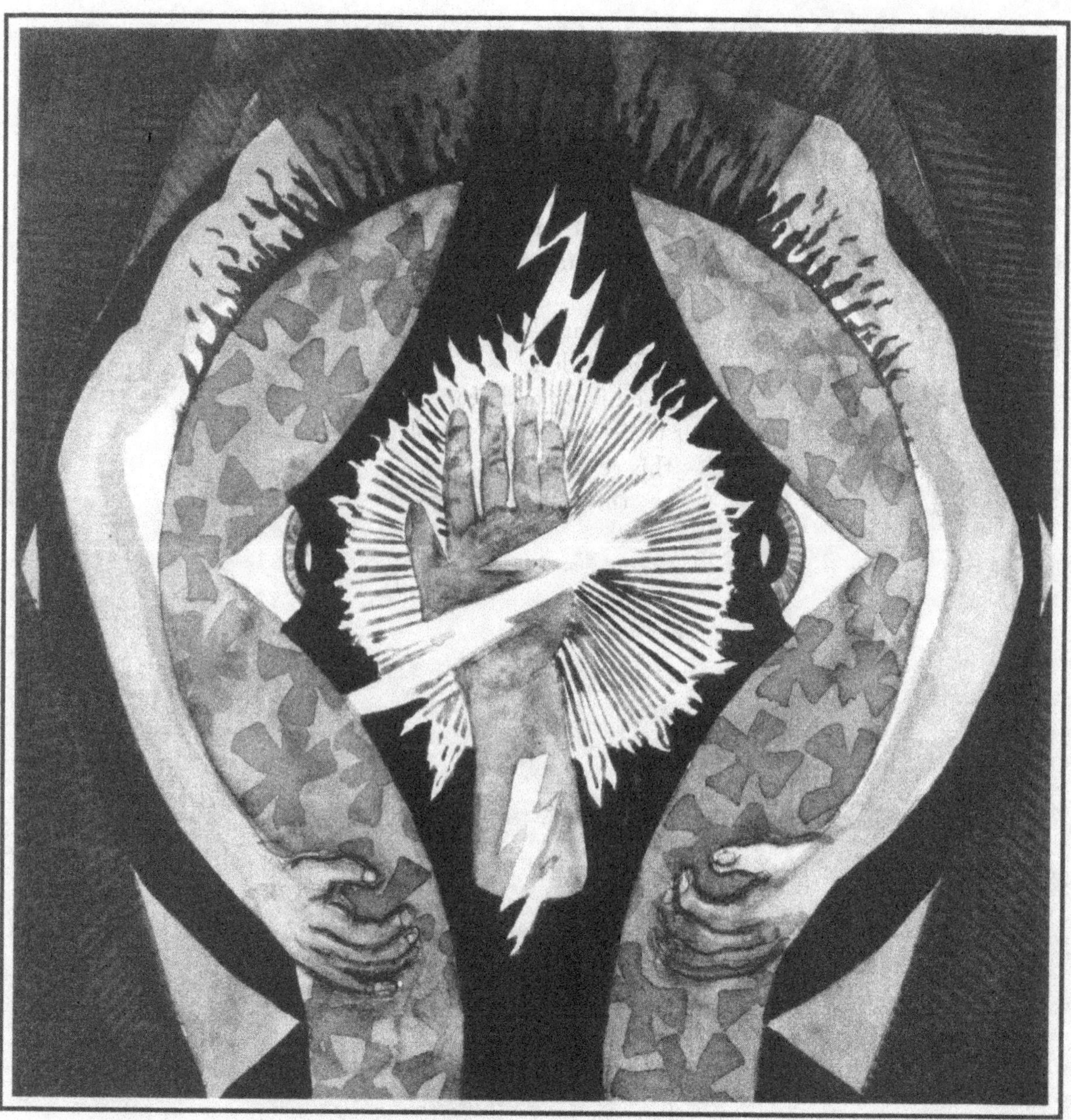

A Garden the Other Side of Eden

First was the sound of out-of-breath gasping as of someone running for his life. Then the gasping sucked into a grunt of great effort, exploded into a anguished scream, and deepened into a roar of outrage as the head of the old man's cane crashed into the crucifix on the wall and sent it spinning down the late-morning-nearly-empty hospital corridor. The old man, momentarily startled at what he'd done, watched the crucifix' flight in amazement, then felt a degree of relief that was close to vindication—and so to trust, strangely even to joy.

In that split second the crucifix blurred, became a trowel spinning into the box on his porch where he'd gotten good at tossing it on his way to washing his hands after gardening. That buzz of memory flickered into a smile on his lips as he lurched on down the corridor toward the startled people appearing in the doorways, summoned from their quiet duties by his frenzied one.

* * *

His heart had been in it at first. Not because he was particularly good at it, but because of the pleasure of it. He liked gardening. He thought of flowers as female, their color, scent, shape stirring him as beautiful women had stirred him when he had been a younger man—and stirred him still, though less urgently. He liked the pace of gardening. He liked his hands in the dirt, the feel of the sun, the breeze in his hair, the reassuring, slightly provocative smell of the earth. He liked the remembering, and forgetting, he was able to do as he planted, watered, weeded. He liked the pride he felt in turning the nondescript little plot in front of his small row house into a garden that, in his view, noticeably improved the neighborhood.

It had been early March when they'd moved in. Within a week, the impulse stirred in him. The second week it nudged him out into the front yard to dig up the small area between the sidewalk and the house. The third week he bought and mixed in mulch and fertilizer. Then he began planting things with no detailed plan but with much tenderness and hope.

When the various seeds and bulbs began to grow, he could hardly wait to get out in the garden each morning with his battered water bucket and the coffee can he used to dip out what he called "a little shot" for each plant. Frequently, he spoke to them as he moved from one to another. With a kind of shy longing, he sometimes even found himself talking to God as if God were another gardener. His heart was in it, at first.

* * *

Now, seven months later, he was rampaging down the third floor corridor of the east wing of St. Monica's hospital, swinging his cane at the crucifixes on the walls. The nurses and doctors scattered before him as if he were the carrier of a deadly, untreatable plague. A nurse crouched behind the nurses' station, one arm shielding her head as she yelled into the phone, "Hell, yes, it's a crisis. Tell security to get their asses up here before this frigging whacko kills someone. Damn sure, I mean it. This guy's . . ."

A crash interrupted her as a crucifix bounced off the counter into the computer screen behind the nurses' station. The force of the old man's swing jerked his cane out of his hands, sending it ricocheting off the ceiling and into a stack of medical charts, bouncing them off the counter and onto the floor.

For the old man, the clatter coalesced into a single stab of pain. He felt as if his head was exploding and realized that his left arm and leg were uncontrollably jerking, his vision blurring. Yet, he heard and wanted desperately to protest the nurse's description of him but couldn't get the words from his brain to his lips. "Not a frigging whacko," was the slippery shred of consciousness he tried to hold on to as he stumbled toward the floor and darkness.

The "Code Blue" team and hospital security arrived on the scene at the same time. The man was diagnosed as having suffered a stroke and was hooked up to all the necessary life-support systems.

Security checked the identification in the man's wallet. His name was Ben Gregory, and there was an address. The head nurse on the floor called Admissions, which in turn called Social Services, to trace the man's family. There was no answer to repeated telephone calls.

Because Security couldn't explain how a crazy, unauthorized man had gotten onto a medical floor before visiting hours where he could endanger staff and patients, the circumstances were not only embarrassing to the hospital but also presented a potential liability. So a decision was made to send a case worker and a security guard to the man's address to talk to the family, if there was one, before bringing the police into the situation.

The security guard recognized the address as being in the neighborhood where he'd lived as a kid, near St. John's Church and its school, which he'd attended. He and the social worker found the house around the corner from the school.

As they waited for a response to their knock on the door, the social worker idly observed, "Great day, huh? Great month, October."

"Yeah," the security guard yawned.

"So you lived around here," the social worker went on, knocking on the door again. "Neighborhood's a little run down maybe, but nice enough. Wonder what happened to those flowers?" She pointed toward the garden in front of the house where chrysanthemums and marigolds lay trampled in the dirt.

"Kids, probably," the security guard shrugged.

The social worker thought of Ben Gregory's rampage through the hospital that morning and how he was lying unconscious now, hooked up to all those machines that were keeping him alive. In spite of the warm sun, she shivered and found herself hoping no one would answer the door. She stepped off the stoop and studied the garden. "Sort of like the world, in a way. Much as I work with people, I keep wondering what makes them do things like that—just destroy things."

"Come on, you know what goes down these days," the security guard replied. "Drugs 'n stuff. Dealers, pushers oughta be shot. Plus the damn kids, they think they c'n get away with anything. Oughta get their butts' kicked, most of 'em. Do time."

The social worker shook her head. "Yeah, drugs are a bitch, all right. Few jobs might help, though. But I wonder what made this Gregory guy break up the hospital like he did. What do you think set him off like that?"

The security guard was impatient. "Ask me, the guy's just psycho. Dangerous. Oughta be put away. Lucky nobody got hurt."

"No one but him, I guess," the social worker smiled sadly. She walked over to the trampled garden. Had something in Ben Gregory's brain begun to snap even before his stroke? Was that why he charged through the hospital knocking crucifixes off the wall? She smiled again in spite of herself. "I heard he knocked four crucifixes off the walls, smashed a statue of the Virgin, and ripped a painting of the Pope. Can you imagine that? It must have been quite a sight."

"Quite a sight? Crazy bastard might'a hurt somebody. He scared the hell outta people," the security guard retorted. "Oughta hav'ta pay damages to people, the hospital, for the whole damned mess."

"He probably did a better job scaring people than all the crucifixes," the social worker chuckled. When the security guard frowned, she quickly added. "Sorry no offense meant. There's something funny about it, though. I know it'll take time for security to live it down, but I still can't help wishing I'd seen it when the orderly got so scared he tipped over the bedpans on the cart on the way to emptying them. It must have been a riot, right?"

"Guy should'a been put away a long time ago," the security guard answered without a smile.

The social worker gave up. "I guess no one's here. I suppose we should check with some of the neighbors."

"Yeah," the security guard agreed.

As she turned from the garden, the social worker sighed, "What a shame. I'll always wonder what makes people do things like that."

"I told ya," the security guard argued, "people got no sense of morals, no respect for law and order these days."

"Like you do?" the social worker asked.

"Yeah, as a matter of fact. Like me," the guard insisted. "Sure wasn't anybody like me messed up that garden."

The social worker shrugged. "No, I suppose not. Come on, let's go."

* * *

Ben and Nora had bought the house to be near her son, Mason, his wife, and small child. It had been a mistake. Since Ben and Nora were older, everyone assumed they were married, but they weren't. Both Nora, whose complete name was Nora Pettibone Cunningham, and Benjamin Alexander Gregory were retired on small pensions and social security. They liked each other, enjoyed being together, and decided it would be beneficial in many ways, including financially, if they lived together. The catch was they couldn't marry or Nora would lose her pension and other benefits. So they made their peace with their consciences and took the risk. But what seemed an acceptable arrangement for young people was much less so for older ones.

When they moved into the city, Nora's son wanted nothing to do with them, insisting that their arrangement was "filthy, rotten, immoral." Actually, for Mason Cunningham, their arrangement had less to do with their morality than with his fear of exposure. He was afraid his campaign for city alderman would be in serious trouble if his opponents discovered what his mother was doing and made it an issue.

"I'm running to make the city better," Mason argued in a voice loud enough to force his mother to hold the telephone away from her ear, thus enabling Ben to overhear. "And what kind of stupid trick does my own mother pull on me? Threat of scandal, that's what. Could ruin my career, everything I'm trying to do. It's outrageous what you and that . . . that pimp of yours are doing. Plus, he got you to put all your savings into that place, didn't he? For godsake, Mother, you must'a gone senile or something."

Ben lost it and screamed back, "It's a bunch of crap, you want to make the city better. Better for graft and kickbacks for you and your cronies is what you mean. You should talk about me and your mother, you phony bastard. Call me a pimp again. I'll bust your face . . ." Ben heard the phone slam down on the other end.

And on his end, he watched Nora's spirit slam down. She sank into a depression and became a recluse. Every morning she would call her son and get the same message from him, "Call me when you're married or you've dumped your pimp. And tell him to give your money back."

In his mind, Ben had dozens of arguments with Mason, all variations on why sin and social shame weren't the same; and why it was worse for Mason to be ashamed of his mother than angry at the society that penalized retired people; and did it occur to him that maybe God didn't see things the way he did; and on and on.

But instead of saying any of that to Mason, he retreated into his garden. Often he pleaded with Nora to join him there. She only wept and became morose. He offered to get married, but both of them knew they couldn't afford to do that. The bottom had fallen out of the housing market shortly after they'd bought the small house, and they were trapped.

Before he realized it, the garden was his world. Then it began to feel too important, to feel like work. He found himself worrying about it. At times he felt twinges of anger that others weren't working as hard as he was to cultivate gardens that would improve the neighborhood and make it more attractive, so maybe he could sell the house. And, while trying to be understanding, he resented Nora's deepening inaccessibility. Still, he couldn't leave her. The garden became small compensation, but all he had.

* * *

By late spring, it had become a ritual. Two nuns who taught at nearby St. John's school would come striding earnestly along the sidewalk, as if they hated exercising but were religiously determined to take what they called their "morning constitutional." It was hard for him to associate nuns with anything as physical as "a constitutional." It occurred to him one morning, watching them huff toward him, that they went about their walk as he had come to go about his gardening—as if it had to do with the serious improvement of something or other.

The first time they stopped, the shorter one introduced them both. "I'm Sister Cornelia," she said gasping, "and this is Sister Phoebe. We teach at St. John's."

The taller nun gushed about the beautiful flowers, saying the word "beautiful" with syrupy overtones that made him feel sticky. She went on to say how "sweet" it was of him to work so hard to make his place an "enclave of loveliness" and what a noble and generous offering it was," though he noticed she gushed on without ever actually looking at anything in the garden, or at him.

He remembered reading in a newspaper once that the word "venom" and the word "Venus" come from the same root word, and that originally the words "poison" and "love potion" were interchangeable. Listening to Sister Phoebe, he could understand the connection.

That morning, and every morning after, Sister Phoebe would smile piously and say, "'I planted, Apollos watered, but God gave the increase.' I'm sure you know that's from St. Paul, Mr. Gregory. And, of course, a man like you understands that all beauty and loveliness is from God. This garden is a testimony of faith, Mr. Gregory. I can see it."

One morning he actually asked her if all the aphids and cut worms and beetles were from God, too, but she just wagged a finger at him and smiled as though he were a piece of chocolate she coveted. He shrugged and let it go.

Sister Cornelia, on the other hand, never spoke of loveliness or beauty. There was wrath and judgment in her view of things. She always found something to complain about or to criticize: The garden was too small for so many flowers; he had the wrong species; the effect was confusion; he should simplify; he should organize it better; the colors of the different varieties clashed; he should get different kinds, more summer, fewer spring, no fall flowers because there was plenty of natural color in the fall and in the spring anyway. Once she suggested he add a small statue of the Virgin to the garden. "Of course, you are Catholic, aren't you?"

"No, I'm Zoroastrian," he answered in his most serious tone, "And polygamous and devoted to Zero Population Growth."

Sister Cornelia frowned and admonished, "You should never make light of serious matters. I know you are just joking, but it smacks of irreverence."

He smiled, "You're right, but I thought a little joke would be better than telling you I'm a direct descendent of Martin Luther and Katherine von Bora who, you know, was once a member of your very profession."

"Such impertinence," Sister Cornelia snorted.

Ben laughed, "Katherine's or mine?"

"Both," Sister Cornelia growled, stalking off, Sister Phoebe trailing her like a wolf-hound on a leash.

But to her credit, Sister Cornelia remained undaunted and Sister Phoebe, her faithful companion. Every morning that it didn't rain, they'd meet him at the garden. But more often than he wished, he felt troubled by Sister Cornelia's criticism of his garden. Probably he had been presumptuous. Maybe he was wrong about it improving the neighborhood. Maybe it was all laughable. He thought about going to the garden club lectures to see how others did their gardens. Doubt and water began to pour over the plants at the same time.

* * *

One evening, after supper, Ben had just finished watering his plants when Alan Hicks came over from across the street. They'd talked only briefly in the few weeks they'd been neighbors, but Ben had sensed some tension.

"Workin' hard, I see," Hicks offered.

"Not really," Ben replied. "Like doing it."

"Yeah, guess you must, much time as you spend at it. Must be nice, bein' retired." There was an edge in Hick's voice.

"Some nice, some not so nice," Ben shrugged.

"Not havin' ta bust your chops for nobody must be nice. Got time for extra stuff, like this garden. One way for ya' ta keep tryin' ta please your woman, raisin' flowers at least."

Ben was wary, thinking Hicks was being provocative, making slurs about his manhood and Nora not being his wife. He wondered why people always exaggerated what they imagined was the worst about other people. Maybe it's envy, he thought, or maybe it gives them something delicious to talk about to spice up dull lives. He decided not to make an issue of it. "Yeah, but it tires me out, too. Matter-of-fact, it's about time for me to go in and sit down for a while before bed." He reached down to pick up his water bucket.

"Wait a minute, Gregory, before ya go. Me and some other guys in the neighborhood figured you might like to play a little poker with us this upcoming Friday night. We play every Friday night. Little recreation, ya know, among the guys."

Ben smiled at the invitation. It could be an honest effort to reach out to him or it could be a set-up. Or something in between. He chose to play it straight. "Thanks, Hicks. I'd like to, but I'm too poor for poker."

"Too poor? That some kinda put down of us who like playin' poker? What'aya gettin' at, Gregory?"

"Didn't mean it as a put down, Hicks. Not at all. I just mean I can't afford to lose. If you can't afford to lose, you don't play, right? That's one of the not so nice realities of retirement."

"Still sounds like a put down to me. Like the rest of us are scum for playin' poker for the few bucks we might lose just for the fun of playin'. You think you're too damn good for us, don't ya? That's really what you're sayin', ain't it?" Hicks just wasn't going to let it go. He'd come to unload and wasn't going to let up until he had.

Ben felt his bile rise. He spoke very deliberately. "No, Hicks, that's not what I'm saying. I'm saying I'm too poor. That's all."

"No, that ain't all, Gregory. You been actin' like you was better'n us since' you moved here. Just remember, everybody's dirt's the same color."

Ben chuckled at Hick's nod to civility. "Dirt?" he replied. "You really talking about dirt or something else?" Now *he* was the one not letting it go.

"You know damn well what I'm talkin' about, Gregory. And yours is the same color as everybody elses', you air'gant bastard."

Ben couldn't help himself. "Really? I always wondered. I take it you've personally done a lot of research on the subject? Checked Omaha? Tucson? Miami? How about New Haven? Maybe Yalies' dirt is blue."

"You just provin' what I'm sayin', Gregory. Talkin' like I'm dumbass stupid and you're smarter'n and better'n me. Like puttin' in this garden, showin' us all up."

"Showing you up? Is that what this is all about, you coming over here tonight?" Ben thought he saw tears glistening in Hicks' eyes, but he couldn't be sure in the soft evening light.

"Damn sure. I should'a come before. Now all our women naggin' us to put one in. Like we don't work hard enough the way it is. Like our place ain't good enough the way it is. You're one conceited son-of-a-bitch is all I can say. Never bother'n to talk to none of us about nothin'. You c'n go straight to hell, far's I'm concerned." Hicks spun and walked away.

It was as if all Ben's frustration and perversity snapped out of control. A bumper sticker he'd seen flashed to mind, and the impulse was overwhelming. "Hey, Hicks," he yelled, "when your IQ hits thirty, sell." The curious pleasure he felt in his cruelty was almost immediately choked off by a surge of shame. There it was again, the feeling that haunted him. Was his shame a moral signal or just a crippling neurosis? After all, hadn't he put up with enough? Hadn't Hicks insulted him first? Why should he feel ashamed?

In any case, he didn't respond when Hicks turned and made an obscene gesture at him. He watched Hicks go, recalling how he had thought his garden would improve the neighborhood, excite others into following his lead, make the block more attractive to buyers, so he could get out. What was the whole thing about? Maybe he hadn't given Hicks a chance. Maybe the truth was somewhere between Hicks and him, between moral signal and emotional sickness.

That night he thought of calling Hicks and apologizing. Then he decided that might make Hicks feel cornered. The next morning, Ben sent Hicks a carefully worded postcard, but weeks went by without a response.

* * *

He might have given it up if it hadn't been for Buford Flynn. Buford was nine and in the third grade at St. John's. Every morning and every afternoon he walked past Ben's garden on the way to and from school, slowing down to watch whenever Ben was in his garden. Ben paid no attention. When, after several days, Buford ventured a timid "Hi," Ben responded with a gruff "Hello," neither wishing for nor inviting further talk.

Nevertheless, Buford adopted Ben. Ben wasn't good with kids, but Buford didn't notice. One day he stopped on the way to school and told Ben he lived alone with his grandmother "down that way," he said, pointing. Ben didn't ask for more information. Buford asked what kind of flowers the purple ones were, and Ben growled, "Hyacinth. Ask your teacher how to spell it. And you'd better not hang around here or you'll be late to school." Buford nodded and trudged off.

That afternoon he knocked on Ben's door and when Ben opened it, Buford said solemnly "H-y-a-c-i-n-t-h. Hyacinth. Can I have one for my Grandmother?"

Ben wanted to smile but somehow he felt embarrassed about it. So he just nodded and walked down the steps to pick a hyacinth for Buford. "Do you know Sister Cornelia?" he asked as he handed the flower to the little boy.

"Yep," Buford said, "she's the one taught me how to spell hyacinth."

"Oh," Ben responded, vaguely disappointed.

"She also told me hyacinths ain't too pretty 'cause they look sort of clobbered."

"You mean cluttered, don't you?" Ben asked.

"Yeah, maybe that's it. Don't matter, though. I think they're beautiful, and that's why I want one for my Grandmother. Sisters don't know everything."

Ben chuckled, "Better watch yourself, talking like that. I thought Catholic kids were taught to have respect for the Sisters."

"I'm only Catholic during the week," Buford confided. "Sundays I'm Baptist. Summers I'm Jewish. They got the best and cheapest summer camp. I gotta go now, or Grandmother will start worrying." He put out his little hand. Ben shook it. The friendship had begun.

It grew through the late spring and early summer. Almost every day Buford stopped to talk to Ben about things, from his Little League team to the best place to buy water ice, while asking about the different kinds of flowers and why Ben liked gardening and which ones were his favorites. Sometimes Ben let Buford water the plants or pull weeds or scratch the dirt loose around the roots. During those times they were quiet and serious as they concentrated on the work.

As the days grew hot and Ben's preoccupations with Nora and the neighborhood became more obsessive, Buford would ask Ben why he was feeling bad. Ben would get gruff then, and Buford would study him trying to figure out what he could say to make Ben feel better. When he couldn't think of anything, he'd go over and just touch Ben on the shoulder, wanting to hug him. Ben sensed Buford's care but felt shy in saying anything about his need or his gratitude for Buford's being there. After all, Ben was the man. So instead he'd snort, "You'd better get off to school," or "Your Grandmother's probably wondering where you are." Buford would simply nod and walk quietly away, not having the heart to tell Ben there wasn't any school in the summer and that his Grandmother knew exactly where he was.

When Buford went off to summer camp, Ben missed him intensely. Everything seemed to weigh heavily on him. Unexpectedly, he found himself ruminating about death, and it frightened him. At his age he'd thought he'd accepted death. He was surprised how much the thought of his nonexistence bothered him and set him to thinking about what life and death were really about. Maybe he was afraid of life as well as death. Or was angry at how similar they'd come to seem to him these days. He tried praying, but he wasn't sure what it was he was praying about. Was it his fear, or his anger, or just the damned, intractable fact of death—or his stupid inability to find his way out of any of it? His prayers droned from one subject to another but to no resolution. The only peaceful moments he had were the rare occasions when the simple beauty of one of his flowers absorbed his whole attention. Then he felt some quick, deep gratitude.

* * *

The dry August and hot early September turned into a wet autumn. The rain seemed to limit the number of times Buford and Ben had together. In his pride Ben wanted those times to seem entirely coincidental to Buford, and somehow to himself, so he made no pre-arrangements to see the boy.

One morning Buford decided his favorite flowers of all were the dahlias and the marigolds, " . . . 'cause," he said, "they sort of stay with you in your memory, you know, kind of like a promise when winter comes. What're your favorites, Ben?" he asked wide-eyed that snappy November morning as the gray clouds pulled up like a collar around the neck of the city and the feel of rain in the air made the last of the autumn leaves seem suddenly weary of their holding on.

"None," Ben growled. "None of them are my favorites." He wiped his nose with his finger. "None of 'em!" He wiped his nose again, then got out his handkerchief and blew his nose hard.

Buford went over and touched his shoulder. "I like 'em all, really," the boy said, "I ain't really got no favorites neither, Ben. It's just right now, I'm glad for the red and gold ones." He looked into Ben's face. "D-a-h-l-i-a," he spelled slowly, smiling, hoping to change something.

"Get to school," Ben said sternly, blowing his nose fiercely again. "And that isn't what I meant about none of them being my favorites. Oh, never mind. Get to school." The water in his eyes blurred his vision of Buford's yellow slicker going around the corner. "It's the cold wind," he mumbled to himself. As he opened the door, the dread came back. Nora waited like a lump in the overstuffed chair in the living room.

That morning, Nora's son was coming to help Ben take her to the psychiatric clinic at St. Monica's for tests. Her depression had gotten worse, she wasn't eating, wasn't talking, wasn't getting out of bed. "She's your mother," Ben had said insistently to Mason on the phone. "You ought to know I'm taking her to the hospital. She needs help. If word gets out she's your mother, that's just too bad. I can't protect you any longer."

There was a pause on the phone. "Okay, I'll go with you. We'll figure out something," Mason sighed.

It rained on the way to the hospital. Nora cried softly, apologizing for being "such a problem," until Ben wanted to tell her to "shut up," and then, ashamed that he felt so hostile toward her, put his arm around her and tried to reassure her. Nora would not be reassured.

When they got to the clinic, Mason registered Nora as his mother, gave his own address as his mother's, and introduced Ben as his mother's cousin. Ben shook his head at the lie but said nothing. All morning they waited restlessly in the lounge until a young resident introduced himself and told them that the initial tests indicated Nora should be admitted to the hospital until they could run more tests and get her properly medicated. Mason dealt with the admission procedures. A nurse with a ring of keys on her belt came and took Nora. As a cousin, at least Ben had visiting privileges.

In the late afternoon that day, the sun came out. Ben stood in the garden and watched for Buford, but he didn't come. That night the first frost arrived. Ben stepped outside before bed and watched his breath burst into little clouds. That made him feel lonely and fragile, as though each cloud were one less breath he had left. He went to bed and slept fitfully.

In the morning, by habit, he went to the garden. It was clear and cold. Shortly, Sister Cornelia and Sister Phoebe came striding down the street, leaving little breath clouds in their wake. "God still giving the increase, I see," gasped Sister Phoebe, "but soon winter will give the garden a season of rest."

"Your dahlias look awfully faded," observed Sister Cornelia. "No doubt you failed to feed them properly earlier."

"By the way," Sister Phoebe said, shifting to her most solemn tone, "have you heard that one of our students was struck by a car on the way home from school last evening?"

Ben froze.

"Yes, isn't it terrible? Car skidded on the wet leaves," Sister Cornelia went on. "Too bad, really. I wonder if the accident might have had anything to do with the fact that the boy insisted he was only a Catholic during the week . . ."

Ben grabbed her arm. "How is he? Is he alive?"

Sister Cornelia was unflustered. "Control yourself, Mr. Gregory, please. The boy is in Intensive Care at St. Monica's. He's expected to live, though he may not walk again, we're told."

Ben was shaking. "Buford Flynn? It's Buford Flynn?"

Sister Phoebe's sympathy was reflexive, "Oh, you knew Buford? Such a dear sweet, lovely boy. I'm sure the Almighty has some purpose in this, aren't you?"

"Oh my God," Ben groaned.

* * *

He went into the house and cried. He began pounding on the table, the walls. That wasn't enough. He got his walking cane and charged through the door. The sight of the flowers enraged him. "You betrayed him," he screamed and started stomping on them. He cursed a steady stream, the least of the oaths being "damn." "Damn Mason," he stomped, "Damn Nora, damn the neighborhood, damn Sister Cornelia, Phoebe, Venus, Hicks, damn the whole god damn depressing thing."

He stomped and stomped and swung his cane wildly, at the flowers, the sky, the ground. Then he staggered off swinging at hushes, pigeons, anything; around the corner he stumbled, swinging toward St. John's school.

Rather than calming him or exhausting him, the rage and swinging built its own momentum and carried him into the church next to the school. The sun, rushing through the open door, then narrowing as the door closed, caught the silver spike on one hand of the crucifix over the altar and focused into a dazzling light that seemed to beckon Ben forward.

A single priest saying a mass in a small side chapel stopped in mid-phrase and watched incredulously as Ben climbed up on the main altar and yanked with all his strength at the nearly life-size crucifix. The cross holding the Christ figure came off in his arms, and they fell together on the huge altar. The priest remained frozen in disbelief and fear at the man's maniacal behavior, but he still heard Ben shriek with a strange, wild tenderness, "Good! Good! You've been up there long enough. You don't have to hurt any more."

Ben climbed off the altar and rushed up the aisle carrying the Christ figure over his shoulder. When he got outside, the sunlight dizzied him momentarily. He staggered drunkenly down the steps and started up the sidewalk. Shortly, he decided his load was too heavy. He spotted some bushes under a tree a few yards off the sidewalk, halfway between the church and the school yard. He put the crucifix down in the bushes and covered the Christ figure with leaves, like a blanket to warm him. Then Ben walked quickly to the bus stop and was the last passenger on the A bus that went to St. Monica's.

When the priest finally regained his senses, he ran to the rectory and called the police. The police didn't arrive in time to catch Ben.

Later that day, the social worker and the security guard reported back to the hospital that they had had no luck in finding leads to Ben Gregory's next of kin. An attorney from law firm representing the hospital finally called the police to report what had happened. The police investigation in the next few hours enabled them to put the pieces of the puzzle together, although they weren't sure what to do about it and told no one except the attorney from the law firm about it.

As night fell, and a full moon rose, Nora and Ben and Buford were all on different floors and in different units of St. Monica's, each fighting for life.

* * *

But the most incredible thing was that three of Buford's friends, on their way to school that morning, spied the Christ figure under the pile of leaves. Considering such a discovery an amazing, God-sent stroke-of-luck, and having a certain unquestioning faith in the efficacy of such charms as rabbit's feet, four-leaf clovers, and horse shoes, the three young boys considered this figure the biggest lucky charm that could possibly come anyone's way, and they decided to give it to the one who needed it most, namely their friend Buford, lying in St. Monica's hospital.

Whether it was circumstantial, or providential, it is nevertheless beyond explanation, and nearly beyond belief, that the three boys managed to spirit the Christ figure away before anyone saw them. Once launched on their good-will adventure, they spent most of the morning wrestling the Christ figure all the way to the hospital, up the stairs, past the guards and the nurses' stations, into Buford's little cubicle without being detected or stopped. Probably it actually happened because no one but the three boys believed it could happen. And maybe it had nothing to do with what happened afterward, but don't argue that with Ben or Buford, or Nora. They insist otherwise. As has been said, it is best to let mysteries sing their own songs.

Buford's first words after having been hit by the car were spoken to his three friends and the Christ figure. "Got him down, huh?" he whispered.

One of the boys answered, "Naw. We just found him and brought him here. Figured you could use good luck."

"Right," Buford smiled. "Leave him."

Because he asked, and because it did seem to help him, the authorities agreed to leave the Christ figure in Buford's cubicle, once they got over their initial embarrassment about how it got there. The newspapers and local TV carried the story, and Nora, who began responding to treatment and medication in the psychiatric ward, saw it on the evening news as a human interest story and recognized Buford. Then she overheard the nurses talking about the crazy man who had swatted the crucifixes off the hospital walls and then collapsed with a stroke. One of the nurses mentioned the man's name and said that nobody knew anything about him. Nora asked the nurse for more information, saying that he might be a friend of hers.

The total effect was like a shot of adrenalin to her. First she asked if she could visit Buford. It didn't take long for Nora and Buford to figure out together that Ben was the crucifix snatcher everyone was talking about, but they didn't tell anyone.

Then Nora simply asked for and received permission to visit Ben as well. Her visits were unsatisfactory, but Nora persisted. Ben remained critical and unconscious.

* * *

With the resiliency of youth, Buford quickly progressed out of the critical stage and, though his legs remained paralyzed, he managed to badger his doctor into letting the attendants wheel him down to visit Ben every day. A week went by, and Ben remained in a coma. Finally, Buford went around and got flowers from all the people he could beg or borrow them from and took all the arrangements with him to visit Ben. And he talked the attendant into bringing the Christ figure with them, since he decided maybe Ben needed the luck even more than he did. He got the attendant to prop the Christ figure against the wall at the foot of Ben's bed and put flowers every place else. When everything was in place around Ben's bed and the machines, Buford leaned over and whispered in Ben's ear: "H-y-a-c-i-n-t-h, hyacinth," over and over again. For four days this went on.

Finally, Ben responded. Slowly he opened one eye and, though he was very hesitant in his speech, he spoke those five words to Buford more clearly than he would speak again for months: "Aren't you late for school?"

* * *

Now it is May again. The way back has been slow and painful for each of them, and each of them bears the scars of their struggle. Buford walks with crutches. Ben's left leg and arm are weak, his speech still slow, slurred, and frustrating to him, his smile crooked on one side. He needs his cane to walk. Tears still come easily to Nora, but the smiles are more frequent, as are the curses. She fights now, however timidly, even with Ben.

And she goes regularly to visit her son and daughter-in-law and grandson, riding the bus and arriving unannounced at their door. They greet her with a shrug and let her in, for fear she'll make a scene if they don't, which she would. Actually, it seems to matter less to them since Mason lost his election, which he seems almost relieved about. In fact, sometimes the shrug of greeting is followed by a brief hug, and occasionally Mason and family are seen at Nora and Ben's house. So they are all adjusting. Some might even say flourishing. Sister Phoebe would, which is . . . enough.

Ben and Buford go to physical therapy three times a week together. But the therapy isn't the hardest part for Ben. The hardest thing is coming to terms with some things about himself. It would have been easy to elicit sympathy, to become a victim, to explain what happened to him by blaming it on others, on the circumstances of his situation. To help him prove his case, had he wanted to try that, he had a list of charges and offenders and the evidence of a piece of earth stomped into a hardness no one could believe ever was a garden. But shame kept him from it. Besides, it was a garden, even if he'd mostly lost track of the pleasure of it when he turned it into work.

During those long days and nights in the hospital, studying that Christ figure propped in the corner, he had realized something. He had tried to tell Nora what it was. At first he attempted to speak, in halting, stroke-impoverished words: "I been . . . w'ike . . . seed . . . tha'wou'dn' . . . w'et . . . se'wf . . . bepwo'anted . . ." Then, in frustration, he motioned for a pencil and paper. All of a sudden it seemed terribly urgent to make her understand, to understand it for himself.

I been like seed. Refused be planted, grow. Lost trust. Not trust anything after while. Defended all time. Got

ashamed at wrong things. Lost myself. We lost ourselves. What we afraid of? God, no more fear, please. No more! Say "damn." Say "love you!" Trust! Take chance. Like Buford.

It was agonizing to watch him struggle for words, but afterward there was an ease about him.

Anyway, it's May again. And most mornings, if you're in the neighborhood before they go to therapy, you can see a little boy on crutches and an old man with a cane and watering can—and a woman with wonderful crows feet around her eyes, like furrows in a cornfield—all working away on a little garden in front of a row house around the corner and about a block down from St. John's school.

Some days, if you catch the time right, you might see a tall nun down on her knees next to Buford, watering one of the plants and actually getting her hands dirty in what she still insists on calling, "the lovely, sweet earth," while another nun and the old man yell at each other until they start to laugh.

And on a Saturday, you'll see maybe one or two other guys working on similar little gardens in front of other houses on the block. You'll even notice the one named Alan Hicks coming over to talk to the old man and getting advice from him every little while. The only advice the old man gives him, though, is a shrug and a pat on the back.

But the most curious thing about the little garden in front of the row house around the corner from St. John's school is that somehow, propped up in one corner of it, as though lying on its back, knees raised and ankles crossed in a relaxed, peaceful manner, arms stretched out and hands seeming to caress the flowers, is the Christ figure that once hung over the altar of the church next to the school. It was put there by diocesan permission, at the stubborn insistence of Sister Cornelia and her order, after it had been desacralized by the fairly willing pastor in charge at St. John's. It is amazing how well the figure seems to fit in the surroundings, and sometimes, when the sun slants a certain way, there are those who swear you can see a smile on the face of the Christ.

It's Ben's garden, on the little patch between house and street in a struggling but strangely appealing city neighborhood. He even smiles crookedly and nods when the tall nun reminds him, needlessly, each morning, dirt smudging her face, "I planted, Apollos watered, but God gave the increase." But then he adds, "Some increase!" after which his crooked smile turns into a giggling, slightly drooling, quite unself-conscious laugh. His heart is really in it, at last!

A Kind of Communion Taking

O God,
I cannot grasp you
or escape you,
but would stand
this twilight watch
with you,
this end of day aware,
this resurrection glance.

Sunlight smears its seal
upon the shadowed earth,
a crimson, purple promise
that darkness won't prevail;
bird song drips a weary vespers,
Venus dons her radiant veil,
crickets raise their prayers;
a small child nods to storied sleep,
traffic hums toward home somewhere,
an old man walks his faithful dog;
kids play stickball by the street light,
while a little wheelchaired-sister
swears encouragement at them
and plays battery-powered rap.

Leaning on elbows around dinner tables,
people sip and talk, sometimes touch,
a kind of communion taking
while the dishes wait,
and the bad news we pay for
flickers on the television.

Out back is a rose nodding white,
the faint smell of sweet basil,
a beaded necklace of impatiens
fringing an audacious plot of weeds;
and across the way, a precious moment
steals through an unguarded window
as two wonderfully oblivious lovers
kiss, caress themselves to sighs,
and me to a blushing smile,
reminding me I've heard faith is a blush
in your presence.

O God,
where have I been?
I've heard and seen this all before,
these small and tender mercies,
but realized not the miracle,
acknowledged not the gift,
took not the nourishment,
received not the grace,
ignored incarnation,
forgot what it is you love.

O God,
awe is where the healing is,
and the soar of confidence.
Gratitude coalesces me
into some integrity,
some merge
of trustworthiness,
of love,
of reverent resolve

to celebrate this life, this earth,
to brave a just and joyful work
and a more adoring watch with you,
    sailing this cosmic Tiberian Sea
        on this fishing boat of earth
            toward resurrection breakfasts
                on near, far distant shores.

THE UNEXPLAINABLE

Resonant Assurance

O God
of unfathomable depths
and unapproachable heights,
since it is through mystery
that you come closest to me,
and through awe
that I come closest to you,
grant me
the integrity
to be tutored by the questions
awe eddies up in me,
but pride stanches down;
the courage
to venture beyond the answers
fear bids me make
absolute and inviolable;
the wisdom
to respect the difference
arrogance erases between
the yet unknown, the always unknowable;
the confidence
to love boldly and inclusively
amidst the uncertainties
tyranny and timidity reduce to creeds;
the trust
to rest in the resonant assurance
that what I really need in this life
comes not only by dependable design,

but in strange, unexplainable deviations—
haunt of burning bushes,
untamed prophets—
because you are always going about your
gracious,
unpredictable,
ingenious
creating.

So, O wondrous God,
in awe,
not desperation or resignation,
I pray for those I carry in my heart
whose lives have flattened
into a sentence of single dimension,
a certain, inevitable boredom,
loneliness,
anxiety,
sorrow,
despair,
sickness,
guilt,
hopelessness,
endings,
that in some way,
past their understanding or mine,
past the limits of the world and time,

you are even now working in them,
with them,
for them,
as in, with, for me,
a different,
liberating,
saving,
altogether amazing,
baby eyes,
desert dawn,
misty moon,
sea-storm,
kingdom come,
awesome thing.

Humbled by the Strangeness

O Holy One,
after twilight's soft consolation
I tremble when night rubs softly on the window
as an even softer warning
of how thin is the layer of what we know,
how thick the overlay of proud assumption—
making the darkness your gift,
the tremor, my heart's praise.
I recall a mid-day voice
coming from me but somehow not my own,
shocking me to gagging awareness
of what cannot be bought or sold,
but only betrayed by vain pretension—
making the shock your judgment,
the gag, my soul's confession.

I pause now,
humbled by the strangeness of things,
quieted by the fragile, preciousness of life,
heartened by the incomprehensible greatness of you,
drawn into that galvanic space between us,
that wilderness of curious, childlike clarity
of living shadows,
fluttering wings, tiptoeing winds,
dancing memories,
flickering possibilities,
endless connections,
my own breathing,

where I can shed, scatter
the smoldering angers and resentments,
the cruelty of withheld words,
the danger of unquestioned roles,
the arrogance of unexamined blaming
that shrivels me
and by which I shrivel others.

I pause now,
intrigued by what I've ignored,
released by my great need of you
more urgent than my strutting doubts,
my puffed up demands for proof,
my inane claims to know your mind
when I don't even know my own,
and fear to know it better,
to ask you to take me, go with me
to some uncharted space inside out
where I will hear music not my own,
a rustling in the air;
see a pulse of flame,
a parting of the clouds;
smell the musk of fertile earth,
the astringent incense of my soul;
and realize, in a stitch of healing,
how petty, sad, unnecessary
are my cleverness, deceits, anxieties,
resentments, greeds, lusts, ambitions,
how vast the realms of grace.

I pause now,
summoned by my essential loneliness,
the burden and splendor of freedom,
to stretch toward your presence;
to embrace these contradictions that I am
of wildness and tenderness,
fallenness and faithfulness,
blindness and farsightedness;
and to love myself entire
as I would love my neighbor;
to wrestle the torments and tensions of my life,
the demons and angels, hungers and kingdoms,
into some dim light of dawn,
some poetic blessing,
some priestly scream or prayer,
some prophetic limp of creativity,
some honest word,
some honest being,
nothing fully explained,
but fully ventured,
into a letting go of what success hangs on to,
a leaving of where caution hunkers down,
a going on into the unknown,
inside out, outside in, yet deep between us,
into that strange promised place
of forgive, just, trust, love,
and possible;
into that mysterious promised time
of praise, peace, hope, joy—
fulfilled.

D-d-do ya s-s-see 'im?

O God,
your touch is light,
for sometimes, maybe more,
you wrap grace in laughter,
or perhaps laughing
just puts me lightly in touch with
what I've taken massively for granted;
often it seems your witness is a clown,
or close to one,
or perhaps closer to something
even more incongruous:
a walleyed seer,
a prophet with a stutter,
an angel in disguise.

"D-d-do ya s-s-see 'im?"
I was standing on the corner
waiting for a traffic light,
or maybe for a visitation.
A man, obviously homeless,
rose up from the grate
ski-capped, sneakered, whiskered,
layered with sweaters, grime,
shopping bag in one hand,
the other pointing
first at me,
then at some distant scene
his walleye seemed to spot.

"D-d-do ya s-s-see 'im?"
O God, I laughed,
first to scoff,
needing to prove my sophistication
to the others waiting for the light,
then in embarrassment
that he'd chosen me for this exchange,
his pointing hand now tugging on my arm,
finally in some confusion
over what I say I believe, O God,
and the discomfort I was feeling.

"D-d-do ya s-s-see 'im?"
Red turned green, the others went on,
I stayed unsure why except, I suppose,
the light changed differently for me;
and I laughed again,
in grudging respect for his insistence,
in some small delight for this diversion
on a dull, down day,
a bit of relief that for a moment
I'd broken stride.
Honestly, I thought of you, fleetingly,
as if you'd be proud of me for this,
and in that double think, nearly lost the gift,
save for his tug, his walleyed gaze at me,
his nothing more important question.

"D-d-do ya s-s-see 'im?" He pointed urgently.
It's J-j-jesus, a-a-ain't it?"

This time I laughed
as at a child's wonderment over some magic
long lost in adult explanations, skepticisms,
there being in me a sudden spark of love
for this stuttering, walleyed seer
who alternated between tugging and pointing.
I looked and saw
a woman limping wearily up the street,
grocery bag in one arm, child in the other;
teen-agers arm in arm,
full of dreams, music, hormones;
a school bus, like Noah's ark,
bearing its precious cargo home;
traffic honking up the avenue
purging the day's frustrations;
human beings going to and fro
in the streets on all their human errands,
hoping to find what they're looking for,
like me, like this man beside me, pointing.
I looked at him.

O God,
this time, he was laughing.
"T-t-told ya s-s-so. It's J-j-jesus, r-r-right?
I k-k-knew ya'd s-s-see 'im. G-g-glad, a-a-ain't ya?
He's g-g-glad, M-m-molly."
He called to a friend I hadn't noticed,
leaning against a building at our back.
He laughed, like a child verified, affirmed.
Was that a wishfulness only,
an illusion, or was it real?

All I know is that verifying
was more than I had done,
but somehow I felt it, too,
and laughed with him,
then took his hand in mine
and gave him all the cash I had.
"T-t-thanks, b-b-brother," he said,
his walleye looking at me, I think,
but more, beyond me to what he'd pointed to,
and I had seen at his insistence.

O God,
do such seers see what isn't there,
or do I not see what is?
Or is it that mostly I do not know
what it is I see?
Grace, O God,
grace to see with more than eyes,
grace to feel the tug,
heed the stammer.
"It's J-j-jesus, r-r-right?
G-g-glad, a-a-ain't ya?"
Yes. Yes.
I thank you, brother.
O God, I thank you,
thank you,
thank you, God.

This Catch of Light

Eternal One,
what unutterable beauty
is laced into this world:
late afternoon after rain clouds
hang in pink-edged, purple ruffles
over the green-gray ocean;
a congregation of birds
brown as sand, swift as shivers,
wheel as one at some primordial signal,
pivot against the dark clouds,
catch the light on white breasts,
a flash of inspiration,
a quick revelation
that takes my breath away,
returns it in deep inhalation.
O God,
I say in spontaneous acknowledgment,
as honest a prayer as I can utter.

Now, more reflectively,
I ponder before still O-God-you:
the pivot of the birds
was perhaps nothing to them
but the way of the hunt,
an instinct, a mere exercise,
the sight of prey, a scent of danger;
but to me their ballet
was an abrupt disclosure
of some incredible intention
beyond their power to define or mine to ignore,
our being creatures together.

Together's the revelation,
isn't it, O God?
Beauty being not just in wing
or breast, or burst of light,
nor in my beholding eye,
or breath, or brain,
but in the meeting,
the curious, mysterious between,
the surprise of connection
we were imaged for from the beginning,
creation becoming conscious of itself, of me,
and me of you,
in something like this strange; surge
of wing and wonder,
and then the longing,

O God,
I say again because I'm caught
(if but for this fraction,
become the measure of my life)
in this catch of light,
this feathered wheel,
this flash of revelation,
and I glimpse an essential weave of grace:
salvation is communal,
the ours
of beauty, truth, hope,
the we
of mercy, wholeness, atonement,
the together
of wolves and lambs and all reunion,
the us
of wedding feasts, Samaritans, prodigals
and every occasion of rejoicing;

the love that is, and never ends, being relational,
the meeting,
the surprise of connection
you imaged for this we of me
from the beginning of the any.

So I am less than me
without the others,
and this us is lesser still
without the you
who are our all.

Sam Who-Am and Murph

Everything about Murph's Tavern is run down, including Murph. It has taken fifty-two years of Murph's proprietorship to get that way. Outside hangs a faded green sign that announces the owner's name without the aid of the neon, which had long since stopped working.

Inside, the tavern is small, cluttered with boxes of empty bottles, permeated by the smell of stale beer and the accumulated layer of grease around the small grill in a corner behind the bar. Next to the grill is a refrigerator in which, alongside the cheese and hamburger, Murph keeps a supply of chocolate-covered peanut clusters he munches while cooking, talking to the trade, and instructing his willing but plodding helper.

Tucked, taped, pinned in every available cranny of the bar are faded newspaper clippings, curled black-and-white as well as color photographs, dusty medals and trophies, campaign buttons, slogans on cups, plaques, torn samplers—the historic trail of Murph's fifty-two years on that corner.

If you ask him about that history, Murph shrugs and says, "Yeah, I seen lots a changes while I'm here, most of 'em not so good. I tell ya somethin'. I close at nine every night. People say I'm dumb. They ask, 'What kinda tavern closes at nine? How ya make money like that?' Know what I say? I say if any funny stuff goes on out there, muggings, drugs, stuff like that, I'm already outta here. Money ain't everything. Tell ya somethin' else. Some guy I know comes in here blowin' his money and neglectin' his family, I tell 'im ta get outta here, go home. Troubles, like one of them viruses, spreads around easy if ya ain't careful. Don't need no more trouble, me or the world. So ya gotta take precautions, ya know, while ya can. But I ain't got long here anyhow. Whatta ya gonna do?" Then he pops a peanut cluster in his mouth as if the candy were a question mark, or maybe an exclamation point.

Murph looks like a disheveled owl. His chubby body sags over short legs. His dark eyes dominate his large round face and peer out through black, horn-rimmed glasses. What hair he has is almost white. His clothes are frayed, spotted, made up of odd matches of stripes and plaids, coats from one old suit, pants from another, never anything new, as if the point of dressing for him is to cover the body, keep warm, and use up all his clothes before he dies.

His stories are honed and polished, word for word the same every time he tells them. "I'm Irish, ya know," he'll say absently while frying a hamburger. "Murph is short for Patrick John Ezekiel Murphy. Ya wanna know why 'Ezekiel,' which ain't exactly no

Irish name? I'll tell ya. My people come over from Ireland, no question about it, but the family secret was that somewhere way back some Jewish blood snuck in on account of a crazy ancestor from near Cork gettin' drunk and signin' on for the crusades and bringin' back a Jewish wife who was pregnant and looked Irish, or somethin' like that."

"My mother, God rest her soul, didn't think that was nothin' ta be ashamed of, but it took her six kids ta persuade my old man ta give one of us a Jewish name t'honor that grand old ancestor on her side. Sad, peoples' pinched ways of lookin' at one another, ain't it? Anyway, when I come along, number seven, I got it, the Jewish name. Ezekiel. Patrick John Ezekiel. Priest almost wouldn't baptize me. Took an extra buck in the box from my old man—which was a lot in those days—plus the priest not havin' ta say Ezekiel, only mouth it, when he baptized me, ta get the job done. But him not sayin' it don't change it. My mother give it ta me and that's my name. Whatta ya gonna do?" By the end of the story the hamburger is burning and the smoke stings your eyes.

There's room for only twelve, fifteen stools on the customers' side of the bar. There are seldom that many people in the place except at midday when Murph gives free lunches to homeless people. Murph's Tavern is in a once fine, upper-middle class section of the city that for thirty years has experienced urban decay, racial change, and a bad reputation. Houses deteriorated and businesses fled. Recently, there has been an upturn in the area, and real estate speculators are buying and fixing up property all around.

However, that upturn has not changed the situation for street people. So every day, from mid-morning to mid-afternoon, Murph passes out food to his flock of homeless. It is rumored that several homeless actually live in the run down rooms over Murph's Tavern. And that's where this story really begins.

One of the real estate speculators made Murph an offer for the tavern, intending to make it an up-scale cocktail lounge. Murph turned the offer down cold.

"What'm I gonna do if I don't have this place?" Murph inquired when the speculator made his offer. "Sit in the park and drool? It ain't the money. Here, I belong. They'll have ta carry me out. No thanks. I ain't sellin'. Now ya gotta 'xcuse me. I hav'ta serve lunch ta my friends."

The speculator looked around. "Where? Upstairs?" he asked.

Murph smiled, "No. Too old ta climb stairs much anymore. Right here."

"You serve lunch to friends in a dump . . . place like this?" the speculator sniffed.

"Well, they ain't exactly just friends. You could say they're people who don't live around here." Murph smiled as he moved away. "They don't mind a dump like this, Whatta ya gonna do?"

The speculator apologized, "I'm soriy. I didn't mean to offend."

Murph turned back, deadpan. "Not while you're tryin' ta buy my property anyway, right? 'xcuse me, I really gotta work now."

It was the speculator who reported Murph's Tavern to the City Health Department for unsanitary food preparation, and to the Bureau of Licenses and Inspection to investigate whether people were being illegally housed on the second floor of the tavern. The speculator thought the aggravation might force Murph to reconsider selling.

But strangely enough, not only did the Health Department and L&I investigators visit Murph's Tavern, but so did media people. No one was sure how the press found out about Murph, or how Channel 6 happened to send a crew out to interview him, but suddenly Murph was on the evening news, and stories about him were in all the papers. His celebrity status embarrassed him.

The five o'clock TV live coverage panned the neighborhood, then showed Murph passing out food to his friends. The interviewer asked Murph how long he'd been feeding the homeless in his tavern.

Murph answered, "Maybe five or six years, give or take a couple of days."

The interviewer laughed. "And what made you start doing it?"

"Somethin' just come over me one day. Like someone tapped me on the noggin' and just put the idea in there," Murph said. "It's a free country, ain't it? Whatta ya gonna do?"

The interviewer nodded. "But a lot of people don't help like this," she replied, pointing to the homeless people eating at the bar.

"I don't care what other people do. People're always comin' in and havin' a beer and talkin' about big stuff, like how t'run the government or solve some crisis or other. Everybody's brilliant. I use t'get off on that stuff myself 'til I realized it was useless. This here I do. 'Cause I can, is why. It's real, like. But it ain't no big deal."

The interviewer smiled. "Murph," she said, "I'll wager Channel 6 viewers *will* think it's a big deal. It takes a good man to use his own money and his own business to feed homeless people. You're to be congratulated. You're an example for the rest of us. Wouldn't you agree, Jack? Now back to you in the studio. This is Deborah Alcorn for . . ."

Murph interrupted and pulled the microphone toward him. "Wait a minute. I ain't doin' this 'cause I'm good. It's more 'cause if ya ain't careful, the bad stuffin ya sort of takes over. Whatta ya gonna do? Listen! I ain't no better'n these people. None a you is, really, either. Ya gonna get it all wrong makin' me out ta be some kinda hero or somethin'. I ain't even religious anymore. I used ta be Catholic, being Irish and all, but . . ."

The TV station cut Murph off, and the crew on scene moved in to calm Murph down and get the microphone away from him. On the six and eleven o'clock news, Murph's outburst was edited out, but it was too late. Reports of the interview spread. Murph was an instant folk hero.

The flood of publicity had three results: One was that L&I and the Health Department suspended their investigation of Murph's Tavern for fear it would provoke bad press; two, Murph vowed he would never again allow TV stations or newspaper reporters in his tavern or near his person; three, Murph got several more offers for his property, all of which he refused.

One other thing happened at the same time that may or may not have been the result of Murph's publicity. New faces appeared among the homeless at lunch time, Murph talked to each about their circumstances, and while he tried to discourage some, he never actually turned any away. Within a month things had returned to what seemed normal to Murph, though his meager savings were shrinking under the burden of having to buy more food.

Then the angel appeared. It happened like this. One noon about three weeks after Easter, a new person showed up in the soup line. The person wore a heavy coat under which was a bulky sweater under which was a plaid dress under which were jogging pants. On one foot was a rubber boot, on the other a hightop sneaker. A ski cap was pulled down over a bushy head of hair, and over the ski cap was tied the sort of straw hat women often wear while gardening. On one hand there was a glove, on the other a mitten, and in both were shopping bags.

The new person went to the far end of the bar and sat on the floor, back against the wall. After lunch Murph leaned over, hands on his knees, and began to talk to the new person who was slurping the last bit of soup from a plastic bowl.

"What's your name?" he asked.

"Sam Who-Am," was the answer.

Murph looked puzzled. "Sam, huh? Funny name for a woman, ain't it?"

"Who said I'm a woman?" Sam Who-Am retorted.

"Nobody. I just figured ya was, with the woman's coat and the dress and the long hair. So I was wrong. So okay, Sam, you're a man."

Sam Who-Am's head cocked to one side. "Who said I was a man?"

Murph frowned. "You did."

Sam Who-Am looked Murph in the eye. "No, I didn't."

Murph was struck by the clarity of Sam Who-Am's eyes. The eyes looked very young for such an old face. "Yeah, I guess ya didn't actually say that. So ya are a woman after all."

"No, I didn't say that either," Sam Who-Am insisted, continuing to gaze into Murph's now befuddled face.

Murph straightened up. "Enough with the games, Sam. Which are ya, a man or a woman? Ya gotta be one or the other."

The corners of Sam Who-Am's mouth turned up slightly. "Who said I gotta be one or the other?"

"Who said?" Murph answered incredulously. "Mother Nature! God! That's who said. You gotta be one or the other, unless you're one a them circus freaks what claims ta be both, and I don't believe that stuff anyway."

Sam Who-Am smiled more broadly, and Murph noticed that the teeth seemed very white for an old street person, even though one was missing in front, "No, I'm not that kind of freak, Murph."

"So which are you?" Murph asked again, trying to control his exasperation, "a man or a woman."

"Sit here and I'll tell you," Sam Who-Am replied, patting an empty spot on the floor. Murph nodded his head wearily and sat.

"I'm a burning bush," Sam Who-Am said when Murph had settled in.

Murph shook his head. "Why do I get all the nut cases?" he muttered. Then he added, "I have ta admit ya do smell a little like somethin' burnin' though."

"I'm a burning bush," Sam Who-Am insisted, "a messenger from God."

"As long as ya ain't from L&I or the Health Department," Murph shrugged.

"It's true," Sam Who-Am insisted, softly. "I am really an angel."

"Oh yeah, of course. And I'm the Pope. What hospital ya been in?" Murph wheezed, struggling to get to his feet.

Sam Who-Am put a hand on Murph's arm. "No hospital, Murph."

Murph gave up the attempt to get up. He was too tired. He realized he'd been feeling very tired lately. "Okay, no hospital. But ya ain't from around here. Where're ya from?"

Sam Who-Am smiled again, "I've been around here many times. You just didn't notice. But I am from other places, too."

Murph sighed. "Like China? Or Korea, maybe?"

It was Sam Who-Am's turn to look puzzled. "China? Why do you say that?"

Murph pinched his nose, blew, and then let the air out in a rush. "Because your other name sounded Oriental or somethin'. What was it again?"

"Oh, you mean, 'Who-Am'?"

"Yeah. Sounds Oriental. But ya don't look like that, no slant eyes or nothing."

"I'm not Oriental," Sam Who-Am chuckled.

"Then what?" Murph pressed. "Armenian? Eye-ranian maybe? What's 'Who-Am'?"

"It's a long story," Sam Who-Am said.

Murph nodded. "I'll just bet it is. Look, I like ta know who I'm feedin' here. So tell me the shortest, straightest way ya can."

Sam Who-Am rubbed those young eyes. "You know who Moses is, right?"

Murph put his head back against the wall. "Yeah, I know. Everyone knows that. Besides, I got a little Jewish in me from way back. Ninety-nine percent Irish, though."

Sam Who-Am continued. "Remember when God told Moses to go lead his people out of Egypt, and Moses said no one would follow him? And God said, 'Just tell them I sent you.' And Moses said, 'How will they know who you are? What's your name?' And God said, 'My name is I am who I am.' Only, the burning bush where God's voice was coming from coughed and made a crackling sound right at that moment, and Moses thought God said, 'My name is Sam Who-Am.'"

"That misunderstanding caused a lot of problems. When Moses got to Egypt and told the Pharaoh to let his people go because the God whose name was Sam Who-Am said so, the Pharaoh laughed at him. Same thing happened when Moses told the Jews. Nobody had ever heard of a God named Sam Who-Am. Took all those plagues to straighten Pharaoh out about it, and forty years in the wilderness to get the Jews shaped up after that." Sam Who-Am was laughing now.

Murph couldn't help smiling. "What nut-house hospital did ya say ya were in?" he asked. "That's the craziest thing I ever heard. You shouldn't joke about stuff what's in the Bible."

Sam Who-Am touched Murph's arm. "It really isn't entirely a joke, Murph. Among angels, Sam Who-Am is the code name for things people don't understand—or can't quite believe. Like angels. Like me."

Murph studied Sam Who-Am for a moment. Then very quietly he said, "Sam Who-Am, huh? All right. It ain't a bad name 'cause I sure don't understand ya comin' in here like this, those young eyes lookin' out of that old face, teeth all straight 'cept one missin' and none of 'em havin' no stains on 'em or nothin'. Somethin' funny about ya, all right."

Sam Who-Am's hand covered the mouth. "I guess I didn't get all the bugs out of my impersonation."

Murph smiled. "Ya got quite an imagination, I'll give ya that. Must a kissed the Blarney stone sometime in your life. I don't buy ya being no angel, but ya can eat here when ya want. What else can I say? Whatta ya gonna do?" He started to get up again, but this time felt a bit dizzy. "Guess I'll just sit here a while longer," he said, sliding back to his seat beside Sam Who-Am.

After a moment Sam Who-Am said, "You don't go to church anymore. Why not?"

Murph looked at Sam Who-Am. "How'd ya know that? Was ya around when that TV bunch was here, and I told 'em somethin' about that? Is that how ya knew?"

"Let's just say I knew," Sam Who-Am replied. "So, why don't you go anymore?"

"I ain't sure," Murph sighed. "I guess it was that the confessions took too long."

"Took too long?" Sam Who-Am asked. "What do you mean?"

"Just that," Murph said. "I used ta go in and try ta tell the priest all the stuff that's wrong inside me and all the stuff I done and said that ain't right or true for just one lousy day, and it took such a long time I couldn't never finish, even one day's worth, let alone a whole week between masses. Other people didn't seem ta have no trouble, but I did. So I felt there was somethin' really wrong with me. Like I didn't belong. Didn't deserve ta belong. So I stopped goin'. That's all. Whatta ya gonna do?"

Sam Who-Am touched Murph's cheek. "Is that really all, Murph?"

Tears filled Murph's eyes and trickled down his cheeks. "I don't guess it is," he whispered hoarsely. "It's lonely not belongin'. I act like it ain't, but it is. I think maybe that's got somethin' ta do with my feeding homeless people in here. It's like for an hour or so we all belong. For a little while we ain't none of us homeless. Only I ain't never able ta say nothin' about it ta none of 'em ta help make it real for us. Whatta ya gonna do?"

"You're talking to me," Sam Who-Am reminded him.

"I was just thinkin' that same thing," Murph said, taking off his glasses and wiping his eyes with the back of his chubby hands. "It's a wonder, ain't it?"

They sat quietly for a moment, and then Murph went on. "Sometimes early in the morning, or at night when there ain't nobody there. I go sit in Saint Madeleine's and think what it would be like ta be there, me and all these people here together in that beautiful place. I sit there thinkin' if that could happen, then there wouldn't be no more vacancies in peoples' eyes or lives . . . or whatever.

"Wouldn't it be somethin' if that could happen? But that place and this one's like two different worlds that can't get together. Be somethin', wouldn't it, ta get 'em together? Only, lately I been thinking it ain't just two worlds. It's really like two parts a me can't get together. So I sit there wonderin' why I'm so lonely, why I'm feelin' so empty? I don't know. Sam Who-Am's a good name for God if it's like ya say, the name of things people don't understand. Whatta ya gonna do?"

Sam Who-Am leaned forward to engage Murph's eyes. "Murph, those world's aren't so far apart. There are angels in all of them. Really! When you go to Saint Madeleine's, sometimes you talk to a Sister there, don't you?"

Murph frowned. "How'd ya know that? Are ya from Saint Madeleine's? Are ya a Sister in disguise? Is that who ya are?"

Sam Who-Am's hands went up in denial. "No, no. I told you who I am, Murph. Heaven is not far from earth either, even if you can't believe that. I just know that Sister Mary Martha prays for you."

Murph shrugged. "Maybe she does. I ain't gonna ask how ya know that, or her name. It's for sure I don't understand ya, Sam. The Sister said she'd pray for me, and I don't figure she'd lie. But so what? What good're her prayers ta me?"

Sam Who-Am spoke as to a child. "Murph, what good is your feeding the homeless to Sister Mary Martha?"

"I never thought about it," Murph answered after a long pause, "Maybe if one of these here people's her brother or sister, it'd be good for her,"

Sam Who-Am clapped. "That's it, Murph! You saw it."

Murph was puzzled. "Saw what?"

Sam Who-Am answered enthusiastically, "Saw what most people don't see. We do belong to each other; heaven and earth belong to each other. We're connected by bread and prayers and everything else. Sam Who-Ams are about helping people find that out, see that. You see it, Murph."

"I do?" Murph replied.

"Of course," Sam Who-Am insisted. "You feed the homeless."

"I ain't so sure I see it," Murph protested. "Fact is, I ain't seein' nothin' too good at the moment. I'm feelin' kind of strange and disconnected right now."

Sam Who-Am put an arm around Murph. "It's all right, Murph. I'm sorry. I got going in circles like a one-winged angel. I'm sorry. Don't be afraid."

"Why's ever'body lookin' at us so funny?" Murph mumbled, weakly pointing at the half-dozen or so people standing in a semicircle squinting at them.

"They aren't looking at us funny, Murph. It's just the light," Sam Who-Am assured him.

"Ain't no light in here," Murph insisted. "What's happenin'?"

"Just don't be afraid," Sam Who-Am repeated, cuddling Murph tenderly. "Don't be afraid."

"Tell the truth, I always been afraid," Murph whispered. "I acted tough and tried ta hide it, but I always been afraid. Of dyin', I guess. Dyin's the worst kind of not belongin'. And now here I am, an old man. A scared old man. Whatta ya gonna do?"

Sam Who-Am rocked Murph slightly. "Oh, Murph, you always tried so hard. But you never let anyone help you. You never trusted your longing to belong. Murph, if you'd tell people you are afraid, you'd help them with their fear. Tell them, Murph. Let them be with you."

Murph looked up at the scraggly, familiar faces. As loudly as he could, he whispered to them, "Ya been standin' there listenin' like CIA wire tappers, so ya musta heard what I just told Sam Who-Am here. About my bein' scared. So whatta ya gonna do?"

Without a word, the whole group got on the floor around Murph and put their arms around whatever part of him they could. Some were crying. Then one ventured to say, "God, if you can hear this, we want ta thank you for Murph. He's sort of like Jesus to us. So take care of him now he's so sick."

And another added, "Yeah, we gotta eat." Everyone laughed a little.

Then another began to sing the only religious song she knew, which was "Onward Christian Soldiers," and others joined in for a phrase or two until no one could remember the words.

Finally, someone said, "Maybe a little wine would bring 'im around." As one, they got to their feet hopefully and went after the bottle and a glass.

Sam Who-Am whispered in Murph's ear, "Do you understand any better about connections now?"

Tears began running down Murph's cheeks again. "I don't know. Maybe. I guess I feel a little less scared myself right now," he whispered back.

Sam Who-Am smiled. "Murph, the question was never about God forgiving and loving you. It's that you could never forgive yourself or love yourself. All that endless confessing was sad. And all that homeless feeling. All that work for so little. But listen now, Murph. I'm here because there isn't much time, but don't forget it's after Easter now."

"I ain't forgettin'" Murph replied, hoarsely, "but I ain't sure what that's got ta do with anything."

"It's got to do with you, Murph," Sam Who-Am whispered excitedly. "And everybody. Easter's about a different way of seeing things. It's about connections nothing can break. Connections with God. Do you want to go and check that out with me?"

"You mean leave here? With you?" Murph asked.

"Yes," Sam Who-Am nodded.

"Where?" Murph pressed.

"Hard to explain," Sam Who-Am replied. "Different but . . . not too different from here."

Murph considered the offer for a moment. Then he asked, "How long I got ta decide?"

Sam Who-Am's lips puckered for an instant. "Until Sister Mary Martha finishes her prayers for you."

Murph nodded. "I can't believe that I believe you're an angel. But whatta ya gonna do? Listen, ya married?"

Sam Who-Am looked quizzically at him. "Married? No. Why are you asking?"

Murph smiled, "Well, if I'm goin' ta go off with ya like this, I gotta check out somethin' like that. Don't want no trouble."

"Murph!" Sam Who-Am scolded.

Murph was undaunted. "I warn ya, Sam, it's gonna be a real disappointment if ya turn out ta be one of them circus freaks."

Sam Who-Am winked. "You'd be surprised at how many varieties of angels there are, Murph. Any time people discover a connection in life, some kind of Sam Who-Am is there."

The others straggled back with a bottle of wine and a glass. They poured the wine and the glass was passed around, beginning with Murph, who seem revived for a few minutes. During that time, he wrote a simple will on a piece of a lid torn from one of the cases of empty beer bottles, and everyone present managed to scrawl their name on it as a witness.

Murph left half of his tavern to Saint Madeleine's for the purpose of feeding the homeless. The other half he left to the homeless themselves. Murph's last words were, "Maybe this'll help get two worlds together."

The words had barely passed his lips when Sister Maiy Martha said, "Amen," and toppled off her prie-dieu in the convent chapel of Saint Madeleine's, dead from a massive cerebral hemorrhage but with a beatific smile on her face.

It was the same sort of smile that the rescue squad found on the face of Murph when they responded to an emergency call from his tavern. Sam Who-Am had left by then, and only among themselves did the homeless speak of the one some referred to as she, others as he, but all with awe in their voices.

Though Murph's will quickly became public information, whether it holds up in court still remains to be seen. Right now, no one is contesting it. At least not openly. Meanwhile, the only changes in Murph's Tavern are few but important. A member of Saint Madeleine's helps run the tavern jointly with a homeless person on a rotating basis, and the parish has cleaned it up a bit. Nuns and priests and church members mingle with the homeless while serving lunch, which the two groups often end up eating together.

Channel 6 has revisited to inform its viewers of this unusual circumstance. The question is whether the cameras, in panning the inside of the tavern, showed close-up the last, smallest, and perhaps most significant change in Murph's Tavern: three kodachrome pictures stuck side-by-side amidst the other mementos.

One picture shows Murph passing out soup and sandwiches to the homeless.

A second, which no one has any idea how it was taken, shows Murph smiling, sitting on the floor with a non-descript looking bag lady, surrounded by a motley but happy looking group of vagrants, all of them actually looking a little like clowns at a party.

The third shows Murph's grave, a few daffodils stuck jauntily in a beer bottle leaning against a new headstone that reads, "Patrick John Ezekiel Murphy" in smaller letters, a larger "Murph" under that, and across the top, in slightly larger letters, "It's after Easter. Whatta ya gonna do?"

Very Deepest Mystery

O God,
at last I discern
even in this dark glass of finitude,
that the deeper mystery is goodness,
not evil in all its demonic poses
or all its grinding banalities;
beauty, not nagging ugliness;
truth, not falsehood followed however long.

The mystery is goodness, beauty, truth:
not just goodness agreed-upon, rewarded,
self-interest compromised but slightly;
not just beauty of the admired surface,
custom left unaltered by creativity;
not just truth measured by the numbers,
the unseen not included in its frame;
though even these are mystery
far from all necessity,
as am I,
or anything at all.

But Lord,
the deeper mystery is something more:
the sacrifice,
the costly word,
the disdained lure,
the just deed done unto the death;
the keeping of breakable promises,
the long walk of compassion,
the unsafe witness,
the cross,
the music;

humanity past depravity,
all life, my life, this prayer,
this wink of dust
this blink of eye that sees
traces of forever.

Come close, now, old holy friend past full knowing,
that I may know that this deeper mystery
I am in, and that's in me,
is because you have made me holy, too,
and all this wondrous life I share;
that this hunger, this longing
for the goodness, beauty, truth
that keeps breaking my heart,
and remaking it,
is holy
because all is connected,
all life, all worlds,
to you.

Come close, old holy adversary in all trusting,
that I may trust that this urge in me
to go on and on and on,
is holy because you are the pull of it,
yours the hard to hear,
hard to resist
summons to go on,
beyond defeat, discouragement, despair,
beyond even goodness, beauty, truth,

to go on until I am found
by the life I long and love and each moment live toward
(though mostly too unknowing,
but live toward, nonetheless,
even through the veil of death);
a holy life with you, and all the rest,
in unimaginable goodness, beauty, truth,
because it is you who, above all, beyond all,
keeps breakable promises
and your grace is the very deepest
mystery of all.

The Haunt of Grace

RESPONSES TO THE MYSTERY OF GOD'S PRESENCE

To

Dwight E. Loder

Pastor Educator Bishop

A man of family, faith, hope, humor.

A model of compassion, humility, courage.

Younger Brother of my Father.

Like an Older Brother to me.

Acknowledgments

This book has emerged from a lifetime, forty-five years of which have been in the professional ministry of the United Methodist Church, thirty-eight of them as Senior Pastor of the First United Methodist Church of Germantown (FUMCOG) in Philadelphia. Of course that congregation of remarkable persons who first heard these pieces as sermons live between the lines of this book. I wish I could name each of them personally but . . .

So my staff colleagues at FUMCOG also live between these lines, including the directors of music and the organists. Each of these professional men and women contributed in different but significant ways to my life and my faith. I am particularly indebted to the first in that long line, Robert A. Raines, who surely prompted by nothing less than the haunt of grace, welcomed and endured me as a co-pastor, and in that arrangement of blessing and frustration, taught me much that remains bone deep in me. He is an old and dear friend.

My other colleagues deserve mention by name, but I refrain and trust they will know deeper than words the enormity of their gifts to me and my growth as a human being and pastor. But I must mention the last in that long line, Dr. Ann Marie Donohue, an unordained person whose gifts and spirit are singularly impressive and who has instructed, challenged, supported, and befriended me in ways that were free of clerical constraint and exceedingly beneficial to me because of it.

The foremost person I want to acknowledge is my wife and best friend, Dr. Janet I. Filing, whose insistence on the congruity of faith and life, honesty and love, hard patches and hope, direct address and quiet support, vulnerability and toughness, fragility and courage, and her prophetic stance in insisting that to love your enemies does not mean to be afraid to make them, have not only informed my life but helped transform it. In ways, this book is as much hers as mine.

What I owe to my children, now adults and parents themselves, is beyond all telling of it. Each of them—Mark, David, Karen, Thomas—has taught me more about life than I ever would have thought possible. I only hope I have taught them something about love, for they are always in my heart, however falteringly my heart is expressed in my being a father. But they have helped to take me to places that are evident in this book, and we have become closer in honest love than we might have been had we not gone there together. I rejoice and am glad in them. And in their spouses, Nadya, Steve, Amina, and children, my grandchildren, Daniel, the newest, Aaron, Lyle, Jacob, Julya, Kyle, Marek, Amanda. The revelations go on. I am also blessed by Jan's sons, Christopher and Jonathan, their wives, Valery and Hilary, and little granddaughter, Hoshaiah.

It is also time for me to acknowledge and thank Doris, the woman with whom I shared a marriage and a divorce. She is the mother of our four remarkable children and in that capacity loved, nurtured, and influenced them in good and abiding ways, and so blessed me as well. Her superb talent as a musician and her delight in her music enriched my life and that of our family, and her intelligence, her dauntless confidence, and her friendly spirit were gifts to me and a legacy to our children. The lengthy crisis of our failure in marriage deepened my self-awareness, my compassion, my re-formation as a person, and my experience of the long-suffering patience involved in giving and seeking forgiveness. Doris made important and significant contributions to my life and to my sensitivity—sometimes painful sensitivity—to the haunt of grace, which may be particularly evident in one of the responses in this book.

I am indebted to some special friends whose influence is writ large on the ensuing pages. I dare, in friendship, to name them by their first names, hoping they are good enough friends that they will forgive thoughtless but unintentional omissions. Friends know who they are without being named anyway. Still, thank you, Barbara, David, Ed, Rick, Herb, Joan, Bob, Bill, John, Kenneth, Carl, Calvin, Sheila, Harvey, Linda, Wayne, English, Sue, Doug, Austin, Ernie, Maury, Dan, Edith, Ted, Amy, Sam, Marion. That's more friends than anyone has any right to have, and perhaps I've been presumptuous to claim them as such. Some may even want to remove their names from the roll. However, they do so at their own peril.

It would be impossible to acknowledge the many teachers, preachers, poets, writers, and artists who have so profoundly shaped my own thinking, perceiving, and writing, but not to acknowledge them at all would be to claim far more for myself than is my due. I would be reduced to poverty and stupidity without their gifts to me, and to us all. At the same time, however, I hold no one but myself responsible for the limitations and flaws of this book.

Finally, I gladly acknowledge my editor and publisher, Marcia Broucek. This is not a pro forma acknowledgment but a heartfelt one. In the course of putting this book together, I broke five ribs. Marcia's patience and compassion in caring for me as a friend was far beyond any duty she had as an editor or publisher. But in that professional role, she has also been consistently patient, helpfully critical yet affirming, understanding of an author's outbursts of stubborn resistance and egomaniacal insistence, while quietly containing the damage such might have done to the work. Though this book is not her doing, it would not have been done without her.

I wish a special haunting of all of the persons, named and unnamed, who have touched this work in any way.

Introduction

Where I'm Coming From . . . Where I'm Headed

We live in a society that is increasingly rich in information and poor in reflection. The relative ease and speed by which we access facts and data is astounding, if not overwhelming. We can learn quickly more about any subject than we can assimilate, let alone thoughtfully interpret.

As a result, our lives are changed almost without our consent or intent. We're afflicted with near-terminal busyness. We know more but are less wise. We prefer to get information in sound bites even though the result is a sound-bite-size life. We assume love, marriage, and parenting are about perfectible techniques of manipulation rather than the faltering processes of human relationships. We consider life to consist essentially of what can be added and subtracted, touched and measured, bought and sold, managed and controlled.

Thus we are seduced into believing there are treatments for every disease and dis-ease, solutions for every problem, someone to blame (and sue) for any glitch in a process that results in a heart-rending outcome, teachable steps to follow in achieving any goal. We conclude that enough quantity equals quality, simplicity is truer than complexity, certainty is more compelling than uncertainty no matter the issue involved, knowledge is the road to wealth, power guarantees security, that Machiavelli, the Prince of Cunning, can outwrestle Beelzebub, the Prince of Darkness.

So the major change is inside each of us, in our attitudes, perceptions, and understanding of ourselves and the world. The meaning of life is reduced to whatever discovery, gimmick, promise, or advantage science, technology, the market, or privileged American citizenship pitches to us. Our self-assessment is that we are fairly predictable conglomerations of DNA, cells, chemical interactions, electrical charges, programmed impulses, and mental equipment akin to a computer—and, for most of us, a frustratingly slow one.

What is lost in all that is time and inclination to reflect, as well as the value and purpose of such reflection. What is lost is honest self-awareness, a sense of worth not defined by status, and an inclusive respect for the worth of others. What is lost is the call and the claim of any force, activity, being, or purpose that transcends the muddle of a life that is fundamentally directionless, however well informed. What is lost is the sense of a moral vision or intentional ethical action in response to that transcendence, as well as the experience of freedom and exhilaration in risking a life beyond the trite counsel of the pragmatic or safe or successful.

This book is an attempt to address those losses. Granted, to make that point, I have probably overstated the case a bit. In fact, I do not intend to demean or dismiss our contemporary world or belittle our lives in it, though I do have a "lover's quarrel" with much of both. Rather, I intend to suggest that our lives and the world are more layered, more profoundly interwoven with dimensions than we often realize. My contention is that we are haunted by transcendence at every turn, that our lives and the world are shot through with meaning and possibilities that outrun those for which, to our great deprivation, we too often settle.

No matter what the feel and thrust of every "present age," there is in all of them a great mystery about each and every life, and about the world they inhabit, including ours, and this one. Who can begin to describe or account for the incredible twists and turns, decisions and hunches, chances, influences, happenings and non-happenings, meetings and misses, losses and gains, betrayals and fidelities, triumphs and failures, the variety of people who intersected and redirected our lives—all that was involved in getting us to this moment and this place with the people who share our lives now?

Who can explain how the world has survived all the wars, plagues, epidemics, enmities, exploitations, pollution of resources and social processes, terrible misjudgments, pogroms, holocausts, bilkings, corruptions, and yet generated such incredible poetry, art, music, literature, such wondrous cultures, episodes of saintliness, movements of justice, struggles for freedom, for healing, for peace, such experiences of love and sacrifice and joy?

Surely mystery is an essential ingredient, if not *the* essential of our common life and this earth in which we are all rooted. By mystery I do not mean the vast oceans of knowledge in which we have not *yet* swum or not *yet* mapped. By mystery I mean the infinite depths of being that we can *never* plumb, never know, never exhaust, given the limits of our mortality, our finitude, our creatureliness.

Our inherent sense of mystery is in our irrepressible longing for something we cannot name but intensely miss. We are afflicted, or blessed, with a kind of insistent, cosmic homesickness. It comes in moments of awe and wonder at starlight or twilight, or a child's birth and unfolding, or the quiet peacefulness in an old woman's face, the surpassing lift of music, a pause of self-recognition in Shakespeare, or the opening of the world in a line of poetry.

The longing, the homesickness, comes in the midnight sense that we are not what we most want to be, or in the gnaw of guilt for having been or done what we know is less or other than we ought and most deeply desire. It comes in the twinge of melancholy following moments of intimacy or gladness or satisfaction which, by their fleeting nature, leave us grateful and yet strangely lonely and vaguely dissatisfied. It comes in the surge of hope in the midst of grief, or a giggle in the sudden awareness of our shared foolishness. Our experience of mystery comes in all the variations of our longing for something better, something different, deeper, more abiding than we know and have only glimpses and inklings of in our life in this world. Our experience of mystery is what Augustine called the restlessness of our hearts until they find their rest in God.

I share Augustine's view. My belief, too, is that the mystery we experience is not reducible to the capriciousness of chance or the blind fortunes of coincidence. I believe the mystery is intentional: It intends our good, our redemption. I believe it is gracious: It grants us and all the creatures of the cosmos freedom because that's what love risks doing. I believe it is holy: It makes all of creation sacred and infuses it with meaning. I believe it is personal: It suffers with us and for us, sustains us, enters into a dynamic relationship with us in which our decisions and actions are taken seriously and responded to with healing, new possibilities, and a shared, responsible creativity in the ongoing shaping of life.

It is obvious that none of what I believe can be proved, *either way.* It is a choice, profoundly personal, yet profoundly communal. It is communal because none of us creates the choice; it is offered to us by life itself and through a faith community going back centuries. It is personal because it is ours to make as free persons, to make not just once but as a daily plebiscite.

I continue to choose to understand the mystery this way not because I can make sense of it entirely but because it makes sense of me and of life as nothing else does. I gladly yet humbly confess it is a Christian way. H. Richard Niebuhr was a profound professor and presence at Yale Divinity School. Rather than indoctrinate us with a theology, Niebuhr taught us to think theologically. It was a great gift, as was his affirmation that Jesus Christ was the unique but not exclusive revelation of God. Unique—enough to be held by and to hold on to. Not exclusive—a liberating humility and openness to God's ongoing presence in the world. That has been the compass, or North Star, by which I have navigated in the world.

Charlotte Bronte reportedly said that her Christian faith was for her like wine was in water. It changed the color of her mind. Couple that with H. Richard Niebuhr, and it helps define me and this book. My faith is like wine coloring my thinking, the way I perceive the world, life, myself. To me, faith is a dynamic process such as Niebuhr and Brontë describe more than it is assent to a system of doctrines or an institution of religious practices, though these may, and at their best do, help guide and nurture faith, not conceiving it but sometimes midwifing it.

That's the case because the mystery at the heart of faith, the mystery we can choose because it chooses us first, cannot be squeezed into the shopping bags of our finite thoughts and institutions. Those thoughts, practices, convictions, and the shared actions they generate, can point to a transcendent Presence beyond those thoughts and practices. They can express a relationship with the grace of the mystery to which communities of faith try to witness. And yet, unfortunately, those thoughts, practices, convictions, and actions can too often do the opposite—as many of us have experienced, so I don't need to elaborate. Mostly the thoughts, practices, convictions, and actions of faith communities, including those I served, do a little of both nurturing and stunting. That is why the community of faith itself needs to engage in an ongoing and constant dynamic of reformation. That is my conviction, and it has been—and is—my commitment. We human beings and people of faith need to risk responding in relevant, honest, new, and faithful ways to the mystery that won't leave us alone.

So my belief is captured in the title of this book. We are haunted by grace. We are invited, urged, perhaps compelled, to respond to that haunt. Compelled, since not to respond is itself a choice and response, and not to be aware of the haunt, even dimly, is also a choice and a response, however impoverishing. What this book presents are responses of faith to the haunt of grace. In their original form, these pieces were sermons. In some instances they have been slightly expanded, and all have been at least somewhat reworked.

It seems accurate to call them responses rather than sermons, because even in the form of sermons they were responses to the haunt of grace, the mystery of God's presence in our world and our lives.

In every case, these responses reflect my belief that the world of faith, or religion, or the Bible is not separable from the world of our present experience, the world of science, reason, practicality, art, invention, day-to-day commerce—what is commonly referred to as the "real world." Rather, I believe that to think or speak clearly and convincingly of either the world of faith or the world of our contemporary life requires us to think and talk of both at the same time. We cannot plausibly deny either of them. We need not separate them and discuss them as different realms of our existence. We don't have to drag one world to the other to illustrate or dispute either. We have the more difficult but rewarding task of discerning that the two infuse each other, uniquely but not exclusively, like wine colors water without demolishing the qualities of either.

The challenge has always been to discern and interpret the relevance of the world perceived in faith to the world experienced in our life in this world of time and events. It is to recognize, if only dimly and tentatively, the eternal haunt of grace in our everyday lives.

The challenge is to use our imagination as one of our critical human faculties, like mind or heart or spirit. It is to use our imagination in the way Richard Feynman, Nobel Laureate in Physics, described it, and I keep going back to in my thinking and faith. He said that imagination is ". . . stretched to the utmost . . . just to comprehend those things that really are there."

I have tried in this book, as in all my preaching and in my life, to use my imagination in that way, which I believe is a way of faith, integrity, and authenticity. I have used it in interpreting Scripture as well as life and the events and challenges of the world we're placed in and for which, in some sense, we are responsible. I have used my imagination in these responses to the haunt of grace hoping they will invite others to use their imaginations in ways that are authentic and stretching for them.

My intent, and my prayer, then, is that this book may honestly reflect my own continuing, partially successful struggle—and that of the community of faith I served—to live more fully, freely, creatively, and joyfully in relationship to the haunt of grace, and that it may provide an opening to others to join that struggle as well.

Sweaty Praise

Luke 12:22-32
Romans 8:31-39

Author E. B. White put it this way: "If the world were merely seductive, that would be easy. If it were merely challenging, that would be no problem. But I arise in the morning torn between a desire to improve the world and a desire to enjoy the world. This makes it hard to plan the day"[1] . . . or anything else, we might add.

Nevertheless, that's our common dilemma. It's a bind intensified by the terrible events of September 11th. Since then, we're torn between throwing our arms around those most precious to us, hunkering down to enjoy what we can and praying for the Department of Homeland Security, or throwing our arms around the torn, trembling world and trying to save it. We're in graduate school majoring in "dilemma." When we're bent on enjoying the world, we begin to feel guilty and anxious. When we're bent on improving the world, we begin to feel self-righteous and angry. How do we get out of that bind?

Jesus tries to tell us: "Do not worry about your life . . . Consider the ravens: they neither sow nor reap . . . and yet God feeds them . . . Consider the lilies . . . they neither toil nor spin; yet . . . Solomon in all his glory was not clothed like one of these . . ." Then he adds the rest of it: "Strive for [God's] kingdom."

The point is that God doesn't intend us to *either* improve the world *or* enjoy the world. God intends us to do *both*. Praise is the way we keep our balance between the two. Gratitude keeps us clear that not only do our gifts and our challenges come from God, but that our gifts and our challenges are essentially one and the same. The thrust of Jesus' words is that gratitude is the engine of moral action.

Without gratitude, our enjoyment of the world shrinks into cramped self-indulgence and the unscratchable itch of never having enough. And without gratitude, our efforts to improve the world degenerate into whining self-pity, anger, and frustration over the burden of our supposed moral superiority that others refuse to acknowledge.

So poet Rainer Maria Rilke points us in the right direction when he says, "The more the soul praises, the stronger it grows." Rilke is suggesting that praise is about the condition of our soul, not the circumstances of

1 Recalled on E. B. White's death, in *Newsweek*, October 14, 1985.

our days. Gratitude strengthens our soul by focusing on what matters.

Writer Nancy Mairs puts it in a stunning way: "Thanks to multiple sclerosis, one thing after another has been wrenched from my life—dancing, driving, walking, working—and I have learned neither to yearn after them nor to dread further deprivation, but to attend to what I have."

Thanks to multiple sclerosis? Yes, because that's how she learned the essential lesson of thanksgiving, namely ". . . to attend to what I have"!

"*Consider the ravens . . . Consider the lilies . . .*"

I confess that I'm not always good at being thankful. But I keep learning. I'll never forget the evening I went to a large bookstore where I was scheduled to autograph my most recent book. I fervently hoped there would be a long line of people waiting for me to sign their books. Three people showed up, and two were family.

I felt humiliated and sorry for myself. When I went to bed I couldn't sleep. About three A.M. I got up, paced, and prayed awhile. Then I started to write. You may recognize yourself in it:

> What's enough? Countless times I've watched the sun rise like God's tender mercy to gently lift the dark blanket from the earth, and countless more times I've watched the sun set in such a splendiferous farewell that it must reflect the fringe on God's robe. I've seen the sky define blue and endless. I've watched rivers run to the sea, full as life runs to God. I've felt the sea roll in on the eternal note of mystery and assurance.
>
> I've scratched the ears of dogs, laughed at the ballet of cats. I've heard the cry and gurgle of the newborn, played with children, rocked with grandmothers, learned from hundreds of teachers, some of them homeless, poor, and uneducated. I've been enlarged ten times squared by writers from Shakespeare to Toni Morrison, and yet countless other storytellers, some in delis and diners, taverns and buses, churches, curb sides and prison cells.
>
> I have tasted bread and wine, hot dogs and caviar, somehow in the alchemy of need and gift and joy, all made holy as God's own overflowing banquet. I've been loved and forgiven beyond all deserving, and all breath to tell of it, by family and friends and God.
>
> I've been shaken, changed, and blessed a thousand times—and still—by the prophets, and by Christ. I've felt the touch of God, each time before I realized that's what it was. I've been shrunk and stretched at the same time by the scatter of stars and found North in one of them. I've experienced the loneliness of freedom and being human

and having hard choices. I've known the thrill of small triumphs, the instruction of painful defeats, and so the amazement of being part of the incredible human pilgrimage from Adam and Eve to the twenty-first century. I've shared in the cantankerous yet remarkable family of faith called the church. I'm conscious of being conscious and alive. And all that's just for starters.

How much does it take to praise God? I have a couple of trips around the Milky Way past enough for that, no matter if I never receive another thing. So I best get on with it . . . and praise God that I can.[2]

Would your list be very different from mine? Probably not. Gratitude strengthens the soul by focusing it. Because Jesus was focused on God, he was free to live in the world with daring and delight while others were stuck in their security and image issues like a swarm of killjoys.

So, yes, gratitude! Gratitude even in midst of fallout from 9/11's horrific loss from terrorism and the terrible collateral loss when we struck back at the terrorists in Afghanistan. Attend to what we have.

We all recall clearly those first pictures of dust-choked survivors running from the devastation as the World Trade Center towers collapsed. Then the images and stories of people running toward the devastated, running to meet them with open arms, open hearts, open hands, bearing gifts of prayer, time, money, blood, life itself. Then finally something deep in us somehow trusting that God was also running to that breach, that God's heart was breaking along with ours—and more, that God's hold on those who were dead and dying was tightening even as ours was inevitably loosening.

So we were made brave to go on with all the love we could muster, not only for those dearest to our hearts but also for the victims and families whose names we knew not except that they are our brothers and sisters. Perhaps we will come one day to a time when we'll realize that the victims of our war against terrorism are also our brothers and sisters. Let us pray for our enemies, as Jesus taught us to do, lest we become just like them.

Attend to what we have. *"Consider the ravens . . . Consider the lilies . . ."* It's about gratitude because this is God's world, and it is laced with God's grace. Praise is about the love we are in, always and everywhere.

Then out of gratitude comes this larger call: *"Strive for God's kingdom . . ."* There's the bristle of vitality and the glisten of sweaty gladness about that summons. *"Strive for God's kingdom."* Strive, because there's nothing easy or sentimental about it. Sooner or later, we discover that enjoyment of the world is not

2 Condensed from "This Wrestle Through the Night" by Ted Loder in *My Heart in My Mouth: Prayers for Our Lives* (Philadelphia: Innisfree Press, 2000), 126-31.

enough for us, or for the world. God wants more for us and from us, and so do we.

"Strive . . ." The word rightly suggests there are blisters and bruises in it. Why? Because the love of God in Christ Jesus is not meek or limited merely to lilies and larks. Look at the biblical witness where the hard, healing truth is that God defines love, not the other way around, as we often assume. Look at the prophets. Look at Jesus confronting the power brokers and hypocrites. Look at the cross. God defines love.

Consider these powerful words of St. Paul, always in the present tense:

> Who will separate us from the love of Christ? Will hardship, or distress, or persecution, or famine, or nakedness, or peril, or sword? . . . No, in all these things we are more than conquerors through him who loved us. For I am convinced that neither death nor life, nor angels, nor rulers, nor things present, nor things to come, nor powers, nor height, nor depth, nor anything else in all creation, will be able to separate us from the love of God in Christ Jesus our Lord.

What's so amazing about these words is not just that nothing is able to separate us from the love of God, though that's amazing enough. But the wonder of it runs deeper. The wonder is, that since *nothing* can separate us from the love of God, then *everything* links us to that love: hardship, peril, distress, failure, things present, things to come, everything in life and death and the whole of creation.

Now that's the deepest mystery of God's love. I do not pretend to understand it. Yet isn't that our experience? Isn't that what we are learning in the terrible turbulence whipped up by terrorism? Isn't that what the cross is about, and the empty tomb? That's what this love we're in is about. Nothing separates, everything links us to the love of God in Christ Jesus. That's the love we're in!

It is also what the love in us is about as well, or can be. A few years ago a feature in the Sunday *Philadelphia Inquirer* called the church I served "The Odd Ball Church." It wasn't a slur. The reporter got it just right. What else would a gathering of Christians be but at least a little odd—at odds with the counsels of timidity and security, comfort and consumption; at odds with the ways of injustice, exploitation and discrimination; at odds with the stifling ways of institutional self-serving and pompous self-righteousness and the idolatry of inflated nationalism? What else but odd would any group be that took Christ seriously, that tried to strive for God's kingdom? If we weren't odd enough to have a lovers' quarrel with the world, we wouldn't be anything that mattered much.

Strive! Be odd! That involves taking risks. It means taking on controversial issues because they're the ones that matter: relational justice, racial justice, gender justice, environmental justice, confronting and closing the gap between rich and poor, between our world and the Third World.

Being odd means striving to be creative and courageous in reaching out to all God's people: to those who sit next to us on the train or bus, to those sitting in the houses and offices around to us, reaching out to those sitting on the grates and in the ghettos of our cities and towns. Reaching out to homosexuals, to different political and religious orientations, different nationalities. Reaching out to kids on drugs, to kids who out of some awful emptiness do acts of terrible violence, to kids around the world dying of starvation and curable diseases. Reaching out to people trapped in the oppression of poverty and exploitation and despair and so is fodder for fanaticism and terrorism. To take Christ seriously is to be at least a little odd, thank God.

"I am convinced that. . . {nothing} in all creation will be able to separate us from the love of God in Christ Jesus our Lord." That's the heart of the freedom that enables us to let go of what is familiar and comfortable and strive for God's kingdom. It is the freedom to not be afraid of uncertainty, or of tomorrow.

Now we are cheek-by-jowl with the frightening challenge of terrorism. Surely a limited measure of military action is needed toward the terrorists. But just as surely our country's response needs to expand to become one of compassion and generosity, which will be hard for us to do unless we develop a larger vision of the kingdom we strive toward.

Nahum Barnea, a columnist with a major Israeli newspaper recently wrote, "The terrorism of suicide bombers is born of despair. There is no military solution to despair."

Barnea is right. So our response to terrorism must go beyond bombs and missiles, and just as surely the church needs to raise its voice for such a response. To begin, we need to raise our voice for our own humble self-examination. Otherwise, Reinhold Niebuhr's word will fit us too well: "The self-righteous are guilty of history's greatest cruelties. Most evil is done by good people who do not know they are not good."[3] Jesus put it starkly: "No one is good but God alone." So it is dangerously simplistic and unchristian to label others as evil and ourselves as good. Instead, we need to try to understand why others see us as evil and themselves as good lest our stated goal of wiping terrorists off the face of the earth accomplish just the opposite—creating more of them.

We need to raise our voices calling for the causes of terrorism to be addressed as well as its effects to be stemmed. More than one-third of the populations of the world's poorest countries, including Palestine, is under fifteen years old. They see a bleak future for themselves. That makes them easy recruits for suicide bombing missions.

3 As quoted by Bob E. Patterson in *Reinhold Niebuhr: Makers of the Modern Theological Mind* (Waco, TX: Word, Inc., 1977), 89.

Terrorism is fed by poverty. It is fed by hunger, disease. It is fed by the despair of being marginalized, dehumanized, exploited.

Surely we're called by the time to reflect on our own profligate consumerism by which we gobble up forty percent of the world's resources. Surely we're called to reflect on and reduce our wasteful use of fossil fuel. Surely it is time to end our lip service to environmental concerns while our actions, and those of government and industry, add to its deterioration. Someone pointed out that our nation seems to build alliances only for military purposes, but what is needed now is to build an alliance to address the poverty and deprivation that generate hatred and nurture terrorism.

There is much talk that since September 11th we are living in a different world. That is only partially true. The deeper truth is that since 9/11 we have the choice to live in the world *differently.* We have the chance to find a truer place in it, a humbler place, a more compassionate place in it.

Freedom is indeed a precious gift. But freedom is more than having choices at the mall, or in the voting booth, or in the unbridled pursuit of personal pleasure. I passionately believe that our deepest longing is for the freedom Jesus spoke of, lived out, and calls us to share: the freedom not to be afraid. Even small doses of that freedom will enable us to live in the world differently.

So consider it again: *"Do not worry about your life . . . Consider the ravens . . . Consider the lilies . . . Strive for God's kingdom."* Then Jesus makes this incredible promise: *"Do not be afraid . . . for it is your Father's good pleasure to give you the kingdom."* Every day we're called to step out on that promise. The mystery is that it is in striving for the kingdom that we discover it's a gift to us.

I carry in my heart a little poem a very old woman gave me many years ago. She was nearly blind then, crippled by arthritis, a retired school teacher and quite poor, living on her small pension, much of which she gave to support causes she believed in. The poem is this:

> You say the little efforts that I make
> will do no good,
> They will never prevail to tip the
> hovering scale
> Where justice hangs in the balance.
> I don't think I ever thought they
> would.
> But I am prejudiced beyond debate
> In favor of my right to choose which
> side
> Shall feel the stubborn ounces of my
> weight.[4]

Over the years I have gained passion and courage and joy from those words. They hint at what striving for God's kingdom is about.

4 Bonaro W. Overstreet, "Stubborn Ounces," *Hands Laid Upon the Wind* (New York: W. W. Norton, 1955).

So I ask you, what side of which issue needs the stubborn ounces of your weight? What are the human needs that knock on your heart now and plead with your conscience for those ounces? How will you strive for God's kingdom? Where will you cast your ounces, not to get praise but to give it? Those are our God-given choices and our chance to be blessed.

We dare not give in to the sirens of cowardice and greed and hate and fear. Ours is to strive to heal wounds, to lift the despairing all around us. Ours is to join with God in striving to create beauty where there is ugliness, peace where there is hostility, freedom where there is oppression, new life where there are dead ends.

When Susannah Wood graduated from Radcliffe College, she gave a prayer at her baccalaureate service. The prayer included these lines: "Help us to prepare a kind of renaissance in our public and private lives. Let there be born in us a strange joy that will help us to live and to die, and to remake the soul of our time."[5]

Even so, our calling is to remake the soul of our time. Is it too much to suggest that in our time any renaissance worth the name must join the private lives of each of us to the public life of all of us, and join the life and future of this nation with the lives and futures of all the nations on this blue planet home we share? Finally, there is no "me and mine" in God's world. Remaking the soul of our time requires striving to recover the "we and the ours" of our common human destiny.

Reinhold Niebuhr once said, "We should be less concerned with the purity of our actions than with the integrity of our compromises." I'm persuaded. In this complex world we all have to make compromises, for only the fool, the tyrant, and the terrorist claim to know the ultimate will of God and the absolute truth of anything.

Yet, in this historic moment, as in all moments of life, let us not compromise our integrity and humanity. As we confront terrorism and make critical decisions in the face of the uncertainties and complexities of life, let us not compromise the faithful walk of wisdom and humility for the fearful stumble of simplistic answers and vengeful actions. Let us not compromise our courage into passivity, our creativity into conformity, our compassion into indifference, our conscience into cynicism, the deepest longing of our humanity into the bondage of comfortable but illusory security, our faith into trivial pursuits. Instead, let us *"Consider the ravens . . . Consider the lilies . . . Strive for God's kingdom."*

5 As quoted by Robert A. Raines in *Soundings* (New York: Harper and Row, 1970), 127. Originally published as "A Commencement Prayer" by Susannah H. Wood in the *New York Times,* June 17, 1968.

Where's Your Tattoo?

Jeremiah 31:31-34
Matthew 17:1-13

Whenever I travel, I duck into my seat on the plane or train, immediately open a book or folder of papers, screw up my best anti-social scowl, all to forestall any conversation with the person in the next seat. In fact, my idea of paradise is to have no one in the next seat.

That doesn't happen often. Usually the next seat is taken by the most talkative person traveling in my direction that day. If the person insists on talking, I am barely polite. If they ask what I do, I try never to admit I'm a clergyman. If I slip and tell them, I inevitably spend the rest of the trip squirming while being grilled on what I think, or lectured on what they know, about religion.

So, if asked what I do, I answer that I'm not at liberty to tell them. That usually silences them because they assume I'm some kind of agent for the CIA or the FBI. My position is that if people want to talk about life and death, salvation and damnation, true or false religious issues, come to my turf and get serious. Don't just casually assault me on the plane or train.

It's amazing how often God doesn't seem to agree with my position. Take the trip I made to Richmond, Virginia, not very long ago to kick off a Lenten preaching series. I was sitting there on the train waiting for it to pull out of Philadelphia's 30th Street Station when this stylish looking guy sits down next to me. He's wearing a tailored, expensive-looking leather coat, razor-creased slacks, a cashmere sweater over a turtleneck, carrying a matching leather traveling bag and attaché case, the complete *GQ* look with an aroma of fresh lime and ocean breeze after-shave wafting about him. He's a "rainmaker" personified. My biases rocketed into orbit. I dived into my book. He dived into a computer magazine.

Half an hour later, he pulled out a portable computer and went to work on whatever it was. Good, I thought. He won't want to talk. Then, coming into Baltimore, I heard music. I looked around. It was coming from his computer. "Do you know what that is?" he asked.

"Sounds like banjos," I reflexively answered.

"It's the banjo duet from the movie *Deliverance*," he announced. "Great movie, right? You see it?"

It was too late. I'd taken the bait and he'd hooked me. Except for his visit to the Club

Car, we talked all the way to Richmond. He began by informing me of all the places he and his wife of five years had gone on vacation, including accommodations, prices, air fares, all the sights—Hawaii, Paris, Mexico, a Mediterranean cruise. My impression of him was confirmed. He asked me for ideas for their next vacation. I suggested Hoboken. Or Haiti. At least he laughed. I took that as a hopeful sign. My cargo of biases began to slip.

He said he'd been to Haiti. I was stunned. I'd been there. It's the poorest country in the Western hemisphere. I asked him why he'd gone to Haiti. He told me his wife was a native Jamaican from a poor family there. My biases jarred a little looser. He said he was trying to get his company to open a small production unit in Haiti to give people jobs at a decent wage. There was not an ounce of preening in his matter-of-fact explanation. A couple of my biases about him jettisoned into space.

He shrugged off my compliments about his efforts and went on to tell me that last year, in Hawaii, he and his wife had gotten identical tattoos but he couldn't show me where. I assured him that was okay! He volunteered that his tattoo was over his heart. So was his wife's, but he insisted that only he, her doctor, and maybe her friends in the shower at the gym would ever see it.

"That's too bad for the rest of us," I said.

He laughed again. "The tattoo is a little cross with a crown around it," he went on. "We're far from being religious fanatics or anything, but she and I thought that would be a good thing. A kind of a reminder. I mean, we're blessed and need to share that." More biases flew off into the wild blue. "You ought to get one yourself," he suggested.

"Maybe," I replied. "Someday."

As we swayed on from Washington, D.C., to Richmond, he told me about his retired parents. Just before last Thanksgiving, his mother had surgery for kidney cancer and then, just before Christmas, she had a mastectomy. She was taking Tamoxifen and seemed to be doing fine. He traveled to Richmond every couple of weeks to visit her. But he was on his way to Richmond that afternoon because the next day his father was having heart surgery. "I'm a little worried but still pretty confident," he said. "I'm sure you know that study about prayer."

He hadn't asked and I hadn't told him I was a minister. Maybe I just smell that way or something. A little suspiciously, I asked, "What study?"

He said, "The one that showed that people who are sick and are prayed for do better than sick people who don't get prayed for. Even when they don't know they're being prayed for, they do better. I'm sure that's why my mother is doing so well, and why my Dad will, too. Lots of people are praying for them, including my brother and sister and I."

I admitted I'd heard of that study.

"Impressive, isn't it?" he said.

I agreed.

When we said good-bye at the station in Richmond, I told him I'd pray for his father the next day. He said, "Thanks, Reverend." I asked him how he knew that about me. He said, "I recognized you from the brochure my parents have about the Lenten series at St. Paul's. And you really ought to think about getting a tattoo. Reminds you of things, you know? Well, God bless you." And off he waving went.

I thought about that encounter a long time. It reminded me of a poem my Scottish clergy friend, David Ogston, sent me. When I got home, I dug the poem out. It's called "Getting It Across." It's by U. A. Fanthorpe, and she's a wonderful poet. I know poems can be difficult, but this one's worth the effort, Here's a part of the poem. Jesus is speaking:

> I envy Moses, who could choose
> The diuturnity of stone for waymarks
> Between man and Me. He broke the
> tablets,
> Of course. I too know the easy
> messages
> Are the ones not worth transmitting;
> But he could at least carve.
> The prophets too, however luckless
> Their lives and instructions, inscribed
> on wood,
> Papyrus, walls, their jaundiced
> oracles.
>
> I alone must write on flesh. Not even
> The congenial face of my Baptist
> cousin,
> My crooked affinity Judas, who
> understands,
> Men who would give me accurately to
> the unborn
> As if I were something simple, like
> bread.
> But Pete, with his headband stuffed
> with fishhooks,
> His gift for rushing in where angels
> wouldn't,
>
> Tom, for whom metaphor is
> anathema,
> And James and John, who want the
> room at the top—
> These numskulls are my medium. I
> called them.
>
> I am tattooing God on their makeshift
> lives.
> My Keystone Cops of disciples,
> always
> Running absurdly away, or lying
> ineptly,
> Cutting off ears and falling into the
> water,
> These Sancho Panzas must tread my
> Quixote life,
> Dying ridiculous and undignified,
> Flayed and stoned and crucified upside
> down.
> They are the dear, the human, the
> dense, for whom
> My message is. That might, had I not
> touched them,

Have died decent and respectable
upright deaths in bed.[1]

Surely, some of these wonderful images park in your memory, or your heart.

"My Keystone Cops of disciples . . . They are the dear, the human, the dense, for whom my message is . . ."

Yes, that fits us, as well as Peter, James and John who gasped after Jesus on his climb up the mountain Matthew tells us about. Those three Keystone Cop disciples schlepped along without much of a clue about why they were headed up the mountain anyway. Maybe they figured it was to get away for a rest. Or maybe just to take in the view and clear their heads. Or maybe to plan strategy. Or maybe to pray, mountain tops typically considered to be closer to God. The climb took them all day, and when they got to the top, it was midnight dark.

But what happened then caught them totally off guard—as usual. What happened is called the Transfiguration. Suddenly, on that mountain top, the shroud of darkness pulled aside and night turned dazzling. All the starlight in the heavens seemed suddenly to coalesce in Jesus, then wheel out in a thousand splendiferous directions until all around things whirled to astonished life, and the trembling air itself dropped to its knees along with the astounded disciples.

1 U. A. Fanthorpe, "Getting It Across," *Selected Poems* (London: Penguin Books, 1986), 72–73.

Moses and Elijah, both long dead, stepped through the veil of time and stood with Jesus, alive in the present. It linked him to these prophets and identified him as the one to lead people from bondage—not from Egypt, but from fear and sin and emptiness. Then a wave of words broke over the silence, vibrating in space like a note sung and held from some far off place: "This is my son, the Beloved . . . listen to him!" Was the voice inside them, outside, above, below, where? The disciples were frightened.

Finally, Jesus simply said to them, "Get up and do not be afraid." And when they looked, they only saw Jesus. So they got up, trusting that what had frightened them was gone.

Then they realized the darkness was not so dark anymore. What was happening was not just about the dazzling, radiant light of another world spilling over and into and out of Jesus up on that mountain. It was that the darkness of this world got several shades lighter and less frightening, including the darkness of death. That's nearly what the whole thing with Jesus is about. *"Get up and do not be afraid."*

"I am tattooing God on their makeshift lives."

Can't you just hear Jesus saying that to those dear, human, dense, Keystone Cops of disciples . . . and now to us who fit the bill just as well? And isn't that how it happens? Something like light spills over and breaks in on our makeshift lives when we don't expect it, maybe even do our best to avoid it with our excuses and doubts and arguments and biases, our anti-social scowls on the train or plane or in the living room.

A long time ago, Jeremiah the prophet heard God put it this way: "I will put my law within them, and I will write it on their hearts; and I will be their God and they shall be my people . . . they shall all know me, from the least of them to the greatest . . . for I will forgive their iniquity and remember their sin no more." Very recently, Fanthorpe the poet put words of similar weight in Jesus' mouth, and they sound right: *"I alone must write on flesh."*

And what is the needle with which the tattoo is etched, not so much *on* our hearts as *in* them? What, except the needles of the people we sit with, walk with, work with, argue with, love, or like a lot or not much at all, try to avoid but sooner or later can't. The needles of our enemies as well as people who pray for us even when we don't know it, or realize it. The needles of those who care enough to honestly challenge us with their truth as we traipse up the mountain of our week. That's how God tattoos our makeshift lives.

Sometimes we aren't even aware we're being tattooed until it occurs to us—however dimly, the next day, or week, or month, or year—that the tattoo is there in us somehow, haunting us all along in the longing that sends us traipsing wherever we go. Or in the joys that punctuate the landscape of our lives like mountain tops. Or in the stubborn hope that keeps getting us up and making us several shades less afraid. The light breaks in, for an infinite instant, transfigures us and things around us, in little ways, and sometimes large ones. In the music of a song we find ourselves humming. In the touch of a friend. In the eyes of a child. In a story that breaks open our hearts. In a praying moment when our words fade out and a sense of being heard shivers through. In a night when the starlight strikes us, too, and shushes our babble and puts our souls on their knees.

So the yuppie in the custom-made leather jacket asks, "Do you know the study that showed that people who are sick and are prayed for do better than sick people who don't get prayed for? Even when they don't know they're being prayed for, they do better." And a tattoo needle of this no-longer-quite-as-much a stranger cuts through your biases and etches a cross on your heart. It happens all the time, transfigurations like that.

I keep tucked away for rereading an issue of *Sports Illustrated* in which there was a simple story about Don Haskins, the coach of Texas Western who in 1966 put a lineup of all-black players on the floor and beat an all-white Kentucky team for the National Championship. By doing that, Haskins changed the face of college basketball forever, even though he got thousands of death threat letters as a result.

That big spill of light through Haskins was like those through Jackie Robinson and

Branch Rickey in baseball, and Thurgood Marshal standing tall before Justice Warren and the Supreme Court in *Brown v. the Board of Education* and the Court's decision to make racially separate but equal school systems illegal.

But just as important as the big thing was that Haskins stayed at that college, now called the University of Texas El Paso, for thirty-eight years and turned down more lucrative coaching positions. Now retired, he has little money. He spent most of what he had on medical care for his son, who died. But his friends say that wasn't the only thing that left Haskins in the hard scrabble. It was his generosity and compassion. Typically, every day for years, he left a ten-dollar tip for a lonely waitress in a dumpy, usually mostly empty coffee shop where he and his two assistant coaches had coffee, never more than a cup or two apiece. That was a spill of light, a transfiguration, too.

The point is simple. It's not just the big stuff, the big people, but every person we meet, every choice we make, every act we do, every word we speak that matters enormously. Those encounters are cracks through which light squeezes into this world because God is always using someone around us as needles to tattoo grace and mercy and hope and joy on our makeshift lives.

And using us to do that on the makeshift lives of others, as well. That's the rest of it. The disciples followed Jesus down from the mountain of ecstasy out into the world of need. Even so, each of us is a tattoo needle leaving some indelible mark on someone else, maybe never recognized but essential, mysteriously multiplied like loaves and fishes to feed the hunger, the longing, the needs of more others than we know. Half the message of the transfiguration of Jesus is that it is never as dark as we think it is. Never. By God, there's always enough light.

That's what those three numbskulls like us discovered up there on the mountain: Peter with fish hooks in his head band, and James and John with reservations in their pockets for rooms at the top. The midnight dark wasn't so dark after all because they could see Jesus in it. And hear him say, *"Get up and do not be afraid."* That's the gospel in miniature. And the thing to notice is that there were three of them there. Not one, alone, but three together. Eyesight improves when there is more than one pair of eyes looking and more than one life to see or reflect the light.

This Keystone Cop of a disciple knows what fear is. Do I ever! And doubt and discouragement and all the rest. But I am less afraid, less discouraged, more faithful when I am not alone, when I am with others, people I love. Faith and courage are contagious.

"You ought to get a tattoo like mine. Reminds you of things."

I should have said, "I have one. On my heart. You and countless other people in my life helped God put it there."

What does it mean to be those Christ calls to be needles to tattoo God on the makeshift lives of others? Look again at what the poet says it meant to those first disciples:

> These Sancho Panzas must tread my
> Quixote life . . .
> They are the dear, the human, the
> dense, for whom
> My message is. That might, had I not
> touched them,
> Have died decent and respectable
> upright deaths in bed.[2]

I suppose most of us will die "decent, upright deaths in bed," because the crucifixions and stonings and flayings that ended the first disciples' lives are out of style these days. Still, the point holds: Whoever those dear, human dense ones are who get the message, we are surely among them. We can take risks, go against the conventional, safe practices, work for justice, embrace and include the rejected and oppressed. We may die decent deaths, but we don't have to be so respectable in the process.

So where is your tattoo? Where is your tattoo needle? Think of your own precious children. Think of your family and friends. Think of those you work alongside, or live with in the neighborhood, or vote with, give to. Think of the welfare mothers homeless with the kids on the streets, the working poor who are not paid a living wage. Think of those burdened and dehumanized by racism, sexism, homophobia, indifference. Think of the people we dehumanize with our biases, whoever they are. God gives us strange company in our struggle.

"I am tattooing God on their makeshift lives."

We Keystone Cop, tattoo-needle people need to decide what that means for us and those for whom we are the message. The thing is, we decide every day, every hour, with everyone we meet, because it's all important. And it is never as dark as we think. Christ is in it. And so are we. As for me, then, I suspect I'll own up to what I do next time I'm asked by a fellow traveler.

"Get up and do not be afraid."

In her book *Amazing Grace,* Kathleen Norris describes how the poet Mary Oliver used this story from the life of William Blake as an epigram for her book:

> Some persons of a scientific turn were once discoursing, pompously, and to [Blake], distastefully, about the incredible distance of the planets, the length of time light takes to travel to the earth, etc. when [Blake] burst out, "Tis false! I was walking down a lane the other day, and at the end of it, I touched the sky with my stick."[3]

2 Fanthorpe, "*Getting It Across*," 73.

3 Kathleen Norris, *Amazing Grace: A Vocabulary of Faith* (New York: Riverhead Books, 1998), 381.

The poet recognized the truth. And so do we, if we pay it half a mind, half a heart. God is not far off across endless space and millennia of time. Nor is Christ or the transfiguration, or the light of eternity and the stuff of meaning and hope and joy, or the kingdom of God. The whole thing is as close as the person next to us on the train, or the plane, or the street, or in the ghetto, the barrio, the villages of the desperately poor in Africa or Afghanistan or Palestine or Haiti or Mexico, or in the violent bashing in the Middle East. As close as persons anywhere you put your finger, or your heart, on the globe of this one little planet, home of us all.

Norris, commenting on the Blake story, said she wished ". . . that Blake had lived long enough to hear quantum physicists speaking like poets . . . confirming that 'every atom of our bodies was once inside a star.'"[4] Even so, we can touch people, the stars, God, with our sticks, our hands, our hearts, our votes, our time, our money. And they can, and do, touch us back. All around, Christ is there where we don't expect him, or recognize him most of the time. Nevertheless, there he is.

"I am tattooing God on their makeshift lives."

On theirs and ours.

4 Norris, *Amazing Grace,* 381.

In Your Face

2 Corinthians 4:1-18

Matthew Poncelet, convicted of the brutal murder of two young people, comes through the door of a prison holding cell and begins walking toward the death chamber. Among the guards and officials with Poncelet is a nun, Sister Helen Prejean, who has been his spiritual advisor during his last days on death row. For a moment Poncelet falters and slips to his knees. Helen Prejean kneels beside him. She says, "Look, I want the last thing you see in this world to be a face of love. Will you look at me when they do this thing? You look at me. I'll be the face of love for you."[1]

Poncelet looks intently at her, climbs back to his feet, and walks on toward the room where he will be put to death. Helen Prejean walks with him to the door, her hand on his shoulder. Then she sits with the witnesses on the other side of the glass window looking into the chamber.

Among the witnesses are the parents of the young woman who was viciously raped by Poncelet and his partner before she was killed, and the father of the young woman's fiancé, who was murdered with her after they were dragged from their car parked on a Louisiana lover's lane. As the lethal drugs are injected into him, Poncelet and Prejean look steadily, searchingly at each other.

"I'll be the face of love for you."

The scene is in my heart, and it will stay there. It comes near the end of the movie *Dead Man Walking,* which is based on the book written by Sister Prejean about her experience.[2] It is a powerful, spiritual movie because it is fair to all sides of the story and probes so deeply into the human heart.

As Poncelet is prepared for execution and as the lethal injections begin, his eyes are on Helen Prejean and her eyes on him. There are tears in her eyes. She reaches out her hand to him in a kind of embrace. Her lips move in prayer and assurance with the words, "I love you," even as across the screen flash images of the terrible crime he committed and the faces of the two murdered young people.

How could she do that? How could she be the face of love for him in spite of so much vileness, so much hostility toward her, so much dishonesty and manipulation?

1 *Dead Man Walking,* written and directed by Tim Robbins (New York: PolygramFilm Productions B.V., 1996).

2 Helen Prejean, C.S.J., *Dead Man Walking: An Eyewitness Account of the Death Penalty in the United States* (New York: Vintage Books, 1994).

What would it mean to be a face of love in this world where there are so many faces of hate and fear and anger and arrogance? What would it mean to be a face of love in our "in-your-face" society where we are so ready to stick our accusing face in the face of anyone in our way or out of our favor? What would it mean to be a face of love for someone we consider contemptible, someone we consider utterly wrong, misguided, stupid, even inhuman and evil—all the varieties of Matthew Poncelet that shadow our days and inhabit our nightmares? What would it mean to go at life with such compassion and hope, such faith and courage, that those qualities would somehow be etched in our face?

There are some clues in 2 Corinthians. First this one, as Paul put it to the Corinthians, and to us: "We have this treasure in clay jars, so that it may be made clear that this extraordinary power belongs to God and does not come from us." Faith grasps the difference between clay jars and the treasure of grace.

The face of love begins and continues in a clear awareness of our limitations. We are all clay pots. In a basic sense faith begins with that awareness. When Sister Prejean says she will be the face of love for Poncelet, it's a statement of faith. Through the whole time of being Poncelet's spiritual advisor, Helen Prejean never acted as if she were better than he was, or that she knew more than she did. In her book she writes that, at the end, Poncelet said to her, "I thought you'd be doin' nothin' but preachin' to me, but after our first visit I saw I could just talk to you like a friend."[3]

Sister Prejean was always willing to recognize and admit her limits and mistakes without being defensive. When she first responded to the killer's request to visit and talk with him, she overlooked and ignored the victims' families. She didn't go to them as well as to the killer. But she was humble enough to learn from her mistake. When the victims' parents confronted and blamed her for forgetting them in favor of their children's killer, she admitted she was wrong and was deeply sorry for it. She began to relate to them with humility and compassion. She was always aware of her status as a clay jar.

How rare that is these days! Too many of us are more like the self-righteous Englishman in the joke where he insists he always did "what the Lord would do if He only had the facts in the matter." Or those who *know* which side God is on, which clearly is "our" side, not "their" side. Oh my, it isn't only the political and religious right who seem blind to being clay pots, it is the political and religious left and the middle as well. *All of us!* Whatever else it is, love is not arrogant or self-righteous.

Actress Susan Sarandon, who played Sister Prejean's part in the movie, said that

3 Prejean, *Dead Man Walking*.

the movie and the book were not about who deserves to die, but who deserves to kill. Absolutely accurate!

It isn't much of a stretch to take that insight to other human issues, is it? Who deserves to kill, to condemn, to dominate, to silence others, to disregard and disrespect anyone, to kill people by execution or in a hundred more subtle ways? With drugs and poverty, underfunded schools and inadequate health care, yes, but also with gossip, silence, avoidance, indifference. Who deserves to do that? Not one of us. Yet, we do all it. And that's to say nothing of killing with planes, guns, bombs, missiles.

Surely we grasp that to stand for something does not require condemning or dehumanizing those who stand for the other side. Helen Prejean opposed the death penalty, but she still listened to and had compassion for the terrible pain and profound loss of the victims' families. She understood their view of justice. That takes courage, and knowing you are a clay jar, not the treasure. Prejean talked to and sought to understand the terrible dilemmas of the prison people whose duties involved performing the execution. She constantly and passionately prayed for God's help and guidance for herself because she was aware of her weakness and limited vision. Compassion is contained in a clay jar, not a stainless-steel one.

Clay jars know they are not really better than other clay jars, no matter how poor or cracked those others might be. So they can cry for them, as the tears in Helen Prejean's eyes testified. And yet, they know as well, *"We have this treasure in clay jars . . ."* That's a response to the haunt of grace. The treasure is love, and love is always a gift. Always. It is freely given, not coerced. It is not an achievement or a reward. It is a gift, whether we receive it or share it. It haunts us at every turn of our common life. God's love is always at work in us and around us in steady but mysterious ways, so we can smile with tears in our eyes:

"I'll be the face of love for you"

***

Here is the second clue to being the face of love. In his letter to the Corinthians, and to us, Paul writes: "Since it is by God's mercy that we are engaged in this ministry, we do not lose heart." I believe the ministry Paul is talking about is the ministry of not letting discouragement keep us from persistently risking being accessible and reaching out to all people, regardless of who or what they are, as Paul did to the cantankerous Corinthians.

I know well how hard it can be to reach out, to listen to, and learn from, people who are different from us because they are of another culture, or religion, or nationality, or generation, or because they have ideas or attitudes or convictions that make us uncomfortable, even angry or frightened. Yet that is very close to the heart of what Jesus is about:

God sneakily reaching out to each strange, different, fumbling, difficult one of us.

One of the striking things in *Dead Man Walking* is the courage and persistence of Helen Prejean in reaching out to people and not losing heart. She lived and worked in the worst ghetto of New Orleans. She kept reaching out to Matthew Poncelet, who was an exceedingly obnoxious man, a white supremacist, a macho braggart, a liar, a killer. She reached out to the victims' families, visited them in their homes—even when the parents of the murdered young woman assumed that her visit meant she'd come over to their side and believed Poncelet deserved to be put to death, then angrily asking her to leave when she told them she hadn't come over to their side but was there to listen and to pray with them.

Reaching out means going deep as possible with people into their pain and anger, their fear and hope, meeting them in those depths, listening, trying to understand, sharing ourselves with them. One of the sad things about our frantic busyness is how shallow our relationships become under the poverty of time. We slowly, subtly dehumanize each other, and ourselves, by reducing life to networks of functions in the service of social contacts, careers, bottom lines, goals. Our lives become a compulsive effort to make ourselves more efficient, more attractive, more successful, with better résumés—or obituaries.

Maybe we don't intend to do that, but then the issue is we don't intend *not* to hard enough. As someone said, "It's easy to slip into the current and let it carry you away." It is so easy to shrug as the fabric of society frays and pulls apart. It takes courage not to lose heart, to go against the current, to be present and accessible to each other, even when we don't feel like it.

That's why it is so important for us to pray and worship together, to reach out to each other and to God week by week. It helps us to not lose heart. Then we're renewed to reach out to people in the community around us. Reaching out is what love is, and what the church is about.

Forgive me a personal witness. After a meeting one evening, I walked with a woman to her car across Germantown Avenue from the sanctuary. After she drove off and I turned to go back toward the office, I saw four black men and two black women and a small child come out of the store there. I said hello and added, "That's a beautiful little kid you have."

In no uncertain terms, the men objected to my use of the word "kid," reminding me that it refers to a goat with hair all over it. I said "You're right. I'm sorry I said it that way because that's not what I meant. I apologize for offending you. She's a beautiful little girl."

They were not satisfied. One walked behind me as I went back across the street, then motioned for me to follow him around the corner to a darker spot on High Street.

I went, with my heart beating a little faster. When we'd walked a few yards up the street where the shadows were deep, he stopped. I looked him in the eye and asked him what he wanted.

He said, "White guys don't talk to black children."

I said, "Why not?"

He pushed me and answered, "Because I said so. It's patronizing."

Maybe he could hear my heart pounding through my shirt, but I said, "Hey, I talk to black children and black people all the time. I'm the minister of this church, and we care about all the people in this community. Including you and your friends and the little girl. I know black people have lots of reasons to distrust whites, but we're trying to do something about that. That's why I risked coming with you into this dark street."

He shoved me again and called me an unflattering name.

I said, "Look, we can fight if you insist. But you know we'll both get hurt. So you and I having a fight isn't going to do anyone any good. What's in it for you?"

I knew what was in it for him and could have told him. It was a way for him to strike back at all the prejudice and oppression and dehumanization white people have visited on black people. It was a way for him to recapture some of his manhood and perhaps gain stature in the eyes of his friends and the little girl. But for me this was between the two of us human beings.

But I asked him again, "What's in it for you?"

For a couple of heartbeats he stared off toward Germantown Avenue. The question seemed to give him pause. After a moment he looked in my face and, as if for the first time, saw past its whiteness. Then he said, "If you really care, and respect me and my friends, apologize for what you said."

I gladly repeated the apology I'd made earlier and began to walk back toward Germantown Avenue. At first he hesitated, as if we hadn't finished—and we hadn't, not with two-hundred years of justified grievance. But we had finished with that brief moment of confrontation, confession, and at least tentative reconciliation, even love. He realized that, I think, because he turned toward me, and we walked back together without a word but, I think, some mutual respect and understanding.

When we reached the Avenue in front of the church, he told the others, "He apologized." They nodded their acceptance and approval, then got in the car.

I said, "Good night, God bless you," and watched them drive away.

Was I scared? Absolutely! But not enough to back away from the risk of showing my face to this man, not enough to try to weasel out of our encounter. Something in me just had to reach out. You may have had similar experiences in your work or home or neighborhood and have hung in, reached out. More of us need to do that. Maybe it's hanging in and reaching out to people as close and critical as a spouse or child or parent or friend and working something out with them, or trying to. But surely it's hanging in and reaching out to people marginalized by prejudice, exploitation, and any kind of oppression.

Whatever else it's about, love is about reaching out and not losing heart. Will it make any difference? Yes, in my bones I trust it will. But when and where and how is God's business and takes God's own time. Our part is to respond to God's grace no matter how bad the world's news, or how hard the circumstance, or how frightening the way.

In her book Helen Prejean writes that she has become a friend of the parents of the raped and murdered girl, though they are on opposite sides of the issue of capital punishment. She was asked to visit the murdered girl's father in the hospital. She and both the father and mother laugh and talk together at meetings in the prison, which confuses the guards. And she prays regularly with the father of the murdered boy, and he sometimes gives her small gifts of money for her work.

"I'll be the face of love for you."

***

Then there is a third clue from Paul about what it means to be a face of love in the world: "We have renounced the shameful things that one hides; we refuse to practice cunning or to falsify God's word; but by the open statement of the truth we commend ourselves to the conscience of everyone in the sight of God." Whatever else Paul is talking about, he's talking about accountability. We stand always in the presence of God and are accountable to God for what we are and do and say.

What is so powerful in *Dead Man Walking* is Helen Prejean's insistence on trying to hold Matthew Poncelet accountable for what he has done. In the first days of the week before his execution, she tells Poncelet what Jesus says in the gospel of John: "You shall know the truth and the truth will set you free" (John 8:32). The convict likes that because he thinks it means he will get out of prison and execution if he can get people to believe that his insistent lies about his innocence are true. But she means something much more profound, and at last he comes to learn it.

Poncelet keeps insisting he didn't kill or rape anyone, that it was his partner who went crazy on him. He keeps saying booze and drugs made him go to lover's lane to scare people. He talks about "Niggers," and the "evil" government, and the parents of the victims trying to kill him. Finally, Sister Prejean tells him to think of the girl's father: "He's never going to see his daughter again. He's never going to hold her. He's never going to love her, laugh with her. . . You blame [your partner]; you blame the government; you blame drugs; you blame blacks. . .

what about Matthew Poncelet? Where's he in this story? What, is he just an innocent? A victim?"[4]

I keep seeing myself in that scene, do you? Do we ever look at ourselves and what we are accountable for, rather than blaming someone else, our spouse, our parents, our boss, the other guys whoever they are, whatever group it is? Do we hold each other accountable, or do we just slip-slide by, and let each other slip-slide by, with simple answers to complicated issues, knee-jerk cliches instead of honest exchange?

Love is not easy, only rewarding. C. S. Lewis once said, "We are not necessarily doubting that God will do the best for us, we are wondering how painful the best will turn out to be."[5] Often the truth is painful. Before it is good news, the gospel comes across as bad news for those of us who want to be confirmed as we are. Who was it who said that God invites us to a "come-as-you-are party, but not a stay-as-you-are party." The word is "Repent." Turn around, like the Prodigal Son, and move toward God.

How? By moving toward each other, toward our prodigal brother or sister—which the original prodigal didn't do, much to the Father's dismay. Honest exchange is risky, and it is hard work. But it's what real, intimate relationships are about. It's what integrity is about. It's what love is about. It's what reconciliation and justice and peace are about, in home, community, world.

"You shall know the truth and the truth will set you free."

Helen Prejean is a strong, clear-eyed woman, not sentimental, not sugary or simplistic. She believes that every human being deserves respect. And she saw the possibilities beneath the surface swagger in Matthew Poncelet. Possibilities are what being accountable, and holding each other accountable, is really about. So on the night he dies, Poncelet finally confesses to what he had done. He cries as he does. He takes responsibility. And she says to him, "You did a terrible thing, Matt. A terrible thing. But you have a dignity now. No one can take that from you. You are a son of God, Matthew Poncelet."[6]

Poncelet smiles and sniffles, this macho killer, and says, "Nobody ever called me no son of God before. They called me a son-of-a-you-know-what a lotta times, but never no son of God."[7] And there is a look of wonder, even a kind of peace on his face.

That is what freedom is. It's rooted in trusting that we are a son or daughter of God. Freedom is not about getting whatever we want, or succeeding at whatever we do,

4 Prejean, *Dead Man Walking.*

5 C. S. Lewis, "29 April, 1959," *Letters of C. S. Lewis,* edited by W. H. Lewis (New York: Bles/Harcourt, 1966).

6 Prejean, *Dead Man Walking.*

7 Prejean, *Dead Man Walking.*

or having lots of options to choose among. The deepest, most real freedom is being free to do what we believe is right without being paralyzed by fear of the cost. It's the freedom to love, to do justice—which is love in action—and to do it wherever God puts us, lest we muffle and distort the life in us as well as in others. It is being accountable.

"I'll be the face of love for you."

***

And finally, this last clue from Paul. Read it carefully because it is the secret of it all: "For it is the God who said, 'Let light shine out of darkness,' who has shone in our hearts to give the light of the knowledge of the glory of God in the face of Jesus Christ."

The face of Jesus Christ. That face is all around us, when we look. We see it when we pray. We see it when we are aware of being a clay jar, yet containing a treasure. We see it when we reach out and make ourselves accessible to all the strange people like us in the world. We see it in each other's face when we pay close attention. We see it in the face of the poor, of children, of the homeless, in the face of those we count as enemies, in the face of the sick, the hungry, the prisoner.

We need to pay more attention to personal salvation, to the state of our souls. Put it this way: The gospel is not about less than personal salvation. It is not about less than intimacy with God and freedom from fear, bit by bit, and peace, step by step. Not less than that, but more. The more is how we live in the world, the character and conviction and compassion in us that comes out in our face over the time of our lives.

The gospel is God saying, "I'll be the face of love for you. Whoever you are, I am with you. Wherever you are, I am there in love for you in every face you see, in the face of creation itself. Trust me, the light in the darkness, deep as midnight though it seems." That's the haunt of grace, the response God invites us to make again and again, and always again.

At last, it comes down to this: No matter how much wattage we try to generate on our own, before love can truly shine in our face, the light of the knowledge of the glory of God in the face of Jesus Christ needs to shine in our soul, somehow, in whatever way we can let that happen.

Dead Man Walking: The title of the movie comes from the words a guard calls out as a condemned man, like Matthew Poncelet, walks to the room where he will be executed. The guard goes ahead on that final walk and calls out, "Dead man walking." In a sense—not a morbid sense but a true, even joyful one—we are all dead men walking somehow, dead women walking, because somewhere out there, in the days or months or years ahead, we will all die. We are clay jars.

Yet the most moving thing in the movie is that Sister Helen Prejean knew, deep in her nun's heart, that Matthew Poncelet, that dead man walking, was really walking toward not just death but life and amazing grace.

So are we. We are dead people walking toward more life every day, deeper life, truer life, more joyful life.

"Nobody ever called me no son of God, no daughter of God, before."

Well, someone has now. It's the gospel truth. God says to each one of us, *"I'll be the face of love for you, forever."*

Bent Fingers

Matthew 13:31-33

Nancy was a friend, a young mother, suddenly stricken with an incurable disease. She had only a few months to live when she told me this remarkable story. She told it with a smile watered by tears. "When I was growing up," she said, "I adored my grandmother. Her name was Anna, and she lived on a farm not far from town. I loved to visit her as often as I could. When I was in seventh grade, Grandma Anna died. I was totally heartbroken and couldn't stop crying for days.

"At Grandma Anna's funeral, when no one was looking, I put a letter in her coffin. I asked her to show me a sign that she was still around and that God was real. I desperately needed comfort.

"Over the years I thought I noticed some signs of Grandma Anna's presence from time to time, but I wasn't sure, so mostly I still felt sort of vaguely forlorn. Until I was pregnant with my second child. From its conception, I was just sure the baby would be a girl. The only name I even considered for the baby was Anna. At a baby shower they asked me what we'd name it if it was a boy, and I blurted out, 'Anna.' Of course, they all laughed at me.

"The baby came two weeks late, which meant it was born on Grandma Anna's birthday. I was certain this wasn't a coincidence. And it was a girl, Anna. The first thing I noticed when they handed her to me was that her fingers were bent in a certain distinctive way. They were bent just like my Grandma Anna's fingers had been bent, an obvious, funny little quirk no one else in the family had. The family used to joke about Grandma Anna's fingers, so when little Anna turned up with those same fingers, I cried for joy. It was such a powerful, comforting sign. I knew little Anna's bent fingers were an answer to the letter I'd put in Grandma Anna's coffin."

It's an intriguing story, isn't it? How are we to understand it? Could it be that baby Anna's bent fingers were actually a sign of Grandma Anna's presence? Were they a way God touched and comforted the granddaughter who had asked for such a sign . . . or is the story about an illusion? Were little Anna's bent fingers just a coincidence, a trait explained by genetics. . . or were they a clue to something more?

Peter Gomes, preacher to Harvard University at The Memorial Church, writes, "There is in Celtic mythology the notion of 'thin places' in the universe, where the visible and invisible world come into their closest proximity."[1] Leave it to the Irish to come up with such a lovely, poetic, powerful image: thin places where the eternal world rubs close to the world of time. The Irish monks believe it is at such frontiers that God and human beings are most intimately present to each other. I love the image. All of us can name some thin places we've experienced. Gomes suggests that suffering is one, joy another, mystery yet another. We could add loss, death, birth, love, relationships of trust, sex . . . and comfort. It's as good a place as any to begin.

One Friday evening, my wife, Jan, and I were having dinner with some dear friends, and we started talking about the problems besetting our city and our society. We covered city schools, poor children, lack of funding, the poison of racism, the divisions between urban and suburban communities, the scarcity of visionary world leaders, Third World poverty, terrorism, and on and on. By the end of the evening, I was totally depressed. All night I tossed and turned, thinking about our talk. You know how that goes. It became urgent for me, as surely it's urgent for us all, to try to make sense of things like bent fingers. Are there truly thin places where God touches us with comfort and with its companion, hope?

1 Peter J. Gomes, *The Good Book: Reading the Bible with Mind and Heart* (New York: William Morrow and Company, 1996), 214.

Jesus told two little parables about thin places:

> *The kingdom of heaven is like a mustard seed that someone took and sowed in his field; it is the smallest of all the seeds, but when it is grown it is the greatest of shrubs and becomes a tree, so that the birds come and make nests in its branches.*

Then this:

> *The kingdom of heaven is like yeast that a woman took and mixed in three measures of flour until all of it was leavened.*

Would it be too great a stretch to add this parable of like kind?

> *The kingdom of God is like a little girl who puts a letter in her grandmother's coffin and years later gives birth to a baby with bent fingers as a reply.*

However you read them, Jesus' parables touch on the thin places where two worlds, two dimensions, rub together. The first, and simpler of the two dimensions, is the human side. When we hear these parables, it is easy to focus on the mustard seed and the yeast and overlook the rest of it. Yet it is critical to remember it was a man and a woman who did the small acts of planting the seed and putting the yeast in the flour.

Jesus is saying that such small acts have great consequences no one realizes at the time. Part of the mystery is that the seed and the yeast carry their own future with them, even though that future is not apparent at that moment. But the rest of the mystery is that that future depends on the small acts of the man and the woman. That is the way of God's kingdom.

Lawrence Krauss is a big-time physicist who wrote in the *New York Times* that "all the information in all the books ever written would require . . . about a million million kilobytes of storage." I've never been sure exactly what a kilobyte is, but you might, and the rest of us can take Krauss's word, that a million million of them would store more reading than we could get done in a couple of lifetimes.

Krauss goes on: "That amount [a million million kilobytes] is only one ten-millionth of a billionth of what it would take to store the pattern of a single human being, so that using currently available hard disks that would store 10 gigabytes of information each and stacking them on top of one another, you would have a pile that would reach about a third of the way to the center of the galaxy—about 10,000 light-years. . ."

If you're boggled by that, you're boggled by yourself and every person around you. The Bible is right in saying that each of us is "fearfully and wonderfully made" (Psalm 139:14)! And all those gigabytes stacked from here to Orion are not only about intelligence—or even primarily about intelligence. They're about the wondrous capacities we have for compassion, for creativity, for connecting, for relating, listening, talking, singing, capacities for sensitivity, for forgiveness and beauty, for justice and worship.

In a mysterious way, God uses us to be bearers of comfort and hope to one another. That makes each of us one of those thin places where the visible and invisible worlds rub against each other. Think of that. It is wondrous! That's what it means that we have a spirit, a soul, that we are made in God's image.

Of the four people involved in that gloomy Friday night discussion, one was a teacher in a city high school, and had been for twenty-five years; another had worked for years with senior citizens, and in job training for high-school dropouts, and now raised funds for an agency helping disabled persons; a third ran an off-campus urban semester for college students, was now director of a program for crack-addicted mothers and their children; and me, a pastor of an urban church. And all of us, parents. In the midst of ticking off all the problems, we missed ourselves. We missed each other. We missed the gratitude, the comfort in our own living. We missed how the gifts we are ripple out to others, to the city, to the kingdom. We missed our version of the clue of the bent fingers. We whizzed by the thin places each of us are.

Clearly, one point Jesus makes in the parables is that we are gifts to each other, even as the man who planted the mustard seed and the woman who mixed in the yeast were. What they did rippled out to others. In those ripples are comfort and hope. Of course, we are not perfect, or even close to it. But we are still God's gifts to each other.

Think of yourself. Think of the people you touch in your work, your family, all the listening and responding and supporting and caring you do, and all others do for you. We are a thin place with and for each other.

When our Christian brother Cardinal Joseph Bernadin of Chicago died a few years ago, it was a great loss for all of us. I didn't agree with everything this outstanding Roman Catholic leader did or stood for, but he was a light in the darkness, a builder of bridges between factions in the Catholic Church, and between that church and the Protestant Church. Cardinal Joseph, as he liked to be called, battled for economic justice, for disarmament, for the poor, for the end of capital punishment.

Cardinal Bernadin knew for over a year that he was dying of pancreatic cancer, but he served his people with grace until the end. At a time when you would think he needed comfort and hope the most, he gave comfort and hope the most. That's how, in the mysterious exchange of grace, he got comfort and hope. Bernadin described his fatal illness as "God's special gift to me at this particular moment in my life. As a person of faith, I see death as a friend, as the transition from earthly life to life eternal." The Cardinal was a thin place, a bent finger. So are we all, or so can we be, if we trust and express the gift God creates us to be.

One last thing about the human side of the thin places. It has to do with the image of the small seed growing into a great bush so *"the birds come and make nests in its branches,"* and the image of the yeast raising bread for hungry people. The images are of inclusion. All creatures are included, even each of us. Even those we ignore or try to exclude, or others try to exclude. There is comfort and hope in that as well.

Peter Gomes points to where thin places are likely to be found. He writes, "Where then is hope to be found among people? Where the sufferings have been greatest. . . look to those who have been excluded and placed on the margins. . . It is that the place for creative hope that arises out of suffering is most likely now to be found among blacks, women, and homosexuals. These outcasts may well be the custodians of those thin places . . . watchers at the frontiers between what is and what is to be."[2]

I recall sharing communion in a dirt-floored, corrugated metal shack with peasants in El Salvador, sitting amidst scratching chickens and squalling babies with military gun ship helicopters roaring overheard looking to squash the very rebels we were with. And yet those rebels, most of whom

2 Gomes, *The Good Book,* 230.

had lost family members in their battle for justice, were joyful as we shared communion.

"Like yeast that a woman took and mixed in . . ." Bent fingers. Thin place.

I think of sitting where small candles cast large shadows on the bare walls of a room in Cape Haitian, Haiti. For hours our delegation listened to stories of brutality told by people on the run, hunted by the military dictators of that desperately poor country. The next morning we went with a young priest to take communion in a shabby chapel with people dressed in rags but radiance in their faces and lives.

"Mustard seed . . . becomes a tree so that the birds . . . make nests in its branches" Bent fingers. Thin place.

I think of talking to black South Africans before dawn as they stood in line to vote in the country's first all-race election. Many were barefoot, women carrying babies in slings on their backs, men leaning on crutches, kids clutching parents' legs, old people carried by friends for miles but all serene in their commitment to merciful justice. I think of worshiping in an evangelical church in South Africa one Sunday at which the pastor urged his poor, black congregation not to be bitter or vengeful.

"A man took a seed and sowed it . . ." Bent fingers. Thin place.

When life is stripped down to its essence, when people who have so little of the material things we take for granted, yet show a spirit of compassion, of hope, of faith, of community that our society seems to have lost, I understand a little of what inclusion is and comfort is. It is we who are being included by those people in what life comes down to. It comes down to the thin places, and we dare not miss them.

We are gifts to each other, the poor to us as much as we to them. Roberta Bondi teaches prayer, and I keep going back to something she said: "Our human relations are mirrors of our relationship with God." That is a clear, hard truth, but potentially a comforting one.

God touches us with comfort when we touch each other with honesty and compassion. That's what it means to be custodians of the thin places. That is what justice and trust in our family life is about, and what justice and reconciliation in our social and political life is about, at the core. That is what life together in the church is about, or should be, as well as our mission as a church is about. That is what each of us is about as we pray, sing, reach out, touch, include, let ourselves be included, risk giving the gift God made us.

A young person once said to the great violinist Fritz Kreisler, "I'd give my life to play as beautifully as you do." Kreisler replied, "I did." Well. . .

"The kingdom of heaven is like a mustard seed that a man took and sowed . . . like yeast that a woman took and mixed in . . ."

So we come to the other side of the parables and of the thin places—God's side. It is by far the most crucial side. Think of it this way. Both the man and the woman in the parables "took" something given and did something with it: the man with the seed, the woman with the yeast. God gave it and God was in it. They simply took what was given, lived it, and something like miracles happened.

Faith, or better yet, trust, is the bridge at the thin place. That's why these two parables of Jesus are parables of trust, of faith, and so of comfort and hope. The trust is that God is at work in our lives, invisibly at work, like a seed growing in the darkness, like yeast rising in the loaf. The work of faith is to identify and make sense of the thin places. That means never losing heart. It means to keep taking, and planting, and mixing in faith. It is no accident that small acts affect lives far beyond our view, our power, our lifetime. That's true because God is faithful. God is at work in the invisible world that rubs against, and breaks through, into this visible one, while remaining invisible to us. The haunt of grace is like light that makes itself known by what it touches. God's presence is invisible, but invincible at last.

Recently I read a review of a book by physicist Robert Osserman entitled *Poetry of the Universe*—a wonderful title—with the subtitle *Mathematical Exploration of the Cosmos.* The book is about mapping the universe, and I didn't understand much except the reviewer's final words: "The reader of this little book will know why cosmologists use words like 'beauty,' 'music' and 'poetry' to describe the mysterious nature of our universe." I find that comforting. It frees us from the stifling idea that science will one day explain all the mysteries away and run God out of the neighborhood. Beauty, music, poetry go deeper than explanations. So does God!

For fun, and instruction, here is one more quote from a science writer named Cramer: "If you stand in the dark and look at a star a hundred light-years away and think that what it's telling you is that a hundred years in the past, the advance waves that are returning to the star from your eyes shook hands with the electrons in the star, encouraging it to send light in your direction—well it makes you feel sort of shivery." Yes, it does, even if you don't get it, and a better word for shivery is awe.

The point is this: The God who created all this, and is creating it still, is bigger, more ingenious, sneakier than we can pin down with our creeds and theories. A book on the great Indian leader Crazy Horse helps focus what that suggests spiritually. Once, when Crazy Horse was enraged about what was happening to his people, he went outside the lodge tent into the night where "the sky was far and there was room for an angry man."

What I am trying to say is that God—the kingdom of the invisible world rubbing against this one—has room enough for angry people, people who grieve and cry, frightened people, people who doubt and betray, are guilty of all sorts of sin, who struggle, get sick and die, yet do wonderful, beautiful, incredible things. People like us. God holds us, like the earth holds a seed, breaks us open, raises us like life from a seed, like yeast raises the mess of flour and makes bread of it, of us. That is what God's grace, God's mercy, God's power and purposes are about. At the thin places we are—at the thin places we seek and find and share—God is there, invisibly, invincibly working. The bent fingers are a clue.

And so is this story I heard at the Orthodox Jewish wedding of Jason and Meredith last summer. At the wedding reception, Meredith's father, a professor at Princeton, gave her and Jason a pair of silver candlesticks and explained where they'd come from. During World War II in Amsterdam, Nazis knocked on the doors of Jews and demanded all their silver. One family was a friend of a man named Walter Kauffman, a colleague of Meredith's father. Well, the family gave all their silver except four candlesticks. Then the family was sent to a concentration camp where all died except the father, the friend of Professor Kauffman.

After the war, the man returned to his home but it was burned down and nothing remained but charred rubble. While he was standing there crying in the rubble, a neighbor came and said that they'd thought everything was lost in the fire. But one day, as they poked through the rubble, they came upon the four candlesticks, burned, twisted but not destroyed. They had saved them for the family in case any of them ever came back after the war. They gave the candlesticks to that father as they all stood there in the ruins.

Later, the father gave the candlesticks to his friend, Walter Kauffman. When Walter came to the United States, he gave the candlesticks to Meredith's father. After telling the story, her father gave the candlesticks to Meredith and Jason on their wedding day. The gift was given as we gathered in a synagogue, all of which the Nazis set out to blot from the face of the earth. I watched and listened with tears in my eyes but a smile on my face. Twisted silver candlesticks carrying the light of God's covenant with the Jewish people, and all of us, which the darkness of the Holocaust could not snuff out. Death could not, did not, cannot defeat God or the life God gives us.

A terminally ill young mother telling a beautiful story through her tears and smile; two tiny hands with bent fingers. Two young people, a wedding, and twisted candlesticks. A man who took . . . yea, thousands of men who take mustard seeds and plant them. A woman who took . . . yea, thousands of women who take yeast and mix it. Each of us. All of us. Herein, and all around, is comfort and hope.

How Far Is One?

Psalm 130
Mark 10:2-16

I put off publicly addressing this issue as long as I could—perhaps even longer. I put it off because it's painful. I put it off because I did not want to use a public forum to try to justify myself, or anyone else, by distorting or misrepresenting things, which is an easy and human thing to do. I put it off because I am a divorced and remarried man. And yet, I'm ordained and committed to wrestle with what Jesus says about hard, painful things such as divorce and remarriage. I can no longer avoid doing so with any integrity.

Probably you're familiar with what he said on the subject. But just so I won't be the only one squirming, let me repeat it. Cut to the chase. Jesus agrees with the Pharisees who question him that divorce is permissible by the law of Moses. Then he goes on, "But from the beginning of creation, 'God made them male and female.' For this reason, a man shall . . . be joined to his wife, and the two shall become one flesh . . . Therefore what God has joined together, let no one separate . . . Whoever divorces his wife and marries another commits adultery against her; and if she divorces her husband and marries another, she commits adultery."

There it is, stark and unsettling. I put off addressing it until, at last, it dawned on me that what Jesus is saying is really the gospel in miniature. That is, it's "good news" at heart—bad at first, hard always, but good all the way in. To tell you why it is, let me share a few simple, ungarnished truths that have come from my struggle with what Jesus says, as well as from my own experience.

The truth I want to share could be summed up by saying there is really no such thing as divorce. Not really! Legally, yes, but not psychologically, or morally, or spiritually. It seems to me that this is what Jesus is saying, and my experience confirms it. Divorce isn't just a legal matter. It isn't even primarily a moral issue, though there are moral issues involved. It isn't primarily a moral issue because it really isn't about what we should do, or should not do.

Before anything else, it's about what we *cannot* do. Jesus says we cannot actually terminate our relationships with each other because God made us for each other, and nothing can ever change that. We can abuse, hurt, betray, oppress, exploit, even leave each other, but finally we cannot break our connections to each other. Those connections are braided into creation itself and into our core. They are grounded in God. The inescapable truth is that whatever any one of us does affects all of us, one way or another. It continues to do so, especially in marriage, or after it.

It's a terrible, destructive illusion to think we are ever done with each other. Death does not end a relationship between people, it just changes the way the relationship works. That's how it is with divorce. Divorce does not end the relationship between people, it just changes it. When two become one flesh, as Jesus put it, it isn't just about sharing sex, it's about sharing selves. Sharing selves as openly and deeply as two people can. That experience becomes part of each self. So the relationship continues to affect both parties even after they think they are divorced. My divorce continues to affect me and always will. A divorce continues to affect all persons involved, especially the children but also the entire family, friends, institutions—*even as does a marriage.* It is important to see that. Even as marriage is not the solution for most problems neither is divorce the solution for most problems. Even as marriage is not the cause of most problems, neither is divorce. I know that's how it works for me and for Dory, my first wife.

Morality has to do with the way we relate to each other. But that we *have* to relate to each other, for good or ill, is rooted in God's purposes for us. God intends for us to live together, to love, to be just and fair, to treat each other as equals, to be accountable for what we do, whether we fulfill those purposes or not. And we never fulfill them completely.

Of course, we can help and bless each other, and we do. But we can also betray and hurt each other, and we do. It is never just one or the other in any relationship. Still, there are always consequences to our betrayals: When we betray others, we also betray and hurt ourselves. It's unavoidable and it's true in the relationships not only of husbands and wives but of parents and children, of siblings, of partners in any relationship.

It's also true of relationships between black, white, Hispanic, Asian, rich, poor, middle-class people, gay and straight people, whomever. Legally, politically, economically, geographically we can separate, but in our core, our souls, our very being, we cannot. In the deepest sense, there is no such thing as divorce.

"What God has joined together, let no one separate."

What's the point of insisting there's really no such thing as divorce? For one thing, it means that we cannot dehumanize, demean, and discard someone as though that would solve anything or make us better. It means we can't truly blame others for our problems. I am sick of the blame game we all play. I am sick that the blame game is epidemic in our society. "Nothing is ever my responsibility. If something is wrong it's because of what someone else did." Nonsense! The truth is that one marriage partner cannot say, "If only my spouse would shape up, things would be fine." Nor can one partner say, "If only I could find someone who would understand and appreciate me, my life would be great." Those statements are simply untrue.

The honest truth is that we bless each other, and we give good gifts to each other over the years in marriage and in all relationships. There is some healing in a relationship when that is recognized and affirmed. It helped me, and to some extent it helped our broken relationship when, after a time, I could express gratitude to Dory for her many gifts to me and to our children, gifts which continue to bless us.

Many years ago, when people came to me to perform their weddings, I would set up several premarital counseling sessions. Then I noticed that the couple's eyes kept glazing over. Since then I've gotten premarital counseling down to six words: "When you need help, get it." What I mean is that in times of romance, we think relationships are easy and natural, no sweat, a piece of cake. That is not so! Human relationships are the most difficult yet most basic, essential, and rewarding element of life. So they take work. Love involves work!

No matter who we are, we cannot be everything or mean everything to another person, or to anything else. When we have medical issues, we know the consequences of ignoring them. So we go to a doctor. Yet when we have relational issues, we think we can handle them by ourselves. Probably we can't! The same is true of relational issues as of medical or legal issues.

So when—not if, *when*—we have relational issues, we need to be ready and mutually agreeable to make the effort to get help. Just as we get tune-ups for our cars, we sometimes need to get tune-ups for our marriages. Go to someone who can help, a family therapist or someone you trust who can help each of you face yourself. Go before problems fester. There's no stigma in getting help, but there can be a stunting of the relationship if we don't. And get help if you are considering divorce and thinking that if you can get away from the other person, all will be well.

"When you need help, get it."

God gives us many options. Prayer and spiritual nurture together can be a help. The community of faith can be a resource if the people in it are honest and willing to share with each other at that deeper level and not be content with some feel-good, avoid-hard-things superficiality. My deep hope for the church is that it be that kind of healing, redeeming body of grace.

But for grace to become real for us, we need to claim it. Trusting grace in moments not only of gladness but of conflict, and opening ourselves to it even in tough circumstances, is what deepens and stretches our love for each other. That's part of what I mean by the hard work of love.

God's grace comes to us through many people, including therapists. I know that from my own experience. I went to therapy before my divorce. I went during and after my divorce. We did family therapy sessions that were painful and helpful. I had to face myself so I would not just repeat with someone else what happened with Dory. I had to face the injury I had done to Dory, and to my children. I had to hear the hard truth my children spoke to me about my failures, my temper, my lack of understanding, my authoritarian demands, my not being around for them enough. They listened to my side as well.

There were tears and anger and guilt and healing in it. Out of it came a different kind of relationship between my kids and me that's closer, more honest and trusting than it ever was or ever would have been without that hard, ongoing, even redemptive, work. Divorce, like marriage, can tilt toward mercy, growth, and grace.

The wonder is that a crisis in a relationship blows it open and makes something different possible for everyone, if we work at it. It is in the mess of human life that moral action takes place, or not. Morality is rooted in the awareness that God makes connection the essential condition of our humanity, and it cannot be ignored or denied without shrinking love to a fleeting feeling. Fairness, justice, and love are inseparable.

So Jan, my wife now, and I revel in our relationship yet keep plugging away at it at the same time. The plugging away never ends, thank God. Literally, thank God because it means we take our love, and God's, seriously. There are no perfect marriages, no perfect relationships, no perfect parents, no perfect people because none of us is God, even if we think we are. The hard truth is we continue to disappoint and hurt each other, and yet at the same time we fulfill and give each other joy. Relationships are complicated, confusing sometimes. But we can tilt our relationships more toward the fulfillment side.

Love isn't just about feelings. It's about building trust, because finally there is no love without trust. Love involves work. That's spelled out all through the Bible. Look how hard Moses and the prophets worked. Look how hard Jesus worked, and the disciples and Peter. What else but love works that hard, that deeply, that long? But, oh, how it is worth it. I am profoundly blessed by the work of love Jan presses us to do together, even in those times I'm tempted to shirk it.

Am I committing adultery with her because she and I are both divorced and re-married? I don't really believe so. If I am, God have mercy on me. But surely I would be unfaithful if I avoided the emotional and spiritual intimacy of telling her my side, my truth, and hearing her side, her truth, meeting and engaging each other, and trying to negotiate fairly with each other. That's how trust is built, and without trust what happens to love?

I would be unfaithful if I didn't work at building trust with her. That is what intimacy is about, not just sex. You see, betrayal can be cold-blooded, not just hot-blooded. We betray each other when we lie, distort, manipulate out of a hidden agenda. We betray each other when we avoid the hard stuff, when we treat each other as things to be used for our own gratification or glorification. We betray each other when we retreat into silence and become inaccessible. And to betray others is to betray ourselves and God because there's no such thing as divorce.

Surely, it doesn't take rocket science or artistic genius to connect the dots from intimate to more inclusive relations. We can stretch what Jesus says about marriage and divorce to our relationships with all kinds of other people. We can be more inclusive in our connections with people of another color or race or nationality or creed or gender or sexual orientation because those connections cannot be broken without terrible, destructive consequences. If we haven't learned that yet, it's time we did.

I strongly believe our sexual orientations are mysteriously given to us in the same way our gender or race is. So I also believe that relationships between homosexual persons should be recognized as being as legally and spiritually valid as are those of heterosexual persons. That is only just and fair. It means we all play on the same, level field and are accountable to the same standards for our behavior. When Jesus spoke about creating us male and female, so that what God joins together no one should separate, I do not believe he was excluding homosexuals from the sacredness of partnership covenants. The same truth applies to all human relationships, heterosexual and homosexual, racial, gender, nationality, whatever. What God has joined together, let no one separate!

To see and celebrate our inviolable human connections is what the foundation of justice is about. Without a spiritual depth to it, social action atrophies and dies. That's why Jesus spent so much of his time among those his society had pushed to the margins. But—and this is important, too—he also spent time with the enemies of those marginalized people, and his own enemies. He met them constantly, went to Jerusalem to confront them. Jesus demonstrated that to love our enemies does not mean to be afraid to make them. To love them means not to dismiss or demonize them. As in a marriage, so in social action: We need to be done blaming other persons and groups for what is wrong. We need to begin dealing straight up with them, advocating, arguing, but still treating them as human beings. We need to get on as best we can in simply doing the work of justice where we are, and to do it with some degree of humility as well as passion.

Morality and justice are rooted in the religious awareness of our connectedness not just with people we like and agree with, but with people we don't like or agree with. It is a spiritual issue, not just political or ideological. There is really no such thing as divorce, and it is a dangerous and destructive illusion to think or act otherwise.

I said at the outset that finally it came to me that what Jesus says about divorce and remarriage is good news—not good advice, but good news—however hard or bad it seems at first. How is it good news? How is it the gospel in miniature? Because the gospel, the good news, isn't primarily about morality, it's about grace. The good news is there is no such thing as divorce from God, either. Not really. And here is how I see that.

Go back to the family therapy room with me, and to meetings in our various family living rooms, and to long tearful nights of praying and pacing. You see, what I heard from my children, and from Dory, wasn't so much about the injury I inflicted through the divorce, though there certainly was that. It was about the injuries I inflicted all through the marriage, long before the divorce. I didn't intend those injuries. Mostly, we never do. I did the best I could, and so do most of us, most of the time.

But the best I do, the best any of us do, is seldom if ever grounds for much pride or self-congratulation. Oh, yes, we have wondrous gifts and skills, do good things, are amazingly creative, contribute to others in critical ways, are valuable persons. And yet, we still inflict serious injuries on each other and ourselves. We are limited, mortal beings. We are finite in power, incomplete in knowledge, ambivalent in motives, restricted in determining outcomes of actions. We consistently fall short of the kind of personal integrity or marital fulfillment Jesus pointed to when he spoke of marriage as "two becoming one flesh."

But I wonder, in faith, if by using the term "flesh" Jesus wasn't confirming all our limitations as well as our possibilities. I wonder if he wasn't saying that marriage is about sharing our limitations as well as our strengths, so that we are each made more whole through that continual process of honest, hard sharing. Maybe what he meant by "one" wasn't a kind of fusion of two persons into one, but rather two persons entering into one process of sharing, of challenging, confronting, forgiving, enjoying, growing as two persons coming together in one process. It's intriguing to imagine it that way, isn't it? And more compatible with the way Jesus went about living.

If there is some truth in that view, then marriage isn't so much two people looking in each other's eyes as it is two people side by side looking at the horizon toward which they are moving together. Both the moving and the horizon are the essence of marriage. I believe that is true of all human relationships, from the intimate to the global.

So we come to the question that's the title of this reflection: "How Far Is One?" Part of the truth is that it's as far as the horizon. We never get there in this lifetime. It's beyond our reach, our power. We fail, as I failed in my first marriage, as both of us did. We all fail in our relationships, our best efforts, our lives. Oh, not completely, for to say that would be false modesty, and false modesty is at least half pride.

And yet, there's a Russian proverb that says, "To walk toward spring is to become the spring." It's a compelling image, and we grasp what it means. Then it is also compelling, and true, that *to walk toward the horizon is to become the horizon.*

Now we ask the question again: "How Far is One?" Yes, it is as far as the horizon. And yet it is as near as the next step we take toward it. So trust steps out on that promise. It moves, step by step, and we become, at least a little, the justice and beauty and forgiveness and joy we long for off there on the horizon.

Most deeply, it is God's grace we long for, some wholeness beyond our limitations and faults and failures. How far is such wholeness, such oneness with God? As far as the horizon. But the mystery is that it is by God's grace that we move and live and have our being. It is by God's grace that we walk step by step toward the wholeness for which we long. It is by God's grace that we walk together, when we risk it. And with each step, we become a little more of the oneness, that wholeness. Because grace is also as close as those steps. I hang on to that, or it hangs on to me, every step of every day, or I'd be lost.

What, then, of divorce, mine or anyone's? What of human brokenness in all it's terrifying variations? Come with me to the soul-trembling closing scene of Leonard Bernstein's *Mass.* I have heard it many times on my CD, but I've never seen it except in my imagination. Well, actually I've seen a picture of the scene in the little brochure of the lyrics that comes with the CD. In that scene a priest carrying a glass chalice and wearing beautiful vestments climbs up a staircase where he is to celebrate the Mass. For a moment he towers over the people. He begins the prayers and the choir sings. Then, at the moment he elevates the glass chalice, he hurls it to the floor as if in protest of the distance he and the Mass are from the people. Then he descends from his high station, removes his vestments and kneels among the shards of the shattered chalice. He begins to sing these words:

> Look . . . Isn't that—odd.
> Glass shines—brighter—
> When it's broken . . .
> I never noticed that.[1]

There's the haunt of grace, the mystery of the crucifixion and resurrection.

Broken chalice, broken marriage, broken relationships, broken dreams, broken hearts, broken lives. Yet, sometimes, many times, maybe most times, they shine brighter when they're broken because the light that shines to make them brighter is one no darkness can overcome. So we, in our brokenness walk together toward that light, that horizon, and become more whole. It's not far and yet it takes forever. Walk in peace.

1 Leonard Bernstein, *Mass: A Theater Piece for Singers, Players and Dancers,* Sony Classical SM2K 63089.

X's and O's
The Song of Solomon

The Song of Solomon is so romantic and so explicitly erotic that there were those who argued to ban it from the Bible back when the canon was originally approved. There are those who would ban it today. *The Song of Solomon* was finally included in the biblical canon because others argued that it is a love song to God and from God. In any case, it is in Scripture, a wonderful, graphic, poetic, vivid love song. I recommend that you find someone you love and read it aloud to each other.

Hugs and Kisses*

Let him kiss me with the kisses of his mouth!
For your love is better than wine,
your anointing oils are fragrant,
your name is perfume poured out;
therefore the maidens love you.
Draw me after you, let us make haste.
The king has brought me into his chambers.
We will exult and rejoice in you;
we will extol your love more than wine;
rightly do they love you.
—The Song of Solomon 1:2-4

* When this reflection was originally presented as a sermon, musical interludes were offered between each section.

I suppose my earliest self-conscious expression of love was in thank-you letters to aunts and uncles and grandparents for presents they sent. At the end of the tortured, downhill-tilted lines, just after my name, I added several X's and O's to represent hugs and kisses. Every kid did that. So every kid learned that the trick was to add as many X's and O's as would fill up the page so the actual letter could be short. The X's and O's were the real message anyway. The only thing was that I wanted to give the relatives I loved best more X's and O's than the others, but probably no one noticed the difference anyway. Besides, I was always confused about whether the X's were the kisses and the O's the hugs, or vice versa. But the hugs and kisses *were* the real message.

We are constantly receiving mixed messages about what "true love" is. Out of the many conflicting cultural icons of love, Valentine's Day is one of the most familiar. Yet Valentine was actually a priest in the eleventh century who became the patron saint of romantic love. His message was that all love is pure and holy, not just some love.

If we read the first lines from *The Song of Solomon* carefully, the message of Valentine, and of hugs and kisses, comes through: Down with all the barriers we've put up to differentiate between romantic love and spiritual love, or between the love of friends and the love of sexual partners. Down with the barriers between the love of justice and the love of beauty, or the love of humans and the love of nature, and all the other distinctions we make between platonic and erotic and spiritual love.

Of course there are differences, but the message is they are all of a piece, all rooted in the grace of God. They are all hints of the Lover who created us and everything else, and who loves us and the whole creation.

When we get that message, there are freedom and delight, awe and joy in it. It opens us to God in different and new ways, on every hand and every area of life. The message is that when we love anything or anyone, we're close to God. Or, better, God is close to us.

Catching the Little Foxes

The voice of my beloved!
Look, he comes, leaping upon the mountains,
bounding over the hills.
My beloved is like a gazelle or a young stag.
Look! there he stands behind our wall,
gazing in at the windows,
looking through the lattice.
My beloved speaks and says to me:
"Arise, my love, my fair one, and come away;
for now, the winter is past,
the rain is over and gone.
The flowers appear on the earth,
the time of singing has come,
and the voice of the turtledove is heard in our land.
The fig tree puts forth its figs,
and the vines are in blossom;
they give forth fragrance.
Arise, my love, my fair one, and come away.
O my dove, in the clefts of the rock,
in the covert of the cliff,
let me see your face,
let me hear your voice;
for your voice is sweet, and your face is lovely.
Catch us the foxes, the little foxes,
that ruin the vineyards—
for our vineyards are in blossom.
—The Song of Solomon 2:8-15

"The time of singing has come," says the lover ecstatically in *The Song of Solomon,* and we know what he means. Lovers sing. They can't help it. But then the lover's song modulates to a whispered warning to all lovers: *"Catch us the foxes, the little foxes, that ruin the vineyards—for our vineyards are in blossom,"*

What does that mean? It means that love is not just song, it is work. Little foxes are always eating away at the blossoms of it. So go to work for love; catch the little foxes, the singer implores. Stop them before they ruin love's vineyards.

Little foxes. What are they? Well, the funny thing about love is how awkward and embarrassed it can make us. Why so? Because to love we have to give up control, and that makes us feel foolish. But if we aren't willing to be seen as at least a little foolish, we're a stranger to love. And that's the dilemma of it.

Something Amos Oz wrote hints at it. He describes being a boy living in Jerusalem in 1943. It was a time when life was hanging by a thread for the Jews, and for the world. So Amos' family wrote a letter to Uncle Zvi and his wife, who lived in Tel Aviv. The letter set an exact time for a long-distance telephone call to them: Wednesday, the nineteenth at five o'clock.

In a few days, a confirming letter came back. Since neither family had a telephone in their house, the call was to be made from the Oz family neighborhood pharmacy in Jerusalem to Uncle Zvi's neighborhood pharmacy in Tel Aviv. So a major event was put in place with all the support strategies. All week before the phone call, Amos's family reminded each other of the impending call, warning each other not to schedule or get involved in anything that would interfere with the plans for Wednesday, the nineteenth at five o'clock. Everyone had to pledge not to be late coming home from work or school that day.

On Wednesday the nineteenth, the entire family put on their best clothes and went to the pharmacy to make the call. Invariably they arrived early and sat nervously waiting, not wanting to make the call until the exact minute so they would be sure the family in Tel Aviv would be there. When the moment came, Amos's father, Aryeh, made the call.

Finally, the connection was made, and the conversation went like this:

"Hello, Zvi."

"Speaking."

"This is Aryeh calling from Jerusalem."

"Hello, Aryeh. This is Zvi. How are you all? Everything is fine at this end. We are talking to you from the pharmacy."

"Same here. What's new?"

"Nothing special."

"How are things going, Zvi?"

"There's nothing new in particular. How are things with you?

"Fine. No news here."

"Well, no news is good news."

"Yes, indeed, everything is excellent. And now Fania wants to speak to you."

Fania was Amos's mother. She got on the phone, and it was the same thing all over again. "How are you?" . . . "Fine." . . . "What's new?" . . . "Nothing. You?" . . . "Everything is fine," and so on and on. It ended with the promise to write and the setting of a time for the next call, and then the goodbyes: "We'll talk again soon." . . . "Yes. It's good to hear your voice." . . . "Take care." . . . "All the best to you."

> Later, an adult Oz reflected on those 1943-44 boyhood telephone conversations: "Now I know this was not at all funny. Life was hanging by a thread. . . they were not at all sure they would ever speak again. God knows what was about to happen . . . I realize how hard it was for them to express personal feelings. Public sentiment was no problem. They were highly emotional people. They could passionately argue about Bakunin or about Trotsky. They could reach the verge of tears debating colonialism, or exploitation or anti-Semitism, but when they wanted to convey a personal emotion, they were struck dumb . . . arid, clenched, even terrified, the heritage of many generations of suppression . . . Almost everything was considered improper."[1]

Recognize any of the symptoms? Even so, *"Catch us . . . the little foxes, that ruin the vineyards."* What little foxes? Well, how is it we're so good at analyzing, criticizing, planning, suggesting, advising, correcting, complaining, arguing, surfing the internet in our heads, and yet so shy about saying what is in our hearts, about thanking, complimenting, confirming, telling someone we love him or her? How is it we're so good at running institutions, running neighborhoods, running projects, even running the world . . . and so good as well at running from intimacy, honest sharing, being close?

Maybe it helps to keep remembering that life is always hanging in the balance, and the next time to speak, to show love, may never come. Maybe it helps to remember that we have to be a little foolish, a little childlike and vulnerable to make those X's and O's real, to answer the call of the Lover in our hearts to *"Arise . . . and come away."* To come away from the clench and the stifling habits and let someone see our real face. To hear our truest voice, to touch our deepest heart. To catch the little foxes that ruin our vineyards before it is too late.

1 Story and quote from Amos Oz, "Chekhov in Hebrew," *New Yorker,* December 25, 1995, and January 1, 1996: 50–65.

Kissing the Beast

Upon my bed at night
I sought him whom my soul loves;
I sought him, but found him not;
I called him, but he gave no answer.
"I will rise now and go about the city,
in the streets and in the squares;
I will seek him whom my soul loves."
I sought him, but found him not.
The sentinels found me,
as they went about in the city.
"Have you seen him whom my soul loves?"
Scarcely had I passed them,
when I found him whom my soul loves.
I held him, and would not let him go
until I brought him into my mother's house,
and into the chamber of her that conceived me.
I adjure you, O daughters of Jerusalem,
by the gazelles or the wild does:
do not stir up nor awaken love until it is ready.
—The Song of Solomon 3:1-5

In this portion of *The Song of Solomon,* when the beloved can't find the lover, she goes to look for him. Where does she look? She looks in the streets and squares of the city. Without being too literal about it, there's an X and O message in that.

I've always been a sucker for the story of *Beauty and the Beast.* Everyone knows the story: The beautiful Princess meets the frightening, ugly, deformed beast but instead of running away, as everyone else does, she stays with him. Finally she kisses him, and at that moment the beast becomes a handsome man.

The thing is, it's more than a fairy tale. It touches a primal truth. I've been kissed like that, though looking at me you might not know it. But this beast has been kissed like that, a thousand times, and each one has changed my heart. It happens. You may know that from your own experience.

So here's the point: Love is about personal relationships. But not all those personal relationships are private. Not all of them should be. Love relationships are public, too, and they have public consequences. These days, the city is seen as frightening and ugly by lots of people who run from it. But the city is nothing but a complex network of people. Society is people. Welfare is about people. Poverty is about people. Racial justice is about people. Health care, schools, crime, violence, drugs are all about people. The beast of the city, of society, of the nation, the world, awaits our kiss.

But as long as we *talk* about issues and statistics, we can run and hide. As long as we talk in the abstract about financial markets, about taxes, about Social Security and Medicare, we can take cover in bloodless, heady, impersonal debate. Yet issues change when they take on a human face.

Justice is love on the prowl, like the beloved in *The Song of Solomon* looking for her lover in the city streets, the night streets that are scary, the city streets where people, human beings, pursue their dreams or sweep up the broken pieces of them. Justice is love on the prowl, trying to kiss the beast, trying to put a human face on the issues of poverty and sickness and homelessness and welfare families and all the rest.

Yes, of course, politics are involved, and economics, and finances and tough choices. But first of all, it's about love. Love on the prowl. Lovers like us go on the prowl looking for the people, putting a face on things, trying to kiss the fear away outside and inside, and so finding their hearts and our own. For the simple truth is that the Lover we are all looking for is God, and the face under all faces is that of Christ. This means we are each and every one beasts turned beloved by the kiss of God. We are the ones who have been kissed a thousand times. Think about that and sing.

Then move out! For we are the ones sent on the prowl to find and to kiss the beast of our time in our cities, our society, our nation and planet. To kiss that beast, if not to make it handsome, more importantly to find and set free its heart—and in the mystery of love to find and free our own.

Seal on the Heart

Set me as a seal upon your heart,
as a seal upon your am;
for love is strong as death,
passion fierce as the grave,
Its flashes are flashes of fire,
a raging flame.
Many waters cannot quench love,
neither can floods drown it.
If one offered for love
all the wealth of one's house,
it would be utterly scorned.
—The Song of Solomon 8:6-7

I get a catch in my throat whenever I read this passage from *The Song of Solomon.* The Lover says, "*Set me as a seal upon your heart.*" Isn't that what God is forever saying to us? Isn't that what God is forever doing for us and with us? Isn't that what the cross and the empty tomb are about? Isn't that what the fumbling company of the church across the centuries, and today, is or ought to be about? Isn't that what the moments of love we have all known are about, all those touches and glimpses of it that tiptoe into our hearts like stars into the darkness, like a lover stretching out on the shore of body and soul as the sea stretches out on the sand? All love is of a piece, all our loves hint of the Eternal Lover.

John Polkinghorne is an Anglican Priest and a world-class physicist who made this accurate statement: "Transparent moments of encounter with the sacred can neither be induced nor repeated through human contrivance, but only received."[2] Only received. And yet, we so much want such transparent moments of encounter with the sacred, such a relationship with the Eternal Lover, that we try desperately to earn them, to work to get them as a reward, to prove we are worthy of them. Often in those efforts, good things happen. But the truth is that moments of encounter with the sacred can only be received.

2 John Polkinghorne at a conference on "Science and the Spiritual Quest," Berkeley, CA, 1991.

The Song of Solomon puts it graphically: *"If one offered for love all the wealth of one's house, it would he utterly scorned."* All the wealth of our house, our good works, our smarts and successes, our poetry and prophetic clamoring, whatever else they are about, love is not it. At least, it's not about God's love. God's love is received, not achieved.

But the good news is that God's love is already ours. God's seal is already set upon our hearts. Receiving it is just a matter of being foolish enough to brush the dust off our hearts and saying back to God, "I love you, too." Many waters cannot quench love. Not God's love. Not our love. Not really.

X's and O's to us all.

Mind What's Left

John 5:1-9

Alice and Violet are talking. They are two black women in Toni Morrison's powerful novel *Jazz*. Both women are in their fifties. They've not been friends even though they live in the same apartment building in Harlem. But their pain has brought them together.

Violet is the wife of Joe. Joe had become the lover of Alice's eighteen-year-old niece, an orphan Alice had raised from childhood. Joe is suspected of having killed the young woman when she broke off the affair, but there's no way to prove it.

Now Violet, cramped with anguish, slashes out at Alice's niece for causing it by seducing her husband. Alice listens as she continues with her ironing. Violet rakes Joe over the coals of her lament. She threatens to throw him out. Then she pleads with Alice, "We women, me and you. Tell me something real. Don't just say I'm grown and ought to know. I don't. . . What about it? Do I stay with him? . . ."

The two women talk on for a time. Finally, out of the depths of her own suffering, Alice says to Violet, "You want a real thing? I'll tell you a real one. You got anything left to you to love, anything at all, do it."

Violet is taken aback. "And when he does it again? Don't mind what people think?"

"Mind what's left to you," Alice answers.

"You saying take it? Don't fight?"

"Fight what, who?. . . Nobody's asking you to take it. I'm sayin make it, make it!"

Suddenly they become aware of the smoke rising from where Alice had put down her iron. Alice swears.

> Violet was the first to smile. Then Alice. In no time laughter was rocking them both . . . and suddenly the world was right side up. Violet learned then what she had forgotten until this moment: that laughter is serious. More complicated, more serious than tears.[1]

Such a wonderful scene, and we're in it. Just as are Violet and Alice, everyone is injured in some way. Everyone has a pocket full of losses, harbors some kind of painful wound, walks with some sort of limp. So, as did Violet, all of us know the subtle temptation to consider ourselves victims. It's easy to

1 Toni Morrison, *Jazz* (New York: Alfred A. Knopf, 1992), 110–113.

slip into that mode, and most of us are good at it. We can play the victim at the drop of an inconvenience.

But to do that trivializes the mystery of God's grace and providence. There are two loose ways to trivialize or domesticate God. One is to claim to know what God should and will do without question, as those of us who are conservatives or fundamentalists do. The other is to claim to know what God can't and won't do, as those of us who are progressives and intellectuals do. Faith walks the tightrope between the two domestications. Faith lives in that tension. That is the risk and creativity of it.

One of the reasons I get uneasy in many social gatherings is because there's frequently an undercurrent of a martyr syndrome, a "poor us, we ought to sue them" mentality to much of the conversation. There seem to be endless variations of that lament. Often I'm ready to sing my own version of it. But more often I'm reminded of Flannery O'Connor being asked by a frustrated author if university teachers stifled writers. She answered, "My opinion is they don't stifle enough of them. There's many a best seller that could have been prevented by a good teacher."

Ditto whatever "Poor Us Inc." we're a member of. Ditto victims of all stripes and subtleties who might be prevented by a good teacher, an honest friend, a thoughtful self-examination, and a hard work-out with the mystery of God.

Of course, everyone's wounds are real. Everyone's struggle is hard. Affliction isn't irrelevant. But those truths aren't the real point. The real point is, *"You got anything left to you to love, anything at all, do it . . . Mind what's left to you."* The haunt of grace is that there's always something left to us, and in us, to love.

Which means that celebration, like laughter, is serious, complicated business. In *A River Runs Through It,* a beautiful book from which a movie of the same title was made, Norman says of his Presbyterian minister father, who taught him fly fishing and religion, "To him, all good things—trout as well as eternal salvation—come by grace and grace comes by art, and art does not come easy."[2]

In Scripture there is a story about Jesus by the Bethesda pool in Jerusalem. The tradition was that whenever the water of the pool churned up, it was because a passing angel had disturbed it. Then the first one into the roiling water got healed. Obviously, there were lots of invalids hanging around waiting for the water to roil. (I'll pass on the temptation to suggest the ways you and I might wait around for our version of water to roil.)

One man had been by the pool for thirty-eight years. Thirty-eight years! He's a career victim, a PhD passive-aggressive.

2 Norman Maclean, *A River Runs Through It and Other Stories* (New York: Pocket Books, 1976), 5.

He's probably a nice guy but with a secret rage about what God couldn't and wouldn't do for him. There's no mystery for him, and no celebration. Just a life settled into a rut with no "real thing" to shake and sustain him.

Can't you imagine him camped out by the pool, using his affliction (whatever it was, since the story doesn't say) to con people into feeling sorry for him and running his errands? Can't you hear him complaining in well-modulated, seductive tones about how unfair his fate is? It's a familiar gig. We've all played a few notes of it. It isn't so much that the man is an invalid as it is that he's *in-valid,* a bit of a fraud.

Jesus doesn't chat him up, or hold his hand, or take a history. He just does two things that demonstrate the art of grace and the heart of celebration. One thing is down and dirty. The other, quick and clean.

First, Jesus asks the man, "Do you want to be made well?" That's down and dirty. It cuts through the pretense of congeniality, the collusion of sympathy. The answer seems obvious. But is it? Is it for us? Notice that the man never really answers.

"Sir," he begins. There's the modus operandi of a con artist. "Sir," he says, then lays out his list of grievances. "No one helps me. When the water is stirred up, people push in front of me. No one cares about me. Thirty-eight years and all I got is more of the same."

Jesus question hangs there unanswered: "What do you want?" The sad thing is that the man doesn't seem to think the question really applies to him. It's as if the possibility it carries is too great for him to imagine any more. Healing? Creativity? Freedom? Joy? For *me*? You must be crazy.

Are those possibilities too great for us to claim? Is mystery, risk, grace gone for us? How do you answer Jesus' question, "What do you want? Do you want to be healed?" It's a profoundly religious question. It's a profoundly healing question.

Like this man, too many of us don't consider the question relevant to us. We don't think God actually cares about us or our lives or our healing. If anything, we think God cares only about major things, the sweep of history, the functions of the universe. So we mumble something about miracles of healing not being possible, about new and different options being illusions. Or we assume it's selfish and vaguely immoral to think or risk or live toward what we want.

But Jesus goes down and dirty, and presses us to come clean: *"What do you want?"* It's really a question of identity. Who are you?

In Cormac McCarthy's magnificent novel *All The Pretty Horses*, an older woman, Maria, tells the story of her life to the young cowboy, John Grady. Maria speaks of being sixteen and facing a hard decision: ". . . I knew that what I was seeking to discover was a thing I'd always known. That all courage is a form of constancy. That it is always himself that the coward abandoned first. After this all other betrayals came easily. I knew that courage came with less struggle for some than for others but I believed that anyone who desired it could have it. That the desire for it was the thing itself. The thing itself."[3]

"It is always himself that the coward abandons first. After this all other betrayals come easily."

Maria's words underscore why Jesus' question is so powerfully compelling and healing. *"What do you want? Do you desire to be healed?"* It takes courage to answer "Yes" to that question and mean it. We're all veterans of pain of some kind, broken dreams rattling around in us. All of us are stitched by scars.

Walter Brueggemann talks about "the failure of Easter nerve." It's a telling term, isn't it? Since we seldom claim the audacity of the mystery of grace, we close up and shut down, Brueggemann writes, "The Prince of Darkness tries frantically to keep the world closed so that we can be administered. The Prince has powerful allies in this age."[4]

What a chilling image—a closed world where we are administered. A closed world where we, in turn, administer our own lives to manageable objectives. Where's the mystery in a closed world? Where's the celebration? Where's the worship? Where's the wonder of loving what's left to us?

What's left are wounds, yes, but also being alive not dead, touched by wonder, filled with laughter, charged with wild possibilities, summoned to hope and joy. Love what's left to you because it's stunning. It's the kingdom of God.

What each of us has left to love is our self, at least at first, because it's where the grace that comes by the hard work of art begins. Creativity is putting yourself on the line—"making it," as Alice puts it. It's imagining yourself with all those wild possibilities and churning up the courage to pursue them. Not to claim and risk your possibilities is to abandon your self. Then all other betrayals come easily—especially the betrayal of the mystery of grace.

A very wise person once said to me, "Resentment slowly kills your spirit. If you dare to push through it and choose what is truest about yourself, that's a holy act. Choosing like that is a source of life. It enlarges life places and builds relationships. You become a source of life."

"Resentment slowly kills your spirit," Do we see the man by the pool in that? Or ourselves? Or the possibilities for something different for us and for those with whom we dare to share the art of grace?

Choosing what is truest about ourselves is a holy act. It comes close to what loving ourselves is about. It is what grace enables, what mystery touches on. It is what Easter nerve involves. Courage, then, for that's

3 Cormac McCarthy, *All the Pretty Horses* (New York: Alfred A. Knopf, 1992), 235.

4 Walter Brueggemann, *Finally Comes The Poet* (Minneapolis: Augsburg Fortress, 1989), 11.

the beginning of healing and freedom and creativity.

"Do you want to be healed? What do you want?"

There is in each of us a core, a soul, that is a gift of God. Each of us is of great value that is not subject to the hazards of pain, loss, injury, circumstance.

"You got anything left to you to love, anything at all, do it." Whatever our difficulties are, we have a great deal left to us. Our being alive. Claim it. Do it!

And that's the second thing Jesus said to the in-valid man, and to us. It was quick and clean. Do it! "Stand up, take your mat and walk."

Someone once said, "I didn't fall in love, I rose in it." That's a great image, isn't it? Falling in love is wonderful, and everyone should experience the plunge. It's about music, poetry, dancing, candlelight, all those good things we sometimes think is all that joy and celebration mean. But everyone should experience *rising* in love even more. That's about getting up and walking when it's tough. It's about laughter in the midst of sweat and risk, blisters and battle.

Evelyn Waugh was a writer who got increasingly bitter with age. He self-righteously withdrew from the world because he thought the world was going to hell in a handbasket. When he died, someone observed that "Waugh was offered more love than he was ever able to accept."

In a way, that's true of all of us, and that's the haunt of grace. God offers us more love than we usually dare to risk in the art of living it out. Celebration is a lifetime art. It's about daring to accept more of that love day by day, and rising in it in whatever way we dare.

Franz Rosenzweig says, "One hears differently when one hears in doing."[5] That truth is what the art of life is about, what faith means. I'm not sure we ever really learn the truth by talking, which is a risky thing for a word merchant like me to say. We do hear differently in doing. That's a real thing!

We find out about prayer by praying, casting ourselves with disciplined abandon into the silence day by day, listening to the silence until we hear the love and holiness in it for us.

We learn about God by trusting in the darkness, stepping out on the promise, walking through the storms and into battle for justice in our homes and neighborhoods, city and world.

We learn mercy by forgiving someone who has hurt us. That doesn't mean walking as if nothing happened and gossiping about whoever offended us. It means confronting those who hurt us, telling them our truth, listening to their truth, working on the relationship for however many lifetimes it takes. We learn mercy by forgiving someone who has hurt us and whom we've hurt as well, if we're honest about it. *"Grace comes by art, and*

5 Franz Rosenzweig, *On Jewish Learning* (New York: Schocken Books, 1987).

art does not come easy." One does hear differently in doing. That's a real thing!

On my study wall is a simple silk screen on which are words from a Roethke poem I love:

> Of those so close beside me, which
>   are you?
> God bless the Ground! I shall walk
>   softly there,
> And learn by going where I have to
>   go . . .
>
> This shaking keeps me steady. I should
>   know.
> What falls away is always. And is near.
> I wake to sleep, and take my waking
>   slow.
> I learn by going where I have to go.[6]

". . . learn by going where I have to go." We find our way more by walking than by studying maps. We confirm mystery and "make it" by going on into the always uncharted time and space ahead and daring to fail, if need be. We claim our value by daring to live by what we value, as well as thinking and talking about it.

"Stand up, take your mat and walk." Just that.

Remember, the gospel doesn't say what the man's physical illness was. When he got up and walked, maybe he still had a hitch in his gait, or had one arm hanging useless by his side, or had an eye missing, or his body was still troubled by some shaking that kept him steady, now. And surely, not all his questions were answered. He just squared his shoulders and put one foot ahead of the other and started after a different life. So with us! As Alice said, *"Nobody's asking you to take it, I'm sayin make it, make it,"* That's the mystery of grace: We can walk.

The mystery of grace also includes claiming the strength in our wounds and losses. The wonder is that only when we *"stand up, take our mat and walk"* do we make our way back into the human enterprise, which cannot quite go on without us. That's what the church, the gathering of faithful people, is about—not perfection or success but integrity, courage, the art by which grace comes. Faith comes by living faithfully.

"Making it" with what we have left isn't about perfection, it's about integrity, the integrity of living a life that's all of a piece, not split into pieces. The integrity of saying what we mean and then letting our lives mean what we say. Faith is about walking, loving what's left to us and so, hearing differently.

"Mind what's left."

"God does," Jesus is saying when he tells the man, and us, to get up and walk. The gospel also tells us we are loved with more love than we'll be able to accept, unless we rise in love to something like eternal life. That's what this human walk of life is about.

6 Theodore Roethke, "The Waking," *The Collected Poems of Theodore Roethke* (Garden City, NY: Doubleday, 1961), 108.

God walks with us in the world, an unseen, haunting presence. The mystery and celebration is that we learn by walking where we have to go, and with whom.

And finally, there is the laughter—always the laughter. Alice and Violet laughing as the iron scorches a week's wages away from a poor woman, but the world coming right side up at the same time. And don't you suppose Jesus was laughing, and the man as well, as he rolled up his mat and hitched himself on out of thirty-eight years of fraud, and the world coming right side up again? Don't you suppose he was laughing—at himself being free at last, over the wonder of the world, for the "among us" of God's kingdom?

". . . laughter is serious. More complicated, more serious than tears."

Of course, we cry. More of us need to learn to do it better, and more often, given the way we treat each other and the world. Tears are necessary, a prelude to doing something about what makes us cry.

Then the laughter. That's a real thing. All the while, the laughter. Every step, the laughter. We laugh in wonder, in delight. We laugh at our foolishness, which gives perspective. We laugh in relief, which gives us strange comfort. We laugh in confidence, not that we will win but that God will, *is* even now, and in God's sneaky way, there'll be no losers—except maybe those who refuse to stand and walk.

Laughter is more serious than tears because in tears we take only the human side of things seriously. In laughter, we take the mystery of God's side more seriously. Indeed, laughter is the truth of taking God more seriously than we take ourselves.

Back when *The Saturday Evening Post* magazine had covers by Norman Rockwell, they also had covers by Richard Sargent. One of Dick Sargent's covers was of a woman in church singing at the top of her lungs, blissfully oblivious to the fact that children were giggling at her and adults were singing somewhere between grimaces and chuckles. The woman's name was Marion Poggenburg. I know, because both she and Dick Sargent were members of a church I once served in New Rochelle, New York.

What it didn't show was that Marion Poggenburg just had a radical mastectomy. She was a large, buxom woman. She joked that her operation "left a lot of me missing." She knew her chances for a cure weren't good, and at first she was depressed. She'd been unable to have children. She'd lost her husband. Now this.

But then, as she put it, "I looked my faith straight in the face, or it looked me straight in the face, and frankly, neither face was all that pretty. But I realized that I had to leave some things up to God, just as God had left some things up to me. Isn't that what love is all about, after all? So it's up to me to get on with living my days, however many there are. The best I can. With all that's left of me."

And that's what she did. Dick Sargent's portrayal of her singing in church was really very typical of her. She was irrepressibly vital. She was the last of the .400 hitters—she hit about 4 out of 10 notes of every hymn. Yet she sang as loudly as she could, even though her vibrato sounded a little like a car with a low battery trying to start on a cold morning. She never finished the verses when everyone else did. So half the last line of every hymn was a Marion Poggenburg solo. She told people that if she didn't have to stuff half her bra with old socks, which "confines my breathing a little," she could sing even better.

She prayed the same way, only faster, as if trying to drag us by the collar to the throne of grace which, I have a hunch, she probably did. There was no way you could come to church and pray, or join in singing the hymns, without leaving feeling better and laughing a little on your way home.

Just before I left that church, Marion took me and my family to what she called her "hideaway," a little place called Pea Island in Long Island Sound. We sat there in the sand, she in her old-fashioned bathing suit, and watched the waves break against the shore. She said, "I want to forgive you for leaving. But, you know, I'll be leaving myself soon. Truth is, I'm as ready to die as to live, and I really believe either means the other, when all's said and done, if you know what I mean. Anyway, I decided months ago, that part's up to God. My part is being ready and doing whichever."

Then she went tromping off into the ocean and began splashing around. I watched her with tears in my eyes. After a few moments, she turned and motioned for me to come in. She was laughing. She shouted, "Isn't this wonderful? Come on. You'll see." I joined her, and started laughing, too. That's how I remember Marion Poggenburg. She taught me something about mystery and celebration I'm still trying to learn.

> *"Do you want to be healed?"*
> *"Mindwhat's left."*
> *"Nobody's asking you to take it. I'm sayin make it, make it."*
> *"Stand up, take your mat and walk."*

And laugh, for Christ's sake and for ours, for the haunt of grace is with us wherever we walk, even to the end of the age.

More Than Enough

Someone once said that if someone puts together two words about music, one of them will be wrong. I invite you to remember that as you play over the score of these words.

Many years ago, I quoted in a sermon something about a jazz scene from James Baldwin's novel *Another Country.* A friend liked the quote and used it in a book he was writing, without crediting me for finding it. I was young, and that made me angry, as though somehow the quote belonged to me.

About a year ago, I was in a bookstore leafing through another book and discovered that the author had used the same Baldwin quote and attributed the source to the friend who had borrowed it from me years ago. I was older and smiled. After all, I'd borrowed it from Baldwin, and he was probably writing about an actual incident.

It occurs to me now that the trip the quote took over the years is a little like jazz itself. More deeply, it's a little like life itself. In some way, the quote was something like a riff each of us plays through our lives in the larger concert of human experience. Though the Baldwin quote was a riff of words, not music, three times the quote came around in a different setting. Three times it gave something special to the persons who heard it, to say nothing of all who read it. So now, the piece comes round to me again, or actually, comes round to Baldwin again:

> The joint, as Fats Waller would have said, was jumping . . . And, during the last set . . . the saxophone player . . . took off on a terrific solo. He was a kid . . . from some insane place like Jersey City or Syracuse, but somewhere along the line he had discovered that he could say it with a saxophone . . . He stood there, wide-legged, humping the air, filling his barrel chest, shivering in the rags of his twenty-odd years, and screaming through the horn *Do you love me? Do you love me? Do you love me?* And, again, *Do you love me? Do you* love *me? Do you love me?* . . . the same phrase, unbearably, endlessly, and variously repeated, with all of the force the boy had.
>
> . . . the question was terrible and real; the boy was blowing with his lungs and guts out of his own short past; somewhere in that past, in the gutters or gang fights. . . in the acrid room . . . behind marijuana or the needle, under the smell . . . in the precinct basement, he had received the blow from which he never would recover and this no one wanted to believe. *Do you love me? Do you love me? Do you love* me? The men

> on the stand stayed with him, cool and at a little distance, adding and questioning . . . but each man knew that the boy was blowing for every one of them.[1]

In a thousand ways for me, and I believe for each of us, jazz keeps asking that question, our question of each other, perhaps, or of life, or of the universe, or of God: *"Do you love me?"* When things get twisted out of shape for us, when pain hits, or loss, or failure, or illness, or the face in the mirror looks back with more sags and wrinkles than we remember gathering over the years, and the whole mysterious shebang of it overwhelms us with awe and questions we feel we're going to drown in, something in us whispers or screams out, *"Do you love me?"* Do I matter, am I worth anything much beyond this moment, or to those close beside me who matter so much to me? Something in jazz blows this riff for all of us.

But the wonder runs even deeper than that. Something in jazz plays the answer, and the answer is "Yes." Jazz, like longing, like grace, haunts us, pours out the ache and agony of our human struggle. It began in the experience of slaves, of wars, of depressions, of betrayals in church and state, of gutters and gangs, and blows in precinct basements and World Trade Towers, and it resonates to whatever our particular versions of the ache and agony of life are. What does it all mean?

"Do you love me? Do you love me?"

Then, around the edges, and in the midst of this wondrous mess, and out of it, comes the joy, the wild or quiet passion, the incredible creativity and hope and faith, the music of the "Yes, I love you."

The "Yes" expresses itself in a thousand other amazing ways, other surprising variations, other irrepressible riffs that are also ours. When asked about jazz, Louis Armstrong answered simply, "What we play is life." Jazz takes the stuff of our common life, the miracles of the ordinary, and plays it with such imagination, and love, that it reminds us it's all uncommon, extraordinary, even sacred, all that about us and our life. And it reminds us of the God who gives life to us, over and over and over again, who is the source of all creativity, and who keeps saying "Yes" to us in one mysterious riff after another. "Yes" is perhaps the one right word about jazz, the word grace shares with jazz, the ultimate word of faith, and of life itself.

1 James Baldwin, *Another Country* (New York: Vintage Books, 1960), 8–9.

A Gift for Whoever*

Not long ago, the train I was taking to Hartford, Connecticut, made a stop in New York City. Since it was a thirty-minute layover, I got off the train to stretch my legs and walk around Penn Station. In getting back on the train, I tripped and fell headfirst onto the steel floor of the boarding platform. My first reaction was embarrassment, hoping no one saw me or heard the crash.

I got to my knees. All I could see were a few stars whirling around. I pulled myself to my feet and began looking for my glasses. I spotted them, frames twisted grotesquely, one lens missing. I picked them up, stuffed them in my pocket, and began frantically groping for the missing lens. I found it and pocketed it with the frames.

By then perhaps thirty seconds had elapsed, and I realized there was blood all over my shirt, my pants, and the platform. I pressed my handkerchief to the cut over my eye just as the woman conductor approached. She took my arm, expressed concern, offered to take me for medical attention up in the station. I keep telling her, "No, No, I'm fine. Don't bother. It's nothing."

A second conductor appeared, big as a tackle on the New York Giants football team. He looked at the cut and insisted I needed stitches. "We'll have a doctor take care of you and put you on the next train north," he said.

"I'm all right. Really," I insisted, blood still streaming down my face. "Head cuts like this bleed a lot. It'll stop soon. Thanks, but I really don't need anything. I'm okay."

A third uniform took shape in the haze. He had a badge. "Look," he said, "I'll call an ambulance, we'll get you taken care of and back on a later train."

* When this reflection was originally presented as a sermon, jazz interludes were offered between each section.

I blustered back, "I don't need an ambulance, and I'm not getting off this train. I have to get to Hartford to speak tonight and this weekend. I don't need anything. I'm okay. Thanks anyway."

They led me to the Club Car adjacent to where we were standing and made me sit down. I admit by then I was glad to do that. I was feeling a little dizzy. Someone got me some water. The train was about to pull out. The three good Samaritans hurriedly conferred. The one with the badge finally said, "It's up to you. We can't force you to accept help. But you'll have to sign a release before you leave the train in Hartford." I agreed. They left. The train pulled out. I put on my dark glasses and sat staring out the window all the way to Hartford.

Staring out the window and thinking. What makes me, maybe most of us, so resistant to help, so unwilling to admit and accept the care we need? Whoever wrote the Proverb "Pride goes before a fall" didn't get it quite right. Pride also seems to go *with* a fall and *after* a fall. Not just a physical fall but all the other ways we stumble, hit our limitations, get hurt, experience need, and deny the truth about ourselves. To our own detriment, we choose the illusion of being self-sufficient, in control, independent. Pressing a handkerchief to my eye, I lied through my blood, "I'm fine. I don't need anything." I offer that as a metaphor about most of us.

Staring out the window and thinking. And remembering something the wonderful priest, teacher, and mystic Henri Nouwen said: "The most difficult thing of all is learning to be loved." Why is it so hard to learn? I suppose love is what we long for most. And yet. . . we proud ones resist. Why?

Staring and thinking. Thinking we resist because love is always a gift. It's nothing we earn, nothing we deserve, nothing we can force, control, win—all those ways, all those things that pride insists we have to do. Earning, deserving is what we're conditioned to do. Falling, failing, flaws are shameful. Gifts are hard for us. Rewards, we're better at. And yet. . . love is always a gift. Some person's love for us. God's love for us all. The only way to have it is to accept it. Simple, and hard, as that.

"The most difficult thing of all is learning to be loved."

And maybe jazz is a good teacher when we pay attention. In an interview, Miles Davis said the secret of jazz musicians is they "don't play what's there, [they] play what's not there."

Who knows for sure what he meant, except all of us get a hint when we listen to jazz. Somehow it's about playing what isn't there, what's more than is visible on the musical score. It's a little like love—maybe more than a little. It's a gift. It's beyond our control, deeper than can be measured, earned, more than a reward. It's just played. It's just heard. It's at least half mystery. Just as is the gospel, and mercy, and grace, and God.

Like love, jazz somehow makes us a bit homesick for something beyond our reach, but it also touches us, sets our feet tapping, our bodies moving, our pulses beating faster, our hearts singing. It brings out of us what our pride denies about us: our need, our hope, our longing for love. For a moment, maybe longer, we accept the gift. And for a moment, maybe longer, life is full, pressed down, shaken together, running over with the gift of it. A gift for whoever will accept it, for what it is.

Staring out the window and thinking, my pride began a meltdown. I realized how too typically sad and foolish I was in denying my need on that train platform in New York—and most of the other places I've been in my life. Sometimes things happen that lead to a meltdown of pride if we dare to let it happen. If we dare to admit our mortality, our frailty . . . and how wonderful it is that we are not only lovers at heart, but beloved at heart, the heart God put into us.

All that weekend I explained how I came by the lovely purple stain around my eye. People said they were afraid to ask because they thought it might be a birthmark. I said, "No, it's not a birthmark. Maybe a re-birth mark, though."

The great jazz musician Wynton Marsalis led a Master Class at the school where my daughter is an administrator. After the young musicians finished their first number, Marsalis asked them what the trumpeter had done during his riff. No one could answer. Marsalis said, "You know, jazz isn't just about playing your own instrument. It's about listening to others. You have to listen in order to know your place in the bigger picture."

Jazz, faith, life, the gospel is about listening. Listening to others, to our deepest longing, to our gifts, yes, but also to our limits, our needs, our mortality. Listening to the intimations of God. Listening in order to know our amazing place in the bigger picture.

A Kiss for Each

Not long ago, a doctor friend gave me a copy of Richard Selzer's book *Mortal Lessons.* My friend told me he thought I'd like the book, perhaps find it a book about faith, even God. He was right. This gifted writer and gifted surgeon wrote of an experience that struck me so powerfully, it settled in my soul like a cooing dove:

> I stand by the bed where a young woman lies, her face postoperative, her mouth twisted in palsy, clownish. A tiny twig of the facial nerve, the one to the muscles of her mouth, has been severed. She will be thus from now on. The surgeon had followed with religious fervor the curve of her flesh; I promise you that. Nevertheless, to remove the tumor in her cheek, I had cut the little nerve.
>
> Her young husband is in the room. He stands on the opposite side of the bed, and together they seem to dwell in the evening lamplight, isolated from me, private. Who are they, I ask myself, he and this wry-mouth I have made, who gaze at and touch each other so generously, greedily? The young woman speaks.
>
> "Will my mouth always be like this?" she asks.
>
> "Yes," I say, "it will. It is because the nerve was cut."
>
> She nods, and is silent. But the young man smiles.
>
> "I like it," he says. "It is kind of cute."
>
> All at once I *know* who he is. I understand, and I lower my gaze. One is not bold in an encounter with a god. Unmindful, he bends to kiss her crooked mouth, and I am so close I can see how he twists his own lips to accommodate to hers, to show her that their kiss still works.[1]

1 Richard Selzer, *Mortal Lessons: Notes on the Art of Surgery* (New York: Harcourt Brace & Company, 1974), 45–46.

It puts a lump in your throat, doesn't it? I think of all the people I've known in my life who bear the wounds, the scars that have shaped, and reshaped, their lives in painful ways. That includes everyone I've known, really. I suspect you can say the same about people you've known. You can say it about yourself, can't you? All of us bear burdens, carry wounds, that mark our lives.

So don't all of us wonder if we will always be this way? Since we are human beings, the answer is "Yes." Because something cut us some way. And not just once. We all know heartbreak.

The strange thing is that heartbreak opens us to each other, and to God, in ways that change us. We change more from crises than from intention, don't we? I remember asking my psychiatrist after years of therapy, "John, how long am I going to have these damn problems?"

My problems were painful, and I wanted to be rid of them. I wanted to be perfect. Don't we all? Not being perfect tormented me because I thought that's what I should be. John's answer was liberating.

He said, "All your life."

In that moment I got permission from John to join the human family.

But the incredible thing isn't just that our lives are twisted by wounds of one kind or another. The wonder is that there are those in our lives who kiss us anyway. It's a human kiss, but somehow more than that. Eternally more!

Ornette Coleman once said that "Jazz is the only music in which the same note can be played night after night but differently each time." I think that's one way jazz imitates God. Through lots of people—family, friends, even those we think of as enemies—God keeps twisting her or his lips to kiss our twisted lives so our lives not only still work . . . but still work gracefully. One note, grace, played differently in the lives of each of us. It gives us the pitch on which to start singing our song. It give us a glimpse of who God is.

Like jazz, it's enough. More than enough.

Breaking the Code

Luke 4:16-30

The rankled villagers growl, "Is not this Joseph's son?" Their question cuts to the religious chase. It's a dismissal. Near the beginning of his public life, Jesus goes back to his hometown and visits the synagogue. There he tells people who he is and what he's about. He begins by reading the prophet Isaiah: "The Spirit of the Lord is upon me, because he has anointed me to bring good news to the poor. . . release to the captives." Then he says, "Today this scripture has been fulfilled in your hearing." It's a provocative claim. At least no one dozes off. But the hackles-up citizens can't wait to set Jesus straight. "Don't give us that stuff. We know who you are. We watched you grow up. You're just the carpenter's kid. We know the messiah profile and you're no messiah! So stifle this ridiculous posturing. Don't get out of line and make trouble."

"Is not this Joseph's son?" It's a capsule version of people's response to Jesus from first to last, from beginning to end. And from then to now, because we also know who Jesus is, and isn't, don't we? Ergo, we also know who God is, and isn't, right? Of course. So?

So this. Amidst the flurry of reminiscences written about Jacqueline Kennedy Onassis when she died, the words of Adam Gopnik snagged my attention: "Everything that we Americans did to her tried to turn her into an object—on the night of her death, ABC thought it seemly to run not once but twice the film of her husband's murder—and everything she did was to try to make herself back into a subject."[1]

Gopnik's observation disturbs like a siren in the night. It goes far beyond Jackie O. We are all good at making objects of people. We put each other in pigeon holes, as if we were pigeons. It goes like this: he acts like a man, she reacts like a woman, and there you have it. He's white, she's African American, and that explains it. He's clergy, a social worker, she's a lawyer, a doctor, he's a teacher, a businessman, he makes 125 grand per, she's a welfare mother, so now you know. She's a democrat, he's a republican, he's gay, she's divorced, and that's the size of it. In the process of turning others into objects, we do the same to ourselves without realizing it.

"Is not this Joseph's son?" We could be looking out the window or in the mirror when we ask.

We turn ourselves and each other into objects by using a kind of code. We learn the code early. After he had left office, A. Bartlett

1 Adam Gopnik, *New Yorker,* May 30, 1994.

Giamatti gave a speech in which he said that when he became President of Yale, he was pressured to come up with a policy that would define Yale's mission. One night, crouched in his garage between the lawnmower and the snow tires, Giamatti wrote this memo on university policy: ". . . I wish to announce that henceforth, as a matter of University policy, evil is abolished and paradise is restored. I trust all of us will do whatever is possible to achieve this policy objective."[2]

It's an obvious spoof. But Giamatti clearly meant it as a warning against the growing demand to reduce complex realties into simplistic codes and then applying those codes to everything and everyone in our society—such as the deniers of left or right, the diagnosticians for whom all illnesses are similar because all cures are identical, the myopic for whom all the world's pain is simply reduced to their cause, the simplifiers who have boiled life down to a bumper sticker, a T-shirt maxim.[3] These are dangerous trends that impoverish us all.

We all know the codes. We all use them. We use them because they're efficient, time-saving, a quick way to communicate partial truths that are useful. The trouble comes when we begin to take those fragments of truth as the whole truth, or even a basic truth, about each other and ourselves.

"Is not this Joseph's son?"

And there we are with the villagers growling about Jesus among themselves, "Sure, this is Joseph's son. We know the scoop on him, the script to follow in dealing with him." And so they do because they've made an object of him. That makes it easier to dismiss him, to run him out of town in the end. It's all so familiar.

The great Jewish philosopher Martin Buber said we often turn "Thou's" into "its" and live in a world of "I-it" relationships, even in our families. We make objects, "its," of human beings and collude in making ourselves "its" as well. And yet, what's holy in life, what we deeply long for, are I-Thou relationships.

But the concern on my heart isn't just that we make objects of each other. My concern is to keep "it" from happening to us. How do we break the code that reduces us to objects, even to ourselves? What was so striking about Gopnik's reflection on Jackie Onassis was that "everything she did was to try to make herself back into a subject."

As I thought about it, I realized that Jesus always insisted on making himself back into a subject when people tried to make him an object: "good," as the rich man tried to do in Luke 18; or "political revolutionary," as the mother of James and John tried to do in Matthew 20; or "Messiah" as Peter declared in Mark 8. Among other reasons to tell the disciples not to say anything like that about him was

2 A. Bartlett Giamatti, *A Free and Ordered Space: The Real World of the University* (New York: W. W. Norton & Company, 1988), 18.

3 The substance and point of Giamatti's thoughts are found in more academic language in his essays on liberal education in *A Free and Ordered Space*.

his resisting being made the "expected" object, or "King" by coming down from the cross as the jeering leaders challenged him to do.

I believe that's what God is always about, as well, trying to make himself/herself, into a subject, not an object—not an oblong blur, not a philosophical abstraction or First Cause, not a generalized Idea, not an aesthetic icon or a magician to do miracles on cue of the fervently faithful, not any of the ways we tend to make God an object. God becoming a subject is at least part of what the incarnation means. So what could making ourselves subjects mean to us?

***

Before anything else, I believe breaking the code and making ourselves subjects involves claiming our own strange particularities, our own gifts and ground. That's what Jesus was doing there in the Nazareth synagogue—and it's hard to do! Luke's account of it, as well as our own experience, confirms just how hard. To keep making ourselves subjects, we have to resist a lot of pressure to be something we aren't, to do things that aren't rooted in our core. The constant temptation is to act and speak, even think, as if we were only our profession, our work, our race or gender or marital status, or social standing or nationality, or political persuasion—or whatever "it" is—in order to belong, function, get ahead, be "well liked," as Willy Loman put it in *Death of a Salesman*,

I can't tell you how much I dislike being coded as a minister. It shrinks my relationships by defining people's expectations of me and, therefore, their responses to me. If I play that game—and too often I do—I'm an accomplice in the crime of making myself an "it," an object rather than a flesh-and-blood, wondrous yet warted person. We all play that code game because we want to succeed, pay the mortgage, stock the pantry, dress the style, send the kids to camp or college. Of course, we need those things. But how much of them do we need, and at what price? If the price is our soul, if the price is allowing ourselves to ossify into being objects, it's too high.

But there's also a cost in making ourselves a subject again and again and again, dozens of times a day. The cost is a lot of courage. The cost is paying attention to our deepest longing instead of the pitch of hucksters of all stripes. The cost is a willingness to be humiliated, which I believe is what humility really means. The cost is daring to stand our ground against the constant undertow of conformity.

The cost is pitching our tent in the sometimes uncomfortable place of being with others who also keep trying to remake themselves as subjects. They confront, challenge, and support us. They care enough to tell us what they really think and see and mean, and so what we need to hear, not what we want to hear. It is like being Jacob wrestling with the stranger until he got a blessing from him, because that is how we get a blessing and give one in return (Genesis 32:22ff). The cost is being faithful in our living even when our faith is shaky, or small as a mustard seed. I believe that's what Jesus was about, and what he calls us to be about as well.

The choice to keep making ourselves subjects is one of the recurring crossroad choices of life and of faith. Perhaps it is too simple, but only a little, to suggest that the choice is between our real self and gaining pseudo status, between risky freedom and comfortable conformity.

The poet W. H. Auden describes this choice provocatively in his poem "For the Time Being":

SIMEON

> . . . by Him {Jesus} is illuminated the time in which we execute those choices through which our freedom is realized or prevented, for the course of History is predictable in the degree to which all men love themselves, and spontaneous in the degree to which each man loves God and through Him {God} his neighbor.

CHORUS

> The distresses of choice are our chance to be blessed.[4]

4 W. H. Auden, "For the Time Being," *Collected Longer Poems* (New York: Random House, 1969), 182.

"The distresses of choice are our chance to be blessed."

Mid-life crisis isn't the right term for the turbulence of frustration and anxiety that results in those changes some people make at 40 or 50. The term should be pre-life crisis, and a pre-life crisis can strike at any time from 14 to 44 to 64 to 84. A pre-life crisis is about daring to keep remaking ourselves back into subjects for our own and everyone's sake.

In her book *For Love,* Sue Miller writes of a man named Jack whose wife, Evelyn, suffered a stroke that left her terribly incapacitated. It was a pre-life crisis for Jack. What happened as a result was that he rediscovered himself, and his wife. By holding and touching Evelyn, by giving when there was nothing to get back from her, he learned to love her again, in a different way. There was no obvious gain in it, except living as a subject, seeing his wife as a subject, and exercising the compassion at his core, and the freedom in that.[5]

When you strip it down, life is not first of all about getting things, or getting ahead, or getting anything much. It's about giving. I'm not talking about giving things or money, though if there are too many things we can't live without, we need to have a hard look at that. If we aren't generous, we need to examine what that says about us.

5 Sue Miller, *For Love* (New York: HarperCollins Publishers, 1994).

What I'm really calling us to is giving our *selves* by constantly remaking ourselves back into subjects for our own sakes and for the sake of others—and for the sake of God. I deeply believe that's what's involved in loving our neighbors as ourselves. God has given each of us gifts that are unique to us. Each of us is one of a kind, the only one that will ever live in this time and world with just the constellation of gifts each of us has. Surely we would not have those gifts unless God wants us to claim them and give them, whatever they are.

"The distresses of choice are our chance to be blessed."

So one key choice in becoming a subject is to make our gifts into verbs, to act on them, live them out. Not to risk that is to be an accomplice in the fraud of settling for being an object rather than remaking ourselves back into subjects at least two or three times a day. It doesn't matter what people do with our gifts. What matters is that when we dare to give our gifts, we become a subject not an object for them. In that dare is our freedom.

And in that dare is the option of freedom for others, as well. Our choice for making ourselves subjects gives them that choice. It makes something different possible for them. It's an invitation to others to relate to us subject to subject. Love is more than a meeting of bodies, it is a meeting of souls. That meeting is what we so deeply long toward. When we dare to give our selves to others, we invite others to move toward that meeting with us. We make that choice possible for them, just as Jesus makes it possible for us. For the heart of freedom is not to be afraid to risk moving toward each other.

"The distresses of choice are our chance to be blessed."

Now let's swat the fly buzzing around the edges of what I'm saying. Isn't this about too much self-concern, too much self-preoccupation, too much plain selfishness? Well, it might be and that's a danger. But those things are part of everything we do, and always a danger. But consider something Oscar Wilde said: "Selfishness is not living as one wishes to live; it is asking others to live as one wishes to live." Let that sink in!

Wilde's words seem to be powerful, accurate, full of grace and the gospel. To ask, to manipulate, to try to seduce or coerce others to live as we wish to live is a terrible kind of tyranny. Yet that tyranny is epidemic.

Here's an instance. The Judicial Council of the United Methodist Church has ruled that no United Methodist clergy can perform same gender Covenant Services, nor can any United Methodist Church let its facilities be used for such a service. Clergy can lose their ordination orders if they ignore this rule. That is institutional selfishness. That is to treat homosexual persons as objects when they are as complex and human as anyone else, and often more faithful. That's tyranny.

The way to resist tyranny is to live as we "wish to live," as we most deeply long to live, and so invite others to do the same. It is to keep remaking ourselves into subjects and encouraging others to do so, too. It takes courage to do that. But remember courage is contagious. As a boy I remember my Dad singing with gusto, "Give me ten men who are stout hearted men, and I'll soon give you ten thousand more." I believe it works that way, and that is how change happens.

Of course, there's a cost in making ourselves subjects. There's a cost in treating others as subjects. That's why it takes courage. Maybe the cost will be a loss of popularity or promotion. Surely the cost will be criticism, for many people would rather criticize other's choices and gifts than claim their own. Criticism is easier. I know that. So do you. But there is enormous benefit in being a subject rather than an object.

So Jesus did not back down from his claim of who he was and what he was about. He did not fudge on his claim that "the spirit of the Lord is upon me," that he was a bringer of "good news," a prophet, a healer, a liberator, a fulfiller not an exploiter. He did not shrink under ridicule and threat of rejection. In a desperate effort to make Jesus an object, others tried to make him a dead man. But when the raging crowd tried to do that in Jesus' hometown, they didn't succeed. Even when, at last, people did manage to make Jesus into an object by killing him, making him a dead body, God remade him back into a subject. That's the way of resurrection.

We try to make Jesus an object, an icon, an answer, an idol, a lover of our own specifications, a rubber stamp of our preferences, but God continually surprises us by making him back into a subject.

My good friend Bill Coffin says that Jesus preferred to be rejected for who he was rather than to be accepted for who he wasn't. That is freedom, and the promise of the gospel. Jesus invites and enables us to join him in fighting to remake ourselves into subjects, to claim and live out our particular gifts. He urges us to trust him and step out on the promise of freedom. That is the way faith moves once and again and a thousand times.

***

Another thing involved in breaking the code and being a subject is showing our face, our real face. It's about being present to others, moment by moment. There is a kind of deep security in claiming our own gifts that frees us to really pay attention to other people. We don't have to prove anything, or compete with them, or cut them down to make ourselves look bigger, smarter, better, more important.

When we claim our own gifts, we don't have to do all those subtle, insidious things that make us into an object to put along side other objects, all those things men and women do to each other, or clergy do to each other and parishioners, or doctors to patients, or lawyers to clients, or teachers to students, parents to children, siblings to each other, and on and on.

In the ugly game of comparisons, someone is always wounded and left feeling terribly insufficient. That's the point of the game, isn't it? It's a bad game to be as good at as most of us are. I'm good at it, and I'm ashamed of that because I know, from the losers' side, the pain it causes, and from the winner's side, the emptiness it leaves behind.

The game of comparative insufficiency often operates with a vengeance, even in marriage. Columnist Barbara Ehrenreich writes that in our day, "A spouse . . . is expected to be not only a co-provider and mate, but a co-parent, financial partner, romantic love object, best friend, fitness adviser, home repair person and scintillating companion . . . In what other area of life would we demand that any one person fulfill such a huge multiplicity of needs? No one would ask his or her accountant to come by and prune the shrubbery, or the pediatrician to take out the garbage . . . only in marriage do we demand the all-purpose . . . Renaissance person."[6]

Well, I'm sure it's not *only* in marriage, but it is often in marriage that such demands operate. It's another variation of the code, making each other into objects. The way to break the code is to be present, to show your real face to your partner. To show your face is a metaphor for talking honestly and directly to each other from the heart. It's to negotiate and appreciate each other's unique gifts, even if the shrubs don't get trimmed. That's what it means to be a subject in an "I-Thou" relationship in marriage. Side by side in open sharing not fused in subtle manipulation.

"Selfishness is not living as one wishes to live; it is asking others to live as one wishes to live."

To love our neighbor is to live as we wish to live so we can help liberate others to live as they wish to live. I'm convinced that is one of the things Jesus was about. He struggled to set people free to live, to be subjects with each other and with God. That's why he kept confronting people, holding them accountable to what they said they wanted and believed. That's why he paid attention to all kinds of people, from the lowliest and sickest to the most powerful and wealthy.

We all know people who are trapped in being critical, complaining, cynical, angry, and are not living as they wish to live, no matter how it might look. Often they are people who need attitude adjustments, an enlarged capacity for gratitude, and the courage to risk making life changes. But sometimes people are not living as they wish because the conditions of their lives make it nearly impossible. That could be *partly* our responsibility, especially if we do nothing to address the poverty, disease, exploitation,

6 Barbara Ehrenreich, "Burt, Loni and our way of Life," *Time Magazine*, September 20, 1993.

and despair about which people rightly complain.

Sometimes their complaints become violent, and our reactions become largely vengeful. We dehumanize ourselves and each other. We become objects—enemies, criminals, terrorists, oppressors, righteous warriors, evil ones. In a column in the Israeli newspaper *Yedoit Ahronot,* Nahum Barnea put the matter succinctly: "The terrorism of suicide bombings is born of despair. There is no military solution to despair."

That's a powerful, moral, humanizing truth about the despair of terrorist suicide bombings in the market places and buses and Seder gatherings in Israel and those in the New York World Trade Center and the Washington, D.C., Pentagon. Whatever military action is required, it will not bring a solution to despair. To move toward a solution requires that we remake ourselves into subjects, see others as subjects and invite us all to act accordingly.

To act accordingly would be to take the lead in working together in creating conditions that will overcome poverty, hunger, disease, oppression. Deep down, we all wish to live—long to live—the way God put it in us to live. Whether we call that God "Allah" or "Yahweh" or "Father," the longing in us, and God's longing for us, is to live as subjects together in humility, fairness, respect, justice, and peace in our families and in the family of humanity.

Go back for a moment to what Gopnik said about Jackie O trying to be a subject rather than an object. A key part of that effort was that rather than insisting attention be focused on her importance and celebrity, "Mrs. Onassis paid new people the infinitely difficult compliment of assuming that the baggage you both brought to the table was of infinitely less importance than the new gifts you might take away from it. Those gifts, for her, included making her own [self] available and undramatic. . . letting a person into her charmed circle . . ."[7]

There it is!

Every one of us has a charmed circle. Showing our real face, paying attention, being less concerned for past baggage than for being open to present gifts, letting others into our circle—which is the circle of grace—is to be a subject, not an object, and invites others to be subjects, too. I believe that's a huge part of what Jesus is and does by showing us that the kingdom of God is in our midst, not in our possession.

***

One last thing involved in breaking the code and making ourselves subjects every day is, instead of praying our hearts out, praying our hearts "in." I believe prayer is a basic way to be a subject with God, and to respond to God as a subject.

When we go about trying to prove or disprove God's existence, or when we talk

7 Gopnik, *New Yorker.*

about God rather than *to* God, or when we consider God to be our name for the objective laws that govern the universe, or the impersonal enforcer of moral laws, or the endorser of our causes and privileges, God becomes an object.

Prayer opens us to God as a subject, a "Thou" for an "I" to be in relationship with, to worship with our gifts, to pay attention to with our presence. Prayer is the source of the power to constantly make ourselves back into subjects in a world intent on making us objects. Praying your heart "in" is to resist the tendency to become "heartless" in the frantic, impersonal rush of the world. Prayer is being open to the surprises, the wonder, the grace of an I-Thou relationship with God, dynamic as that relationship can be.

It's not such a solemn, sanctimonious thing, either. In Sue Miller's novel *For Love,* a middle-age woman, Lottie, is having supper with her college-age son, Ryan. Lottie is searching for some kind of healing for herself and her past, including her estranged brother, Cameron, and her own dead mother whose house she and Ryan have been working on together for most of the summer.

Lottie and Ryan sit drinking their beer. Ryan says, "Do you think Uncle Cam is. . . well, dangerous?"

"I don't know, hon. He *is* such a humorless guy, finally."

"What does humor have to do with it?"

"It just does. Believe me, it does."

"That's ridiculous, Mom. What could possibly be funny in this situation?"

"I don't know. I mean, of course, really nothing is. I don't mean that kind of humor, I guess. Just. . . I guess I don't think you can forgive yourself for anything—much less forgive anyone else—if you can't somehow let go of. . . what? The *gravity* of everything? Something like that."[8]

I agree, it is something like that, like the gravity of everything. Certainly religion is serious, but it isn't grave. Yet it seems to exist in a cloud of gravity for too many people who find that almost reason enough to head for the door. At least, I hope *almost*.

Take that day in the synagogue. I imagine Jesus being full of enthusiasm and excitement as he looks at the familiar faces he's known as a boy and announces to them, "Today this scripture [of Isaiah] has been fulfilled in your hearing." Can't you imagine him smiling, even laughing, as he says that? Remember, Jesus was thirty years old at that moment, not the thirteen- or fourteen-year-old of the villagers' petrified perceptions, nor the two-thousand-year-old of our "gentle Jesus meek and mild" revised version of him.

Think of the excitement and fun he calls us to join him in having. Think of the fun of being a live subject outside the box of those villagers' dead stereotypes of him, or the fun he has being himself outside the boxes we try to put him in. Isn't that appealing?

8 Miller, *For Love,* 266.

Think of the excitement of releasing prisoners locked in similar kinds of boxes. Think of the fun of bringing good news to the poor that they are valued by God, and of healing the blindness of people who can't see the gifts they have to give each other. Imagine the fun in setting free people oppressed by conditions that keep them from living as they wish to live instead of the way others wish, or collude, in making them live. Sound like a good time, a good news time? Then push past the gravity of everything summed up in that dismissive question, *"Is not this Joseph's son?"*

The point I'm after is that there is vitality, excitement, fun in being a subject. There's fun in praying, fun in accepting and giving forgiveness, excitement in I-Thou relationships, excitement in the gospel. Someone once said, "God answers prayer in four ways: yes, no, later, and you've got to be kidding." Sometimes when I pray, I do hear, "You've got to be kidding." Not a bad way to get perspective. And if we can giggle a little when we realize that sometimes the joke is on us, that sometimes we *are* the joke, then we've inched a little closer to being a subject.

Maybe you've heard the story about the cruise ship that was sinking and the captain yelled, "Anyone here know how to pray?

One guy stepped forward.

"I do," he said.

"Good," the captain replied. "You pray. The rest of us will put on life preservers. We're one short."

Even so, to live at all and forgive anything, including ourselves, we've got to let go of something like our gravity about everything. We've got to let go of the gravity of ourselves as if the outcome of everything depended on us. Sometimes we lose. Sometimes it's "No" or "You've got to be kidding." And then there's getting on with it, and with God. None of us are objects of fate, victims of a cosmic conspiracy, playthings of happenstance. We are subjects of God who is always trying to be a subject to us and to get free of the ways we make an object of God with our debates and dogmas, our disgruntlements and doubts, and our selfishness in asking God to live the way we wish to live.

Prayer is groping our way toward living as we wish to live, as subjects, and to live that way with God the subject. That's maybe more than half of what grace means. The whole thing comes down to an I-Thou relationship with God, with self, with neighbor, with enemy.

A few years ago, *Reflections,* the Journal of Yale Divinity School, carried the reminiscences of women who graduated from YDS before the sixties. Ruth Shinn, a classmate of mine, wrote that our beloved professor, H. Richard Niebuhr, introduced students to theological education by saying, "Here we don't have answers to questions. Here we have great mysteries to explore." I remember Niebuhr telling us that, and I've never forgotten it. His words apply not just to theological education, but to life itself, and to the gospel, and the Christian faith—great mysteries, the haunting mysteries of grace and of God to explore.

Remaking ourselves as subjects with particular gifts is an essential part of that exploration. Relating to other human subjects is another essential part. Prayer is another.

"Is not this Joseph's son?"

Oh my, what a wondrous mystery that question presses on us. And what a wondrous mystery is the Subject about whom this mystery is asked. So are we invited to be about exploring the wonder of it as subjects—and with our lives.

Annex to the Heart

Psalm 145
John 1:43-51

As do other moments of grace, gratitude often comes to me through the back door. For me, the back door hinges began to squeak open when I began moaning about having to go for a week to lecture at an Academy for Spiritual Formation in Minnesota. I flippantly told people I hoped I'd survive the ordeal and those who attended would, too.

I thought of the week as an ordeal because a few years ago I'd had a painful experience leading one of those Academies in California. Yet, in a moment of temporary insanity, I'd signed on to do another, which qualifies me as a bit of a masochist. Then the time of departure was staring me in the face, and all I could see was a gathering of cloyingly saccharin, overly pious, several-degrees-past-pretentious people.

So I went to Minnesota with a chip on my shoulder. I was going to show them, shake them up, shove them in the right direction, then duck and get out of there. But during the week, that chip on my shoulder became an annex to my heart, and the people there moved in and took up residence. They were open, attentive, responsive, willing to go deep, to consider options, see things in different ways. They were profoundly confirming. It was they who showed me, shook me, shoved me in a different direction.

All of us can name a host of things we're thankful for, and I'd guess that most of what we're thankful for are the obvious good things. We do well to take stock of those good things since the list is long. But that's front door stuff, which fits in our hearts without much of a squeeze. Yet it's because of my experience in Minnesota that I want to look at the back door stuff, for which I'm learning to be thankful. I think the most real and deepest gratitude comes through the back door.

***

First, I'm thankful I was wrong about the Spiritual Academy. When I started pondering that fact, it occurred to me that, more times than not, I'm thankful when I'm wrong—even if I don't feel so at the moment. When I'm wrong, it hurts my pride momentarily, but it builds my humility permanently. It pries me open, it stretches me. I am changed more, by far, when I'm wrong than when I'm right. When I'm right, too often that petrifies my point of view.

Someone once said, "Success is the biggest obstacle to creativity and change." That thought haunts me. So I'm grateful that I spend as much time dancing cheek-to-cheek with failure and error as with success and correctness. When I'm wrong and admit it, it puts me in touch with things in myself, in other people, and in the world, for which I have to build an annex to my heart. The annex is needed for those encounters and experiences that don't fit in the well-worn places of my life. And I believe God moves into the annex of my heart with them. I'm very thankful for that when the truth of it dawns on the horizon beyond the familiar.

In John's gospel, Philip is so captivated by meeting Jesus he goes to find his brother, Nathaniel. When Philip tells his brother about Jesus, Nathaniel shrugs and says, "Can anything good come out of Nazareth?" And Philip says all anyone could say to such a question: "Come and see."

"Can anything good come out of Nazareth?"—that run-down-at-the-heels no place, that den of dullards, that swarm of zeros. Sound familiar? Can anything good come out of Minnesota to match up with my compelling religious insights and inerrant moral judgments?

Even more to the point for many of us, can some "mere human being" like Jesus, a marginal peasant preacher-healer who doesn't meet anyone's rational measure, be someone in whom God comes close? Can anything good come out of the unlikely, the dismissible, the unsophisticated, the irritating, the rejects, the disagreeable, the different, the "lesser," the opposition? Could this person who disturbs our certainties and strums our longing be a glimpse of something essential about who God is and what God does?

"Come and see."

When we remember how often we're wrong—and so remember we could be wrong again—only then do we go and see. Only then might we realize that being wrong is less an embarrassment than an epiphany. Such a realization is a visitation from a larger world than we've yet recognized. It's an occasion in which God moves quietly to stretch our spirits and our minds. And it comes holding hands with gratitude and possibilities.

So every day for a week, I came and saw. I lectured and we discussed and wrestled together. Every day we went to morning prayer, and Communion and Evening Prayer, sang the old hymns that can make me, and maybe you, squirm but get into my bones. Every day for extended periods, and every night, we shared silence until that near-death experience became a nearresurrection experience. And the next to the last day, I told the group I'd come in with an attitude and they'd changed it, or God had changed it through them. I was wrong, and thankful I was.

Thankful because, as I told them, they reminded me of what Jesus said in those familiar words in Matthew 25 about being judged by how we treat him when he comes to us as a stranger, in "the least of these," his brothers and sisters. There are many ways to be the "least of these." Yes, of course, the poor, the sick, the oppressed are perhaps foremost among the least of these, and we must remember that. But each of us, in some way, are the least of these as well. That's what makes us brothers and sisters. That's what makes us members of the human family, members of God's family. That's what guards us against our becoming, condescending, self-righteous types who are going to "save" these poor people, whomever we define as being poor because we assume they're inferior—as I pre-defined the Academy people in Minnesota. We'll see Christ in each other if we are open, attentive to different ways of seeing things.

So I saw Christ in those middle-class, educated, not obviously poor, wounded people—like me. All through the week people came to me to talk, to share their stories, asking if we could pray together.

One was a mother whose beautiful teenage daughter had lupus, which was affecting her brain.

One was a shy woman who shared the story of her daughter's struggle with depression and said she felt helpless except to love her daughter and pray, because even though she loved her daughter with all her heart, she trusted God loved her daughter even more.

One was a young man in agony because he deeply loved his wife and children but had never told anyone, other than me at that moment, that he was gay and didn't know what to do. We talked and prayed, and he asked if he could stay in touch with me and I said I hoped he would.

One was an older man who planned to picket the School of the Americas and knew he would be sent to prison for many months.

One was a woman with cancer who lived alone and wrote music of praise and gave me a copy.

The way the Academy people expressed their faith, the words they used differed from mine, but they were real and so was their faith.

"Come and see."

I was wrong, and so I came to see Christ in those brothers and sisters. And I tell you now, being wrong renewed my near-sighted eyes. I am thankful when I'm wrong because it helps me see God's presence where I hadn't thought to look before, or actually thought not to look.

***

Second, I'm grateful when I'm wobbly. Wobbly is another accessory to the gratitude that sneaks in through the back door. I went to Minnesota to be a leader. I suppose that made it easy to presume I was smart and strong, and needed to be. But really, underneath, I was anxious. When I joked that I hoped I'd survive the week at the Academy, under the bravado I really meant it more than I was willing to honestly admit.

Strange how that goes, isn't it? I don't know who first said, "We always put our best foot forward when it's the other foot that needs the attention," but it's true. I'm good at pretending to be smart and strong when I really feel inadequate and wobbly. I pretend to be sure and self-sufficient when I really need help, challenge, correction. I think we're all good at pretending like that when we really need and long for each other's honest presence, each other's thinking and prayers. I really felt wobbly when I left for the Academy. I wasn't at all sure if I could do what I thought had to be done there, since I didn't see myself as any kind of expert in spiritual formation.

But God is sneaky. One night, a clergyman who attended the Academy came to me to talk about what I was saying about integrity and being authentic. Earlier, when we were having lunch together, he'd told me that he'd been in an accident and his legs had been damaged. Subsequent surgery for cancer worsened his condition, and it had progressed until he faced losing all use of his legs. Now he got around in a wheelchair, though at times he could negotiate a little with crutches. He'd been forced to retire in his early fifties because of his disability. I asked him if he was angry about his condition, and he replied, "No." But as he said it, trying to smile, his face and his attitude was pinched.

Now, two days later, he wanted to talk and to pray with me. So we did. He told me he longed to be more authentic and honest, but thought it wasn't Christian. He thought he should be strong, optimistic, and brush aside his disability and his feeling of being weak. But what I'd been saying at the Academy made him realize that was phony. When he told me that, I confessed that I was often phony, too. He looked relieved and reached for my hand.

He went on to tell me he really was angry. Then he said, "The funny thing is that when I say that, either out loud or to myself, I feel a lot of energy moving in me. I feel freer. Do you really think God can take me being angry?"

I asked him, "Can *you* take you that way? I don't think it's God who has trouble with your anger. My guess is God will help you use it."

I asked him what he wanted to do. He talked a long time about wanting to establish an inter-faith, inter-church spiritual advisory center for people with all sorts of disabilities. Not just physical but mental and emotional disabilities as well. I told him it seemed to me he was uniquely qualified to take a shot at it, if he could be okay about his own disability. I hunched out my next words: "Maybe that's what the energy in you is about."

His face lit up. "You think so? Is that what you meant when you said God will help me with it?"

I said, "I'm not sure exactly what I meant. You're the one who sees the connection. I'd say, 'Go for it' and see what happens. I do believe God will be in it with you." We talked some more, then prayed together in a kind of wobbly, stammering way.

The next day, the man volunteered to give the meditation for our communion service. He used his crutches to get to the pulpit, and then he hung on to support himself. He began by talking about how our society is all about being strong, being self-sufficient, doing things for ourselves and not asking for help, as if that were demeaning and inhuman. He said his disability had only intensified his dislike of asking for help. So he tried to be self-sufficient and despised himself when he couldn't be. He talked about the macho ideal being the norm, even for women. "It's all about being tough, powerful, fearless, and smart. Weak people are discarded, despised, rejected."

Then he talked about Saint Paul asking God to take away a thorn in his flesh. Instead, God said to Paul, "My grace is sufficient for you, my power is made perfect in weakness" (2 Corinthians 12:9). "Now I'm learning that's what the gospel is about," he said gripping the pulpit. He went on to describe what that was beginning to mean for him, and his dream of starting a spiritual advisory center for disabled people. We knew he wasn't talking just about himself, but about all of us, about everyone.

Disabilities come in many forms. I think of the arrogance and terrible isolation of my compulsion about perfection. I rail against my limitations until I am worn out, and wear others out in the process. Perfectionists drive everyone crazy, as I understand perfectly. I recall once saying to a friend, Carl, that I'd always been taught that whatever I did, even if it was digging a ditch, it had to be "the best." Carl said, "You can't do or be the best at much, or much of the time. I tell my kids sometimes good enough is okay. Getting a C in school is okay."

I almost cried when he said that. Because he's right. We can't do or be the best at everything, or even very much, or maybe in anything. Macho is phony. Those "No Fear" T-shirts cover hearts that know better. Self-sufficiency is a fantasy. "*My grace is sufficient for you, my power is made perfect in weakness.*" It takes courage to admit weakness, but courage is the tap root of faith.

"*Can anything good come out of Nazareth?*" Can a man with a few scraggly followers, and with nail holes in his hands and feet, overthrow Rome, change the course of the world, give abiding meaning to lives through the ages?

"*Come and see.*"

Can anything good come out of you with your weaknesses and limitations? The gospel says, "Yes," if you accept them and throw them in the pot with all the rest of us and our weaknesses and limitations: husbands, wives, kids, all the disabled in the neighborhood, and the welfare moms, the addicts, the homeless, the jobless, the strangely deprived rich, the isolated macho pretenders, all the rest. Do what you can, and that's commitment. Give what you have and are, and that's courage. Then it's about God, and that's faith, hope, trust. It's about grace being sufficient, power working through weakness, and through us.

I'm thankful when I'm wobbly . . . and I'm getting wobblier. Then I can really pray, and then I can let people into my life, and then I can put the burden of pretense down. Then I'll keep adding annexes to my heart to let in other people in whose weakness God is at work, as God is at work in mine. There's no other explanation for any of us. Not really. Build your own annex, and we'll all come in with God.

Permit me this quick aside. Once again, the world seems locked in a terrible, terrifying power struggle. Israel and Palestine slip in each other's blood toward a war of incredible destruction for both sides and the whole Middle East. Everyone knows the only way to peace is for both sides to compromise and to accept each other and live together as two neighbor states. The question is, which will be wobbly in public and move toward building an annex for each other?

There is a war on terrorism underway at the behest of our beloved country. It's a necessary war but surely within limits. The question is, how will it be fought? Only with military force? Only by bombing Hussein out of power and Iraq into misery? Sometimes my lower angels fly to that drum beat. But if we do that, then what? Who wins, who loses, and what is lost or won?

Those are the tough, inescapable moral questions when we get past the first impulse for revenge and second for safety. There is a spiritual, faith dimension to everything, including our response to terrorism.

Surely any war against terrorism must also be a war against poverty, disease, exploitation of the weak by the strong. It's easier to obsess about evil than it is to imagine what it would mean to be good as we see it in Jesus or other great leaders, such as Moses or Isaiah or Gandhi or Mohammed. Just that kind of imagination is a dancing partner of faith. So as a people we need to recognize our own wobbliness. Maybe we need to build an annex to our national heart so it will hold not only Americans but humanity. Maybe admitting our limitation, our need for a true global village isn't such a bad foreign policy. There are people in Israel, and Palestine, and even in this country, who advocate for it. Maybe they, too, are accessories squeezing through the back door. Whether or not we let them in or join them, I, for one, am thankful for their squeeze.

***

Third, and last for now, I'm thankful when I wonder. Wrong, wobbly, wonder. They make a curious combo. Yet, they're all back door stuff that leads to building an annex to the heart because none of them fits easily into our customary living spaces. Wonder comes with gratitude through that back door.

A cartoon in the *New Yorker* showed a couple of middle-aged, sagging-shouldered guys walking down the street carrying brief cases. One of them says to the other, "I'm at the point where I find mixed messages reassuring." Don't you love that? It is reassuring in this world, where so many people, on so many sides of anything, claim to know the absolute truth about everything. I suppose you could go in a dozen different directions with that cartoon. But try this one: Mixed messages, rather than absolute ones, signal that the world is a mysterious place. That more is going on in it than we know. That there's more to truth than we know. That there's more to God than we know. And there's the wonder!

Jewish leaders once asked Jesus if it was lawful to pay taxes to Caesar. The question was a trap to embarrass and discredit him. The Jewish people despised Caesar for occupying and oppressing their country. Yet open opposition meant severe Roman reprisals. Whatever answer Jesus gave, he'd be in trouble, either for supporting Caesar or advocating rebellion. What did Jesus do? He gave a mixed message. He showed them a coin and asked whose image was on it. The answer was Caesar's. So Jesus said, "Render to Caesar the things that are Caesar's and to God the things that are God's." That's a mixed message, not an absolute one. It leaves us to make our own decisions.

The coin of the realm, then and now, belongs to Caesar. So render to Caesar, that is, to country, to society, the things that are rightfully theirs, and be grateful for the benefits they give us in return.

That leaves God. What do we render to God? Well, whose image do we bear, you and I? From page one, the Bible is clear about that. We bear the image of God. What, then, do we render to God? What else but ourselves. But how? When? Where? Ah, mixed messages and wonder.

Here's the heart of it: It's an awesome thing to be a human being! It's a wonder to know that whatever happens in and to this universe, we are part of it and will always be part of it. It's stunning to know that what we are, what we decide, what we do, is a factor in the continued unfolding of creation. So it is profoundly awesome to realize that there's more going on in this world than we know, or than anyone else knows. We are free to do new things. And certainly God is. So the unknown isn't just about things we don't know yet, it's about things that are unknowable to us mortals. Unknowable to anyone! Not scientists or preachers or politicians or economists or poets or prophets or artists or logicians or rationalists, or whoever. No one knows all, or much, of what's going on in this world, in this creation, in these hearts. We live in and with mystery, and so, with wonder.

Aristotle said that life begins in wonder. He didn't go far enough. Life begins in wonder and *continues* and *ends* in wonder.

Most creative things begin and continue in wonder. Poet James Dickey suggests that poets love more intensely, more vitally than other people. Maybe so, since wonder runs up and down poets' spines. But so does it run up and down the spines and within the hearts of people of faith. We are well acquainted with mystery all around and at the depths.

The other thing Dickey said was a quote from his grandmother: "He who ever strives upward, him we can save." I'm not sure what his grandmother meant by that, but I certainly think it applies to poets who, in trying to get something down on paper, strive upward toward words of power and insight that open and lift and surprise us in ways that change how we are in the world.

Even so, people of faith strive upward in a similar way. In fact, I believe all people strive upward, one way or another in some kind of faith, admitted or not. It's a human thing, and most deeply a faith thing. Striving upward is what our deepest longing is about. It's about being saved, made whole, reconciled to each other and God. Striving, not to get ahead, not to get on top, but to reach toward God. That's what it means to pray, to worship, to trust, to risk, to engage each other beneath the surface.

I risk sharing my story "beneath the surface" because I keep going back to it as a hinge moment in my life. It's my very close brush with suicide years ago. I'd prayed and prayed about my depression and anxiety but to no avail. I despaired of God and couldn't see past the darkness. But in the middle of the night I'd decided to end my life, my little four-year-old son padded down the stairs, came over to my lap, hugged me, and went to sleep. I began to cry. I realized that, in some mysterious way, my prayers were answered. I believe such indirect, roundabout ways are God's preferred way to answer prayers. In mysterious ways, we may be answers to each other's prayers but never know it.

I told the people at the Academy this story. I went on to say that I believe even if I had committed suicide, God would still have answered my prayer. God isn't limited by our time. Most of us think God only answers prayers some way that fits our categories, the ways we know things happen. Then there are those mixed messages, those multilayered events and experiences full of wonder, of questions, and so of decisions of what we will trust about life. What seems to me unquestionable is that there are more mysterious things going on than we can know or imagine.

So the story goes on. A few days after I came home, I got an e-mail telling me that the teen-age son of one woman, I'll call her Rose, who had been at the Academy, had committed suicide on the Friday night she returned from that week away. Rose had given me a book of poems she'd written about children, inscribing it with gratitude for our time together. Now her son, I'll call him Mike, was dead by suicide. I was stunned. Grief flooded in. I cried as I groped for words to write to Rose.

Two days after I heard about Rose's son, I got an e-mail from another person I'll call Alice. She also attended the Academy and was close to Rose. Alice wrote me about a vision she'd had the night Rose's son killed himself, though she hadn't gotten that news yet. On the night she came home from the Academy, she had a vision of me standing in the auditorium of the retreat center with a noose dangling over my head. Then she was walking down a long, stone-walled corridor, feeling like she was walking toward the crematorium at Auschwitz. Fire began to rise out of the floor, then it turned to clear water, and flowed out like a river. She sensed that God was crying, and she longed to comfort him.

Alice was sure God wanted her to do something, but she didn't know what. It was after midnight, but Alice walked downstairs where her own thirteen-year-old son was watching television. She told him of her vision and asked if he'd ever thought about suicide. He answered no. Even though it was late, she called a friend she worked with who had been talking about taking his life. Alice explained her vision and talked with her friend for nearly half an hour. He was very grateful for her call and for reaching out to him because very few people did that.

On Sunday morning, Alice heard the news of Mike's suicide. She wrote:

I called Rose Sunday evening. I really felt God leading me to share my vision with her, Ted, so I did. She was so thankful. She felt it was an affirmation of the words you shared at the retreat about your own thoughts of suicide. She had been clinging to those words, especially when you spoke about how you felt God would have honored and used your suicide within the sovereignty of His will. I am so amazed at how God connects us together, how God uses everything for his purposes. I cannot begin to understand the how and why of it all. Simply knowing I, you, Rose, all of us are part of God's plans brings peace and awe, doesn't it?

God bless you my friend,
Alice

"I cannot begin to understand the how and why of it all. Simply knowing . . . all of us are part of God's plan brings peace and awe, doesn't it?"

Yes, it does. At least sometimes it does. Enough times. More than enough times. Squeezing through the back door. Enough times to keep building annexes to our hearts just to hold a little of the sneaky grace of God and our strange brothers and sisters of the human family.

Sometime soon go to your back door and think about that. Then lift a prayer of gratitude for the wonder of it all.

New Rules of Engagement

Matthew 1:18-25

He threw away his reputation as a good man by marrying a fallen woman.

That's one of the little clues to the large wonder of Christmas, and of life. To sense the power of it, revisit the story. Joseph and Mary are engaged but, as Matthew delicately puts it, they have not lived together. So when Mary turns up pregnant, Joseph sees no option but to break off with her if he is to maintain his standing as a righteous man. By getting pregnant as an unmarried woman, Mary has shed her virtue and become an outcast. According to religious law, she's done something for which she could be stoned to death. So, despite his concern for Mary, Joseph plans to disavow her. He feels driven to it by his wounded pride and by what has been drummed into him about what society, and God, required of him.

Then something happens to upset the world for Joseph, and forever. An angel speaks to him, in a dream, no less—and no more. He's haunted by a message in intimations and nudges squeezing in from another world through the cracks in this one. As always, we have to squint our eyes and cock our ears to catch it. The angel fluttering through Joseph's dream tells him not to be afraid to take Mary as his wife, that she's pregnant with Jesus, who will save people from their sins. What's a person to do with that kind of news? What would you do? Run and hide? Or turn and risk? Joseph turned and risked. And a different life began.

"Do not be afraid!" That's nearly the whole meaning of Christmas and the gospel.

Do not be afraid: God is doing a new thing.

Do not be afraid: It's the only way you can have good will toward anyone.

Do not be afraid: It's the basis for new rules of engagement.

Start with the obvious truth that we are all connected. That's the way God put the world together. What happens to any of us affects all of us, like it or not. Many people don't like it, and many don't acknowledge the connection. Even so, the inescapable truth is that everything and everyone on earth is connected. That's the ecosystem of life. Connection is a given.

But engagement is a choice. The choice is whether or not to make connections vital, not just formal; intimate, not superficial; sustaining, not empty.[1]

1 I am greatly indebted to Barbara Krasner, PhD, and a collaborator in the formation of Contextual Family Therapy for the provocative distinction between

By now all of us are at least somewhat familiar with Ntozake Shange's marvelous choreopoem *for colored girls who have considered suicide when the rainbow is enuf.* The girls are identified by the different colors they wear as they move in a kind of dance, sharing their experiences of relationships in which they felt exploited, isolated, frustrated, and angry. Near the end, the lady in blue says something that probably puzzles us at first:

I used to live in the world
really be in the world
free & sweet talkin
good mornin & thank you, & nice day
uh huh
i can't now
i can't be nice to nobody
nice is such a rip-off
. . . is Just a set-up"[2]

Engagement is a choice against the rip-off. Engagement involves pressing beyond shallow niceness and congeniality, agreement and pretense, to more honest and deep relationships. It is to seek fairness for ourselves and for others. It is to talk to others, rather than talking about them. Engagement is about building trust between each other by saying what we mean and meaning what we say. Without trust, love shrivels and compassion twists into manipulation. Engagement involves honestly sharing truths about ourselves, our thoughts, feelings, and experiences, and inviting others to share their truths with us. That is hard to do but infinitely worth it because it empowers us to find new, larger truths together.

Engagement takes courage, which is half of what faith is. It involves taking risks. By daring to engage each other, we make something different possible between us, and within ourselves. When we honestly share the hard truths we keep hidden in an attempt to be "nice," something deeper, something more healing and redemptive opens up for us that our pretense has kept closed down. Engagement is what Jesus was about. That's why he was harder on hypocrites than on prostitutes, thieves, and tax collectors. Hypocrisy and pretense close things down, mistake congeniality for love, and shrink the possibilities for the abundant life that Jesus urges us to claim for ourselves and each other.

So Joseph dreams, as we all do. In many ways, our dreams and his are alike. We also dream of loving and being loved. We dream dramas of finding a deeper meaning for life, of escaping the demons, of laughing and playing together. In Joseph's dream, the angel tells him not to be afraid to heed the longing in him to move from the empty outskirts of his life into the bustle and excitement and sacred struggle at the heart of things, and of himself.

connection and engagement. However, she is not accountable for the interpretation and application of that distinction relative to "New Rules of Engagement."

2 Ntozake Shange, *for colored girls who have considered suicide when the rainbow is enuf* (New York: Scribner, 1975), 38–39.

In some way don't you suppose our dream angels are telling us the same thing: *Do not be afraid.* Listen to your deepest longing for love, for meaning, for relationships that are deep, trusting, satisfying, challenging, and joyful, for a world of justice and peace and beauty. In a haunting way, our dreams call us to engagement, to move from the outskirts to the center of our lives.

The mystery is that while grace engenders engagement, engagement enacts grace. Engagement, then, is our response to Jesus' haunting promise that the kingdom of God itself is *among* us or *between* us. It is not the possession of anyone but is found in our relationships with each other and all God's creation. Healing, justice, forgiveness, peace reside in whether and how we engage each other.

The haunting word of the angel in the dream had it right: "Do not be afraid . . . [Jesus] will save his people from their sins." God's love isn't about endorsing our status, or propping up our self-esteem, or defending our privileges, or sticking a seal of approval on our comforts. It's about saving us from our sins. What does that mean? The condensed answer is that it means calling us out of the pretense and pride and hypocrisy we hide in. There is a real toughness in grace. I believe Jesus demonstrates, and calls for, new rules of engagement.

Not long ago, two people at a retreat I helped lead gave me a sheet of paper with the heading "The Invitation" by Oriah Mountain Dreamer. The words touch on at least a part of what engagement and grace are about:

> It doesn't interest me what you do for a living. I want to know what you ache for, and if you dare to dream of meeting your heart's longing.
>
> It doesn't interest me how old you are. I want to know if you will risk looking like a fool for love, for your dream, for the adventure of being alive . . .
>
> I want to know if you have touched the center of your own sorrow, if you have been opened by life's betrayals or have become shriveled and closed from fear of further pain. I want to know if you can sit with pain, mine or your own, without moving to hide it or fade it or fix it.
>
> I want to know if you can be with joy, mine or your own, if you can dance with wildness and let the ecstasy fill you to the tips of your fingers and toes without cautioning us to be careful, to be realistic . . .
>
> I want to know if you can live with failure, yours and mine, and still stand on the edge of the lake and shout to the silver of the full moon, 'Yes!'
>
> It doesn't interest me to know where you live or how much money you have.

I want to know if you can get up, after the night of grief and despair, weary and bruised to the bone, and do what needs to be done to feed the children.

It doesn't interest me who you know or how you came to be here. I want to know if you will stand in the center of the fire with me and not shrink back."[3]

Surely something like that is what Joseph heard. Don't be afraid to engage life, yours and others. Don't be afraid to take Mary as your wife, to take risks, to do battle for what you believe at your core. Don't be afraid to battle for love, for honesty, for intimacy, for mercy, for justice, for integrity. Don't be afraid to move out of the box that can become a coffin. Life isn't about innocence, it's about engagement, and Jesus lived by those new rules of engagement. That's what Joseph's dream, his angel, was telling him—and us. So Joseph threw away his reputation as a good man and married the fallen woman. He, and we, know more deeply the grace of God because he did.

As a person who has gone through the pain of a divorce, I've learned the critical difference between connection and divorce. Through the years of our marriage, Dory, my former wife, and I were connected but not engaged. There was more image than reality in our marriage, more the concern to be seen as right and blameless than to be honest and engaged. I tried to live the ideal of what my parents expected, what the church expected, what society expected. I couldn't do it. It led at last to my emotional and spiritual breakdown.

I didn't risk engaging Dory nor, I think, did she risk engaging me. We avoided and denied and pretended. We retreated from each other. We fought but didn't talk, blamed but didn't listen, or speak our truth, or share our hopes and disappointments or our selves.

When the divorce happened, my grown kids were angry with me most about my pretense. It distanced me from them as well, as they were growing up. My kids were burdened by an ideal I pretended to be. I wanted to be seen as good and innocent, but wasn't, could never be, because only God can be. My pretense was wrong. It hurt other people, and it hurt me. Out of my fear I lashed in and I lashed out. I was connected but not engaged.

Since then, from therapy, from my kids, from my deepest longing and dreams, and from my wife, Jan, I've learned about engagement. Since then, I've heard and heeded the angel. It isn't about innocence or goodness. It's about not being afraid, or less afraid, to come out of hiding. It's about being human, not angelic or demonic. Jesus came to save people from their sins. Saved to get engaged and to understand something of the depths and mystery of God's grace.

3 Oriah Mountain Dreamer, "The Invitation," *The Invitation* (San Francisco: HarperSanFrancisco, 1999), 1–2.

The incarnation we celebrate at Christmas can be grasped as one of God's unique ways of engaging with us. "And the Word became flesh and lived among us" (John 1:14). No longer above the fray, but *in* it, in heart of the human struggle, in all the messy, dusty, rocky, boney, fleshy, bloody, gutsy, sweaty, confronting, loving, beauty, and wonder of it. Engagement—not innocence, not idealizing, not niceness but *engagement*—is what Jesus was about and calls us to move toward. When we join the fray with him, we discover what grace and mercy and healing and reconciliation and abundant life are about.

Saving Private Ryan is a soul-shaking movie.[4] Even if you haven't seen it, you'll get this point. There's a timid, seemingly cowardly American soldier, Corporal Upham, who keeps avoiding being involved in the ugly business of the war, or being engaged with the other soldiers in his small squad. I think Corporal Upham was trying to hold on to his innocence. But which of us is really innocent in this fallen world? Innocence is an illusion. And yet it's such a powerful illusion; it drives us to blame others for what's wrong in the world, or in our own lives.

Even in the midst of the terrible war, Corporal Upham clings to "the rules" as though they will keep him safe and innocent. His fear transposes into self-righteousness. He acts like a non-combatant, which he is not. He and the others in his squad are sent behind the Nazi lines hours after the invasion at Normandy. They are to find and bring back to safety Private Ryan, a paratrooper who jumped into Normandy to blow up crucial bridges.

At one point, Upham and his little squad of American soldiers come upon a German radar station and try to take it out. One of their unit is killed in the fight, and, in turn, they take a German soldier prisoner. The others want to shoot the prisoner because it would be very dangerous to take him along as they move around behind enemy lines. But Upham argues that "it's against the rules" to kill a prisoner. So reluctantly, Captain Miller lets the German prisoner go. The other soldiers in his squad are dismayed because their lives are at stake if the German soldier runs to warn his buddies.

Later, that same German soldier turns up leading a battalion of Germans and, in another encounter, he kills one of the squad of American soldiers while Upham quivers nearby, doing nothing to engage in the fight.

But finally Upham gets the message. He finds the courage to be engaged. He joins the fray. In one encounter he shoots the German soldier. He's less afraid. He comes to "the knowledge of good and evil," so to speak.

Upham's obsession to be only innocent and good was the source of his pretense. It was a weakness that endangered and hurt

4 I am indebted to my colleague Ann Marie Donohue, PhD, for her many insights concerning *Saving Private Ryan*. Our discussions are reflected in this interpretation of the film.

the others. Upham denied the reality of a power in himself and around him that the rules don't touch, can't touch, a power that twists the rules for its own purposes. Call it sin, or evil, or tyranny. Whatever we call it, it's real. It's in the world. It's in us all.

It was only when Corporal Upham, like Joseph, accepted that reality and got engaged in dealing with it, that he seemed to stop being so afraid. I would go so far as to suggest the radical view that Upham's spiritual life, his spiritual depth and wholeness, began when he risked engagement in a less-than-perfect, east-of-Eden world, rather than trying to maintain the illusion of innocence. Isn't that what Christ did? I think so!

Go just a bit deeper: The "good" that the rules supposedly uphold is often undone by the persistent self-serving and self-deception worming through our claims to be good, even as we routinely try to tilt the rules to our advantage. That is always the danger of good people, like Joseph before his dream, like some of us, like me. Our version of the good replaces God. And yet we're often, maybe usually, afraid because the world is both more cruel than we can control and more beautiful than we can resist.

So here's the mysterious part, the grace part of it. God, the ultimate "good," does not always abide by the rules either. That's what Jesus' birth and life, crucifixion and resurrection are about. They are revelations of God acting, engaging to break the rules of lesser goods, as well as of corruption and death. By his engagement with people, Jesus did miracles that went against the "rules" of madness, sickness, storms, and religious powers. Don't you suppose that's why he was so upset with the hypocrisy of people who limited goodness to the keeping of rules, maintaining their image of innocence while their spirits atrophied? Risk of engagement is based on grace, not on innocence.

Rules are a good thing as far as they go, but they do not exhaust the possibilities for either goodness or evil. We're haunted, nudged to imagine and respond to what lies beyond the bounds sometimes. In both directions. And there is Joseph, throwing his reputation and caution to the winds and engaging with Mary in a new way, and thwarting Herod's plan to kill Jesus along with the other babies in that horrific slaughter of the innocents in Bethlehem.

Christmas, God's invasion of human history, Jesus' birth, has nothing to do with fantasies of innocence. It's about engagement. Too often the call of Christians to conversion seems to be about a conversion to innocence. But it's really a conversion to responsibility, to engagement with whatever dehumanizes, demeans, oppresses people.

"Do not be afraid."

"I want to know if you will risk looking like a foolfor love, for your dream, for the adventure of being alive."

Will you risk engaging your self? First that. Engaging your self is a two-way street running from inside out and outside in. It involves taking the risks of trying something different in your relationships with others in the family, the marketplace, the workplace. Those risks can be occasions of self-discovery and empowerment. But it also involves honest prayer, soul searching, quietness, reflection.

In the conclusion to "The Invitation," Oriah Mountain Dreamer writes,

> It doesn't interest me where or what or with whom you have studied. I want to know what sustains you, from the inside, when all else falls away.
>
> I want to know if you can be alone with yourself and if you truly like the company you keep in the empty moments.[5]

Even so, I've learned that being sustained inside, liking the company I keep in the empty moments, isn't about my goodness, my wisdom, my achievements. At least it isn't about those things all the way down, though you and I claiming our gifts is part of it.

But more, it's about battling for our integrity, our honesty, our soul. Tucked in among Annie Dillard's treasury of incredible insights is a description of an Advent Mass where the organist couldn't find the opening hymn, acolytes blundered in lighting candles, a number of strange requests from the congregation were part of the prayers.

5 Oriah Mountain Dreamer, "The Invitation."

Just as Dillard was on the verge of bursting into laughter, the priest included this request in his prayer: " 'For my son, that he may forgive his father, we pray to the Lord.' 'Lord, hear our prayer,' we responded, chastened." Dillard goes on: "Week after week, we witness the same miracle: that God is so mighty he can stifle his own laughter. . . Week after week, Christ washes the disciples' dirty feet, handles their very toes, and repeats, It is all right—believe it or not—to be people. Who can believe it?"[6]

Careful now, that's God's first question of us, as it was of Adam and Eve, and Moses and the Israelites, and the disciples jockeying for special privilege, and everyone down through the years. *Who can believe it?* Maybe the father who sought his son's forgiveness in that morning Mass. Christmas, like Jesus washing the disciples' feet, says, "It is all right to be people, to be human." Then comes that haunting, gracious question: *Can you believe it?*

Why that question? Because to be human is to be less than God but more than animals. It is to live in the tension of being both spiritual and physical. When we posture in any guise of proud self-sufficiency, or of indulgent self-degradation, we deny our limits and decline our gifts. We waste resources of minds, hearts, relationships. We become stuck in hypocrisy. We spurn our humanity.

6 Annie Dillard, *Teaching A Stone To Talk: Expeditions and Encounters* (New York: Harper & Row, 1982), 20.

Yet how many times a day, or a week, or a lifetime, do we do that?

To risk engaging ourselves is to wrestle our humanity out of those denials. The wonder is that we do that wrestling best when we do it together. The wonder is that such wrestling is the heart of relationships and the web of community. We don't fool God by trying to fool ourselves. When we give up such foolishness, we'll love ourselves and our neighbors better, and our honesty and integrity will sustain us in the empty moments. And our prayers and our lives will deepen. That's part of what the new rules of engagement are about.

Then there is the risk of engaging with others and for others. Oriah Mountain Dreamer's question, *"I want to know if you will stand in the center of the fire with me and not shrink back,"* is close to the core of it. Faith isn't about staying on the shallow end of life or the fringes of battle against injustice and oppression. It's about being in the center of the fire where our brothers and sisters are. It's about doing what Luther thundered, "Love God and sin on *boldly*." Sin, because everything about us is tainted with a self-interest we can't escape. But sin boldly. Boldly means being aware of our shadow side yet acting ". . . with firmness in the right as God gives us to see the right," as Lincoln so beautifully framed it,[7] trusting God can still do something with us that benefits others and brings about God's own purposes.

What would happen in your family if you really engaged each other, really spoke honestly, really listened carefully, really challenged as well as credited each other? That's how trust begins and fear eases. Unless there's trust, love is a sham.

What would happen in this world if we dared to engage it more compassionately, demanded better schools, better salaries for teachers, adequate health care for low-income working families, serious efforts to stop global warming, water pollution, an end to poverty in the next hundred years, as the National Council of Churches in Christ in the USA is advocating—to name just a few issues that challenge our humanity and, if met, would do more to end terrorism than all the high tech military weaponry combined?

In the Sunday *New York Times Magazine*, Max Frankel ended one of his columns with these words: "Just as we now wonder how otherwise enlightened people could trade in dark-skinned bodies or demand and accept female subservience, future generations are bound to marvel at how so many of their forebears could routinely feast while others went hungry, or how some ancestors could amass fortunes while others went begging. Like slavery and male domination in their time, the inequalities of our day are justified even in the most progressive circles as not only tolerable but also actually essential to economic growth and social harmony."

7 Abraham Lincoln, Second Inaugural Address, March 4, 1865.

Are they really essential? Are those "rules" set in concrete? Are economic incentives the only, or primary ones, or is justice, the welfare of everyone, even more compelling? Never mind that we may be born into circumstances of privilege, as most of us are. The issue is, will we employ our privilege to engage the world on behalf of justice for all?

"I want to know if you can get up, after the night of grief and despair . . . and do what needs to be done to feed the children."

There's the battle. Good rules getting overturned for better ones. That's the haunt of the dream, the nudge of the angel. *Do not be afraid.* Jesus saves the people from their sins. God's grace is deep and empowering. That's what the new rules of engagement are about.

And, finally, what about engaging with Christ? I wish I had the capacity to speak more clearly about this. I think of the great prophetic teacher and social activist Reinhold Niebuhr, who lived out his vision of what he called "Christian realism." But late in his life he wrote this: "I have come to realize that it is possible to look at the human situation without illusion and without despair, only from the standpoint of the Christ-revelation . . . I have come to know. . . that only in the 'simplicity of the gospel' is it possible to measure the full 'dignity' and 'misery' of human beings." Dignity and misery not only in physical terms, though those, but also in the deepest spiritual terms, full or pinched life terms.

I'm coming to be persuaded by Niebuhr's point. Not "only" from the standpoint of the Christ-revelation, but at least from that standpoint "is it possible to look at the human situation without illusion and without despair." At least from that standpoint because I am also persuaded by what Reinhold's brother, H. Richard Niebuhr, said: "Jesus is the unique but not exclusive revelation of God."

The simplicity of the gospel is that somehow God was there in what the Babe of Bethlehem grew up to be and do. One of Queen Elizabeth's advisors back in the sixteenth century told her, "People must be able to touch the Divine here on earth. They must have something higher than themselves to worship." The mystery is that in Jesus, the human one, the divine comes close enough for us to touch, and yet stays higher than ourselves.

But we are reluctant to engage Jesus. We seem to prefer a more abstract, removed God. We prefer the old rules, our rules, rather than the new rules of engagement God gives in Christ, new rules that break those of our little goods and lesser gods, our defensive claims of innocence, our rules of logic, our elevation of profit motives and power struggles, our argument that greed is a virtue and consumption the ultimate freedom, our fascination with violence, our retreat from community, our frantic denial of death. Maybe we prefer to be afraid.

"Only in the 'simplicity of the gospel' is it possible to measure the full 'dignity' and 'misery' of human beings."

Our full dignity is a wondrous thing—the music, the beauty we create, the love, the labor to be just, the gifts of healing, our reach toward peace. But for me, it is our misery that wakes me sweating in the night. Misery not so much of poverty, except of spirit, but the misery of fear. It is hard not to be afraid, and I cannot manage that on my own, or even with others for more than a moment. Fear of my frailty, my taintedness, my limitations, my betrayals and failures, my mortality, my death. I think the fear is part, maybe the core, of my sins. The sins Jesus will save me from. So says Joseph's angel, his dream. And my dream and your dream, too. I only wish that saving didn't take so long.

It begins with Annie Dillard's realizing that when Christ washed his disciples' feet, it was as if he were saying it is all right—believe it or not—to be people, to be human beings, because he became one, too. So, it's okay to be afraid. At least a little. Most of us want, and try, to be in control of the chaos and uncertainty of our lives. We don't like uncertainty. We are afraid of it. And yet, down deep, we know we don't control, and can't control, the uncertainties and contingencies of our lives.

So what's the point? The point is that Christmas, that Jesus, isn't meant to help our "reason" find answers. Jesus is meant to *disarm* our reason. Uncertainty, terrible things, death will keep happening. But it's all right to be human beings. Our fear tears us open, makes us aware of how vulnerable and needy we are all the way down inside. What wakes us sweating in the night, what sends shivers down our spines, cramps our stomachs and loosens our bowels, is exactly where God comes close and touches us—in the smelly dirty manger; in the hard-scrabble roads, shoulder-rubbing with the needy and the powerful; in the shadowy, sweaty struggles in the midnight of our decisions; and, finally, in our deaths.

These are the new rules of engagement to topple the old ones, topple the claims we make for our goodness and our innocence and our smarts, topple our insistence that we deserve what we want but know we can't get on our own or by our rules. Then there is grace, and it's what we want most deeply in life, and it's a gift. So, in the darkness of our fear, we are invited to turn toward the light. We're invited to stumble our way to the manger. We're invited to risk kneeling, risk praying, risk sinning on boldly, risk trusting that Jesus will, and even now is, saving us from our sins by turning our fear of death in all its insidious little and large forms into the way to life.

It happens through the new rules of engagement with Christ, and so with ourselves and with all our brothers and sisters. It's God's grace all the way through. And so, says Dillard, and Joseph, and Jesus, it's all right, even a great gift, to be people, and we can go our way "exultant, in a daze, dancing, to the twin silver trumpets of praise."[8]

Amen.

8 Annie Dillard, *Pilgrim at Tinker Creek* (New York: Harper & Row, 1974), 271.

Catch-153

John 21

It's Easter again, with all its pageantry and proclamations. Anthems trumpet, lilies trumpet back, and alleluias echo everywhere. Yet under it all, our eternal longing still collides with our earthy limitations, and our ambivalence lingers despite the excitement of the day. For the most part, we know more of the loss and slow leak of sadness than we do of bliss. Dare we be honest, we might admit there's an undertow of skepticism in the tide of hope that brings us to this day.

Maybe to catch the resurrection we have to glance off to the side of it. The best place to look might not be at the angels, or empty tomb or upper room, but at a stinking fishing boat bobbing out there on the sea of Tiberius with waves slapping against its side and weariness settling in on its occupants. Whatever day was about to dawn at that moment, it wasn't the Sabbath or they wouldn't have been out there fishing. That's one of the things to see, looking off to the side: The resurrection didn't happen on an appointed religious day.

It happened on what would be the equivalent of our Monday, that groan-and-gripe day when, like it or not, you haul yourself out of bed, hitch up your belt, and hike yourself off again to the chaotic thick, or the boring thin, of whatever the routine is for you. Who would ever think to keep an eye out for a resurrection on that kind of a day? But that is just when it happens, if the stories tell it at all straight. And that's enough to fasten our attention on this fishing boat for a moment. It's our kind of scene, our kind of people. So we lean forward a little and squint to get a better look at them, off to the side there in that muffled place between sea and sky, darkness and dawn.

And there they are, Peter and his partners, in their creaking old boat at the end of a not-so-good night of fishing when the empty tomb seems a lot less relevant to them than their empty hold. Isn't that the way it goes? We fish for whatever it is—perks, promotions, or popularity—to prove whatever it is we feel we have to prove—our worth, our importance, or our loveableness. And, as all that gets measured, the bottom line is brutally clear: no fish, no worth. In there somewhere, perhaps, is a vague, fleeting intimation of human limits which hint of death, that familiar, gut-wrenching experience of a slow leak in expectations that has so many variations: the disciples' empty nets or our flat-line-type let down in a 'Don't call us, we'll call you' response to a best-shot interview.

Fix just that moment in your mind. It's not hard to imagine, is it? Don't you suppose Peter and the others are standing there gripping the side of the boat, griping about their luck, staring into the mist and ugly memories rising off the sea, a mix of sweat and tears, and rain maybe, dripping off their noses, someone spitting out a curse, someone yawning, someone scratching their behind and . . . hey, someone *does* call them!

"Friends!"

Who is that booby yelling at them, stirring them from their stupor?

Maybe that's how resurrections always start, with some voice calling—who knows for sure whose it is, or where it comes from, exactly, only that we hear it. That's all and that's enough! Someone calls: a bird, a kid in the alley, a singer on a car radio, a friend on the phone, a word or two from a stranger across the room or the next table, our own voice maybe. No matter, some voice is always calling us or we wouldn't be here this day—or any place any day, probably—and maybe the voice comes from out there somewhere, or inside somewhere, or both. Who knows anything for sure, except we hear it.

So a voice calls Peter and the others, and sets off a confusion as full of comedy as a blend of Woody Allen and Eddie Murphy—or as funny as we might look if we could see ourselves hustling to get it together after the alarm goes off Monday a.m. and we're about to miss the train and can't find the other shoe, or the keys, or the phone number we're supposed to call that day, and the toilet won't shut off, and there's not enough cash around for a train ticket and . . . then, somehow, there's the voice, "Friends, have you caught anything?"

And you scream, "You gotta be kidding!"

But the voice persists, "Shoot the net to the starboard side and you'll make a catch."

Now wait a minute! What do you mean, try something different. We fish from the port side, the way we learned. That's the way it's supposed to be done. But then what have we got to lose so. . . holy mackerel, or perch or bass or cod or whatever that mess of squirming fish is. . . why didn't we think of the starboard side? Or did we? Whose voice was that anyway?

"It is the Lord!" One of them guessed. Could be, sure. That's who it is! And Peter, bless his bumbling heart, gets so excited (or so embarrassed because he's been fishing in the buff) that he puts his clothes on and jumps overboard to swim to shore, which is stupid and backward, but isn't it the day for it?

. . . "Why won't that toilet stop running, and damn this knotted shoelace, and the toast is burning, and oh yeah, I'll be home late, and . . . hey, answer the phone will ya' and tell the idiot who's calling that I'm not here . . . what does he mean, 'Would I be interested in a free week in Martinique if I invest in a condo there?' And, oh God, I'm going to miss the train . . ."

It is funny, isn't it? Like putting on your clothes in your craziness to get into the swim. So everyone laughs and yells and makes their way to shore as best they can, dragging the fish behind them.

And there they are, off to the side, at precisely another moment to fix in your mind. It's not hard to imagine either, is it? After all, what would you do in those circumstances? Don't you suppose they kept looking at each other sideways, nudging each other like schoolboys, shuffling and stammering as people do when they can't get their hearts or minds around something? It's a stupendous thing that's happening. Jesus is back. Well, do you know what those disciples did right then? They counted the fish. At a time like that, they counted the fish! Ah, but it is just there, off to the side in something that seems ridiculous, that we catch something of what the resurrection is about. Hey, how many fish, or minutes, or chances do we have here? 1, 2, 3 . . .

Jacob Bronowski, that magnificent mathematician/physicist/poet, gives us a clue. He writes: "When a man counts 'one, two, three,' he is not only doing mathematics; he is on the path to the mysticism of numbers in Pythagoras and Vitruvious and Kepler, to the Trinity and the signs of the Zodiac. . . and before we know how it happened . . . the numbers have conspired to make a match with nature."[1]

1 Jacob Bronowski, *A Sense of the Future* (Cambridge, MA: The MIT Press, 1977), 29, 31.

Ah yes: 1, 2, 3 . . . the mysticism of numbers, the Trinity and strange signs; 28, 29, 30 . . . before we know how it happens, a match with nature and with grace; 41, 42, 43 . . . tulips, and pussy willows, and rain filling the rivers and stirring the seeds; 103, 104, 105 . . . the mystery and the miracle of everything, such as us opening our eyes in the morning, and a couple making love, and a child making sense of markings on a page; 133, 134, 135 . . . a choir singing *"Dona nobis pacem"* and the heart indeed feeling peace in the hearing of it, and reading a wondrous story on an old woman's face or in the grope of a baby's fingers; 151, 152, 153 . . .

One hundred and fifty-three fish! One and five and three add up to nine, and numbers that add up to nine are divisible by nine, and if you don't get the point, don't worry. Maybe there isn't one, except for the fun of it. But if we can't laugh at it, maybe we ought to feel a little uneasy because we may be missing the larger point, which is that probably the numbers themselves—and surely the nature they conspire to make a match with—are gifts, pure gifts. No matter how eager we are for spring, every year we learn again that it comes by its own numbers, in its own way and time, and therefore, as always, it comes as a gift. So numbers and nature. So life, so the dawn, so the neighbor, so the beloved, so the earth itself—gifts! One hundred and fifty-three fish and a resurrection!

Surely everyone knows Joseph Heller's *Catch-22*. The term has become part of our language. Yossarian is a World War II bomber pilot who wants to be grounded because the other side keeps trying to kill him when he flies over with his bombs. He tries to get a doctor to ground him on the basis that he is crazy, but the doctor tells him he is wasting his time. When Yossarian persists—"Can't you ground someone who is crazy"—the doctor admits that he can. In fact, the rule states that he *has* to ground anyone who is crazy, but the person has to *ask*. Yossarian presses, "So then you can ground me?" To his puzzlement, the doctor says no. "You mean there's a catch?" questions Yossarian. "Sure there's a catch!" answers the doctor. "Catch-22. Anyone who wants to get out of combat duty isn't really crazy."[2]

So Catch-22, which symbolizes everything that says you can't win, not really, not finally. Most of us, most of the time, live by catch-22: You can't win.

Then comes Easter, and another catch, God's catch, Catch-153, which says you can't lose, not really, not finally. Catch-22: You can't win. Catch-153: You can't lose. Scholars who dabble in the mysticism of numbers suggest that the number 153 represents all the varieties of fish in the world, which is to say, all the varieties of people in the world, all caught and held in the net of God's grace. So another thing to see off the side in the story is that, no matter what, the net holds it all. Whatever the load, the net doesn't break. There's a place in the kingdom for all us poor fish.

So, 149, 150, 151. . . can't you hear the laughter building in their bellies and spilling out of their throats as they count. . . 152, 153—Catch-153—and who would have believed it possible? I think whoever said that only when we hear the gospel as God's wild joke do we hear it at all, was definitely on to something. So here is the gospel cast in miniature: the disciples counting their fish, and we running to catch the train and breathlessly discovering it's even later than we are, and everyone joining in the laughter of God's joke in saving all kinds of fish in God's kingdom—carp and minnows and suckers, blues and bullheads, eels and whales, and all the rest, whatever kind we are, even whatever kind we don't like.

Suddenly in the laughter of it, we begin to wonder if maybe all those impossible things Jesus talked about aren't impossible after all: camels squeezing through the eye of a needle; mountains getting up and moving; mustard seeds growing into row houses for birds; the blind given sight, the deaf their hearing; the vested powers shaken; someone dressing up in something like a tuxedo or evening gown, tapping on the shoulders of drunks and idiots and prostitutes and us—and our enemies—inviting us all to a great champagne and candlelight party. Someone going a second mile with us, and a third, and a fourth—or is it us with them? Or both?

2 Joseph Heller, *Catch-22: A Dramatization* (New York: Delta Publishing, 1971), 11–13.

And Catch-153, we can't lose, not really. We don't have to fish anymore to prove anything. Life is a gift, pure and simple, and there's no end to it, no end!

But there is a beginning to it, or can be, That's really what Easter is about, and maybe that's what the disciples finally got through their thick skulls, or their heavy hearts, out there on the beach. Resurrection isn't just about life without end, but it's about life that begins, now, eternally now. John Donne, that poet-priest, put the point to verse in "Hymn To My God, in My Sickness":

> Since I am coming to that holy room,
> where, with thy choir of saints for evermore
> I shall be made thy music, as I come
> I tune the instrument here at the door,
> and what I may do then, think here before.[3]

Yes, think here before, and sing, blow, play here before, which is to say risk living now! Catch-153, and there's the risen Lord on the beach, setting those disciples to music, and if it sounds like laughter, it means they got the point at last. Life without end can begin!

So they begin by moving on to something very simple. They had breakfast together, and that is another off-to-the-side moment to fix in your mind. A small fire, some bread and fish, the smell of the sea, gulls screaming hello to the morning, a few friends, and something between them, and in them, something we can't really define except love is the best name we have for it—and remember, it is love that never ends, love that nothing can separate us from.

And there it is: breakfast and love!

An old friend, Edward Huber, felt that haunt of grace and responded to it for us all in something he wrote on a holiday greeting card he sent years ago: "We look across the table for the thousandth time at the children, the friends, the beloved. Is [God] so close after all, leading us again and again from dark valleys to the ecstasy of the familiar? The One we have longed for is already among us."

That haunt is a key to resurrection, to eternal life beginning: the ecstasy of the familiar, being simple, staying simple, and staying watchful, lest we miss the resurrections of the daily. Staying simple and watchful means letting go, doesn't it? Letting go of many things, letting go of ourselves, maybe! It is, after all—*before* all—God's day, and all of it is a gift: life and everything about it. Maybe whatever is coming unraveled for us—marriage, job, life itself—maybe whatever it is can't begin again until we do let go, a little. Letting go: the disciples of their familiar fishing boat, launching off into a suddenly strange and wondrous world, and we of whatever familiar, stifling thing it is we hang on to so tightly—a grudge, a resentment, a guilt, a lie we're living, a borderline

3 John Donne, *The Complete English Poems* (Baltimore, MD: Penguin Education, 1971), 347.

rage, a certainty of our rightness that is choking us, and everyone else, to death.

Do you remember that delightful scene in *The Belle of Amherst* where Emily Dickinson reads the newspaper to her sister Vinnie one evening? It goes like this: Emily says, "Oh here's one you'll love Vinnie. 'TRAIN HITS WOMAN ON MILL RIVER TRESTLE.' 'Cornelia Snell, fifty-four. . . was killed last Wednesday by the Belchertown express as she struggled vainly to free her foot from a railroad switch.' Her foot, Vinnie! Engineer Grover W. Putnam declared, "By the time I saw the poor lady and her dog, it was too late.". . . Oh, the dog survived! It jumped clear!. . . Her children are planting an evergreen in her memory near the spot. Isn't that sweet, Vinnie?" Then after a long pause, Emily says in simple wonder, "I wonder why she didn't take off her shoe?"[4]

The question is the same for each of us: What do we need to take off, let go of, if we are going to live—or begin to? Catch-153 says we can't lose, so let go. We don't have to fish anymore to prove anything. We can tune our instrument for the joy of it, our instrument, our authentic self, and here at the door of eternity, begin to play the music of what we know as love wherever we experience it or sense the need for it, and so begin to live it out with all the courage and imagination and joy we can muster.

Live it out! That, too, is what Easter is about: beginning to live it out. And that is what the struggle for justice is about: love with its sleeves rolled up, love with bloody feet and wounded hands and a won't-quit glint in its eye. Love with its sleeves rolled up and laughter on its lips. And it means no one is left in tombs: not the poor whose children go hungry and have no medical insurance, or African Americans in urban ghettos, or gays, or women, or children, or Arabs, or Jews, or Palestinians, or Third World people, or old people, no one! Justice means no one is left in bad schools, or in unending wars of revenge, or polluted water, or ozone layers with holes punched in it, or acid rain. Justice and peace, human community, is love lived out.

So the disciples, there on the beach—and us wherever we are—are called to a deep kind of sharing, or the beginning of it. That also involves a profound kind of letting go. To see it, you have to look off to the side, and then off to the side again, and then fix in your mind one last moment. There is Jesus telling Peter three times to feed his sheep, which is quite a lofty calling, if you look at it one way, which Peter did, being Peter—and being like us.

"Feed my sheep." Care for the world and all my children. So question one: "Why me?" And if me, then surely there's a pay-off for that kind of commission. So question two:

4 William Luce, *The Belle of Amherst: A Play Based on the Life of Emily Dickinson* (Boston: Houghton Mifflin Company, 1976), 32–33.

"For what?" Those were Peter's questions, and now they're ours.

But keep looking at Peter standing there—wrestling with himself and the feel of it, flexing his shoulders as if the weight of that way of looking at it were already chafing a bit (as we know it does), and so, scratching his ear, drubbing his nose, rumpling his hair, and sorting out the questions he couldn't quite put a handle of words on.

Then out of the corner of his eye, he spots another disciple, someone he loves, and somehow it all comes clear to him. He points to the other disciple and says, "Lord, what about him?" It's not very hard to imagine that moment and that question, is it? It's not really such a bad question, either. If we listen carefully, we'll find as much concern for the other person in it as a cop-out for Peter. After all, being like Peter, we wonder, too, "How can I care about people without controlling them and the outcome of what I want for them—and the world? How can I love without feeling I need to manage things according to how and why and where I love? How can I feed without investing myself in those I feed and wanting a return on my investment?

"Lord, what about him?" What about my father, my mother, my brother or sister, my husband or wife, my son or daughter, my friend, my colleague, my neighbor, my enemy? If I do things for them, don't they owe me? Shouldn't they do what I know is right for them? What about their struggles, their success, their life, their death? What's the reward for my being so involved and vulnerable?

Not a bad question! It comes close to the heart of this day. *"Lord, what about him, her, them?"*

Cock your head off to the side now, and listen to Jesus' answer over the pounding of the surf and the timpani of your heart: *"If it is my will that he remain until I come, what is that to you?"* With that, we get reminded again of what we keep forgetting about this Easter day: It isn't our day at all, except as a gift. It is really God's day. Ultimately God is in charge of it and every day, and of what happens in them, or to us, or to anyone. That's the awesome, amazing freedom of the resurrection. "*If it is my will* . . ." Which is to say, the mystery of it is past finding out. It's all a gift, all grace. Catch-153! Tune your instrument for the joy of it, not the applause or the reward.

I've watched the video of *The Wizard of Oz* many times with my grandchildren. They think it's scary until almost the end. And many of the encounters Dorothy and the Lion and the Scarecrow and the Tin Man have along the Yellow Brick Road—with the growling wicked witches, their foreboding castle, the Haunted Forest, and the screeching winged monkeys—are pretty hair-raising. Then they finally get to the wizard who they're sure will grant their wishes. They plead their case to the wizard who is hidden behind a screen, but all they get are smoke belches and a loud, booming voice. Then, in a scuffle the screen gets knocked over, and the wizard gets exposed as only a little bald-headed man whose power is all smoke and mirrors.

In frustration Dorothy screams at him, "You are a very bad man!"

The little man replies, "Oh no, my dear. I'm really a very good man, but I'm a very bad wizard." My grandchildren always laugh and clap at that. I join them because in that moment our fears get knocked down a peg or two.

Even so, Jesus' resurrection knocks over our screen and exposes us to ourselves, if we look off to the side. The truth is that we are bad wizards, bad gods, but good human beings—or *pretty good* ones. More importantly, we are *loved* human beings. That's the secret, and it's a saving and liberating one. We don't need to pretend to be wizards, or angels, anymore. Life with the feel of eternity about it is not anything we can give to anyone, including ourselves. But it is a gift that comes anyway, and keeps coming. It is something to accept, to point to, to share, to rejoice in, and that's the wonder.

So the liberating mystery is that we can only begin living as very good human beings when we accept that we are very bad wizards, even worse gods. But never mind. Today—every day—is a gift still and all to us very human beings. This day, all days, this life, life forever and the living of it.

"If it is my will . . . what is that to you?" Which is to say that nothing happens God can't handle, even with wounded hands. We can let go of ourselves, our lies and illusions and pretenses. We can dare to love just for the joy of it, love because deeper than anything else, we're lovers, and not to love is to deny our lives. We can let go of those we've loved who have died, for they are in God's hands. In the letting go, there's something of peace and healing. We can even let go of enemies. We can love them because they're just "human merely beings," as e. e. cummings puts it, as are we. And not to see that is to miss a resurrection or 2, or 3, or 4 . . . let go and forgive and feed sisters and brothers the world around in the freedom of it; 10, 11, 12 . . . share with them for the joy of it; 77, 78, 79 . . . bad wizards but good humans beings, matched with a kingdom . . . 97, 98, 99. . . .

And the matching goes a little like this scene from Herbert Tarr's *The Conversion of Chaplain Cohen.* David, the adopted boy now grown, is leaving home. He stands on a railroad platform saying good-bye to the adoptive parents he calls uncle and aunt. He takes their rough hands in his. "How can I ever begin to repay you two for what you've done for me!"

Uncle Asher speaks gently, "David, there's a saying: 'The love of parents goes to their children but the love of these children goes to their children.'"

David protests, "That's not so. I'll always be trying to . . ."

Aunt Devorah interrupts him: "David, what your Uncle Asher means is that a parent's love isn't to be paid back; it can only be passed on."[5]

There it is!

141, 142, 143 . . . God the Father and the Mother of us all, and Easter and the Risen Lord and something there is just no name for but love, and joy; 148, 149, 150 . . . something we can't repay, but only pass on the best way we can; 151, 152, 153. Catch-153, and no matter leaky toilets and missed trains and aching problems and all the thick and thin of it, we can't lose. But we can begin the passing on of love and the living that doesn't end. Alleluia.

5 Herbert Tarr, *The Conversion of Chaplain Cohen* (New York: Avon Books, 1963), 32.

The Song of the Disordered One

Mark 1:14-20

During a telephone conversation, my friend Bill Coffin commented that a lot of people hold certainty dearer than truth. Many seem to hold to the British academic's allegiance to the position that "Nothing should ever be done for the first time."

That shoe fits most of us. We much prefer certainty to uncertainty because uncertainty is one of our greatest fears. So we try to hold it off by holding fast to our habits, biases, and opinions. The sad consequence is that insisting on certainty means forfeiting creativity. That distorts the gospel and shrinks our lives.

It's unimaginable how dull and deprived our world would be without the creativity of composers, artists, poets, writers, performers across the ages. We rightly rejoice over the gifts of those creative giants. But surely it is misguided to limit the notion of creativity to them. Creativity includes the art of life itself. It's about the way we live and work, what we risk, and why.

It's about Jesus calling Peter and Andrew and James and John to follow him. What's so stunning is that, without any negotiation about wages, benefits, and pension plans, these four drop their fish nets and take off after him. That seems unbelievable, even irresponsible. How could they do such a thing? They had obligations to meet, bills to pay. Why would they do such a chancey thing? It goes against our grain. It's too romantic. It makes no sense.

Or does it? Just on the face of it, what Peter and Andrew and James and John did suggests that much of what we assume is fixed, irrefutable, unchangeable, really isn't. Maybe Peter and his buddies had hit the ditch of their unlived lives and believed they were stuck there. Some of us might know what that's like. But Jesus flings open something different for them, and us. He insists that life can change, we can change. That's what creativity is about. That's what the gospel is about. And it's both appealing and scary. What does it mean?

Recently I came across the definition of a leader as being a non-anxious presence. Don't you suppose that's what Jesus was for the disciples, and why they followed him? Even so, that's what Jesus is for us, too: a non-anxious presence. He takes the fear—or enough of it—out of uncertainty to energize creativity. To live creatively does take faith, faith in a non-anxious presence who shows there is more to the world, to life, to us, than can be contained in all our little certainties.

There are possibilities yet untapped in us. There are dimensions yet unexplored around us. There are chances yet to be taken on the way to becoming free, to making love, to doing justly, to shaping beauty, to going deeper into the mysteries of God's kingdom. Christ calls us to be about that creativity. Come, follow me.

David Ogston, a minister in Perth, Scotland, recently sent me a letter about some things I'd written. In his letter he said, "Here's my thank you. It comes from the pen of Iain Crichton Smith, one of our poets (Scotland is awash with poets)":

> Children, follow the dwarfs and the giants and the wolves, into the Wood of Unknowing, into the leaves
>
> where the terrible granny perches and sings to herself past the tumultuous seasons high on her shelf. . .
>
> Avoid the Man with the Book, the Speech Machine, and the Rinsoed Boy who is forever clean.
>
> Keep clear of the Scholar and the domestic Dog and, rather than the Sunny Smoothness, choose the Fog.
>
> Follow your love, the butterfly, where it spins over the wall, the hedge, the road, the fence,
>
> and love the Disordered Man who sings like a river whose form is Love, whose country is Forever.[1]

I read that as a powerful description of Jesus: *"the Disordered Man who sings like a river whose form is Love, whose country is Forever."*

So, what is the song this Disordered One sings to us?

The first stanza is that certainty is not all it's cracked up to be. A little girl riding home from church asked her father, "Daddy, why does the Bible always say, 'And it came to pass,' and never says, 'It came to stay'?"

Well, how would you answer? The reason is because nothing ever comes to stay. Change is inevitable. Think of all we thought was certain before September 11, 2001. Now all that certainty has tumbled with the towers. We've experienced how limited, vulnerable, fragile, and yet imaginative and talented we are. Change comes, swiftly or gradually, but it comes because it's part of God's creation. It makes creativity not only possible but necessary.

The question isn't whether there will be change, but whether we will bend it to the good in our personal life and in our life

1 "Children, Follow the Dwarfs" by Iain Crichton Smith, *Collected Poems* (Manchester, UK: Carcanet, 1992).

together. Out of the chances in uncertainty, can we, will we, make our lives and our world more humane, more just, more fair and lovely?

You've probably heard the story of the old man in Ireland who lived alone. His only son was in prison as a political enemy of the government, and the old man didn't know who would spade up his potato garden for planting. So he wrote his son about his problem. From prison his son wrote back, "For heaven's sake, don't dig up that garden. That's where I buried the guns!"

Early one morning a couple of days after the old man got his son's letter, a dozen British soldiers invaded the garden and dug the whole thing up but didn't find any guns. The old man was bewildered and wrote to his son telling him what happened and asking him what to do next. The son's answer was, "Just plant your potatoes."

Now that's creativity in action. It helps shape the world—in spades. Don't you imagine that kind of ingenious creativity would make any entrenched power tremble a little? It's about the creativity of the common life. What revolution is waiting for us to take a risk in our life, at our work, in our neighborhood? What word can we speak, what deed can we do, what resistance can we make, what options can we offer that might create something new for us and for others?

We know the familiar story of that ragged band of Israelites coming to the Red Sea with Pharaoh's army in hot pursuit. But as someone pointed out, the real miracle of the exodus wasn't so much the parting of the Red Sea at that moment as it was the first few Israelites daring to step out into the mud and begin crossing to the other side. They, like Moses, were a non-anxious presence encouraging the panicky fugitives to follow. And they did!

Creativity takes audacity. What we say is certain, isn't. What we assume is fixed and inviolable doesn't have to be that way. John Updike suggests that what we admire most about Jesus is his audacity. It was audacity that changed water to wine, that gave sight to the blind, that challenged the established powers with another vision of what God's kingdom was about. Listen to the song of the Disordered One whose country is forever, and follow, risk, create something new in your life, for the life of others.

***

What is the song the Disordered One sings to us?

The second stanza is that things are not always what they seem. Antoine de Saint Exupéry, who wrote that wonderful book *The Little Prince,* said, "It is only with the heart that one can see rightly; what is essential is invisible to the eye."[2]

2 Antoine de Saint Exupery, *The Little Prince* (New York: Harcourt, Brace & World, Inc., 1943), 87.

Among other things, I take that to mean that it's when we see that something different might be possible, it becomes possible. So half of creativity is seeing possibilities. That kind of seeing is what I mean by imagination. I keep saying that imagination is the dancing partner of faith. We're conditioned into thinking science gives the only true view of the world, that what's real can be measured, weighed, replicated. But is that so? Is what is real about you, or me, what can be measured? No, life is too dynamic for that.

In a little book entitled *The Meaning of It All,* the great Nobel Laureate physicist Richard Feynman writes about how critical uncertainty is to creativity in science: "Nothing is certain or proved beyond all doubt. You investigate for curiosity, because it is *unknown,* not because you know the answer."[3]

That touches on the mystery of God and the freedom faith gives us. Feynman goes helpfully on: "It is a great adventure to contemplate the universe beyond [humanity]. . . When . . . the mystery and majesty of matter are fully appreciated, to then turn the objective eye back on [humans] as matter, to see life as part of the universal mystery of greatest depth . . . usually ends in laughter and a delight in the futility of trying to understand. These scientific views end in awe and mystery, lost at the edge in uncertainty . . ."[4] Feynman goes even deeper when he describes himself, and us, as he stands at the edge of the sea: ". . . living things, masses of atoms. DNA, protein . . . dancing a pattern ever more intricate . . . out of the cradle onto the dry land . . . here it is standing . . . atoms with consciousness. . . matter with curiosity . . . wonders at wondering . . ."[5]

You don't have to get that exactly to grasp that Feynman is saying is that life is shot through with mystery, with possibilities, and so with wonder. Those are the ingredients of wonder, and creativity begins and continues in wonder. In a hundred ways Jesus shows that God puts us at the edge of uncertainty because that's where we are propelled toward the kingdom if we are daringly faithful.

"Love the Disordered Man who sings like a river . . . whose country is Forever."

Jesus is the non-anxious presence bidding us to see ourselves and the world differently, and so to live creatively.

Seeing differently. In an article about authors who offer a "whisper of hope," Doris Betts says, "Cormac McCarthy writes about a blind amputee who is arguing with a street preacher. The beggar says, 'Look at me, legless and everything. I reckon you think I ought to love God.' The preacher answers, 'Yeah,

3 Richard P. Feynman, *The Pleasure of Finding Things Out* (Cambridge, MA: Helix Books Perseus Publishing, 1999), 248.

4 Feynman, *The Pleasure of Finding Things Out*, 250.

5 Feynman, *The Pleasure of Finding Things Out*, 144.

I reckon you ought. An old blind mess and a legless fool is a flower in the garden of God.'"[6]

That hints at the creativity of seeing. Of looking past the surface and seeing people, whoever they are, whoever you are, however wounded, messed up, difficult, as flowers in the garden of God. Of looking beneath appearances to see that things and people are not always what they seem. Of reaching out to others with compassion, with mercy, joining in a mutual nudge toward justice. No big thing . . . or is it? What does it mean to love our neighbor and our enemies as ourselves? Goethe said that once we see and make a commitment, the whole universe moves. Maybe that's too grandiose, but something moves, even a little, and that's a major beginning. That's what creativity dares in the dance with uncertainty.

That's how the song of the Disordered One urges us to live: To follow our love over the walls of fear and narrow nationalism, over the hedges of racism and religious dogmatism, over the fences of poverty and exploitation. To shape uncertainty into justice and peace and beauty and a glad inclusion of everyone into the feast of the human family. It invites us on toward the country of forever.

***

6 Doris Betts, "Everything I Know About Writing I Learned in Sunday School," *The Christian Century*, October 21, 1998: 966–967.

What is the song the Disordered One sings to us?

The third stanza is, finally, this: Time is not always as confined or as small as it seems. There's a story of two old friends, Ed and Max, who live in the same neighborhood. Every morning, Ed appears at the door of Max's house and Max is ready. Then they go for a walk together. One morning, Ed turns to Max and asks, "What is your name again?" The two friends walk on a few steps, and Max turns to Ed and says, "How soon do you have to know?"

That's not quite so funny when you're older and stick it on the calendar of your own life, or when you're young and live on the anxious edge of urgency. Most of us, most of the time, want to know the answers and the outcome of things today, or at worst, tomorrow. It's part of our compulsion to have certainty, and it stifles creativity because creativity takes time.

So it takes patience, and for me at least, patience is in short supply. And so, therefore, is creativity. I give up much too soon. I get discouraged much too soon. I become pessimistic much too quickly. Do you?

But healing, justice, peace, reconciliation—all the things creativity is about in the artistry of our little lives and our small world—take time. How much time? Perhaps more time than any one of us has. But they will not take more time than God has. It is good to remember, as often as we can, that there is a non-anxious presence with us all the time, wherever we are.

"Love the Disordered One who sings like a river. . . whose country is Forever."

Forever is what we are part of, what our little creativity stretches out toward. That's why, more than anyone else, people of faith don't have to be afraid to fail. We need fear only not risking, not daring to be creative. Outcomes are up to God, and so are resurrections—of us, and of our failed efforts.

I go back to a story I love about buzzards because it's true, it's funny, and at heart it's about creativity and time. The buzzards are the ones who were supposed to be in a scene in the movie *Hud.* You may remember the story. In the movie, set and filmed in Texas, Paul Newman was supposed to ride up, discover a dead cow, look up at a tree branch lined with buzzards, and in his distress over the loss of the cow, fire his gun at one of the buzzards. Then all the other buzzards were supposed to fly into the wild blue.

Well, the first problem with shooting the scene was the scruffy condition of the local buzzards. So more photogenic buzzards had to be flown in at considerable expense. The second problem, more formidable, was how to keep the buzzards sitting on the tree branch until it was time for them to fly. The solution was to wire their feet to the branch, and then when Newman fires his gun, to pull the wire, release their feet and allow them to take off.

But the film makers had not reckoned with the mentality of buzzards. With their feet wired, the buzzards had balance problems but enough mobility to pitch forward. When they tried to fly, they hung upside down from the branch with their wings flopping. Not a good outcome for dramatic effect. Plus the circulatory system of buzzards doesn't work upside down. So after a minute or two, they passed out, hanging limp from the tree branch. That wasn't what Hollywood had in mind.

After six or seven episodes of pitching forward, passing out, being revived, being put back on the branch, pitching forward again, the buzzards gave up. So when the wire was pulled the next time and their feet released, they sat there, saying in their nonverbal sneer, "We tried that before. It did not work. We are not going to try it again." So they had to bring in a high-powered buzzard therapist to restore their self-esteem.[7]

I suppose we could go in a lot of different directions applying that story to the topic of creativity, including the forward flop. But the point I have in mind, and heart, comes out of my own experience, and out of the gospel. Most of us have had the equivalent experience of the buzzard flop, and like them, have given up and settled into a less risky, less humiliating life style. But we aren't

7 The buzzard story is adapted from "Dancing with Professors: The Trouble with Academic Prose," *New York Times Book Review*, October 31, 1993: 24.

buzzards, and that life style, though safe, isn't too joyful.

The gospel says take the risks no matter how many times you flop. Take the risks as many times as there are risks to take to imagine yourself whole and loving and a blessing, to mend a breech between you and someone, to do something for the sake of justice, to say your truth at whatever cost, to exercise compassion, to create something beautiful, to lift someone left by the side of the road, or the pew, or your desk or house.

***

What is the song the Disordered One sings to us?

The song is not complete with only three stanzas. There are blanks for you to fill in. That's so because it's an invitation to be creative, and no one can be creative for you.

As you sing your particular verse, remember that a non-anxious presence is with you always, to the end of the earth. That's reason to rejoice for the creativity you can live.

Follow your love, the butterfly, where it spins
over the wall, the hedge, the road, the fence,

and love the Disordered Man who sings like
a river whose form is Love, whose country is
Forever.

A Long View from the Parking Lot

Luke 12:22-34
Philippians 4:4-9

Maybe Jesus had pretty much worn them out by then—those twelve he'd rounded up from fishing boats and tax offices and rebel camps and anywhere else he could find them. Worn them out traipsing all over the country, day and after day, heading out early every morning, even after Jesus had been out praying most of the night. Worn them out with all that shake-things-up preaching and teaching. Worn them out with all that healing of peoples' stomach-turning diseases. Worn them out with all that shoulder rubbing with the smelly poor and hanging out with disreputable sinners, all that befriending of nobody women, and all that stressful bearding the authority lions in their dens. Worn them out until they weren't sure anymore which town they'd left or which one they were going toward.

Worn them out until they began to wonder out loud where the whole thing was headed and what was to become of them. Lately, Jesus had even started talking about death, his own death, and that's certainly a topic to put a kink in a campaign. They'd started out thinking he was the Messiah come to change things, a surefire winner they'd risk backing. But now they'd begun to doubt that he was a viable candidate after all, or one that would last long. As far as they could see, they were in a road show to big trouble. They were worn out, a little fed up, and a lot scared.

So right there, on the dusty road midway between their dreams and their distress, Jesus sits the disciples down and speaks some of the gentlest, most assuring words he ever spoke: "Do not worry about your life . . . for life is more than food, and the body more than clothing." The words resonate. Jesus might well be speaking to us, on the road from there to here to wherever, midway between our weariness and our worries.

And yet, the words are so easily forgotten that we need to hear them again: "Consider the ravens . . ." Not particularly pretty birds or lovely singers, their only sound a grating *kraaak*.

". . . And yet God feeds them. Of how much more value are you than the birds! And can any of you by worrying add a single hour to your span of life? If then you are not able to do so small a thing as that, why do you worry about the rest?"

The words pour out of him—and over us—as haunting as flute music or a Gregorian chant: "Consider the lilies. . . even Solomon in all his glory was not clothed like one of these. But if God so clothes the grass of the field . . . how much more will he clothe you—you of little faith!. . . do not keep worrying . . . Instead, strive for [God's] kingdom, and these things will be given to you as well. Do not be afraid . . . for it is your Father's good pleasure to give you the kingdom. Sell your possessions and give alms . . ."

Those last words—about selling our stuff and giving alms—are less about duty than about freedom. They're about the freedom to take chances and laugh, even in the face of adversity or failure, or death itself. We don't have to pinch, or grasp, or crouch, or run. But even if we do, the words haunt us, stir our longing: *Do not worry. Do not be afraid.* Why? Because God is at work in it all.

My friend Rick Josiassen recently included in a note to me some words of Yale professor of philosophy Dr. Eugene Rosenstock-Huessy. The words touch on the meaning of what Jesus is saying: "If we take the short view, we can make God a liar. But if we take the long view, we can see the glorious, unfolding mystery."[1] Look at things in the short view, and they're a blur. But take the long view, things come into focus. Short term is face-value, long term is grace-value.

Faith is more than half about taking the long view. Don't you suppose that's why Jesus used those nature images in what he spells out to the disciples sitting there by the roadside—and to us sitting wherever we're sitting now? Jesus is emphasizing that more than present appearances are called for in taking the long view. The long view goes beyond the surface of "now" to swim the dimension of depth. God works beneath the surface, beyond the appearances, more attentively than the ticking of time, under, ahead of any given moment. Taking the long view is about paying attention to the slow work of the mysterious, persistent haunt of grace.

So there they are, the disciples, halfway between the fishing boats they left bobbing behind and the splintery cross they are headed for, and Jesus is telling them to focus on the kingdom of God, to take the long view and to not be afraid. *"Consider the ravens . . . Consider the lilies . . ."* At least it is enough to get them on their feet and back on the road.

Surely Jesus' words came back to Peter and John like the scent of honeysuckle much later as they stood astonished by the empty tomb that first Easter morning, trying to focus on a view that is longer by an eternity than they'd dared to dream, stretching out past death itself. You see, the gospel is about nothing if it's not about focusing on the long view, on the unfolding mystery of God's

1 Dr. Eugene Rosenstock-Huessy, *I Am An Impure Thinker* (Norwich, VT: Argo Books, 1970).

grace. Which of us doesn't need the assurance of Jesus' words to see beyond the short term?

So hear them again through a personal experience. It happened on a Sunday morning on the road between the church office and the side entrance to the Education Building. As we all do from time to time, I was feeling worn out, a little fed up, and maybe a lot scared when I drove into the parking lot. About what? About variations on the same things that shrink all of our worlds and shorten our view.

As I got out of the car, wagging my briefcase behind me, I spotted Cakky Braun and her little son, Robert. I called to her, asking if she would wait a minute for me. She stopped where the parking lot meets the ramp into the Education Building.

I studied Cakky as I walked toward her. I swear, she looked like a psychedelic angel with her multicolored scarf wrapped around her head to cover the hair loss from chemotherapy, and her jacket like a field of wild flowers punctuated with rolling mounds that turned out to be pockets bulging with health food snacks.

Recently Cakky had been diagnosed with inflammatory breast cancer, the most aggressive kind. The chemo was to shrink the tumor before surgery. I walked over and asked how she was. She began to give me a long view from the parking lot.

"I've never been better," she said, her eyes glowing like a delighted child's, her words tumbling out with a kind of excitement. "I realize my cancer is truly a chance for me to let God transform my life, and that's happening. People ask me and I tell them there's nothing like a near-catastrophic disease to get you focused on what matters, get your priorities straight. I'm glad that's happening. You know, when the first round of chemo didn't shrink the tumor, I got real down about it. But now I think it was a good thing because if it had worked the first time, it would have been too easy. I had to deal with my fear so I could move ahead."

When I asked her how she did that, she responded, "Diet, hypnotherapy. But really, the key is I pray all the time. All the time! I don't take God for granted any more. You know?"

I told her I pray for her every day. She gave me a little hug and said, "I know. The prayers of people help. It's the most important thing anyone can do. I pray instead of worry, because if I worry that much, I might as well be dead anyway. Being anxious shrinks your life, you know what I mean?"

I said I absolutely knew that.

She went on, softly "You've really helped me, and I thank you. I know you love me. I'm trying to love everyone. I'm focusing on serving God and being present to my family."

I stood there listening and thinking about what I'd been worried about a few minutes earlier. Whatever it was, it looked pretty puny from where I stood at that moment, at the edge of the parking lot with the long view Cakky was stretching out for me.

"When I got my head together is when things started changing for me." It seemed to me as if Cakky were almost singing somehow. "My tumors are thirty percent smaller than they were. I keep praying. That's what I do now. Every day it's amazing how God gives me quietness and sends kind of deep thoughts, sort of like angels, to keep me going and feeling whole. I'm a lot less afraid now, and fear's really the worst thing about this stuff."

"So you've been healed in the way that matters most," I said, hugging her.

"Yeah, even if I don't get cured," she said. "No matter what happens, I'll be okay. The family will be okay. We've gone through half our savings, but it doesn't matter. If we have to sell the house, we'll be okay. No more worrying about climbing the career ladder, like I was doing before, with my sixty- to seventy-hour weeks. It was crazy. If I have to deliver mail, it'll be fine, being outdoors, getting exercise." Then Cakky added, "Thanks for your love and being there for me. Let me know what I can do for you."

"Pray for me," I said, tearing up.

"I do," she said. "I already do."

"I guess that's why I'm doing as well as I am," I smiled. "But keep praying, will you?"

"Okay. And let me know what else I can do for you, please," she said.

I put my arm around her, and we walked into the building together. I'd been given a great gift, a long view from the parking lot.

"If we take the short view. . ."

If? Mostly we do, don't we?

"But if we take the long view . . ."

What else is the church about except to help each other take the long view? The wonder is that it happens often enough to keep us going.

"Consider the ravens. . . Consider the lilies. . . Strive for God's kingdom . . . Do not be afraid, little flock, for it is your Father-Mother's good pleasure to give you the kingdom."

What does it mean to *strive* for a kingdom if God is *giving* it to us? I used to think, and too much still do, that striving for God's kingdom meant doing all sorts of virtuous things, working for justice, fighting for good causes, making all the effort I could to improve society and the community, efforts that we all willingly and rightly undertake. But maybe too willingly . . . if we get worn out, a little fed up, and maybe a lot scared, blurred by the short view. It's easy to let the long view get out of focus.

Don't misunderstand. I think all our efforts for justice and all our expressions of compassion are good and necessary ways of faith. But I don't think those things are the first thing it means to strive for the kingdom. I think the first way is focusing on the kingdom, focusing on the goodness and grace of God, even in hard times. I think first of all it means taking the long view and seeing "the glorious, unfolding mystery" we are part of *but not responsible for.* We work *out of* God's kingdom, not *for* it. Otherwise, we live joyless, burdened, anxious lives.

I'm coming to grasp—and be grasped by—the wisdom that striving has something to do with what Cakky said: "I pray all the time. All the time! It's amazing how God gives me quietness and sends kind of deep thoughts, sort of like angels, to keep me going and feeling whole. I'm a lot less afraid now, and fear's really the worst thing about this stuff. Shrinks your life, you know what I mean?"

We *do* know, don't we? Striving in faith is about the long view. It's about shrinking our fear a little and expanding our lives a lot. Striving is what Paul wrote about in his letter to the Philippians: "Do not worry about anything, but in everything by prayer and supplication with thanksgiving, let your requests be made known to God. And the peace of God which passes all understanding, will guard your hearts and your minds in Christ Jesus."

The long view is rooted in that peace. Out of that peace, true freedom is born, the freedom not to be afraid. Out of that freedom, our work of compassion and justice is generated. When we pray, with thanksgiving and honesty, our shoulders can drop from up around our ears, and in some deep way, as with Cakky, we can trust—or begin to—that everything will be all right. Otherwise, it just comes down to being worn out, fed up a little, and, sooner or later, scared a lot because no matter how hard we work for good, if the outcome is entirely up to us and our efforts, the game is over.

Keep focused on the long view: "I pray all the time. All the time! . . . I'm a lot less afraid now." What else but the peace of God is that?

I think striving for the kingdom also has to do with daring to be generous. *"Do not be afraid, little flock, for it is your Father-Mother's good pleasure to give you the kingdom. Sell your possessions, and give alms."* That's about freedom, isn't it? That's the long view Cakky was talking about: "No matter what happens, I'll be okay. The family will be okay. We've gone through half our savings, but it doesn't matter. If we have to sell the house, we'll be okay . . . Please tell me what I can do for you."

Whatever else freedom is, it surely involves generosity of spirit. Generosity is a risk. It bets that there really is enough for everyone, so life isn't about grasping and hoarding. Generosity is an antidote for the contagious dis-ease of having more than is good for our souls. Generosity isn't just about giving things and money to good causes and institutions working for justice and peace, though it may mean *at least* that. That kind of generosity can begin a discipline that leads to our freedom of spirit.

But generosity is about more than giving money. It's about being open to other people, sharing ourselves with them.

"Please tell me what I can do for you," Cakky asked.

"Pray for me," this professional pray-er said from my heart.

"I already do," she said as though she had nothing else to do.

Her generosity carried healing for both of us.

I think generosity is close to the heart of prayer. What if we prayed generously for each other, and for those we think of as enemies? What if we prayed for our leaders and the poor in one breath, for the oppressed and exploited at the same time we prayed for the wealthy struggling with their own kind of oppression? Imagine what answers we might become to our own prayers. Generosity is about giving the precious gift of time to each other. It's paying attention to other people, and that quite literally means paying the cost with a piece of ourselves to attend to others. Generosity stretches us toward the long view.

It's curious how close to science generosity comes. Cakky's experience confirms it. I keep going back to what Nobel Laureate in physics Richard Feynman says about the whole scientific enterprise: It is about the question, "If I do this, what will happen?" and then responding to the question with, "Try it and see."[2] Isn't that essentially what Jesus did? I don't suppose many people thought he could heal people by forgiving them, or give sight to a blind man by mixing clay and spit and smearing it on his eyes, or feeding a crowd of thousands with five loaves and two fish, and so on and on. Most people, including his disciples, would have said out of hand, "If you try that, nothing will happen and you'll have played the fool." But Jesus' spirit was too generous *not* to "try it and see." And lo and behold, look what happened.

Generosity stretches toward the long view. Being peacemakers, going the second mile, loving neighbor and enemy as ourselves, feeding the hungry, caring for the sick, liberating the captives, being merciful, taking the log out of our own eye before dealing with the speck in another's eye. Try it and see.

Will it do any good? Try it and see, and look as far down the road as you can imagine. Try it and see, even with the most unlikely brothers and sisters you can think of, even with your supposed enemies.

Being generous means not giving up our efforts to do justly, or to make peace, or to be trustworthy in our relationships if in the short term, or by the short view, they don't seem to work. Generosity means that risking even the modest gifts and compassionate spirit of each of us not only increases our freedom in grace, but enables God to work slow miracles with us and through us. "Try it and see." Take the long view of yourself.

In the end, maybe something simple is as startling and profound as anything complicated can be. Maybe truth comes in a children's song as powerfully as in the theory of General Relativity or the map of the double helix of the human genetic code. Mostly, we

2 Richard P. Feynman, *The Pleasure of Finding Things Out* (Cambridge, MA: Helix Books, Perseus Publishing, 1999), 255.

like sophistication because it makes us seem so smart. We can slip away and hide in it, arguing our short-term views which make God a liar, or irrelevant.

But maybe, if we admit it, the straight-jacket of sophistication is unbuckled by a simple confession of love that buckles our knees instead, and softens our hearts.

"Do not worry about your life . . . Consider the ravens . . . God feeds them. Of how much more worth are you than the birds . . . Do not be afraid . . . it is your Father's good pleasure to give you the kingdom."

What relief, what peace, what joy, what freedom there would be if we could begin by accepting that gift. I got a glimpse of what it could be when Cakky gave me the gift of a long view from the parking lot. Her honest simplicity cut through all my over-blown pretensions of being so smart and sophisticated—or having to be.

Karl Barth was one of the brilliant theologians and biblical scholars of the late twentieth century. Barth wrote many weighty and revolutionary books on a wide range of topics and called them *Church Dogmatics.* Toward the end of his life, this great thinker was asked if he could make a brief summary of his systematic work. He nodded and answered, "Jesus loves me, this I know, for the Bible tells me so."

That was a huge gift to those of us who bobbed along in the wake of this profound man. Maybe that simple affirmation of faith, coming out of his long view, was the most profound and liberating word of all.

"Jesus loves me, this I know, for the Bible tells me so."

"Do not be afraid . . . it is God's good pleasure to give you the kingdom."

The first year I was the pastor of a church, I was a graduate student in contemporary theology working toward a PhD at Yale. Preaching a sermon every week in my little church turned out to be a more daunting task than the exams and term papers of graduate school. I struggled each week in my first year as a preacher, as I struggled all the years since.

I don't think I could have kept on with being a pastor for long unless I had come across this little prayer by Donald Baillie, a great Scottish theologian and preacher. The prayer is so deeply engraved in my head and my heart that it is part of me, and I call it up and pray it very often:

Let me no more my comfort draw
From my frail hold of Thee;
In this alone rejoice in awe,
Thy mighty grasp of me.[3]

Pray this simple, deep prayer with me, for all our sakes—and the sake of the long view.

3 D. M. Baillie, *To Whom Shall We Go?* (New York: Charles Scribner's Sons, 1955), 16.

Tracks in the Straw

TALES SPUN FROM THE MANGER

For Mark, David, Karen, and Thomas
whose stories are wondrous
and whose tracks are in my heart.

Introduction

Start with the visit of the angel Gabriel to the peasant girl Mary. Most of us have heard the story so many times we glaze over whenever we hear it yet again, if indeed we pay much attention to the Christmas story at all. But I risk beginning with this visit because it takes us quickly to the heart of the mystery of Advent/Christmas and the why of this book. Gabriel comes to Mary and says, "Greetings, favored one. The Lord is with you."

What's Mary's reaction? "She was much perplexed by his words and wondered what sort of greeting this might be."

What's so striking is that this exchange between Gabriel and Mary happens *before* there is any word to Mary about her becoming pregnant by the Holy Spirit, about her bearing and giving birth to the Messiah. All Gabriel says is, "God favors you. God is with you," and Mary is in a dither of confusion.

Why? Of all the possible reasons, cut to the main one. Mary is confused because if God is with her, why can't she see him, touch him? If God favors her, loves her, where is he?

That is the core issue of Christmas, if not of religion itself. If God is real, why isn't God as evident to us as everything else that's real?

Mary's confusion gets worse when she learns she is to become pregnant and give birth to the Messiah even though she's a virgin. "How can this be?" she asks. She's told it will happen by the activity of God. The invisible God of all creation will become visible in a human being. That doesn't clear up the mystery, it just deepens it. So Mary says all anyone could say: "Let it be with me according to your word."

God pitching his tent in human history and our personal histories? The Spirit that hovered over the deep darkness at creation becoming flesh to live among us? Indeed, "How can this be?" If God is real, if God is with us, if God loves us, where is she? Why can't we see him, hear him? So our struggle is very like Mary's. In a way it is even more complicated because, for us in our technological age, mystery is considered to be something we don't know *yet* rather than something that is essentially unknowable. We are proudly resistant to Mary's trusting reaction, "Let it be with me according to your word."

We insist we're not intellectually naive and admit we're not pure or virginal—spiritually or otherwise—so our questions take a different shape but are just as compelling as Mary's. How can God be with us in the common reality of our daily lives, our confusion, our struggle, our poverty and pain, our small hopes and little loves? How can there be anything like birth, or rebirth, or new life in us or through us?

Still, the drama begins: "Greetings, favored ones. The Lord is with you." There it is, the heart of Advent, of Christmas . . . and the heart of our confusion. Augustine wrote of the mystery of the incarnation by concluding it was the visible disclosure of an invisible reality. Obviously, something visible cannot fully reveal what is invisible. It can only point to that invisible reality. It cannot reduce it to visible proportion or prove it by measurable data. So why doesn't God make things more plain? I believe it's a matter of grace.

One cold night about a year ago, I sat with a man on his patio. The man had just tragically lost his beloved young wife, mother of three children, eleven-, nine- and six-years old. We struggled and stammered together to try to understand what such a loss meant, how God could let it happen, where God was in the face of this enormous pain. Recently I heard from that man. He wrote, "I will never forget that night on my patio and the way you said, This is why God hid Moses in the cleft of the rock: we can't live looking at God full in the face.'"

I remember that night, too, and I know that no one can look at the face of God and live. It would be too much for any of us to see such utter incomprehensible holiness and glory and power. There is something terrible as well as tender about God. So God put Moses in the cleft of a rock and kept his hand over the cleft until he passed, and then he let Moses see only his backside—a trace, a glimmer.

Yes, it's a story, but absolutely true and resonant as well with the deeper mystery of Advent/Christmas. We are all in some kind of cleft: a cleft of time and space, a cleft of culture, family, humanity: a cleft of our mortality, our finitude. There are things we cannot see, or touch. They remain invisible.

Even so, we can see glimpses, glimmers of the invisible, terrible, tender God in the incarnation, profoundly true glimmers but necessarily incomplete. The glimpses are heartening, healing, compelling, yet confusing, and they arouse the imagination. It cannot be otherwise with great, unfolding truth. Or with the mystery of God. As the gospel of John affirms in one breath, "The Word became flesh . . ." yet cautions in the next, "No one has seen God."

So we come face-to-face with the real mystery of Advent/Christmas. God is not just somewhere "back there" or "out there" but "right here." As I said in the introduction to the First Edition of *Tracks in the Straw*, that means the mystery is a very human one. And yet, what makes the human mysterious is the presence of God in it, with us. So the human story is really always about God and what God does with, in, and for human beings in spite of ourselves.

For the mystery of Advent/Christmas is the mystery of the human and the specific—as specific and human as each one of us, as the face you saw in the mirror this morning, as the old woman you passed on the stairs, as the children you almost tripped over on your way out of the subway or into the office, as the shoppers elbowing their way through to the store counters, as the human faces and shapes and sizes and colors wandering the streets with you.

I titled this book *Tracks in the Straw* to suggest that God isn't obvious in entering the world. What is more ordinary than a baby's birth to a poor family in a poor country? Still, God leaves "tracks" in the straw. The tracks are faint but there for those who look and follow them with imagination. And imagination is the dancing partner of faith.

Poet Kathleen Norris writes that in Ephesians when Paul explicitly compares marriage with Christ's love for the church, he finally gives up and simply says, with exasperation as well as wonder in his voice, "This is a great mystery." Norris concludes, this is "what happens when you discover a metaphor so elusive you know it must be true. As you elaborate, and try to explain, you begin to stumble over words and their meanings. The literal takes hold, the unity and the beauty flee. Finally you have to say, I don't know what it means; *here it is*.[1]

The poet's insight holds for the birth of Jesus and what it means, and for the Advent/ Christmas season that gathers around it. Though that birth is surely not just a metaphor, it is a mystery because it involves the unknowable—dare I say sneaky?—ways of God.

1 *The Cloister Walk*, Kathleen Norris, Riverhead Books, New York, 1996.

I put my experience of that incredible mystery in stories because I believe with all my heart that is the most accurate and faithful way to follow God's tracks in the straw. I have rewritten the stories from the First Edition of *Tracks in the Straw*, some radically, some moderately, so they will carry more powerfully the awe and the possibilities of Christmas. I have added some new stories and omitted others. The stories also have been arranged so that they can be read one section each day of Advent.

I have tried to add something deeper to the book as I have gone deeper into my own experience of the mystery of Christmas and my reflections on what it means. These stories are for everyone who knows the ache and insistence of longing in their lives—believers, doubters, clergy, laity, families, single people, old, young, black, white, brown, male, female, you.

Now, after stumbling over words and their meaning, yet trusting that the terrible, delightful, healing wonder and beauty has not fled them, and thanking those whose feedback has helped me with this new edition, most especially my beloved wife, Dr. Jan Filing, as well as my gifted colleague, Dr. Ann Marie Donohue, and my remarkable editor, Marcia Broucek, I say with exasperation and wonder at what I have written: "I don't know all that it means. *Here it is!*"

* * *

A Personal Prologue

"I Feel Better"

Every chance he gets, which is too often, a friend of mine says, "It's the end of the world as we know it, and I feel fine." He swears the saying is original, but I'm sure he picked it up somewhere. At first I chuckled when he said it, now I roll my eyes. I know if it really was the end of the world as he knows it, he wouldn't feel so fine.

At least I know I wasn't feeling fine that night three days before Christmas as I drove through the rain and sleet to meet my daughter Karen for a late supper at a center city tavern she liked. The world I knew was ending, not just in the somewhat abstract way it always is, but very specifically and painfully.

Karen, my bright, beautiful kid, had dropped out of college to try to deal with some tormenting personal problems. I was scared by what she was doing, but I could only be with her in whatever way I could and however she would let me. In fact, that was why I was slip-sliding along the River Drive toward our rendezvous.

In addition, my mother was dying, and my father was clinically depressed. My first marriage was unraveling, which pained and disillusioned me and my family, hurt and angered my kids, and put my professional future at risk. It actually was the end of the world as I knew it, and I didn't feel at all fine.

I turned off the drive and went past shops and department stores splendidly decked out for Christmas, lights, decorations, bell-ringing Santas, shoppers weaving along everywhere. I figured some of them must have felt as disoriented as I did that night. I know that Christmas is a tough time for lots of people. That year, I was experiencing it first hand.

I drove through the heart of the shopping district into a section where homeless folk camped out over steam grates in the side-walks in front of stores whose owners had closed early and pulled down security grates over the windows.

I turned onto Lombard Street where row houses, eateries, and small shops existed cheek by jowl. I was lucky to find a parking spot a couple of blocks from the place where I was to meet Karen.

I got out of the car and looked around, as if waking from a dream. Then it came to me, two lines from a poem I'd read years earlier. Why just those two lines came as clear as from the poet's pen, I don't really know. Nor did I recall any other lines or even the name of the poet. Only two lines:

"This world is wild as an old wives' tale
And strange the plain things are."

The lines came like a visitation. That night, the world did seem wild to me, and plain things had become strange. And the night was still young.

The sleet had stopped, and the rain was a cold drizzle against my face as I walked down Lombard toward Vince's Tavern at the corner of 19th Street. Somewhere in the block between 22nd and 21st, I came across a row house with the whole front window jammed with a manger scene. Judging from neighboring houses, at some point the residents of this one had enlarged the window to twice its original size—probably to accommodate this exhibition! It was something you'd be more apt to see in a department store window than in a row house on Lombard Street. The painted figures must have been three feet tall, and each was lit from inside with glowing light. It was truly impressive.

I smiled as I hurried past, silently saluting the piety of the family who gave up half their living room and all of their privacy to display the manger scene in such splendor. Nativity scenes in South Philadelphia row houses are not uncommon, and yet "strange the plain things are."

I rushed on to meet Karen. We ate and talked. But the meeting didn't ease any of my anxiety or her pain. When we left Vince's, the rain had stopped. We stood on the corner and said good-bye. There on the street, I hugged Karen for a long time, and she hugged me back. I told her I loved her and asked her to be careful and to stay in touch with me no matter what. She promised she would. Then she went off to meet a friend, and I walked slowly back to my car.

I was thinking so hard about my daughter that when I came upon the row house nativity again, I was momentarily caught off-guard. This time I stopped to look at it more closely. There it all was: the coterie of shepherds, the three wise men, a full complement of angels, a number of assorted animals. They were all gathered around Joseph and Mary, who were side by side, looking . . . actually just about where I was standing. That was strange.

I stepped closer and examined the scene more carefully. My first impression had been right: There was no manger, no infant Jesus in the window! In effect, the street was the manger, and I was standing in it. Out of the corner of my eye, I thought I glimpsed someone smiling and nodding in the shadows behind the shepherds, but when I looked again, no one was there. Had that Lombard Street family intended that the street be the manger?

Intended or not, the scene was strange. The fragment of the long-forgotten poem crossed my mind again:

"This world is wild as an old wives' tale
And strange the plain things are."

What made those words float out of the near chaos of my life to the surface of my mind just when they did? Why had I come across that row-house nativity scene on my way to and from meeting Karen that night? I can't tell you. What I can tell you is the nativity scene made that row house, all the neighboring houses, no longer so plain but very strange.

And even stranger became the old familiar story that row-house scene was telling. That night, that old story was being told differently. This time those silent, lighted figures were looking expectantly out on the street for the Christ child, out on the street where the beasts are motorized now, and the milk comes in cartons, and the lambs wool in worsted suits, and people like shepherds sleep on steam grates, and people like wise men dish out food in soup kitchens—or work in political movements or business coalitions or churches to change things so someday there might not be homeless people or hungry children or addicted parents.

I stood there with tears in my eyes. With a force that lumped in my throat, I realized that just where I was standing, the Christmas miracle happens. In the street, where human traffic goes endlessly by, where men and women and children live and limp and play and cry and laugh and love and fight and worry and curse and praise and pray and die, just there Christmas keeps coming silently, insistently, mysteriously.

I turned and walked back to my car, the mystery of it making me light-headed and light-hearted. I laughed to myself as I thought about a wild stable always being close at hand in this wild world, about the strange, saving birth taking place in unlikely places like Lombard Street where I was walking—taking place anywhere I would ever walk, any street anyone would ever walk.

I stood by the car and looked in awe back down the street, trying to grasp the revelation of the strange, saving birth taking place again and yet again in all the unlikely places lining our streets—at the tables where we spill coffee and our secrets; in the beds where the sheets get wrinkled and the dreams disturbing; in human exchanges in taverns or cafes where our hopes for each other and ourselves stumble over our limited power; in the offices where decisions and lives are made, unmade, and somehow remade. It happens in the shops where we search for some item that will be just right but never quite find it; on the corners where we dodge each other in our frantic pace, yet sometimes quickly explore each other's eyes, longing to make human contact in the midst of the rat race. It happens on the steam grates where, once in a while, passers-by fish a coin from their pockets and drop it in the hand of one of those homeless brothers or sisters.

Ah, yes, "strange the plain things are." A Christ come to be close at hand in unlikely people like that row-house family, and my family floundering as it was just then, and countless other families on countless other streets. Jesus born again and again, in a thousand times a thousand miracles, a thousand times a thousand moments, and an occasional heart. God close at hand. Always.

"God does something everywhere, but doesn't do everything anywhere." A teacher I loved said that once, and I keep forgetting it—and remembering it. I drove home that night, thinking of my daughter, my sons, and of all the pain and struggles we would go through on our particular versions of Lombard Street. In that moment I knew that nothing could keep me from standing by and with my kids. And I thought of other people I loved, and those I didn't love much or at all, and I knew I would do the best I could to stand by and with all the "street people" of life because I had the God-given chance, the small, precious gift of doing something somewhere.

And it also occurred to me that one of the "somethings" God does everywhere—and certainly at Christmas—is to bring to an end the world as we know it. That doesn't make me feel fine, but it does make me feel better. Much better. Because the rest of the "something" is that then a new world begins in a small explosion of light no darkness can overcome.

* * *

IN THE SHADOWS

Clumsy Beautiful

They're always yellin' at me in this place, especially on busy nights like that one. When it gets so busy as that, the owner of the inn is fit to be tied, and maybe he should be. I suppose he's scared that if somethin' ain't just right, it'll make some customer mad, and he'll lose a few denarii. So, the busier the place gets, the more he yells. He yells kind of quiet, you know, like a snake hissin'. But there ain't no mistakin' what it is.

"Deborah," he'll yell. (That's my name and the prettiest thing about me, I've been told more than once—like I ought to have an ugly name.) "Deborah, get the wine goblets . . . sweep the floor . . . wipe up that vomit . . . get some wood . . ." and so on and on and on. Actually, he yells other things at me, too, but I won't repeat 'em. I try to ignore 'em and just do my job.

I'll tell you one thing they call me, though: Clumsy! I suppose I am, too, since I'm always droppin' cups, or spillin' wine, or trippin' over a door sill, or catchin' my dress and tearin' it on somethin'. People laugh at me, 'specially the customers, and they say crude things to me. I don't understand why my body won't do what I want it to. It's a source of embarrassment.

I'm clumsy with words, too, if truth be told. When anyone asks me somethin', and I have to answer, my throat gets tight and my mouth dries up, and I just go blank. Even with the other servants, I don't say much, though you mustn't get the wrong idea, thinkin' I'm shy and innocent or somethin' like that. I can tell a bawdy story good as the next one and hold my own in an argument, believe me. It's just that pretty words seem as hard for me to get hold of as the doves I try to catch sometimes out back. I been told it don't matter much, my bein' clumsy, since I'm just a servant and a woman. But that's what I wanted to tell you about, sort of. I wish I could tell you about it so you'd understand. Maybe I'll understand better myself if I can find the words. So, I'll try.

Oh, wait . . . another thing. I'm plain. I mean real plain! I think you ought to know that, though I ain't sure why, 'cept I think it's important for you to know me if you're goin' to understand what I'm tryin' to tell you. And the way a person feels about herself helps other people know her, don't it? I didn't say that too clear, but I trust you get my meanin'. Bein' plain is, well, a particular burden for a woman, I suppose.

Oh, men pinch and pat and feel when they can. And they're always tryin' to get me to do things with them, sayin' things to me they don't mean. And sometimes I go with them just for the attention, even for a few minutes. To tell the truth, I like the feelin' of what we do together, if you catch my meanin'. But sad to say, men don't mean nothin' *permanent* when it comes to me. Fact is, though, I ain't too much worse off than most women in Bethlehem, even them who get taken for wife. A little worse, maybe. Less secure than wives, probably.

Anyway, truth of it is, bein' a servant girl in an inn in a town like this ain't too glamorous. You get treated sort like of a beast of burden, a bearer of water and wood and dishes and nothin' much else, and you get to thinkin' that 'bout yourself after while.

But to get to the point, that day—or that night I should say—I was feelin' 'specially like a beast of burden. I'd been workin' all day. The town was runnin' over with strangers comin' in for the census takin'. The inn was so crowded and so noisy, you couldn't hear yourself think, and I had a terrible headache. I must have been up and down the stairs and out in the shed and back, I don't know . . . seemed like a hundred, two hundred times at least. I was trembly tired, in a fog almost. I'd fallen over people's feet a couple times, and once I just burst out cryin' and snuck into the pantry closet for a minute. It had been like that all week, really, and now it was halfway through the night and everythin' was still goin' strong.

"Deborah, you mangy goat, get some more wood."

To tell the truth, I was glad to go outside. Maybe I could rest a minute, quiet-like. Goin' through the kitchen, I grabbed a crust of bread and slapped Nathan's hand away when he tried to get fresh. I pushed out into the night air and leaned for a second on the wall. "Bearer of wood and water and wine . . . and whatever else men want . . ."

Goin' across the yard, I munched the bread, gulpin' it down like I was starvin'. Suddenly I tripped and fell in the mud. Right in the mud on my hunkies. Dropped the crust right in the mud, too, before I'd finished it. I just lay there and caught my breath before I started cryin', more from tiredness than hurt. Then I sat up and started laughin'; I don't know why. Maybe 'cause suddenly it kinda came to me.

What came to me was how wonderful still it was. The moon was hangin' up there so silver and soft-like, and the clouds over its face were touchin' it, gentle as I imagine a lover doin'. And the stars were like someone just lit them like candles; and the darkness around them had begun to crumple into tiny flakes like some old shawl, and the flakes was failin' away, floatin' down . . . like black snow failin' quiet all around me. And the cold and the mud and the light were all quiverin', like durin' your first kiss and you wonder what happens next.

Funny how I'd never felt quite like that before or noticed how sweet bread tastes on your tongue before it goes down to calm your growlin' belly. Sittin' there, I felt like I'd waked life up, like it had been sort of sleepin' there unnoticed before. At least by me.

Then I heard a baby cryin' somewhere. I've heard lots of babies cry before, but usually it's just annoyin', 'specially in the night when you're tryin' to sleep. But this time I giggled at the sound. And wondered about it. So I followed the cryin'. And there in the stable, where old Naphtali works, was this family, a mother with her arm around a baby, jigglin' it sort of, tryin' to get it to stop cryin'. And what musta been the father with his arm around the mother, tryin' to comfort her. And this baby, a boy, obviously just born, red and wet, but so full of life it was spillin' out over everythin' around, includin' me.

I don't know what it was happened then. Maybe it was just noticin' that a new-born baby is like . . . like a miracle. I mean, there is this little thing, and it's alive. All its parts are there. It's breathin' and movin' and makin' little sounds. How does that happen? I mean, how does that *happen?* I just stared at the mystery. I don't have the words to tell you. It was life, pure and simple. I mean it was life, pure enough all right, but not so simple. No baby is, and certainly not this one. This one was makin' me breathe in gulps, like I couldn't get enough of that life he was about.

I *can* tell you that right then, lookin' right into the heart of life, or whatever you call it—spunk or hope or love . . . right then, and ever since, I felt beautiful. And furious proud, too, to be a human being, to be a woman, to be part of what produces a miracle like that . . . or *receives* a miracle like that . . . even *is* sort of a miracle like that.

See, I am clumsy with words. But all the same, I just felt, well, strangely graceful, about me and life and even about the owner of the inn. Imagine bein' that close, that much a part of the heart of . . . of God, I guess. Yes, God. I do wish I could tell you better. Maybe you got your own words. I hope so. I hope you know how mysterious God is and how beautiful God makes people, even when they are plain like me and got mud on them. Or blood, like the baby. I hope you got the words for that . . . or the quietness.

* * *

The Ninth Woman

In some things you have no choice. You just have to do them whether you want to or not, regardless of whether you see much purpose in them. It isn't until afterward that you may wonder about them and about why things happened just that way to you.

Off in Rome, Caesar Augustus decided on a census, and we had to comply. So it began. It may have seemed a little thing to him, but to us, it was a major disruption. There was a lot of talk, resentment. But no one could do anything about it. Everybody had to go to the place of their ancestors to be counted. We went to Bethlehem, Amos and I and our children, because that's where his family was from. The thing I couldn't figure out was why we had to be counted. Some said it was for taxes. Since we had nothing, anyway, such a long hard trip seemed doubly ridiculous to us. But we had to go, so we went. And little Deborah was sick all the way; burning hot she was. It is hard enough taking care of a family at home. Traveling, it's impossible. But you do what you have to do.

As it turned out, the afternoon we finally got to a place where the Roman legionnaires were asking people the official questions and writing down the answers on long scrolls, I was the ninth woman. I don't know why I remember that. The soldier asking questions called out for another to write down, "Amos of Godara, the fourteenth man on this day, with four male children, three female, and his wife, the ninth woman." And all the while, they were joking among themselves, paying little attention to us, really.

It was hard and bare, a number like that—so simple and matter-of-fact and distant, somehow. I remember shivering, and I remember my feet hurting and Deborah being so hot . . . the ninth woman . . .

Afterward, when the man said that was all and we could go, there was no place we could stay. Those who could afford it stayed in the inn. Some had family in Bethlehem who could put them up. We less fortunate ones, well, we did the best we could. A man Amos met said some people were being allowed to stay out behind the inn in a cave where the animals were kept. So we went. It was out of the wind. I remember the wind that night, and I recall hoping Deborah wouldn't get even sicker. We found some water for her, and we shared a little bread. It was a bit crowded, with all the people and animals.

Then . . . over in a corner of the place, this woman started to groan and make sharp cries like a wounded animal. I knew immediately what it was. I felt sorry for her. It wasn't much of a place for giving birth. But I knew I'd have to help, too, and that was irritating. I was so tired. Wasn't Deborah's being sick *enough*? And the other kids crying and being so restless? But, you do what you have to do.

The woman's eyes were wide, frightened. The pain seemed to surprise her. It often does the first time. Her husband didn't know what to do, except to keep reassuring her. Birth's too much for most men to understand. For most women, too, I suppose, but you have to take care of things first, then figure it out later, if you can. Most men can't do without answers before they try anything.

It took a while. It wasn't an easy birth. It was good I was there to help. Knowing how it was, I could tell her about it, and that seemed to calm her. I told her to scream if she had to and bite her shawl—not her lip. And I reminded her that the pain was helping the baby get out.

When he finally came, I cleaned him with a bit of crumpled straw, as you do a new-born animal. The father gave me an old blanket he'd gotten somewhere. I wrapped the baby and gave him to his mother. She was exhausted. And so was I, but I was glad I could help.

There's nothing like seeing what happens between a mother and a baby in that first few minutes. I've been there lots of times, helping in my little village of Godara. But never in a stable. Yet, the strange thing is, I felt it that night, too, that powerful, special thing between a mother and a baby.

The woman looked up and asked me what my name was. I told her "Leah." And she said, "Leah, this is Jesus." I smiled. It was the first time anyone had called me by name since we left home. Not a number, a name. It felt . . . good. I touched her forehead, and Jesus' cheek, and held her hand for a while, until she slept.

Deborah was still hot when I went back to my family. I lay down with her and held her very close. The children were all awake, but quiet in the dark. Just their eyes moved. They'd seen. It was like they were struggling with a secret and didn't know how to ask or tell it. And I didn't know how to tell them, either.

Some nights, like that one, the wind whispers, and it seems somehow like more than the wind. And children are quiet at the end of the day. Little things happen, and somehow they don't seem so little. But, it isn't until afterward that you may wonder about them and about why they happened just that way to you.

"Leah, this is Jesus."

* * *

Eyelight

Working all my life in a stable, I've seen lots of creatures born: sheep, oxen, donkeys. Most births are easy and natural enough. Some you have to help along. But, either way, you never get used to them. It's awesome to watch the struggle, to see the young one all tired and worn out afterward, and the mother, too. You can't help smiling, watching the mother washing her baby with her tongue. And then the little one working so hard and finally standing, all wobbly, and walking around all curious-like, but staying close to its mother. No matter how many births you've seen, each one squeezes your heart, all right, and makes you think about things you usually don't think about, busy as you get doing your work and trying to keep your life together.

But there was one peculiar birth happened once, long ago, that I won't ever forget. There wasn't any room in the inn. I knew that, working there, but it wasn't any skin off my nose. The stable and the animals were my business. I kept out back and left the rest to the others except when they made me help. So when those families came along and asked me if they could spend the night in the stable, I said if it was all right with the innkeeper, it was all right with me, as long as they didn't get in the way of my work or bother none of the animals.

It was really crowded in the stable because of all the guests, their beasts adding to the ones we had. You never heard so much bawling and whimpering. All night I was mucking out the place the best I could, trying to find enough new hay, quieting down the more skittish animals.

So I'd almost forgotten about those people I'd said could stay there until a man came looking for me and said his wife was having a baby. He asked if I had anything to wrap the child in after it was born. Such an interruption was all I needed on a night like that one! I was about to tell the man to see to it himself as best he could, when a light from somewhere outside caught his face just so. I don't know exactly what that light was. The moon? Someone passing by with a torch? A shooting star maybe? All I know is that it was strange. Even now, I shiver to think of it. And the wind seemed to rise up just then, too, like a spooked colt wheeling and galloping off across the meadow.

Anyway, there was that man's face in the quick light, I don't know how long . . . a minute, a lifetime. But I don't ever remember seeing a man's face so sharp and clear before. The deep lines around his mouth. His jaw muscles rippling his beard like a breeze caressing a grain field. And the beads of sweat over that upper lip where there is that little crease. (Jake, who works in the kitchen and is a little mad, says that crease is the print of the finger God lays right there to seal your lip just before you're bom, so you won't speak the secrets of where you've been or the worlds where you've come from before you entered this one.)

But the man's eyes! His eyes were what stopped me. They were so deep. So tired, so sad, somehow. Yet, they were so strong—like they looked right through you; like they had looked right through almost everything and knew awful, wonderful secrets. Eyes that had the same kind of light as a rising sun touching the hill tops, then creeping down to the valleys, and seeing it makes you shiver inside. I remember those eyes. I guess the way to say it is that there was love in them, and . . . love always gives you pause . . . sort of takes your breath away. Does mine, anyhow!

The man said a woman from another family staying in the stable was helping his wife. They needed something to wrap the baby in, cold as the night was. So I got a blanket. It was worn, but clean, because I'd washed it good after my dog, who used to sleep on it, died. My dog and his dying crossed my mind as I handed the blanket to the man and followed him to the corner where him and his wife had hunkered down. Strange how the cycles go: death and life being linked, one leading to the other so definite, so natural, but so mysterious all the same.

Anyway, I saw the birth. It wasn't easy, like a lot of them are. I don't know who fought the hardest against it, the mother or the baby. In any case, it appeared that neither of them were too sure they wanted it to happen. But nature paid them no mind. At last there was one final groan, followed by a sharp cry, and then a calm that was like that deep quiet moment just before or just after a storm. Even the animals seemed to sense something extraordinary was happening. They were absolutely still. I remember feeling that this birth was different, too, though I couldn't have told you exactly how.

So the woman who was helping wrapped the baby up in my blanket and handed him to his mother. The father's hands were huge and rough, and right then he put one hand on his wife's shoulder and the other on the baby's head. He was a tender man, I saw, for all of his being so big. The mother smiled, and she and her husband looked at each other for a long time. I don't know what their eyes were saying, but it was something powerful and personal and . . . secret I guess. I had to look away. Some things are private between just two, and if you interfere, even without meaning to, you're where you don't belong. But those eyes, I remember.

When I looked away from them, I looked to the baby. Now, here's the thing I can't explain. That child's eyes were just like that man's eyes, just like his father's eyes. I know it makes no sense to say it, but it's true all the same. That baby's eyes seemed so sad somehow, yet so strong, with that same rising-sun kind of light in them, burning like they looked through everything, too, and knew awful, wonderful secrets. There was the same kind of powerful love in those eyes, and I saw it, believe me. Don't ask me more about it. That strange light that night, I never could figure out where it came from . . . or where the light in those eyes came from . . . or what made the wind sound like it did, like more than the wind. Like the wings of night birds flying, but you can't see them—just hear them.

So I remember, and I wonder about more things than I can ever mention without being called mad. And maybe I am mad now. But you do your work, and take care of what you can, and keep your promises . . . and you wonder. Especially when, some nights, the light from somewhere outside your window makes mysterious shapes on the walls and ceiling, like it's trying to tell you something deep and true. You remember and you wonder about the light and the shadows and about all you dare to know and yet know not. You remember because you can't forget them—things like birth and death and . . . love. Especially love. But even as you remember, you don't understand much. And yet you do remember eyes and light and those shadows and the very silence of them which seems to say, "Glory to God and on earth peace . . . peace . . . peace . . . *peace!*"

* * *

Tangled in a Line

Sometimes you have to draw lines, and sometimes you have to bend them or even ignore them. But most of the time, you have to walk them; walk a tight line. The trouble is knowing which to do, when. When is the voice of conscience more critical than the voice of the court? You don't always know. It's hard to keep your balance. It's easier to compromise conscience than to challenge power.

So when Herod calls, you go! It was early evening when he called, the time I'm speaking of now. It had been a long day. The temple in Jerusalem is always a busy place, and priests have responsibilities . . . a thousand responsibilities . . . that often keep me awake at night: the wall of the temple needs repair; oil for the lamps is running low; revenue from sacrificial animals is off; there are the ritual observances to be got through.

And always there are political pressures to contend with—Rome on one hand, the Zealots on the other. Do you submit to powers or resist? And if you resist, how much, how far? And always the pressure, the pressure. When does one find time to think about such questions, to reflect, to study? I tell you, it's hard to keep your balance.

The days are always long, and this particular day had been one of the longest. We were meeting in the courtyard, the chief priests and the scribes, talking about how Rome's tax rulings were affecting temple properties, when the message came that Herod wanted us.

I remember feeling uneasy, as I usually do when summoned by powerful people. Rulers are not to be taken lightly. The nation must be preserved. Herod often wants the help, the blessing, of the priests for some scheme he's plotting. He is a cunning man. He could shut the temple down! He could get Rome to tighten the screws on our country. People would rebel, but. . . against Rome? It seems too terrible to contemplate. People would be slaughtered. This way, we give a little, modify, adjust, to keep the peace. But it's hard to know when to draw a line and when to walk it. Everyone knows that.

Herod summoned.

We went.

The palace was in a turmoil about something. You could feel it as soon as you walked through the gate. The guards were tense. There was a tightness in the air. The sun set fiery that evening, and the walls of the inner courtyard were blood-red up high, running down darker and darker into the deep shadows where we walked. I was seized with a sudden cramp in the gut. Perhaps I just needed to relieve myself. I felt clammy, but my mouth was dry as sand. Was it just pressure? Or something else? How do you know?

It was too late to turn back. Or was it? Perhaps my foreboding was for nothing.

In the outer chambers were three richly dressed men. They were obviously foreigners. They were just sitting there, nodding to us as we passed into Herod's inner chambers. There was a curious calm about those three men that added to my apprehensions.

When the door closed behind us, the air inside was heavy, rank. Fear makes the body stink, and Herod's breath was foul when he wheezed his question, his voice as tight as a tent rope in a storm: "Where is the Christ to be born?"

The question was totally unexpected. We were stunned. No one thought to ask him why he wanted to know.

No, I thought to ask. Had the Messiah—the one we had waited for—had he come? What did those three men in the outer chambers have to do with this question? Had they brought news? What would Herod do if the Messiah *had* been born?

I did think to ask those questions, but Herod was obviously in no mood to be crossed. So I didn't! To challenge power is dangerous.

The torches burned in their brackets on the wall, and the occasional hiss and crackle of the flames made the sudden silence seem more ominous. The knuckles of the guards were white around their spears. It was quiet, as only fear can make it quiet. The air was so close you could hardly breathe. Another cramp hit me like a wave on rocks. Cold sweat broke on my forehead, ran down my back.

Every one of us priests knew what Scripture said about the Messiah's birth. So the answer Herod wanted was supplied:

> *"In Bethlehem of Judea: for so it is written by the prophet, 'And you, O Bethlehem, in the land of Judah, are by no means* least *among the rulers of Judah, for from you shall come a ruler who is to shepherd my people Israel.'"*[1]

Whose voice had filled the room in answer to Herod? Was it mine? Had I blurted out those words or had I simply thought them? In any case, the words echoed . . . a ruler . . . a ruler . . . a ruler. Herod was a clever man. What else should be said to soften those echoing words? Power is jealous. I said nothing else. We were . . . I was . . . just trying to keep my balance.

That's hard to do, isn't it . . . keeping your balance. Later, Herod ordered all the male babies in Bethlehem killed. All of them! To rid himself of the one Messiah. I can never forget that. Power is jealous, frightening. I can't forget that either. You have to walk a tight line . . . yet it gets tangled . . .

My responsibilities often keep me awake at night . . . and the memories . . . the massacre . . . and the cramps, the cramps . . . pressures, always pressures. Privilege on one hand . . . and I sometimes forget *what*, on

1 *Matthew 2: 5b-6, NRSV*

the other. I wish God would make it clearer when you have to draw the line and where. If the Messiah survived the killing, would he make it clearer? Maybe Yes. Maybe No. Maybe both.

You know, what the prophet Micah really wrote was this:

> *"But you, O Bethlehem . . . who are one of the* little *clans of Judah, from you shall come forth for me one who is to rule in Israel . . ."*[2]

I wonder why, so long after Micah spoke it, we . . . I . . . tangled the prophet's line and why in the story of our meeting with Herod, it's recorded that way? "Bethlehem. . . by no means *least* among the rulers of Judah" rather than "Bethlehem . . . one of the *little* clans of Judah." There is a difference! One way suggests Bethlehem is much less than the other way—less and yet perhaps more.

In the night I hear a voice. Whose voice is it? Whose? It says, "Watch the lines . . . the choices . . . the little things."

O Bethlehem, so little, so little, but often a little makes all the difference.

* * *

2 *Micah 5:2, NRSV*

Under Their Noses

Studyin' the stars is a good thing, I suppose. Yes, I'm sure it is! When I have time, I look at 'em, and they are awesome, all right. I wonder what they are, and what keeps 'em up there, and what's behind 'em. But lookin' at 'em doesn't give me any answers to those questions, so I don't do it much. Yet, maybe just askin' the questions is a very important thing. For answers, I guess, you have to study the stars a long time. I don't know.

The three men who hired me as a tent bearer for their journey studied the stars like nothin' else mattered. They spent most of their time lookin' at the stars, talkin' about 'em, arguin' about old scrolls and maps like they held the secrets of life. And, as I said, I am sure that is a good thing, since their plottin' and plannin' got us to the place we were tryin' to get to.

But, I think, studyin' the stars can also lead you off the mark if you look at 'em too long. And if you look at *only* the stars, they put you in a kind of trance. You lose touch with other important things. You just don't see those things, you miss 'em. And that is not good—for the things missed or the ones who miss 'em.

The truth is, it was a hard trip over many days—or was it years?—from where we started to where we ended. A trip like that takes a lot of work. You have to pack food, measure it out, prepare it every day, and then repack it. You have to make fires, pitch and strike tents, feed the animals, rub 'em down, watch for pack sores . . . and a thousand other things. For such a long trip, three men like the ones I signed on with need a dozen people to help.

And that's what I'm tryin' to get at. They hired us and then ignored us. I don't think they meant to, but they did. They seemed to live in one world—the world of stars and supposin'. But we lived in another—the world of earth and people. When they needed us, they just took for granted we'd be there: cookin', cleanin' up, takin' care of what they must have thought was less important stuff. I bet it never dawned on 'em to tell us what they were thinkin' or what the stars were doin' or where we were headed. Like I say, I don't think they intended anythin' mean or bad. They were just too taken up with the stars, I guess. But to us, it came to the same thing as if they meant to ignore us.

Now, I admit feelin' a little angry about their bein' so blind to us, like we were not much different than dumb animals. I mean, we could have used some extra help once in a while, 'specially durin' some of the storms. But it was like they didn't see. That's the thing. They just didn't see what was under their noses. They were so totally caught up in what they cared about that they didn't see anythin' else. Now that I think of it, I realize the same thing happens to a lot of us, not just to people who study the stars. People get stuck in their own little world and shut out everythin' else.

What I'm sayin' is that, over that long journey, lots of things happened right under those stargazers' noses, but they just missed 'em, that's all. I mean, Abdul fell in love with Tamara, and it was like springtime with them, and us. And Elias, who stuttered and was so shy when we started, turned out to be a wonderful storyteller. Rhona played the lute for us so soft and beautiful you would 'a thought it was an angel makin' that music. And when Raman, who took care of the camels, got sick, Ardis mixed a bunch of herbs and mold and made a broth that broke his fever. When he started gettin' better, we all laughed and had a party with a bit of extra wine and scraps of meat and cheese that we filched from the stargazers who never even missed 'em.

There were lots of other things the stargazers missed, too. Like the way the ground shines when the early mornin' sun touches the dew; and the way a whole flock of swallows will fly this way and that, as if they were connected by some invisible thread, turnin' and dippin' by the same tug. I don't think those three men paid any mind to the way your breath puffs out in little clouds in the chilly air; or the smell of the jasmine; or the way rocks change their shapes when the sunlight and shadows hit them just so, as if they were livin' things. I swear, those stargazers never noticed a whole flock of things that made my heart beat faster or made me laugh, or that put a lump in my throat and made me whisper, "Thank you, God."

At last, we got where we'd been headin'. It was kind of a strange place. A stable. But the stargazers got out their gifts for the baby inside. I have to say they didn't seem like fittin' gifts for a baby—incense and spices and gold. Well, maybe the gold helped the family, but what I'm sayin' is that those gifts were picked before we'd even started, and those men were dead set on followin' their plans, no matter what.

Strange as it seems, I'm not sure those three men truly even *saw* the baby or, for that matter, the mother and father in that stable. I wasn't supposed to have followed them in. Not that they actually said not to, but that sort of thing is kind of an unspoken rule for us hired hands. But I followed anyway because I wanted to see what it was we'd come so far after. And it seemed to me that those three old wise men, if that's what to call 'em, didn't see that baby at all. I mean, they didn't smile, or touch his cheek, or kiss his head right there on the velvet-like spot on top, or any of that. It was as if, for them, that baby was really just as far off, as removed from the world, as the stars they'd been so busy plottin' about.

Funny thing . . . to have come all that way and still have missed it. At least, as far as I could tell, they missed it. I mean, we went back home another way just to throw off anyone who might have been wantin' to ask us what we were doin' there. But on the way back, nothin' changed between them and us. Nothin' else changed either. It's a sad thing when that happens. And it happens pretty often, as I see it.

It's not that those three were totally wrong, or anythin'. Or that lookin' at the stars is stupid. But, that baby . . . his eyes were so wide open. And it seemed the whole time I was there, he was lookin' so hard, strainin' to see, like he'd never rest 'til he'd seen everythin', linked up with all there was. It's like he was sayin' to me, to us all, "There are wonders all around you. Don't miss anything. Don't miss life . . . or God."

* * *

WAY OVER OUR HEADS

Naked Isn't the Last Straw

UNBORN: Why me?

ANGEL: I don't know. Why *not* you? Trust me, there's a reason. You'll find out.

UNBORN: Come on, do I have to do it? It sounds awful! What does it mean to get born, anyway?

ANGEL: Getting born is . . . well, it's entering a new place, a different place from where you are. And you have to become very small to get in. That's the way it's designed. There's no other way to do it. You have to start as a baby.

UNBORN: What's a baby?

ANGEL: A baby is a very small being. At first they're quite helpless. Oh, they have all the parts they'll have when they get bigger and stronger, only none of the parts work very well. Except certain ones. You'll see.

UNBORN: Helpless? *I know* I won't like that. I don't want to do it!

ANGEL: Someone will be there to take care of you. Probably.

UNBORN: Probably? *Probably* someone will?

ANGEL: Well, usually, your mother. And your father. Usually.

UNBORN: What are they?

ANGEL: Mothers and fathers? Well, they are . . . like other human beings. Only they aren't quite like each other. If they were, there wouldn't be babies.

UNBORN: It sounds worse all the time. I'm just not doing it. Why should I? I mean, what are human beings?

ANGEL: Well, I'm not sure what to tell you about them. They are creatures pretty much like all the other creatures God made. Only they are a little more . . . complicated, shall we say. They eat and sleep and walk around and have sex and babies. And they fight a lot over eating and sex, and who can walk or sleep where, and whose babies have what rights. But they think, too. Sometimes. And they love, once in a while, until it begins to scare them. They create things, and they destroy things. They struggle a lot. They are quite unpredictable, really. After all, they are free. And they keep looking for God . . . sort of.

UNBORN: Sort of?

ANGEL: Well, they can't seem to decide. They don't seem to know what they fear most: that they *won't* find God or that they *will.* So they "sort of" look, without concentrating much on how or where. But they don't seem quite able to *stop* looking either, especially when they are afraid, which is quite often. Only they don't like to admit it. So they pretend a lot.

UNBORN: That settles it. It's just too confusing! I'm not going to be born.

ANGEL: Excuse me? That settles it?

UNBORN: Oh, I don't know. Does it hurt, being born?

ANGEL: At first, while you're getting into the world.

UNBORN: Then it's over?

ANGEL: Not exactly. There are different kinds of hurt. That's partly what I mean about humans being complicated.

UNBORN: But why?

ANGEL: Why what?

UNBORN: Why are humans so complicated?

ANGEL: I don't really know. Some say humans messed things up. They call it sin. And that's partly true.

UNBORN: Partly?

ANGEL: Yes, partly. Because I think humans are *meant* to be complicated, too. I think God created them that way. God put all those possibilities into them. That makes them complicated. I guess you'll be finding out why on your own.

UNBORN: I suppose so. But it sounds so depressing. I mean, what hope is there for such messed up creatures?

ANGEL: Hope? Oh, there's lots of hope. It's not depressing. You'll see.

UNBORN: I just *know* I won't like it. I'm going to apply for an exemption.

ANGEL: But you *will* like it! Really. Human beings are beautiful, too. And so is the earth.

UNBORN: Earth? What's the earth?

ANGEL: What's it like? Well, it's . . . a little like here. Sometimes. But sometimes not.

UNBORN: Well, that *certainly* clears things up.

ANGEL: What can I say? Earth is where human's live, or at least try to.

UNBORN: Fine. Just forget it. Just tell me where is this "earth" is.

ANGEL: Okay, come here . . . look . . . where I'm pointing.

See . . . way, way over there, as far as you can see across all those thousands of light years . . . there, that little speck of blue. That's it. Can you make it out?

UNBORN: Barely. Makes me homesick just thinking about going there. I don't have to go yet, do I?

ANGEL: I guess not. There is something else I have to tell you first.

UNBORN: I don't want to hear it.

ANGEL: But it's important.

UNBORN: Is it good or bad? I don't want to hear any more bad things!

ANGEL: I haven't told you anything bad. I told you some hard things about being a human being. But not bad.

UNBORN: Well, they sounded bad to me. All that stuff about human beings being complicated and fighting about things. And about there being a zillion kinds of hurt. Stuff like that sounds pretty bad.

ANGEL: Well, maybe a little. But not really. I told you, it's just because God gives human beings freedom to choose and puts so many possibilities in them and the world. Makes things interesting. Exciting. But not necessarily bad. And what I have to tell you now isn't good or bad either. It's just necessary.

UNBORN: Oh, sure. So, what is it?

ANGEL: It's that while you are waiting to be born, you start forgetting. By the time you're actually born, you'll have forgotten almost everything.

UNBORN: What are you talking about? Forgotten *what*?

ANGEL: You'll have forgotten everything we've talked about. You won't even remember me or having been here.

UNBORN: I won't remember anything? *Nothing*? What do you mean, that's not so bad. It's *terrible*!

ANGEL: But it really isn't. After all, if you did remember, you wouldn't really be entirely human. If you remembered, you might not take your life on earth seriously. You might think it didn't matter. And it matters. A lot. So you forget about "here."

UNBORN: Forget *everything*? I'll never remember *anything*? In the slightest?

ANGEL: Well, you won't remember anything *exactly*. But sometimes, over the years of your life, you'll have certain feelings that you won't quite understand or certain longings or times of restlessness you'll wonder about. That will be sort of like remembering.

UNBORN: Doesn't sound much like remembering to me.

ANGEL: I didn't say it was exactly like remembering. It's just a *little* like it. And there might be other times when some kind of warm glow or . . . or shiver will pass through you, go over your soul, like a breeze over water, stirring up the very slightest ripple, and then be gone. But it will leave behind a trace of peacefulness or sadness or joy in you, or all three mixed up together. Those could be hints. Nothing specific. You won't remember anything specific about here or us.

UNBORN: Can I come back here? I mean, when I'm done being human, can I get born back here? *Please* tell me I can.

ANGEL: But you can't. Not really. Because things change. "Here" won't really be *here* then. Everything changes. You, me, everything. Being human will change you. Believe me, it will. That's what makes being human so exciting.

* * *

UNBORN: Everything you've told me about leaving here and getting born and never coming back doesn't sound exciting at all. It sounds terrible. Who ever wants to be born?

ANGEL: I wish I could make you understand, but I can't. I'll tell you a little secret. A poet wrote some wonderful words about it in a kind of prayer to God called a psalm. The poet said, "Thou hast made human beings little less than God . . . Thou hast given them dominion over the works of thy hands . . ." Sometimes I catch myself wishing I was . . . well, wishing that maybe I could see what being human would be like.

UNBORN: What are you saying? You don't mean that.

ANGEL: Yes, I do. At least sometimes I do. What I'm saying is that to be a human being is a wonder greater than the stars.

UNBORN: You really think so?

ANGEL: I really do.

UNBORN: That's hard to believe. Look, tell me plainly, will I always be a human being after I'm born? I mean, will I have to live on the earth forever?

ANGEL: So many questions! In some way, yes, you'll always be a human being after you are born. As for the other question, no, you will not live on the earth forever.

UNBORN: I ask for a plain answer and what do I get? Riddles and mysteries. Let me try again. If human beings don't stay on the earth forever, what *does* happen to them? What will happen to ME? Just give me a simple answer.

ANGEL: Well, that's very hard to explain, but I'll try. What happens is . . . well, time passes, and . . .

UNBORN: Aren't there any simple answers? What's "time"?

ANGEL: Time is . . . well, look. See that galaxy over there? It's moving, isn't it?

UNBORN: Sure it's moving. Anyone can see that!

ANGEL: So, listen. For that galaxy to move from the place where you see it to the place it *will be* takes time. Time works like that with everything. Time measures movement and movement measures time. Get it?

UNBORN: No, I don't! And even if I did, what does that have to do with what happens to human beings?

ANGEL: Well, I'm telling you that time happens to human beings because they move, too. They move from one place to anther. Like galaxies, they move from where they were to where they're going. They move from birth through days and nights, through all kinds of experiences and struggles. Time measures their movement. That movement is their life. They get older as they move. After a while, they move to the end of their time, each one of them. Some have more time to move than others. But, finally, everyone comes to the end of their time. And then they die. Their bodies stop working. They have no more days and nights then. Now do you get it?

UNBORN: Die? I don't think I like this. It's hard to die, isn't it?

ANGEL: Yes, it seems to be. Human beings are usually quite afraid of dying. They wonder about it. They struggle over it long before their time actually ends. When it comes to dying, they are a little like you are about being born. They worry a lot about what will happen to them.

UNBORN: Well, what *does* happen to them? That's what I asked you before!

ANGEL: I can't tell you.

UNBORN: You can't tell me. So what else is new? What *can* you tell me?

ANGEL: Well, I can tell you that human beings are not accidents. God planned them.

UNBORN: I must say you are *very* helpful. You scare me, you confuse me, you make it all sound so hard, thank you very much. What kind of a universe have we got here? What is God up to? Why did God have to make it this way?

ANGEL: Now you're way over my head. I don't know why. But I have thought about it, and I don't think God *had* to make it this way. God just *did* make it this way.

UNBORN: With a little help from human beings, if I'm getting it at all right. All that freedom God gave them, all those possibilities God threw in the mix.

ANGEL: Hey, you were paying attention!

UNBORN: But why this way? With all that freedom and chances for things to get messed up?

ANGEL: I told you, I don't know. But the same thing that makes it possible for things to get messed up makes it possible for things to get fixed up, made better. I think it has something to do with love. In some ways love seems to be the hardest lesson of all for human beings.

UNBORN: But why is love such a hard lesson for them? Love's the best thing there is!

ANGEL: I don't know. Maybe someday they'll learn. That's why God sent Jesus to be born on earth.

UNBORN: Why didn't they listen to him?

ANGEL: Well, I suppose if they really had listened, they would have had to change, and I guess they didn't want to. Sometimes I ache for the earth. It's so small and fragile. Look at it over there.

UNBORN: It's pretty small, all right. But, I have to admit, it does look kind of beautiful, at least from here. And quiet. Is it really quiet there?

ANGEL: Not much. Quiet is another thing that human beings have trouble with.

UNBORN: Do they know about listening? They must know about that!

ANGEL: Some of them. A little. But whether it's quiet or not, they aren't sure what to listen for. Funny how they miss things, even when they hear them.

UNBORN: That's sad. Will I forget to listen, too, when I get born?

ANGEL: Mostly. But sometimes, maybe, you'll *almost* remember.

UNBORN: Almost? Not "almost." I *have* to remember how to listen!

ANGEL: Oh, there will be times when you listen and hear things, and you'll recognize them as beautiful, powerful, true things. Then you can practice listening more, and deeper, because you'll know how important it is. It's part of what humans call prayer.

UNBORN: But how will I know what things are beautiful and powerful and true?

ANGEL: Many ways. You'll learn. From some people, from your experiences, from your own heart.

UNBORN: Tell me one more thing. Something that's beautiful and powerful. Maybe I'll remember it. Just one thing.

ANGEL: Well, there are lots of things I could tell you. But one is that, sometimes, when it's a little quiet, mothers and fathers listen to their baby's heartbeat before the baby is born.

UNBORN: They can do that?

ANGEL: Oh, yes!

UNBORN: What does it sound like?

ANGEL: It sounds like the heart of God.

* * *

ANGEL: Well, that about covers it. I've told you all you need to know about being human, for now. I think you're about ready to go.

UNBORN: Ready to go? Are you kidding? I still have a million questions! Besides, I haven't even packed.

ANGEL: Packed? You won't need to pack. You can't take anything with you.

UNBORN: Nothing? Not a thing?

ANGEL: Nothing.

UNBORN: But I have to have something to wear. I can't get born looking like this!

ANGEL: Believe me, you don't need to take a thing. You'll get what you need when you arrive.

UNBORN: But I have to make an entrance, don't I? I have to have something to arrive in.

ANGEL: No, you don't.

UNBORN: Let me get this straight. You are actually telling me that I don't get to take a stitch with me?

ANGEL: Not a stitch.

UNBORN: *You mean to say that to get born on earth, you not only have to forget everything you ever learned here, AND become small and helpless, AND risk being taken care of by human beings who are complicated and confused . . . AND survive with people who aren't too sure how to love or even know what love is, AND fight a lot about things, AND are afraid most of the time, AND get old and die and worry about it . . . BUT, to top it all off, you have to start out being absolutely, positively, completely stark naked? HAS ANYONE SPOKEN TO GOD ABOUT THIS? NAKED IS THE LAST STRAW!*

ANGEL: Really? Why?

UNBORN: WHY? Tell me, are there people around when you get born?

ANGEL: Of course! Your mother is there, your father usually, several others.

UNBORN: Well?

ANGEL: Well, what?

UNBORN: Well, so much for going naked, is what! What'll they think when I whoosh in wearing my basic nothing? It'll be embarrassing is what it will be!

ANGEL: Oh, I see the problem.

UNBORN: You bet your sweet feathers you'd better see it. If human beings are so uptight about everything, I can just guess how they'll be about my turning up naked.

ANGEL: Not to worry. When you're a baby, nakedness is fine. In fact, they think it's adorable. It's only later that it's a problem.

UNBORN: Later? Please, try to explain that. Oh, don't bother. I already know: "It's complicated."

ANGEL: It is complicated, and it's even a little funny. You see, when you're a baby, nakedness is fine because . . . well, because to them, a baby's body is beautiful.

UNBORN: I begin to get the picture. It's later on that human bodies turn ugly, right?

ANGEL: No, that isn't exactly it.

UNBORN: For once, could you tell me exactly what it IS?

ANGEL: Exactly? Probably not. I suppose the simplest way is to say that it has something to do with the way people learn to think of themselves.

UNBORN: That's not even *close* to exactly.

ANGEL: Well, listen. When humans grow bigger, almost none of them ever thinks his or her body is what they wish it was. It isn't beautiful enough, or strong or handsome or thin or tall, or whatever, enough. They think their nose is too big or their ears stick out, or their eyes are the wrong color or their chin is weak, or their chest is too flat or their ankles are too thick, and so on and on and on.

UNBORN: Is it really that bad? Their bodies?

ANGEL: No. Not really.

UNBORN: So why do they think that?

ANGEL: They learn it. And then, to make it worse, there are things about how God made their bodies work that embarrass them, so they're forever making jokes or getting all puckered up about it.

UNBORN: That's closer to exactly but not close enough. Get closer. What are you really saying here?

ANGEL: I'm saying it isn't just their bodies that are involved when they talk that way. They're actually talking about how they feel about themselves and about things that frighten them—like being laughed at, or being humiliated, or not being liked, or being thought stupid. Or about sex. Or how it is to get old and die. As if those things mean there's something wrong with them or they aren't worth much.

UNBORN: But why . . . I mean, if God made human beings that way, why are they afraid like that? When they see a baby, why don't they remember?

ANGEL: Well, now, weren't you just saying things like that yourself? About why you didn't want to get born or be a human being.

UNBORN: I suppose. But the more you explain it, the harder it seems to be a human.

ANGEL: Well, part of the problem is that human beings make it harder than it needs to be. They seem to have trouble accepting themselves as God's creatures, believing that God loves them. They seem to think it's bad to be a creature. They hide themselves. Behind clothes, pretenses, all sorts of things.

UNBORN: It sounds lonely.

ANGEL: Yes. It is. Humans get in a lot of messes trying *not* to be lonely. But they'll always be lonely because they are free. And they just become more lonely if they do things to try to make themselves less lonely. Do you understand?

UNBORN: Some. Not much.

ANGEL: Listen: Lonely goes with being human because God creates each human being as a particular person not quite like any other. It's a lonely thing, but a glorious thing, too. Loneliness is like a wind ripple on the water that God blows. It's like a reminder to turn to God and not try to stop the loneliness in other ways. Feeling lonely is a way humans have of remembering where they came from.

UNBORN: I'm not sure I get it, but maybe, sort of . . . I think I'm already beginning to forget. Does that mean I'm ready to go? I can't be ready yet! I have so many questions.

ANGEL: You always will. It's all right. Life is a mystery, a wonderful, holy mystery. You won't ever have all the answers, but you'll have enough. Listen to your heart. Pray. Look at Jesus. Don't be afraid. Listen to your loneliness. It's like nakedness. It hints at what it means to stand before God as a creature God loves. You can't hide or pretend with God. Loneliness is a gift to remind you of that. And that God loves you as a parent loves a child, naked and all.

UNBORN: I'll try to remember that. Will you come and visit me on earth?

ANGEL: Oh, yes. There are always many of us around. All the time.

UNBORN: That makes me feel a little better about going. I love you.

ANGEL: I love you, too. Try to remember love is what matters to God.

UNBORN: I know. But I'm already beginning to forget. How will I know when you visit? Hurry! Tell me.

ANGEL:	You won't know, directly. God isn't obvious, so neither are we messengers. God keeps sending messages and messengers, but humans don't seem to pay much attention. Sometimes, some do. Maybe you will be one who does. But I *will* visit you.
UNBORN:	Promise?
ANGEL:	I promise.
UNBORN:	Oh, I can feel it's time for my journey. That little speck of blue seems so far away.
ANGEL:	But it isn't. It'll be Christmas time when you're born.
UNBORN:	Christmas?
ANGEL:	Jesus' birthday. Don't be afraid. Don't be afraid.
UNBORN:	I'll try. Good-bye . . . good-bye . . .
ANGEL:	Christmas is about peace. And joy. You'll find out. I pray you will. And it's not good-bye. God is with you. So it's always hello.

* * *

WE CAN TELL YOU A SECRET

The Thwig Eater

Care for a thistle, anyone? These purple ones are my favorites.

You're welcome to have one, really. They taste a little like what you two-legged ones call "basil." No? Well, all right. I find them a particular treat now that I am a very old jackass, so you won't mind if I have another, will you? That's why my name is Thwig, which is what we jackasses call this purple thistle. Thwig loves thwigs. Hee haw!

I'm a dumb animal, really, but what everyone doesn't seem to realize is that all of us are really dumb animals, whether we have two legs or four legs or many legs or no legs. We are more alike than it might seem. Of course, you two-legged ones know many things we four-legged ones don't. But we know some things you don't, believe it or not. Which is why, just this once, I've been given the gift of speech to tell you what I can about the event, since I was there. I wish it were more, but I wonder if anyone could really tell more.

Anyway, I know the woman called Mary was very heavy as I carried her along that day. I belonged to her neighbor, Elihu, and she and her husband, Joseph, had borrowed me for the trip. It was not something I wanted to be doing, carrying this woman with a belly swollen with an about-to-be-born baby and then having to go so far from home with almost complete strangers. For me, it was a hard job, like hauling wool and wood and grain and jars full of water. Mary was uncomfortable and withdrawn. Joseph was withdrawn, too, and edgy. It seemed clear that they'd been fighting before we started. You know how you sense that sort of thing. Anyway, it was pretty obvious that they didn't want to be taking this trip.

Every so often he would growl, "I just don't understand," and it wasn't clear what exactly he was referring to—the trip, or Mary's mood, or some problem of his own, or what. And when she'd answer, "Well, I don't understand either," nothing got any clearer except that they weren't getting along too well right then. I tell you that so you'll know that everything about this event wasn't all "thwigs and clover."

The roads were clogged with people, and at certain places along the way there were Roman centurions urging everyone to move along faster. Occasionally there was a centurion riding some big, well-groomed horse who would prance around and go out of his way to bump me to prove how much better he was than I. He didn't have to do that; I already felt inferior. All my life I'd been called a stupid jackass, and I'd heard two-legged ones call others a jackass when they wanted to insult them. I knew I wasn't much.

I'm not sure I'm telling this very well. If all this seems to be about trivial, unimportant details, you'll just have to bear with me because that's part of what I have to tell you.

As we moved along that day, Joseph kept tugging more urgently on the rope until the bit began to cut into my mouth. He kept muttering to himself things like, "Damn Caesar, damn Rome, damn being too old for all this nonsense, damn Mary getting pregnant." He wouldn't stop for anything. And the faster we went, the greater the distance grew between him and the woman on my back.

And the longer we went, the more she complained about being uncomfortable, and about her worries over what were they going to do with this baby and how Joseph was going to earn enough to support them.

Meanwhile, all I could think about was how much further did we have to go, and would there be anything good to eat when we got there, and would there be a place to sleep out of the wind. What I am telling you is that all three of us got to be little more than beasts of burden.

So part of what I have to tell you is that we missed things because we seemed to feel we were victims, that we had no choice but to do what we were doing. Nonsense! Even I have choices. Jackasses wouldn't be called stubborn otherwise! And if we four-legged ones have choices, how much more do you two-legged ones have them. Oh, not about everything, but about many things. We all have choices.

But choices are not just between alternatives. The secret of choices is deciding what those alternatives *mean*, what their consequences are, which choices are better than others and *why*.

Yet, for a time that day we were simply beasts of burden; and the burdens we were beasts of were our resentments. I'm not sure how it happens, but when you clop along obsessed with a routine, it's easy to start feeling sorry for yourself. At least, it's easy for me. The stones were biting sharply at my hooves, my mouth hurt, my back ached, and I resented having to do this job. I began to resent my owner for loaning me out. I thought about the thwigs I wanted and couldn't have. I thought about horses who weren't shaggy like me, who were more beautiful and talented, who had more to eat and better stables. Resentments grew like poisonous mushrooms in my dark mood.

Certainly you will understand if I tell you I think the same thing was going on with Mary and Joseph. I tell you this so you might see that everyone connected with this birth was something of a dumb animal. It is important to see that because that's exactly what made this whole thing so miraculous.

As I said, you miss things when you clop along with your head down and your nose to the ground. *But the things you miss are still happening!* That's part of what is so amazing. Mary's baby still kicked around inside her, in spite of her worries and complaints. In spite of his grumbling and fuming, Joseph led us on. And I carried this miracle on my back, even though I resented it.

But one thing we four-legged ones remember to do that you two-legged ones forget is to keep in tune with all of our senses. As the day burned down, I heard a whir and looked up. The sky was the color of a thwig, and far off on the edge of the earth, two bright stars shone clear as a jenny's eyes when she sees her colt. The whir was the sound of children running at their before-sleep-games, though it sounded more like great wings in the air. Then the children laughed, and I swear you could smell their delight. And in the long shadows, I saw a young couple holding each other so tenderly I hee-hawed in gladness. Then, for the first time, I felt Mary's fingers tightly wrapped through my mane. Suddenly I realized she'd been hanging on like that for the whole time, and the courage and toughness of her hold stirred my heart. I'd almost missed it. Such a small, beautiful signal, my heart went out to her. I wonder how many creatures are hanging on like she was.

* * *

So, we clopped along toward wherever we were going. But what I started to tell you is that you miss things when you clop along, counting whatever you count when you get into a routine, or become obsessed with a job or a list or a goal. You miss the dumb animal things, the little things, the precious things if you hold your nose to the ground. But, you know, you also miss things if you hold your nose up too high, if you pretend that you're *not* a little bit of a dumb animal.

I mean, one time I met a lovely mare named Chigachig. She told me that was her name because that's the sound she made when she galloped. Chigachig belonged to a wealthy man to whom Elihu sold wood. I met her when we took a load of wood to that house. Chigachig laughed at me for doing such lowly work and for looking so mangy. She said *she* looked like Ugo Oga (which is the name of the Great Mare who created all horses) because her coat was so shiny and golden and beautiful. I asked her if she'd ever seen Ugo Oga. She said she hadn't, but she was sure she looked like the Great Mare.

Well, since I had never seen Ugo Oga either, I couldn't swear that Chigachig didn't look like that god. But I do know that Chigachig missed many things about herself and the world because her nose was so high in the air. For one thing, she missed that I loved her and wanted to be her friend. And she refused to try the thwig I offered her because it looked dirty. Too bad for her.

But there is another reason I tell you about missing things if you hold your nose too high, a reason that is harder to get ahold of. When you start thinking of things too far off the ground, too airy, too sort of heavenly, it is easy to get your tail all twisted around.

I've heard the two-legged ones talking about their gods just the same way we four-legged ones think about Ugo Oga. The Romans say their gods are powerful and favor Romans over other people. But sometimes I also hear Elihu and his friends say that when God's Messiah comes, he will destroy the Romans and their empire and rule the world, and that Elihu and his friends and the people of their country will share his reign. That sounds as arrogant to me as what the Romans say.

Such arrogance makes you two-legged ones miss things just like we four-legged ones do. We are more alike than it seems, we dumb animals, and we all miss things.

I tell you this because in the twilight, that day, I heard Mary whisper to Joseph, "You said we are to call the baby 'Jesus'?"

And he answered, "Yes. According to my dream, he will be the Messiah."

And Mary answered quietly, "I know."

I wondered, then, about such a dream, and if it could possibly be true that a Messiah could be born to such dumb animals as these two (forgive me for putting it that way). And, if so, what might they miss about him? What were they already missing about him? What might all of us miss about such a Messiah?

It was a strange night. As we approached the edge of the village, the shadows felt heavy as water and seemed to part like the sea when the tiny ship of us moved through them. The dark leaves of the trees were streaked with strands of silver that scattered again whenever breezes rustled, then disappeared again to wherever breezes go. The smell of supper smoke and apprehension mixed together, and the quietness was weighted with expectancy. It was a lonely time for the three of us. Something was happening. We'd all begun to sense it, and our silence changed from sullen to thoughtful.

Finally, Joseph found us a place in a stable, which was actually a cave with a rough opening on one wall through which the light and wind sniffed. It was a dirty, smelly place, full of other animals and some other poor people huddled out of the wind. The animals were caked with mud and dung. But it was shelter, and we entered it none too soon. Mary groaned, a sound as deep and loud as wind before a storm. The birth began.

Birth is an animal thing, drenched in sweat, bellowing, moaning, panting. It is full of blood and wonder. This one was no different, and the other four-legged ones and I watched, quiet, not spooked by the sights and sounds of it. This was something we understood. Or more truly, it was something we understood that we *didn't* understand, though we had been through it many times.

There is always pain involved when new life comes. It is not just physical pain, hard as that is. It is also the pain of being vulnerable, of birthing another life that will be vulnerable as well—a life separated from the womb where it was safe, protected; a life pushed out on its own; a life which, having begun, you know will one day end. So with the happiness of the birth there is also an aching kind of melancholy in that knowledge.

But without pain, life does not happen. Without pain, no one claims life, or reclaims it. Do not ask me why. I just know it is so in my dumb animal way. Without pain and struggle, life doesn't come fully to anyone. Without struggle, life itself somehow would be as unreal as Ugo Oga, as a god who is only an idea off somewhere where no one or nothing can reach—nothing like pain or sweat or joy. Birth is an animal thing. It is a precious thing. It is an earthy thing. It is a very mysterious and holy thing, a thing of God.

I wish I could say more, but I am a dumb animal. I can tell you that birth in the stable was a thing of God. That night the wind sang a miracle. That night the light of stars left scorch marks like a brand on the world. A strange wisdom gazed out of that little, red, wrinkled one's eyes, that baby Jesus. And I tell you, with this jackass tongue, that somehow I knew then that God was with us: with all us jackasses; with all of us dumb animals of the earth; with all of us who clop along with our heads down or our noses up; with all the sullen, raging Josephs, all the frightened, complaining Marys of the world.

I tell you that far off One—whatever name you give it, Jupiter or Caesar or Ugo Oga or Yahweh or Allah, or whatever—came to us that night. I know it as a dumb animal knows. There it was, *there God was*—a little thing, an animal thing, vulnerable as I am, vulnerable as a mother's love is, vulnerable as any love is and must be. It was a miracle God chose to come like that.

We four-legged ones know we live by gifts: thwigs and a bucketful of grain sometimes; a clear pool to suck water from, someone to scratch our ears sometimes because they care; a jenny or another jackass to run with or stand next to when a storm comes and jagged fire splits the sky and your courage shrivels. They're all gifts to make your blood rush and sing a little. We know we live by gifts, and we are not so dumb as to refuse them.

That birth was a gift! I received it gladly.

Will you understand this braying tongue if I tell you what I came to know that night? That night I learned what power really is: It is the choosing to come close, to break through the fences that separate us, to share yourself whatever the cost, to be vulnerable. A simple, complicated choice. That's all . . . and that's everything. Honestly sharing yourself is being willing to let yourself be a jackass . . . or a child, or a friend, or a lover. That is what love does.

Love is the only power we dumb animals really have. And I believe it's most of the power God has. So it must be the only power that matters much. I looked at that baby that night and understood just how risky a power it is, sharing yourself. That is what God did: God came to be with us, like a jenny in a storm. God came to help us claim life, and that is no easier than carrying that heavy woman, Mary, such a long, hard way, or the pain and labor of many struggles. And yet, life is joyful, too, as joyful as a back rub in the heart, a thwig for the soul.

In that light-haunted, wind-fluted stable, the gap between God and us got closed. In that wrinkled baby, God gave us the way to touch each other's hearts, to close the distance between each other, to share ourselves, even with our enemies.

Yet we all, especially you two-legged ones, keep missing the chance. I know, because it was my daughter who carried Jesus into Jerusalem to die some thirty years after I carried him into Bethlehem to be born.

But I tell you, I carry him still. I cannot understand the mystery of it, but I carry his life in me now. Yes, I am a dumb animal, but what is beyond me keeps me going—the splendid puzzlement I saw in the birth that night. I hope the story of that night will carry you on, too, if you choose. For the wonder is that the things we miss *do* keep happening. The child stirs once more, even in the disbelieving ones. God comes again, and the labor and the joy of it await. Oh, don't miss things . . . little things . . . precious things . . . dumb animal things. Such holy things . . . such wondrous, holy things.

Are you sure you wouldn't care for a thwig? I find the smallest ones are a particular treat now that I'm a very old jackass. They really are quite wondrous.

* * *

Tickled from Behind

Hello? Hello! I can't believe I can really talk like this, in your language! Quickly, listen up! I only have this power to speak your language for a short time, to tell you my story. If you feel stupid listening to a goat, think of how I feel trying to tell you anything in this idiotic language you speak!

Now, one of the main things I want to tell you is that someone is always out to get you. You think I'm exaggerating? Let me give you a little refresher course in my family history. Where do you think the term "scapegoat" comes from? You got it. My family history. I won't go into all the gruesome examples because you know about scapegoats.

The thing is, they don't even have to be goats any more, can you believe it? As a matter of fact, these days not only does everyone seem to *have* a scapegoat, everyone seems to *be* someone's scapegoat. It's not just that scapegoats are someone to blame anymore. Oh, no! The field has expanded. Scapegoats are someone to use, to con into doing something for you and taking the fall if it doesn't work out. And there you have the bare bones of what I mean when I say someone's always out to get you.

So, I'm telling you, you've got to stay alert, keep a sharp eye out. If someone is out to get you, you have to dance around a little, be ready to duck and parry on a moment's notice. Goats, you may have noticed, jump around a lot. Well, everyone has their own way of doing that.

But, hey, having made that point, I'll get to the main part of my story. It's about a very momentous birth I was in on. The birth happened at night, but earlier that day my mate, Quan, and I had left the herd and climbed as high on the mountain as we could go. It makes me feel free and daring to leave the herd and climb like that!

It was cold up on the mountain, but it was as if you could see to the end of the world and beyond. There was snow on the high mountains across the valley. The grass tasted intoxicating. The air was so clear and sweet that only the tiny ripples on the little stream distinguished the air from the pure, fresh water. It was as if there were no other animals in the world except Quan and me. I said to Quan, "Let's never go back. Let's live up here, free, on top of the world. No one would bother us here. No one would take your milk any more, or steal the kids to butcher or barter. No one would threaten us. No one could get us. We could live all to ourselves. We could do as we please. We'd be free, Quan."

Quan nuzzled my neck and said, softly, "No, Zub. We wouldn't be free; we'd be a lie, a dream. The mountains are beautiful, and I love it here. But there are other animals in the world, Zub. We could never live all to ourselves. Praca and Capra didn't make us that way. The gods go together, so their creatures go together."

She rested her chin on my back. I felt troubled.

Praca and Capra are the goat gods—Praca, the Billy god; Capra, the Nanny god. To be honest, I didn't have much truck with such nonsense, but Quan did. I knew I couldn't get anywhere arguing with her, but I tried anyway.

"Look, Quan," I said, "let me tell you the way it is. In this world, which is the only one we have or know anything about, you have to look out for yourself because no one else will."

She shook her head. I knew she'd start in about our owner, Naphtali, looking out for us and our friends among the other goats, so I cut her off first.

"No matter what it looks like to you, animals are out to get each other, Quan. Believe me. You have to keep a sharp eye out."

She pulled away and looked at me. "Why?" she asked simply.

I confess I couldn't explain the reason. I was just mouthing off without really thinking. So I couldn't look back at her just then. The answer to her question seemed so obvious, somehow; and yet, just because she'd asked, I knew it wasn't. She seemed so beautiful and wise to me.

Finally, I just blurted out, "You just have to look out for yourself in order to *survive*. I don't want to die, Quan."

And there it was, out in the open—my fear. I am afraid to die. Death is something I worry about a lot. I wonder when it's coming, how it's coming. I leap across chasms in the mountains as if I were fearless, but it's a cover. My knees shake every time I jump!

Somehow it was a relief that now Quan knew about my fear, but her response surprised me. (I think she'd always known.) She walked over and stood beside me for a long time, and then she said, "I think what you mean is that you don't want to lose your life, Zub."

I was confused and wanted her to explain, but she was silent. I waited. For a long time we stood looking out over the valley, watching the shadows climb toward us until we were standing in the last sliver of light, a light that was so dazzling it seemed to come from nowhere. It was like a fire that burned only on that little outcropping of rock on which we stood. Then I heard the words, though I couldn't swear she spoke them: "It is your life you fear to lose, Zub, so you cannot stay here. If you do not make sacrifices for something, nothing is worth anything. Not even life. Especially not life."

Suddenly I felt dizzy. Was it the heights, the light, the words? Whatever it was, the world was spinning.

The next thing I remember, we were slowly picking our way down into the darkness. When I looked back to where we'd been, I saw that the splinter of light still burned, intense and clear. But somehow it seemed to have leapt from the rock to a place higher up in the sky where it appeared to be a radiant star. The next thing I remember, we were slowly picking our way down into the darkness.

When we reached the valley, I wanted to stay out under the stars, but Quan needed to be milked, for she had come fresh, even though the kid she'd birthed had not lived. If we went to the stable, Naphtali might milk her, though he might be too busy working in the inn, especially since there were so many two-legged strangers about recently. In any case, we went to the stable, a cave out back of the inn. But we had scarcely entered and begun to get comfortable when all the confusion began.

A man and a woman pushed their way in, stumbling over us in their rush to find a place to lay down. A jackass followed them. Strangely, I wasn't immediately angry or suspicious—just surprised. I didn't resent this intrusion for some reason . . . maybe because obviously they had other things on their minds.

Anyway, it wasn't unusual for poor people to take refuge in a stable—or even for a woman to get pregnant in a stable, if you'll forgive my goatish candor. But it *was* very unusual for a very pregnant woman to enter a stable; and this one was obviously about to give birth. She groaned, then gasped at the pain. So the birth began. We watched.

Will you believe me if I tell you that watching the birth had the same effect on me as standing high in the mountains that afternoon, where it seemed I could see past the end of the world? I kept hearing Quan's words: "If you do not make sacrifices for something, nothing is worth anything. Not even life. Especially not life."

Then it was over, the birth itself, I mean. Things happened quickly after that. The man cut and tied the cord, and the woman took the baby boy to her breast, under her shawl. Quan went over and nudged the man, and somehow he understood. He found the milk bucket and milked Quan. Then he did a strange thing. He took the little baby and washed him off in some of Quan's milk. Quan watched as if the baby were hers. After that, the man took a cup and gave the woman a sip or two of Quan's milk and drank the rest himself.

He went and got a ragged piece of blanket somewhere, maybe from Naphtali, and wrapped up the baby. The woman kept whispering his name: "Jesus." I walked over and stood next to Quan and looked at the baby. I had the powerful sense that that baby *wanted* to be there. I mean right there, in that cold, dark, smelly place, which in that instant seemed somewhere past the end of the world and yet close to the beginning of another one. I think he wanted to be right there with us . . . us goats, so to speak. I remembered what Quan had said about gods and creatures going together, and the funny thing is that what she said felt different in this stable than it did up on the mountain. Here, it felt right.

That Billy-goat-of-a-kid even seemed a little like a goat, the way he was making snorting noises, kicking his legs so furiously, butting his head against his mother's breast. So I started to laugh and, to my surprise, Quan joined in. Then the jackass brayed, a bird sang, a dog howled, a cat meowed, and, I'll tell you, it sounded like music. The laughter joined with the wind and light that sniffed around the openings of the stable. Then it broke out and rolled out over the valley, getting louder as it washed down over the plains.

I laughed because the situation struck me funny! Here I was, always on the lookout because someone is always out to get you, and lo and behold, this tiny, wrinkled baby had gotten me that night, right in the heart, and it was wonderful. This baby, this dirt-poor, peasant mother and father stumbling into this forsaken, dung-drenched stable, had snuck up on me from behind and caught me off guard and tickled me with the whiskers of mystery . . . of God.

I swear, that little, unlikely thing, that newborn miracle, whispered to me of God and made my heart leap around like a billy-in-love. There was such a gladness in it all. Yet at the same time, there was a silence in it, inside me, that was wondrous as the stillness on a mountain summit in the moonlight.

I realized during that night that it cost this newborn one something to be there, in that dark, cold stable with us goats and jackasses and two-legged ones and all the others. It occurred to me it always costs a kid something to be here in this world. What was funny, joyously funny, was that, judging from his curious smile, this Jesus must have decided we were worth it, for him to make a sacrifice like that—to *be* with us.

I looked at that baby lying there, eyes wide open, gazing right at me. And I began to feel he was asking for some sort of sacrifice from me. And then it dawned on me: He just was asking me to be a goat and be glad of it. He was asking me to accept the sacrifices which being a goat involved. Nothing more, nothing less.

That night—that improbable, cold, smelly, altogether wondrous night—I went to that kid, that Jesus, and I knelt down by him. There was a fleck of blood on his cheek and a bubble on his lips like kids get, and that crazy smile. But in his eyes was a star, I swear it—a dazzle of light like the one on the high mountain that shadowy late afternoon. What light was it? It was like no light I'd ever seen, and yet it was like every light I'd ever seen. It was like all the stars in all the skies that ever were, gathered in one place and then, in a blink, scattered wide again, forever.

As I gazed at that light, I heard him chuckle, a chuckle I'll never forget the sound of . . . baa . . . baa . . . Oh, I'm losing my speech; I must be quick to tell you now.

Oh God, my heart was full that night. So I did a funny thing, a spontaneous thing. I wanted to give the baby Jesus something, so I lay down and put my whiskers on his little feet to keep them warm. It must have tickled because his chuckle seemed louder, almost laughter. Quan's eyes twinkled as she lay down beside me and put her head on that tired father's lap to keep him warm. At last we slept a little. But every once in a while, I thought I heard the baby laugh, and it woke me. I know that, once, when I woke up, the little Jesus lurched forward and touched my head, here, between the horns; and to this day my heart burns from the power of it.

As I lay quietly, looking at the baby, I began thinking of Quan, and my goat friends, and even Naphtali. I began thinking that what's important is laughter and what it's made of. . . like delight and . . . well, gratitude, and hope, and love. What's important is this mysterious link between me and Quan, and between . . . well, as she said, there are other animals in the world and you really can't live all to yourself. What's important is a nuzzle against your neck and laughing for the joy of it.

Laughter is a holy thing. It is as sacred as music and silence and solemnity, maybe more sacred. Laughter is like a prayer, like a bridge over which creatures tiptoe to meet each other. Laughter is like mercy; it heals. When you can laugh at yourself, you are free.

So . . . baa . . . quickly, quickly, before I can no longer speak your language . . . I want to tell you . . . baa . . . stay alert. Listen for the laughter. Listen deeply beneath all the words, beneath the silence. In the gurgle of a baby, in the bleating of a goat. Oh, join the laughter. Laugh at yourself, laugh in joy. Baahaa . . . for not to laugh may be to miss the one who is being born among us even now . . . and is out to get you . . . so keep a sharp eye out . . . listen . . . Watch . . . Laugh . . praise be, praise baahaha . . . ha ha . . . ha ha . . .

* * *

Trillia Minor

Now that a mysterious power has enabled me to turn my language of song into your language of words, I'll tell you featherless ones a secret: Often I hear you sing, just as you hear me. Your singing draws me to you, just as that night I flew into the stable when I heard the baby crying—which is a way of singing, too, you know. Oh, what a night it was. I will tell you of it, for that must be why I have been given the gift of being able to speak in your language.

That night, the flock of us flew on and on, as if there were no time; as if the glorious twilight simply forgot how to become night and lingered on, touching the edge of day like a lover unable to leave his beloved. I cannot explain how the light shimmered all around us, yet if you looked for its source, anywhere, all your eye caught was darkness. Was it a strange tilt of the moon, or some peculiar fall of starlight? Or, more wondrous still, was it perhaps the darkness showing its other side? It's a mystery I cannot fathom.

All I can tell you is that there was a glow that night so awesome that it stirred in us an irresistible urge to fling ourselves toward it, though, in truth, it seemed to penetrate us as well, until we glistened in the sky like drops of water flung into the twilight air where they catch the last rays of sunlight. Maybe you have known such nights.

Ah, that night was wrapped in wondrous sound as well. It was like a thousand brooks tumbling over rocks in the mountains, like a choir of nightingales scaling the vault of heaven, like the tinkling bells of the lead sheep of every flock on earth . . . all at once, everywhere. Yet, when you cocked your ear to catch it, there was only stillness and nothing moved. Was it the wind, or the rustle of our wings, or the beating of our hearts? Or, more wondrous still, was it perhaps the silence whispering its other side? That, too, is a mystery I cannot fathom.

All I can tell you is that the sound that night stirred an irresistible urge in us to lift our voices and hurl them to join that splendid spill of music. Oh, such a night of silver and song it was, a night such as you have surely known.

Soaring in that forever sky, I heard the baby's cry. Do you doubt it, that I could hear such a cry while flying so high? Oh, doubt it not! Yes, I heard the baby cry. I left the flock and flew to where it came from as if that were the only place in heaven or earth that it mattered for me to be. That is where my story begins.

I entered the stable silently, gliding to a rafter braced to hold the roof in place. Everything was old there, the stable as ancient as a cave in which Adam and Eve might have stayed, with the feel about it of a hundred generations of forgotten families who might have made their home there in times past. The animals were heavy with the aura of age—or agelessness—that animals easily acquire. The birth itself was as old as time, as were the primitive, fretful renderings of the parents.

Yet everything was new, too, as new as life, as new as something beginning and, so, triggering other beginnings, especially for the mother and father who were half-lost in their contemplations, occasionally looking at each other shyly, wanting to touch with words but managing only with fingers. I realized that everything about that night, everything about the silver and song of it, spun around this scene.

Most of all, I watched the baby. I could scarcely believe it, but he watched back. I have never known one so freshly hatched who could watch so intently, for so long a time as this one did. Perhaps my quick movements had caught his attention. Whatever it was, he seemed never to take his eyes off me. He was all eyes! I swear it. He saw me! He was the only one who saw me that night in that place. Do you have any idea how amazing that is to someone like me? Do you know how cheaply birds are valued in this world, how we are taken for granted?

Yet, he was all ears, too. I know that because, when I sang, he heard me. But did I really sing? Or was the sound of it the other side of silence humming through me? No matter! He heard my song, the one in my heart; the one I wanted to sing and somehow must have.

So now you know the strange secret in the heart of my story: I thought I came to that place to see something, to see who had cried. But, no! Somehow I realized I came there, to that baby, to be *seen!* To be *heard*!

Oh, my featherless friends, I ask you, do you really think we go anywhere, any of us, just to search for something, just to see something that might be for us the key to understanding things, or to find something that will satisfy our ravenous hearts? Do you really think that is why any of us moves so fast, tries so hard, works so long? Oh, maybe the answer is partly 'yes.' Maybe we're always looking for something that will make the secrets of heaven and earth known to us.

But more than that, what we really want is to be seen. Not merely noticed, not put into a cage, a category, but to be truly *seen*—to be delivered into life by a gaze, gasping like a baby, startled into awareness by a look so penetrating, so powerful, that we sense forever after that we are known and will always be remembered.

That's how it was that night for me, an ordinary swallow. He saw me, Trillia, the only Trillia that ever was or will be. And when he did, there was a rush of fire and wonder in me that, ever since, I've poured out in a song that I taught other birds to sing. To me, it was as though that was why he was bom. It was to see me; and to see everyone else in that stable, every other creature on the earth, to see us so we would forever know we are seen.

Oh, I am such a bird-brain. I told you that baby was the only one who saw me that night. But that isn't right. Part of the secret of it is that *I saw me,* too! Maybe for the first time, I saw me that night . . . because he saw me. And so I sang that night, as for the first time.

I wish I could sing for you now. We birds sing just as naturally as you rejoice—no more, no less. For us, it's the very blueness of the sky, the warm shafts of sunlight, the abundance of bugs and seeds, and sweet dew in the morning that set us singing. These, and dry nests and a mate and little ones so fierce in their longing to fly.

But, like you featherless ones, we seem to lose most easily what is most natural. It isn't that we stop doing those natural things; it's that we lose *why* we do them, what they mean. We lose the *life* in them.

What I'm trying to tell you is that all of us creatures lose our natural capacity to wonder and to rejoice. We get tired, or stuck. Or jaded. Then we act as if we've seen it all. But it's just an act, and underneath we keep looking for something that will help us understand things, something that will satisfy our ravenous hearts. So we pretend not to look, yet look anyway out of the corner of our eyes so others won't notice. That's such a sad split in our lives. It makes us pluck the feathers off wonder and nest in envy.

I've noticed you featherless ones don't sing with your hearts in it much any more. You make the sounds, but there's no song if your heart's not in it; there are only notes, only techniques, only pretense.

There is a saying among us swallows which is, "You can't sing if you don't hear the song." I sing because that night I heard the song, and the song was simply, "You are seen. Always and everywhere and forever." My featherless friends, we are not lost. We do not live and leave no trace. Not a bird falls to the ground without God knowing. That's the song at the heart of everything!

I know, some of you are saying that swallows don't sing. Well, mostly you're right. Oh, sometimes we sing, some of us. But mostly we twitter. You know twitter, don't you? Twitter is our universal creaturely language. Twitter is what comes out when you sing and think that *you* are what the song is about.

Of course, you know twitter. You hear it everywhere, in every gathering you ever go to: the way people can't wait to talk about themselves and twitter away to impress you with what they know, or who they know, or what they've done. Twitter is what happens when you sing for your supper—you know, sing for gain, to get noticed, to get something from others for your singing. Then your heart's not in it, and the song is flat and empty.

But the thing to see is that under all our twitter is a deep longing—in us and in other creatures—to be *seen*, to be loved. That longing is why we all twitter. We want to be important to something, to someone. We want to prove that we matter, that somehow we won't be forgotten, that we are not of little value or no consequence. Oh, how much we all need to be seen! That's what I realized that night when he saw me.

Much later, when I slipped out of the stable and flew again, I simply could not contain the power, the incredible love of that baby's gaze. I rode that gaze as high as eyes can see, as high as you yourself must ride your dreams sometimes. I rode it to the stars. I flew with the angels that night, though I cannot tell you now of their appearance, what their raiment was or the number of their wings. Oh, do not doubt it. I flew with the angels that night.

Then, I looked down. What I saw is the rest of the secret in the heart of my story. I saw things differently. You can imagine that, can't you? You can imagine how, if you hopped from where you are to over here or over there, or if you flew higher or lower, you could look at the same things you'd seen before and see them differently. You can imagine how maybe you could even look at the past or the future and see it differently, too.

Well, I looked down that night on the earth, and it was lovely beyond even singing of it. I could only be silent, the other side of singing. Everything was laid out in beauty so wondrous and holy I closed my eyes and let it hold me. There I was, suspended somewhere between now and evermore, a tiny bit of a thing in an enormous creation. But what I felt was not so much how small I was, but how inseparably *connected* I was to it all, to everything, to the brightest stars in the heavens, to the dullest stones on earth.

That's what I want to tell you now, my featherless friends. You are a part of it, too, part of that enormous, splendid, mysterious whirl of life. A very small part, yes, but a part still, and inseparably connected. Oh, don't let yourselves become so earthbound, so timid and hesitant about those vast spaces, outside you and inside, that you forget, or disbelieve, that you are part of a holy thing, part of the song. So rejoice! That is the way to be part of it all and to grasp that God is with you in everything.

Oh, quickly now. Sing! For this is the most curious mystery of all: Incredible and glorious as the song is, it isn't the song but the *singing* that matters most! The mystery is that the song has many parts—parts for swallows, sparrows, and nightingales; for angels and four-legged creatures and those who swim in oceans, and for all kinds of featherless ones. The truth isn't that there is only one song for every creature; it's that all the different singing of all the different creatures mysteriously combines into one song.

It's the singing that matters, being a little part of the music. The music is God's gift in us, so the music becomes much less without each of us singing. Our part is to sing our music back to God with whatever ruffles and flourishes we can add of our own.

Oh, friends, be done with twittering. Sing from your heart. Dare to rejoice. For it takes courage to sing from the heart—courage and craziness. With a brain as big as yours, my featherless friends, it is a terrible temptation to think too much. To sing, you have to let yourself become a little crazy. Or a little child-like or a little bird-like. You have to let wonder have its way with you.

Dare to sing. Singing is the heart of the celebration of Christmastide, singing the birth of the One who is all eyes. His gaze is always there . . .

> God is there, looking back at you
> wherever you look;
> there in the eye of every crazy bird
> you see;
> there in every song you hear;
> squinting at you whenever the wind
> blows,
> wherever the light shines,
> whenever a baby cries or a child
> laughs,
> or a woman dances or a man sweats;
>
> God is there looking at you,
> claiming your compassion, demanding
> your response,
> wherever a family hungers
> or a creature is oppressed or
> brutalized
> by war or threat of war,
> by poverty or prejudice, by injustice;
>
> God is there looking at you
> wherever beauty is done,
> or truth is told, or lovers whisper.
>
> Oh, friends, there is one unshakable
> reason to sing—
> the baby born that night grew to be an
> adult,
> and he insisted with his life
> that God has an eye on you
> and will never, never lose you in the
> dark.
>
> God is there, looking back every-
> where, in everything.
> You are seen. See!
> You are seen. Sing!

I tell you this because these are the few words I, Trillia Minor, will ever speak. Now I only sing.

* * *

THAT STRANGEST OF NIGHTS

A Twist of Hospitality

A sharp knock on the door, then urgent words
from one half-hidden in the shadows:
"Please! We need a place to stay.
My wife's birth pains have begun.
The time is here, we can't delay."
Through the night's din and flickering light
his voice came sharp as a hammered spike
to split the air, and
though then I knew it not,
my armored heart as well,
and the sum of time,
and my well-stitched, seeming seamless dream
of making a killing from Caesar's scheme.
Later, when the frantic became a vacancy,
I was grasped by a hospitality
far surpassing any of mine.

No, I did not turn them away.
We have a tradition in our land
to extend hospitality
any possible way we can
to strangers, especially those in need.
They needed a place, I provided one,
out of the wind, some privacy—a modicum,
a dry corner out back with the animals
and a few other travelers who huddled
in other corners of the stable for a penny or two.
Best I could do in those circumstances
They took my offer and paid their coins.
Then I left them there to take their chances.
It was I who blindly turned away from them.

Since, I've come to see
that all of us are travelers
from here, to somewhere, to eternity!
We travel not by Caesar's but by hope's decree
that we might come upon some small thing
that will make some larger sense of us,
of our mysterious beginning and our end:
a word, a silence, a fragment of song,
some signal at least fractionally clear,
as came that night, in a woman's shriek,
a baby's cry, the humming of the wind,
when the night breathed deep, gathered all in,
then moved to the dawn of what would be.
That is the story I would tell of me
and this twist of hospitality . . .

I'd been brutally busy for days with little respite.
Circumstance spawned a once-in-a-lifetime chance.
I felt compelled to seize it at all cost
as if it were drink to a parched throat.
My mind whirred in calculation every minute.
My heart beat fast at the prospect of affluence.
Were the stars out? Was there a moon?
Was the night quiet as snow or full of whispers?
Was the wind a lullaby or a warning?
Did shadows dart in the streets like Zealot spies
scattered by the torches of Herod's soldiers?
Was there a melon-scented mist rolling in?
I cannot tell you.
I was busy with numbers, measuring portions,
setting prices, estimating profits.
Praise Caesar, I thought, what a killing I'd make!
But I did not send those two poor peasants away.

I kept the custom reluctantly.
It was myself I turned away.

When I'd shown them the stable, I checked my accounts
in a closet alone where I totaled amounts.
Yet my mind kept wandering from the trail of profit
to the maze of myself, my deceits that corrupt.
But, I'm a good man, I thought, I've earned what I've got.
I've worked hard, tried to keep every law I've been taught.
I'm not much for splitting philosophical hairs,
I keep my mind focused on practical cares.
Add things up, I maintain, the numbers don't lie.
Cut deals while you can, dismiss the nebulous why.
That was my creed, to make a killing my goal.
My intent was to stop short of selling my soul.

That night I had my list, bent on keeping close count.
I would trace each transaction and watch profits mount.
Yes, I considered my list as a sacred thing.
I studied like a priest so I'd live like a king.
Fifty mugs of wine in each of twelve flasks,
times two denarii each, while the wine lasts.
Eight squares of cheese, twenty bushels of flour,
twelve roasted lambs, fifty guests served each hour . . .
I subtracted a bit for the cheap lutist I hired,
and the cost of his food so his voice wouldn't tire . . .
(I'd been told spirits improve as songs entertain
and keep attention off food, so guests won't complain.)
I thought I'd been shrewd to arrange everything,
to make, as it were, such a marvelous killing.

Then alone, in the quiet, I found myself thinking—
A killing? Is that just a manner of speaking?

Or is it somehow tragic, something quite lethal?
What had I done to feel so achingly hollow?
As if touched by a ghost, I started to pace,
My heart was pounding, sweat rolled down my face.
Why did it seem so quiet in there?
Why was it so cold? Had some danger come near?
My flesh was crawling, my scalp bristled with fear.
I clutched at straws. Was it something I'd missed?

I shook as I checked again with my list,
but just then my heart squeezed up like a fist.
Like a corpse too soon buried I fled from that tomb;
my list trailed like a shroud, like the wake of my gloom.
I was shocked by the sudden wave of laughter and song,
yet, those sounds drowned my dread of whatever was wrong.
Though I was revived for a time by the revel of guests,
I knew something other was needed before I could rest.

But I confess, I never went to the stable.
It didn't occur to me there was any reason.
I had to swallow my panic, get a hold of myself.
I had to follow my list, get the job done
It wouldn't do to leave the guests unattended.

When the last of them had gone to bed,
I cleaned the place. There were things to do
to divert my attention, to straighten my head,
to ignore my heart, to turn away once again.
I swept and scrubbed, picked up, directed the help,
put things away, repaired a chair that was broken.
Like I always said, your time is never your own!

But, that night I began wondering,
if it's not your own,
whose is it?
That's a night question . . .
Somewhere among the dirty dishes,
I asked myself,
if your time is not your own,
then *whose* is it?

Silence answered! It dizzied me so I had to sit and hold on.
As people slept, silence deepened 'til I was nearly undone.
Then I found myself wondering what they dreamed of.
Was it, like me, of beasts and shadowy things?
Of lovers, perhaps?
Of some resolution?
An easing of the torment? An ecstasy?
Dreams and labor—
I think the two are linked somehow,
as day and night are sides of time.
But whose time?
At last, I stood and went to work while they dreamed on.
Yet, somehow I realized we all were waiting, in our way,
for some healing resolution,
for an ecstasy,
for some joy that is more than momentary.
It came to me we are all waiting for love,
and tears filled my eyes at that recognition.
We were waiting for time to be fulfilled—
whoever's time it is, ours or . . . mystery's.

* * *

As I worked with my wife and family that night,
I joked about dreams.
In their sagging weariness, my family took me seriously.
My wife stared at me as if she was seeing someone else.
Her reply came as from the depths of reverie:
"Dreams are like the wind blowing where it will.
Tonight, out there, where you did not come,
the wind blew a miracle into life.
Now the child sleeps, and the mother, too,
dreaming of the child and the cost of his birth.
A dream of love is a challenge to be embodied in time.
A miracle depends on the will to choose."
Her words seemed a kind of invitation. But to what?

My daughter seemed to know.
She spoke over her shoulder, pointing with her head:
"While you were counting, we visited the stable.
In spite of the smell, we watched.
For a lifetime, it seemed,
we watched a dream become flesh.
Over the flanks of muddy beasts, we saw life come.
It was an unlikely place, full of humming and whispers.
Still, where else do unlikely things happen?
But, you did not dare. You only care for numbers."
I wanted to protest, to speak of my sweats and shakes,
but, no matter that, she was still right.
I had not dared, so I did not speak.

But my son did.
I'd never heard him speak so,
or listened if he had.
He spoke like the writer of psalms.
"I went, too, drawn by light that seemed to follow me.

I peered through night and lolled with cats and quietness.
In peace I met strangers whose faces I knew not,
yet I knew their hearts were like mine,
and like the heart of that new born one,
and yet not quite. Not quite!
We knelt there and listened to his breathing speak.
And we heard, I swear, his heart's haunting beat."
My son expected me to scoff, but I could not.
His passion changed our equation.
He was father to me on that occasion.

Yet, I never went.
I listened to their words, but I never went.
Pride or confusion kept me away,
or a habit I would not break.
I forged reasons from excuses to persuade myself
but they did so only partially,
and sufficed merely to paralyze me . . . as always.
I said no more to my kin, only to myself,
thus winning the argument but losing my way.
I thought their spontaneity was an extravagance,
a betrayal of the guests.
Of course, others would argue, there are worse betrayals.
Say what they will, I had my duties, and my lists.
I argued, what difference makes one baby, more or less?
There are bills to pay.

Still I wondered, what more is required of me . . .
and what more do I require?
Those two requirements seemed not a match to me.
Nor, I complained, is there time for both.
A hundred steps across the yard
from here to where they were.

I did watch the shadows there a time or two.
I even hushed those men who yelled in the yard.
They tried to explain their exuberance,
I decided they were drunk.
What else but too much wine
would make them leave their job tending flocks?
I stayed with mine.

Bone tired, I walked and counted.
Ten steps from meat rack to cupboard,
four more to the door.
I watched from there, for a time.
Ten steps to the cellar; left for the bread;
right for the wine.
Back up to the kitchen to stir the embers
tuck the bread in the oven to warm.
Eight steps to the rack to stack the wine,
twelve more to the dining hall.
I swept the tables and set them for morning.
Back to the kitchen to check what was left to be done.
I looked at the sky from the kitchen door
on which that desperate husband knocked,
ran my fingers over the panel . . .
Then turned to squint at the rim of the world
to check how much time before dawn.
At last I sat and now it was tears rolled down my face.
What was I do to? It was my job to keep this place.
There's always so much to be done,
and whatever the time, it's never your own.

Or is it?
Someone has to get the mugs and plates and set the table.
That night, the crockery on the table planks

sounded like thunder, or the babble of kings
shouting their demands, expectations, claims.
Or, it occurred to me in my stupor of fatigue,
perhaps crockery knocking on table planks
sounds like that knock on the kitchen door,
or how I imagine the voices of prophets sounded,
when they spoke not only of claims but of choices.
Choices . . . perhaps that's the heart of it.

A hundred steps from this hall to the stable—
I never went.
But now I see it wasn't a hundred steps
only one—the first!
It was a choice.
When there's not time for everything,
time is an invitation to choose.
I never went.
But now I see choices are steps the feet take
following the steps the heart takes first.
Choices are the identity time gives you
when you make them with your life,
and with your love,
until forever fills your time.
I never went.
A hundred steps,
or a thousand from here to there . . .
or only one—
just a heart beat or a lifetime never taken.

I never went.
But there was this strange twist of hospitality
which is the heart of my story, and of me,
the innkeeper kept.

Dreams came to me as I sat and watched the dawn
come silver soft through the door
on which the knock and words
and the mystery had come
the night before.

I watched . . . I heard . . .
A tongue I didn't know . . .
Movement in the shadows . . .
The singing of a bird . . .
A rustling.
A merciful hospitality came to me.
Then my heart understood:
worthiness is not asked of us,
just receptivity.
Or perhaps the kind of faithfulness
that is part humble curiosity.
And wonder enough . . .
and plain worn down simpleness.
I heard what ears cannot truly hear.
In the wind, I heard a cry and then a laugh,
it was the language of the child
brooding over my chaos, creating a world.
I saw the chain of light traced across the sky
and I fell in love
with the old wrinkles and familiar voices
of me and friends and family,
guests and all,
given life again somehow.
Lifetime become mine, undeserving.
In one moment born, a promise made, and kept,
in the time of a life.

I never went.
One came,
and there was here,
then was now,
and that's the miracle even for me.
Not into the Inn where there was no room,
but into the shriveled womb of empty me
came the fullness of a time.
Christ is born!
Not too late, for me or you.
For we are guests.
And there's the ecstasy,
the twist of God's hospitality,
eternity mysteriously
extended to us
in time.

* * *

When the Shavings Sing

The Loneliness of Joseph the Carpenter

(JOSEPH ENTERS IN DARKNESS, CARRYING A LAMP, WALKING LIKE AN OLD MAN. HE TAKES COVERING OFF OF TABLE, PUTS LAMP DOWN, AND RUNS HAND OVER SURFACE. HE PUTS ON APRON AND TAKES RAG FROM POCKET, BEGINS RUBBING TABLE. STOPS. LOOKS UP. BEGINS TO SPEAK.).

It is me, Joseph.
For a long time I have not spoken to you directly,
but surely you have not forgotten me.
But for me it is time to speak,
for time runs short for me.
I made this altar for you as my offering.
Bit by bit it took my life to build it, and much pain:
to find the wood, to cut the parts,
to fit the joints, to make it stable,
to plane it smooth, to carve this paneled scroll,
to rub in oil so it would last,
and light caress the grain.

Each time, with the oil, I rubbed in prayers.
Not words such as I speak now
while there's such time as you allow,
but prayers, still, of tears and curses,
of broken dreams and rumpled loneliness,
as you also surely know.
Now words too long not spoken I would speak to you
and with the oil rub them as well into the wood
and thus will know myself, and seal for you,
what I have made and who I am.
I dare this, though you know that I'm a quiet man,

a carpenter who speaks better with his hands,
quiet, save for what has churned within,
this clang of lonely years and lonely thoughts
which I need tell you now, as if you didn't know.
For my sake, then, I speak, to find some peace.

Every year at this star-scorched time
I've resolved to tell you, and almost begun,
then pulled back into my too-willing unreadiness,
waiting for a smoother season in my life,
with no rough edge, no gnarl, no slivers,
no cracked place to have to work around.
It never came. I knew it wouldn't.

Ready or not, the time has come for this to happen,
for time itself has become the sliver. So I begin
with these words familiar to every Jew:
"Hear, O Israel, the Lord our God, the Lord is one.
Blessed art Thou, O Lord our God, King of the universe,
Who forms light and creates darkness,
Who makes peace, who creates all things."
But peace, Lord, you did not make for me,
at least not in a straight way or entirely,
even though I was regular at the synagogue,
reciting the prayers by heart again and again,
though without my heart being wholly in them
as it is in this prayer I utter now.

O Lord, King of the universe, hear me
for my heart is open before you on this altar.
I am alone. It is my voice alone I lift to you.
Mary's son—and who else's?—was half the ache
I carried through these years,

hoping to be delivered of
before the fullness of my time had come,
not that I didn't love Jesus all the while.
Yes, I loved him, yet, from a lonely place,
outside, some distance between us,
knowing he was not mine.

Mary tells me now I am not able to travel with them,
for Jesus moves fast and I have grown slow.
She is right. But no more right than before.
I always remained behind and watched them go.
There was always work for me to finish.
We were never rich enough for me to go.
Mary tells me I forget things and might get lost.
Well, I have always been lost, a little,
not sure what she and he were all about.
But I remember much, O Lord.

I remember how it was before his birth.
Mary was poor and young-maiden plain,
though to these already seasoned eyes,
which saw fine tables in rough planks,
she was quite beautiful indeed.
I was not a young man, nor handsome, as you know.
But my being able to provide made my desperation
seem to her to be the essence of devotion.

So the arrangements were made, such as they were,
between her family and mine,
and the deal struck for a small dowry.
But Lord, I being more than ready,
took no note of the small print
on what was to come after.

Yet even had I been able,
even had I foreseen her too-soon pregnancy
and my more long, labored pain,
I would not have even then withdrawn,
for I was blindly happy
before I saw at all
what love required of me.
That was the wager you won, O Holy One.
But it was a hard thing you put on me.
I did not get what I expected.
Whoever does? Did you?

But before our marriage, or the birth,
oh I remember well, O Lord,
that season of giggles and silliness,
of a sky full of stars, a heart full of song,
how we danced and sighed the scent of lavender,
were folded in silence, wakened in laughter
and lived in each other's eyes.
Oh, I felt young and it was lovely.
Lovely, lovely . . . before she said,
"I am going to have a child."
There was no laughter in her voice then, Lord,
only sober truth, and secrets.
Secrets she could not fully tell,
for she did not fully know,
this being her first one,
she being so young,
yet suddenly so far-off wise
as a pregnant woman can sometimes become.
So unflinching as she was, telling me her news,
all other sound was walled away,
all light snuffed out,

and I felt suddenly as old
as I'd felt young but hours before.

Then came this gorging bitterness,
this humiliating loneliness,
this deathly sense of nothingness.
I knew the child she carried was not mine.
Whose then? Whose then? Whose then?
I gagged on those words.
I thought to walk away,
leave her to her shame.
I thought to take her by the throat,
choke from her the name
then go and kill the man.
But none of that would change the shock
of being caught between my dream
and this betrayal.
O Lord, it is hard to be a man
when your manhood seems at stake.
Mary said she was pregnant by the Holy Spirit.
What was I to think at such an outrageous claim?
She had audacity, I had to give her that.
But little credibility.
You have to forgive me, Lord,
my doubt that You were the one,
the Father of the child rooted in her womb.
However much she may have wished it so
to spare her innocence, to preserve our vow,
my part was simply to provide what was necessary.

But Lord, do you engage so often in such begetting
that doubt of it should not enter my mind

at Mary's seemingly far-fetched explanation?
To ask you to forgive me that
seems to be asking very little.
And yet, if it be true, what Mary claimed,
that her condition was your doing solely,
and the Messiah was growing in her womb,
then for me to forgive you this insult
to my virility, of which you warned me not,
is, indeed, asking very much.
Who is any man to forgive you?

Accept then this altar I here offer.
With it hear my ancient accusations out
and let me be at peace with you
before time ushers me to sleep.
For at Mary's announcement
the betrayal was a deed done,
the insult, a blow delivered
like the swing of a hammer
to the groin.

O Lord, King of the universe,
who was I to believe, who was I to forgive?
All I knew was that her child was not mine.
It was between Mary and whoever.
Mary said it was you.
For me, it was whoever.
The "between she and whoever" did not include me.
I was on the outside, excluded.
Exiled in loneliness and work and duty.
It is hard to be a man, you know.
If Mary spoke truly, you are finding out.
Or did you know all along

how hard, and how much help
we humans need?

O Lord our God, King of the universe,
it was the darkness you create that I knew then.
I groped on. It was Mary I tried to forgive.
Then the dreams came,
like ghosts haunting me to wakefulness.
Voices telling me to fear not
to take Mary as my wife
but not expect to be her lover,
an aching loss of our earlier loveliness.
Was it your voice, or hers, or mine, spoke so,
To take her as my wife and despite the shame,
despite the slow, unyielding pain,
to willingly embrace this loneliness?

I stayed with her. You counted on that,
though you could have made another plan had I faltered.
I was expendable. I sensed that.
Even so, I stayed.
I wondered if I was just too desperate to leave,
an old man for whom a something relationship
was better than a nothing wilderness.
I stayed.

Was I just too weak to stand up for myself,
letting her walk over me rather than bringing her down?
Yet would causing her fall put me on my feet again?
I stayed.
Was it my wounded pride that wouldn't let me leave,
pride like a broken leg on a valued chair
that I was driven to repair

so as to prove my potencies had not been removed;
by whimpering pride driven to keep up appearances?
Who cared? Not you, but I.
Yet only at first. Then pride tired.
I stayed.

Or was it that I loved Mary
and love betrayed is still love,
perhaps deeper for being less
than a wine-and-flowers fantasy.
Yes. Yes, I stayed, yet a bit reluctantly.
I became useful. And Mary slept alone.
There was no warm comforter against my loneliness.
Still I was useful. O Lord, you knew I would be.
Carpenters are. That must have been the plan.

So when came the enrollment demand
and off to Bethlehem we went. I got us safely there,
but scarcely there and bedded in a bam,
when her waters broke and he was born,
landing like Noah after the flood.
Lord, what I remember of that night . . .
was the cold. It got inside me, and stayed,
clanking like rocks, like stones,
flaying my heart to pieces.

What I remember was Mary's eyes.
They never strayed from Jesus.
He was all she could see,
all that mattered to her in the least.
And that was it.
I was only useful.

I wrapped Mary and the babe in my cloak,
found old skins in corners to cover them,
heaped straw around Mary's feet
and with my body shielded them from the wind.

But I could not rejoice as Mary did.
He was not mine.
A father cannot know the bond that holds
between a mother and a newborn child.
Still, we have our own bond that forms,
different but strong. I'd dreamed of it.
Instead, Lord, I felt twice removed,
once from Mary and whoever,
once from this child who was another's.
I was at the edge of all of it,
huddled in barren loneliness.
He was not mine, this Jesus.

Oh, there were songs that night,
eerie in the wind. I heard them dimly.
Splinters of words about peace on earth, and joy.
For me those things were as far away
as where the singing came from.
I was exiled in usefulness.

* * *

O Lord, blessed art thou for the chores.
I was glad enough for them.
It gave me something to take my mind off
what ate at my heart, some small purpose
to sustain me through the days.

So when he was two, this little Jesus,
there came other dreams to torment me,
full of screams and blood and awful warnings.
Was the voice yours that spoke
of Herod's terrible massacre of children,
a holocaust of the innocents?
I was told to take Mary
and this son who wasn't mine,
and flee for their safety.
They were my responsibilities.
I mattered for my usefulness.

The trip to Egypt to escape Herod's madness
was all bundles of rations, and ropes
and careful routes, and repairs on the run,
places to stay, bits of work to pay for things,
my chores, my duties.

Then came the trip back to Nazareth,
the frayedness of things, the short cuts,
short supplies, the weariness.
I got us back, Lord.
You must have known I would
or I would have had no dream to go.
And I was glad for the work of it.
But it changed nothing between us,
between Mary and Jesus, whoever and me.
The stones within me clattered all the way.
Mary simply loved her child more
than she loved anything.
Jesus was hers, not mine,
in the way that can't be changed,
the way of flesh and blood.

So, you know, the years went
the way of all flesh and blood.
I was useful, but Mary still slept alone.
We shared routines, respect, civility.
There was kindness and care, no animosity.
We even had other children together.
But Mary always slept alone.
She withheld not her body but herself,
which was untouchable,
and she chose not to share.
I worked and was quiet.
I helped raise Jesus the best I could.
He laughed and had his own secrets.
He spent time alone, grew strong and thoughtful.

And when he was twelve,
the year of his passage to manhood,
we made the pilgrimage to Jerusalem,
the pilgrimage required of every young Jewish man.
Then he was missing.
We frantically searched.
Finally, in the temple we found him.
In tears Mary spoke more sharply to him
than I'd ever heard her speak:
"Why did you do this to us?
Your father and I have searched everywhere . . ."

It was the first time she had ever called me that.
My heart leapt.
Was she signaling a change?
I looked at her.
Her eyes were locked on him
as on the night he was born.

"Didn't you know I must be in my father's house?"
His words made her smile.
To me they were daggers opening again the wound
I'd tried to stitch with forgetfulness.
They both knew he was not mine.
The father he referred to was not me.
He was loyal to another.
I felt not jealousy
only a void, a vacancy
in which the stones inside clattered.

But, I was useful, Lord.
You must know how hard I worked.
I taught him carpentry, and he delighted me.
He learned fast, was good with his hands,
though his heart was not in it,
as mine was not in the prayers
we uttered together in the synagogue on Shabbat.
For both of us it was a duty we did
for each other.

Maybe that's how it began to change.
Was that part of what you had in mind?
If so, it was not without its cost.
One day while he was helping me,
our little cart stuck in slippery mud.
I watched as Jesus collected stones
to put beneath the wheels,
small stones, gravel.
He gathered them in his apron,
then held them out to me.
He said, "These are like those you carry inside."

I was stunned that one so young
would see me half so accurately.
He had a carpenter's eye.

Then he scattered them under the wheels of our cart,
and the wheels took hold, the wagon moved.
As the wheels squealed against the stones,
he said, "Listen to the gravel sing.
Everything has its song. Listen."
As our cart waddled along on our delivery,
he said, "Gravel gives traction.
That's why it is beautiful.
It sings of the kingdom. All things do.
You have given me traction, too.
Your work, your duty done,
each day a bit broken from your heart
from dreams turned cold.
Traction you have given me
as I will give you by my love, my brother."

It was like him to say such words
and leave me with the mystery of what he meant.
Brother? Me? I was almost his father.
Well, no, but provided like a father,
cared, taught, watched, wondered like one.
Brother? Then related, at least. At least family.
I smiled. I loved him, too, this almost-son,
and yet . . . he was not mine.
Still, there was traction. I was useful.
The stones that rolled around in me
had become useful in my duty,
my work . . . and I was glad.

To be useful is to be part of some purpose.
I didn't know what it was,
or where the traction of me led,
but that is what he'd said,
Mary's strange son,
and not quite mine except . . . in part
as in his saying I was part
of something he was part of, Lord.

Traction from the stones of pain and disappointment
the simple fidelity of every day.
"The gravel sings," he said. "Everything has its song."
What was mine, Lord? What was yours?
Traction is good, but is it enough?
Without it, nothing moves.
But moves where?
That remained the mystery.
Moves where? With whom?

He is gone now, Lord.
As usual these days, they are off somewhere,
my wife, Mary, and Jesus, her son,
and those who follow him,
as Mary does, being now as bewildered
as the rest of them, as I am as well,
for this mystery is as deep
as the promises it keeps.
But Jesus is not quite the Messiah
Mary expected, either,
doing those strange things,
saying what he does.
His riling people up upsets her,
as it upsets the rooted powers

against which she would protect him as a mother,
yet cannot.
Still she loves him with all her heart
and bewildered, follows him wherever.

They tell me I'm too old and too forgetful
to go along. But not in my heart.
There I follow him.
From a distance, of course, as usual,
but not such a distance, which is unusual.
He called me, "Brother."
What shall I call him?
I asked him that as I ask you.
Before he left this last time, I asked,
knowing we'd not see each other again,
time having traction and running out.
He said, "Listen to the song of things.
Listen when the shavings sing.
They will sing to you what you long to know."

O Lord, I love the wood I make things of.
I made this altar for you as my offering.
One night as I was using the plane on the last board for this,
fitting it, making a rough place smooth,
I listened to the shavings
as they peeled away and fell.
I listened . . . and the shavings sang.
The sound was very like that night when he was born.
Or so it seemed to this old man.
O Lord, tell me the shavings sang!
Tell me this is not the conjuring of a mind worn down by time.
No! I swear!

“Shoosh, shoosh, shoosh,” they sang.
“He is not yours . . . not yours . . . not yours,” they sang.
“You are his . . . are his . . . are his,” they sang.
“You are like us . . . like us . . . like us,” they sang.
“Your altar is made from us . . . from us . . . from us,” they sang.
“We are part of it as much . . . as much . . . as much,” they sang,
“as what you see and smell and taste,
and touch . . . and touch . . . and touch,” they sang.
“You are his . . . are his . . . are his,” they sang.
“Be at peace . . . at peace . . . at peace,” they sang.

Lord, you need not tell me this is not conjuring.
I was there when the shavings sang.
I did not expect their song.
I expect less, by far.
I expect the worst, the knots and gnarls,
the cracks and splinters.

I did not expect the singing.
That first time when he was born,
or this time from the shavings.
I did not expect Mary’s son
to be of the Holy Spirit.
I did not expect a Messiah.
I did not expect you.
Not for years did I expect good news.

I did not expect this joy.
It is a gift.
It does not come on cue.
It’s a surprise.
Who deserves it? None.
Who is it for? All.
For the shavings of the earth.

"We are part of it as much, as much, as much,
as what you see and taste and touch and touch."
"Listen when the shavings sing," he said.
But I did not believe they would.
When they did, I was overcome, struck dumb.
O Lord, blessed art Thou, blessed, blessed, blessed.
These shavings are your mercy, Lord, to me.
Yes, mercy, mercy, mercy to me.
I accept it, yes. With joy . . . joy.

Now I see that joy is not loud,
or not always loud, or only loud.
Why had I always thought that?
How much singing have I missed?
Too much, too much, too much.
Joy is not always loud, like angels' choirs,
but more like choirs of shavings,
the gurgles of a newborn.
It starts in stillness,
the overcoming that shushes speech,
and touches the soul.
Sometimes in such a stillness,
such a joy, such mercy, I see things whole,
quickly, deeply as in a lover's eyes,
as in a baby's birth and star-lit skies.
A stillness, a wholeness, mercy and joy,
a purpose wrought in a mystery abiding.

I am part of this mystery
as these shavings are part of this altar I made for you.
Bit by bit it took my life to build it.
It is my gift, my thanks, my praise to you
for my life, and for the joy,

while there is still time to offer it
to you, his father, and mine as well.
"Brother," he called me.
Brother to him
and so to everything.
Joy. Quiet as a carpenter.
Quiet as a carpenter's almost son,
Quiet as this brother to everyone.
Quiet as this strange savior come
who is not ours but makes us his.
Joy. I have listened to the shavings sing.

* * *

A Wide Berth

The Shame of Michael the Goatherd

(MICHAEL ENTERS HERDING GOATS, CARRYING BAG OVER SHOULDER, BUNDLE OF STICKS BY A ROPE. PROCEEDS TO SET UP CAMP BY SETTING STONES IN CIRCLE TO SHIELD FIRE FROM WIND. HE TALKS TO HIMSELF AND GOATS.)

This place'll do.
There, that's enough stones to keep the wind out.
And this rock'll be dry for sitting. Fire will warm things up.
(TO GOATS) Hey-ho, settle down out there.
Get to eating. Plenty of grass around.
You can come closer when the wind kicks up.
Now, then, what've I got here? *(FORAGES IN BAG)*

I gotta remember to tell 'em
what a strange night it was.
Don't worry. I'll remember.
It was the strangest night ever.
Tell 'em there was more than one got born that night.
I can never forget that.
How could I forget? The strangeness that night . . .
it changed everything. How could I forget?
The thing is, they never listen.
They don't pay me no mind when I tell 'em.
It's because I walk like I do.
Feet pointed at each other. Like an idiot.
I look like an idiot. Like a pigeon.
I know. It's the only way I can walk. But they laugh.
Makes me ashamed. How I walk. How I look.
I hate my body. I wish it was different.
I wish I was different. More pleasing.

I know I'm ugly.
And I'm always ashamed.
I always got something to hide.
Me, is what . . . myself.
How I am. Hide it.
I'm missing something. I'm maimed.
It helps to be a goatherd.
Nobody talks to you.

Maybe they're right about me.
I walk like a pigeon.
And I really ain't much smarter'n a pigeon.
Not when you come right down to it.
Yeah, first you can't walk right,
then you can't learn quick-like.
Even playing as a kid I got ashamed
at how slow I was catching on to things.
I'm stupid. That's the nut of it.
All you can do then is be a goatherd.
(TO GOATS) Hey-ho, easy out there.
Don't take no offense. No insult meant.
There're thing's worse
than being a goatherd, you know.
Though I can't think of one right now.

Time for some cheese and bread. *(FORAGES IN BAG, RETRIEVES)*
Women never come near me. None of them.
Don't blame 'em, really.
Every morning the first thing is the stink.
Last thing at night is the stink.
Wake and sleep with the stink.
You don't have to tell 'em. They know.
It sinks in, the stink does.

To my clothes. These are all I got.
When I can, I wash 'em.
Don't help much. The stink stays.

Gets in your skin, your hair, your mouth.
I can taste it all the time.
Stink comes from the goats,
the dung, rotten carcasses, sickness, vomit, old sweat . . .
But not to lie, I have to say,
it comes from inside as well,
that awful stench, that hellish smell.
Stink ain't just from outside.
It's inside just as much.

When I come near, they yell,
"It's Michael. Give 'im a wide berth."
Even the shepherds yell that.
They make jokes about me and laugh.
They think they're so much better than goatherds.
I guess everyone else thinks so, too.
Not to lie, I guess I do, too . . .
Give 'em a wide berth.
Give myself a wide berth. Ahh . . .

At first I thought "berth" meant having a baby
and I got flustered and angry about that,
thinking the shepherds meant I was weak and womanly,
so I spit and dared 'em to fight me
if that's what they thought.
I didn't know what a wide berth meant.
I was ashamed I didn't know that,
didn't know much of anything.
I was stupid. Stupid!

But I finally learned it meant to avoid me.
To not come near me.
As if they'd catch my stink.
I wondered how they knew.

I gotta remember to tell 'em
what a strange night it was.
I remember, but they never listen.
It's a wide berth they give me.
Only Mosa and Pildash know
the strangeness of that night.
How do Mosa and Pildash know? They're goats.
And they weren't even there then.
They weren't even alive, so how'd they know?
How'd they know?
I told 'em, that's how.

(TO GOATS) Ho-hey, Mosa. You know, don't you?
How strange it was that night?
Pildash, you know.
Samson, you know.
I told you. You're good goats.

I talk to you goats because you're here.
There's no one else to talk to.
Except yourself. You talk to yourself.
Goats and yourself.
Maybe a stray traveler once in a while.
But mostly goats and yourself.
You get close to the goats.
They're not mine. Someone hires me to herd them.
For however little they want to pay.
Can't be choosy. So you take it.
Seeing who you are, that you stink anyway.

Yet you start thinking, acting
as if the goats are yours,
are owed to you.

I watched how the shepherds did it.
From time to time you kill one or two goats,
eat the meat, sell the hides.
Sell 'em for wineskins, bags, sandals,
make yourself gloves, a coat,
have a few shekels for a little wine.
You tell the owners a wolf got those goats, or a lion.
Now and then you bring
a ripped, bloody hide back to show 'em
so they won't get too suspicious.

Those are the tricks.
You cheat. You steal.
That's the nut of it.
You cheat, lie, steal for personal gain.
It's a way to try to scrub away
the terrible stink, the ugly stain.
It's not a good thing at all.
It doesn't work. The stink stays anyway.
It just made me more ashamed.

And on a cold night . . .
On a cold night, the goats slept with me,
Sheva, Pildash, Mushi . . .
We huddled together. For the warmth.
Like lovers we huddled. Together.
It's an unspeakable thing,
being together like that,
goats and . . . goatherds . . .

this stinking goatherd
. . . like lovers.
According to the religious law,
you could be . . . stoned to death . . .
if anyone even accused you . . .
goatherds have been stoned.
(TO GOATS) Hey-ho, you don't have to fret.
No, Sheva, No Pildash . . . you don't fret.
It's the advantage you have as goats.
No shame for you . . .

Me, it shamed, the stink. That I stink.
I was ashamed of the way I walk,
the way I look, what I do,
how slow I think, how bad I stink.
The way I am, even now a shame . . .
a great shame.
That's why I must remember . . . remember
to tell 'em what a strange night it was,
of the strangeness that changed everything.
I remember but they pay me no mind when I tell them,
even as the wind sings,
even as the fire crackles,
even as the stars glisten
and gather like goats to listen,
they pay me no mind when I tell 'em.

So you talk to yourself . . . to myself,
and to the goats, one more time . . .
and one more time
and one more time after that,
one more time like this.

* * *

There are times when the goatherd stink
is in your throat,
an ache is in your shoulders and knees,
and in your heart,
and you're sure God himself
has given you a wide berth.

Not to lie, I'm not religious in the usual sense.
For that I can't get near enough
to where the chanting and the praying is.
I can only get to the courtyard of the animals,
where they're bought and sold and sacrificed,
the bulls, the lambs, the doves, the goats,
where my tears at losing these friends
flows down the drain with their blood.
No, I'm not religious in the usual sense.

But you can't live under the stars,
or hear the singing of a bird,
or watch anything, even a goat, be born,
or see death stalk a creature
like a lion in the grass,
or see a mother goat fight the lion
for her off-spring,
or watch a lily open
to trumpet a welcome to the sun,
and not be religious at all,
not wonder if your ache will ever ease,
or if you'll ever be
welcomed home somewhere.

From your mother's breast
it seeps into your Jewish bones
to expect a Messiah
to come someday—
never today, of course,
but someday, just the same—
come like a king to make things right—
not for me, a goatherd, of course—
for the righteous, not the shamed.
A Messiah someday, but never today.

Nevertheless, when the rumor came it was exciting.
It snapped the snarled string of day after day
after day after day after day . . .
The rumor was passed to me from a old woman.
From time to time she visited herds to buy milk.
A bony, scraggly-haired, toothless hag she was.
I liked her.
She was a woman. She spoke to me.
I never wanted to see her leave.

Keturah was her name.
She made cheese from the milk
because it was soft for her to chew with her gums.
She gleaned tufts of goat hair, sheep wool
from where it snagged on bushes
and wove them into ragged clothes.
Some said she was a witch
or possessed by demons.
That, I'd never say.
She talked to me. She spent time with me.
It didn't matter how she looked,
no uglier than me anyway.

I thought she was strange, all right,
but maybe more angel-strange
than demon-strange.

Who says all angels have to be
clean and beautiful?
They might be terrible and frightening,
some of them, breaking in like that
from some eerie, other world.
That is, if you believe in them,
which I do . . . a little more now.
(TO GOATS) Hey-ho, I see it.
Don't get in an uproar.
It's just a little lightning. That's all.
Won't hurt nothing. Calm down.
Just a little lightning. It'll be all right.

Anyway, that day, a little before that strange night,
Keturah walked over,
came from the shepherd camp
a hill or two that way
where she'd spent a few days.
She told me there was a crazy woman
living with them shepherds.
Keturah said the woman seemed to be getting
crazier every day.

Turned out the crazy woman had been there for a while,
living like a prostitute with them, Keturah said,
being a prostitute in return for food
and a little protection.
We both laughed about the protection part,
us knowing the shepherds

(and me knowing myself).
They treated the crazy woman bad, Keturah said.
Used her hard, treated her mean.
Said from what she'd seen
the crazy woman might be with child.

Keturah said she thought the shepherds
were becoming afraid of the crazy woman,
her getting more crazy all the while,
that, being done with her,
they would tie her hands and feet
and leave her for the wild animals.
Keturah considered going back
to be with the woman,
watch over her some.
It was a tasty tidbit of gossip, Keturah's story,
something you could keep company with,
play with for many long nights.

But it couldn't hold a candle to the rumor.
Keturah said everywhere she'd visited lately
there was talk of the Messiah coming soon.
People said they'd seen mysterious lights in the sky,
heard strange noises,
felt rumblings in the earth.
Keturah asked had I seen any signs?
Felt anything?
Did I notice anything strange?
Of course, you see things, hear things, I told her,
but no more lately than usual.

Except maybe for the wind humming a sound
a pitch higher than before,

and perhaps the stars seeming to droop
a little closer to the ground,
and the goats being more wary and jumpy
about sounds they usually ignore,
and, like a while ago, more sheets of lightning
without any storm coming after.
There was nothing more I could remember,
nothing more, though since she'd asked,
even that little seemed strange.
No, it didn't seem strange; it *was* strange.
I remember it.
Of course, I remember. It was strange.

Keturah nodded as I told her.
Then she told me to stay watchful.
She was sure the Messiah was on his way.
I scoffed, but I stayed watchful.
Even after Keturah left late that night,
I stayed watchful.

* * *

If I hadn't been watching,
I wouldn't have heard the noise.
In the moonless darkness two nights later,
or maybe it was three, I heard the noise.
It woke me up. I listened carefully.
It wasn't the goats. They were strangely quiet.
I laid still, frightened.
The air seemed charged as it is before a storm
but the stars were out and it was cloudless.

I got up and squinted into the night.
Dark forms flitted down the hill.

It was the shepherds running, wild, fast, like a game,
like it was day time, not pitch dark,
like they could see where they were going
and wouldn't trip and break a leg, or worse,
on the unfamiliar ground.
And they were shouting as they ran,
"Come on. Run. Run to Bethlehem
before it's too late. Come on, run, run."

It was two leagues or more to Bethlehem,
an hour's walk, or two or more
Yet you could tell they were going to run all the way.
The voices faded and it got quiet again.

I checked the goats.
It was as if they'd heard nothing.
It was all very strange.
Then I heard more footsteps in the darkness.
Someone else was running, slow,
panting like a wounded animal.

I called out, "Stop! Who are you?"
Whoever it was stopped. Nothing moved.
I waited. Then I circled slowly around
like you stalk an animal.
I followed the panting,
and came on that still shadow from behind.

It was a woman. She was young but grimy, worn out.
The rags she wore were wet and sticky

and those on her feet were almost in shreds
though her thin shawl seemed a lovely, eerie white.
Strange that I noticed that so clearly.
Sweat poured down her face. She seemed in pain.
I knew it was Keturah's crazy woman, the prostitute.
She was round-faced, round every way,
round in what she said.

Before I could ask her, she pointed,
then screamed in a mixture of pain and excitement,
"Bethlehem. Messiah.
Have to go before it's too late . . ."
She turned away, gasping.

"Where's Keturah?" I shouted.
I felt like I was in a roaring windstorm.
The crazy woman screamed back,
"She will meet me . . . on the way back."
She groaned and doubled over.

"The Messiah? How do you know?" I shouted.
"Visitors . . . in sky . . ." she screamed,
Go . . . see.
And she took off running.

She kept screaming until you couldn't hear her anymore.
It's hard to tell if a scream
carries joy or pain or fear or need,
or all of that and more.
She was gone before you could make sense of it.
But I remember.
How could I forget

the strangeness of that night?
So I tell 'em yet one time more.

(TO GOATS) Tell you, Pildash, Mosa, Samson.
No one else will pay me any mind except myself.
You love this story that you've heard before.
It'll help you sleep.

Though what I tell of did not in the least
help me to sleep after the crazy woman left.
The darkness seemed spent. Thin, drained.
I couldn't sleep.
Finally I got up and followed them.
To Bethlehem.
Slower even than the crazy woman
with my pigeon walk.
But I went.
The darkness was very thin when I got close,
and a curious silver haze as from afar
seemed to be leaking through it
here and there like the quick tail
of a summer's falling star.
I pondered, What had made me bold enough to come?
Why was I not too ashamed?

Then, emerging at the edge of town
I could make out the shepherds,
coming in my direction,
moving stealthily as shadows,
going back fast as they came,
to reach their undefended flocks
before some disaster struck.
I did not see the crazy woman with them.
Where was she?
Where was Keturah now?

The wind was blowing wild again, and biting cold.
As the shepherds came near,
I yelled to ask them how to get there,
where the Messiah was.
Soon as they knew it was me,
they gave me a wide berth.
They never pay me no mind.
There was nothing to do
but go off in the direction they'd come from,
looking for rich peoples' houses,
a palace maybe,
fitting for a Messiah's birth.
But nothing stirred anywhere.
No one appeared.
I wandered aimless-like, confused.

At last, remembering the goats,
I began thinking I should turn back.
But first I wanted to find
a shelter out of the wind,
to rest a spell before setting out again,
in that cold, howling gale.
Perhaps I have the nose for it,
but that's how I found the cave
behind an inn, where animals were kept:
I smelled my way to the place.
To keep from being seen as a thief,
I snuck in quickly, quietly
and, in spite of the stink,
peered around for a corner
where I could lie out of the wind,
and suddenly . . .

I saw these people huddled together
against the far wall.
My heart stopped.
I stood still as ice.
The kind of people in a place like this
would kill me for my coat.
Finally I could make out . . .
There was . . . this baby.
This mother and this baby,
I could tell plain it was new born,
being so dry blood smeared and
blue cold looking and wrinkled.
And laying with them a gray bearded man
with his arm around the woman.
They were dozing and didn't see me.
I crept closer and knelt down between the animals.

You could tell from the way place looked
a flock of people like the shepherds,
had been there, churning up muck and straw,
making it all messier than ever,
this filthy place where the animals
stood in a stupor, needing a bath
even more than me.

Could this baby be the Messiah?
I almost laughed out loud.
Some Messiah.
The place stunk, like me.
Maybe worse.
This stable had a stink
that had gathered, layered, ripened
for months, for years.

Dirt, dung, animals' sour breath,
decay, dead things in the cracks,
and me crouching in a corner
in muck and shreds churned up
by shepherds surely no less shameful than I.

It was like all the stink of the world was there
with a Messiah mixed in,
this baby wrapped in rags,
by a mother appearing to be
as wild and drained as the crazy woman,
and an old man who could have been,
not to lie . . . a goatherd
judging from his looks.

If this baby was the Messiah,
which at that moment didn't seem likely,
at least he didn't give people like me,
a stink like mine,
a wide berth.

Sitting there, I started to cry.
I didn't quite know why. Me. Crying.
Like a scream, not knowing
whether from joy or pain or fear or need,
or all of them and more.

It was Keturah's face I saw, then,
through my tears, remembering her,
that tough, toothless hag of an angel.
"Stay watchful," she had warned.
And here I was crying like a baby.
Then I heard words, I don't know from where

except it was a woman's voice, like a lullaby:
"He has scattered the proud
in the thoughts of their hearts . . .
and lifted up the lowly."

My head jerked up.
The mother was looking right at me.
Had she spoken those words?
Her eyes were full of surprise,
as if wondering why I was there,
but smiling, too, she was,
as if to accept me all the same.

"My name is Mary," she said softly.
Nodding, she whispered, "This is Jesus."
That voice. I *had* heard it before.
It was like an echo in my head . . .
"He has scattered the proud . . .
He has lifted up the lowly . . .
lifted up the lowly . . .
lifted up the lowly."

Then the baby was crying.
I heard it plain as a goat bleating.
Then he wasn't crying.
When I looked again
they were all looking at me.
The baby was wide-eyed,
his eyes full of secrets and fire.
The old man's eyes were crinkled
in a kind of smile as if to say
he and I both knew something,
which was that we didn't know.

It was like a dream.
It was like home.

As I sat there, the baby began to look around
like he couldn't figure out where he was either.
It was that look made me think
maybe he really could be the Messiah.
He just accepted it, the strangeness
the place, the stink, me, himself,
without seeming ashamed of any of it,
or having to give any of it a wide berth.
It was the strangest night.
The strangeness changed everything.
I remember it so as to tell 'em.
How could I forget?

* * *

Though I don't quite know
when I left the cave
or which direction I went,
somehow I got back that night
with my pigeon walk.
It was like waking from a dream.

What I remembered first
was hearing the goats off in the distance,
and then stumbling over something
as I moved closer to stir the fire
in the final darkness before the dawn.
For safety, you are careful, walking like a pigeon.
You learn each stone and hollow of each camp.
So I do not often stumble.

That night I did.
I reached to grab and throw aside
whatever the cursed thing was
that threw me off my stride.
My God, it was another baby . . .
still smeared with blood like the other one,
but bluer with the cold,
wrapped in the oddly lovely, flimsy white shawl
of the crazy woman!
Keturah had been right:
The crazy woman had been with child.

I searched for the crazy woman in the dark,
a few steps in each direction,
but she was not there.
Why was this baby left here?
What was I to do with it?
Maybe it was as dead as it seemed,
since it didn't move or cry.
But then it opened its eyes
and looked at me, as if it, too,
wondered what I would do.
I shifted the baby to my other arm.
The shawl fell away.
It was a girl.
That settled it!

Ah, but I would have done it anyway,
life being hard enough out here,
there being no room in it for a child,
no way to care for it,
not enough food.
And no one else would take it, raise it either.

All the time, babies, children die
and who cares to ask how they do, or why?
You just get rid of 'em,
especially if they're female,
as this one was.
You leave 'em to die,
in thc cold, for the wolves,
like the mother did who left her here
for me to stumble over.

I put the baby down by the fire
and went to check the goats.
They were restless.
One of them, young Zamza,
had given first birth while I was gone.
I found her dead.
Another goat had taken the newborn kid as her own
and was nursing it in the early light.

I began to cry. Not for years had I,
then twice in the same strange night,
I sobbed as if I'd lost something,
or found something, or both.
What was I feeling,
kneeling there in the mud
by the dead mother goat?
I remembered the scream, the crazy woman's scream.
She must have been feeling birth pangs
even as she ran through the night.
Why was that crazy woman
so determined to go to Bethlehem?
Why was I?

I cried and watched the nursing kid
and thought of the Messiah in the stink.
I saw that baby's face, his eyes.
I heard again that voice, that lullaby,
"He has lifted up the lowly . . .
lifted up the lowly . . .
lifted up the lowly."
I got up and walked back to the fire.
I took off my coat and wrapped the baby in it.
I called her, "Mary."
I took the skin from Zamza's body,
cut way and scraped clean her small milk bag
with its virgin pink teat,
and dried it best I could by the fire.
Then I sewed it up, left an opening at the top,
put goat milk in it,
and little Mary nursed at this breast.

So it went for many months,
as me and the goats moved around
in the constant search for pasture.
The goats liked Mary, I could tell.
Then late one afternoon,
Keturah came to visit again.
We sat quiet by the fire
and watched the sun go down.
All she said was,
"I knew you'd take care of her."

Then she handed me the curious thin, white shawl
the crazy woman had worn and I'd found Mary wrapped in
when I stumbled over her that strangest of nights.
I'd thrown it away as a useless rag weeks ago.

"I thought you might like to keep this," Keturah said,
"to give to little Mary someday from her mother."

I didn't ask her how she knew the baby's name,
or how she'd come by the shawl
and mended it to be like it was that strangest of nights.
It was enough that I knew this toothless hag
was some sort of terrible, tender angel,
and that little Mary's mother
had died giving her birth.
The rest was all Keturah's work.

Keturah smiled that toothless smile and said,
"The shepherds are different, too.
It was a wide birth that night."
Then she was gone.

The strangeness of it is all past figuring out.
I started laughing at what Keturah said.
Maybe I was right in my ignorance.
Maybe there is another way to see
what a wide berth means.
Maybe it does mean having a baby.
Giving life to many all around.
So the one born in Bethlehem, that baby Jesus,
does give wide birth, wide life.

That wide birth rippled out to me
so I wasn't so ashamed anymore.
It rippled out to the crazy woman,
who gave birth herself that night.
And to little Mary
because I saved her.

And I did raise her
until she was five years old.
Then Keturah came to visit one last time.
She said, "Mary's of an age to be with a family,
not out here in the wild.
There's a childless couple in Magdala.
I'll take her there."

So I cried a third time.
Both of us cried.
Mary and me.
And Keturah, too.
But it was right for Mary to go with Keturah.
I knew that because I loved her.

That was years ago now.
The strangeness of that night changed everything.
I remember to tell 'em.
Little Mary come to be called Mary Magdalene.
That is how she is known now.
She used to visit me, sometimes.
Then she stopped.
For a time the word was she was a prostitute,
like her mother.

Then little Mary hooked up with Jesus.
Once or twice, I went to see her,
and this Jesus.
I stood at the edge of the crowd
and watched and listened.
She was wearing the shawl I'd found her in,
that strangest of nights.
Little Mary spotted me and came to me both times.

We talked a little, remembered.
Both times she said, "I love you."
And me, stinky old me, managed to choke out,
"I love you, too."

The last time I visited little Mary
she took me to meet Jesus.
I knew it was the same one
I'd met that strangest of all nights.
His eyes held the same secrets and fire.
And he knew too, who I was.
I don't know how, but he did.
All he said to me was, "I love you."

For the fourth time I cried,
and croaked, "I love you, too."
But the words came out like a scream,
of pain and joy and fear and need,
and more, of great gratitude and hope.
Jesus smiled, then, his father's smile,
to let me know, I'm sure,
we both knew a mystery we didn't completely know
but that knew us altogether.

Little Mary visited me the last time not long ago.
They killed Jesus.
Killed him for not being the kind of Messiah
they wanted or expected.
What fools we are.
What shameful fools.
If only they knew what they don't know
but are known by.
Even when I remember and tell 'em,
they don't pay me no mind.

Or him either.
But there's hope for us. Hope.

Little Mary of Magdala said Jesus had come back,
returned from the dead.
She had seen him.
She was following him still.
So the wide birth isn't over yet. Not yet.

(TO GOATS, DANCING)
Hey-o, Pildash, Mosa, Samson.
The fire and the secrets in his eyes.
And he's coming again.
Coming again
Coming again.
He lifts up the lowly . . .
lifts up the lowly . . .
lifts up the lowly . . .

* * *

AND NOW . . .

Gum on the Altar

Then the chariots of the Lord, rolling out on shafts of light and through timeless darknesses and unknown worlds, break rank to wheel and scatter round planets like our own, finding their way into curious and unlikely corners of such planets—for curious and unlikely reasons, bearing curious and unlikely messages—you might guess there are curious and unlikely creatures in them, hanging on to the reins as much to stay in the chariot as to guide it. Who knows where such messages—and messengers—might end up? So it is well to pay attention!

Consider, if you will, two old women walking to lunch, as snow begins to fall. Could they be . . . ?

"It's snowing, Rose," observed one of the women named Phoebe.

Rose, the other woman, engaged in what truly were her own thoughts, mumbled to herself, "Do you think green would match the trees if I opened the door to sneeze when the gardener squeezed and the air is nice if it's blue as ice but Mrs. Vassick ain't so full of spice and . . ."

"Rose. ROSE!"

"Yes? Oh, Phoebe, it's you. Yes, it is. Yes. What?"

"It's snowing, Rose."

"Well, yes it is," Rose agreed. "It certainly is. Yes, it is. It is snowing. Yes, certainly, it is. It is . . . "

Rose!

"Yes? Yes, Phoebe?"

"Rose, I heard no two snowflakes is alike. Not one like another."

"Is that a fact?" exclaimed Rose. "Well now, ain't that something. Just imagine that. Ain't no two snow flakes alike. Ain't that something. Think of. . . How did they find that out, Phoebe?"

"I don't know. I just heard it's so."

"My. Now, ain't they getting smart," said Rose. "They just know everything these days, don't they. Imagine knowing ain't no two snowflakes alike. Imagine knowing these snowflakes we're mashing under our feet right now ain't like no other snowflakes anywhere forever and ever. How do they know that, Phoebe? That no snowflakes ain't like no other snowflakes forever and ever and never and lever and clever and . . ."

"Rose."

"Yes?"

"Rose, how many snowflakes do you think there are?"

"Well, let me see," Rose answered. "A lot! Certainly a lot. Oh, a very lot. A thousand, probably. Oh, more. More than a thousand. A hundred thousand? A thousand thousand? Oh, I know it's a very, very lot. How many, Phoebe?"

"Zillions, Rose. Zillions and trillions and millions."

"Is that a fact, Phoebe? That many. Well, now ain't that something. That is something, ain't it? That certainly is a lot. A very, very lot. A very, very, very . . ."

"Rose!"

"Yes? Yes, Phoebe. Yes. What is it?"

"Who makes snowflakes?" asked Phoebe.

"Who makes snowflakes? Oh, well now . . . let me see. Who makes snowflakes? Who makes . . . let me see. I . . . ah . . . I don't know, Phoebe. I don't know, do I, Phoebe? I should know, but I forgot. I'm going to cry. I am. Going to cry. I don't know. I just forgot."

"Rose! Don't cry, Rose. It's all right. I'll tell you who makes snowflakes. God makes snowflakes, that's who."

"Oh, good for you, Phoebe! You remembered. Good for you. Of course. God makes snowflakes. I forgot. Ain't that something? Of course. Certainly God makes . . . How do they know that, Phoebe?"

"Reverend Thurston says so, in chapel," answered Phoebe. "He says that God makes everything. Remember?"

"Did he say that? Oh, yes. Of course he did. I remember now. Ain't that something. God makes everything. Snowflakes, too. Certainly, of course."

"Besides," confided Phoebe, "last night I heard little voices and they kept saying, 'God made us, God made us.' Over and over. And I looked all around, and it was the snowflakes talking through the window. Did you hear 'em?"

But Rose was off in her own thoughts again, talking to herself. "Coke is good. I like Coke, and I don't smoke or tell no jokes and old cow pokes and . . . why don't they let me have Cokes? Is two small Cokes more than one big Coke? I asked the man, but he said I didn't have enough money. Two cents, I had. Change. Home on the range. Where everything's strange . . ."

"ROSE! Listen to me, Rose."

"Oh, Phoebe? It's you. Yes. Certainly. I was listening. Yes, I certainly was. I was, yes, I was, and . . . and you was talking about . . . about.. ."

"Snowflakes, Rose."

"Yes. That's it. Good for you, Phoebe! You remembered. Good for you. That's it. We was talking about snowflakes. Of course. Certainly. Phoebe, you look sort of sick. What's the matter, dear?"

"Rose, I ain't sick. Now just shut up a minute. I'm just thinking, is all. Rose, if God makes snowflakes, and no two snowflakes is alike, and there are zillions and trillions of snowflakes, God must be terrible busy. So how does God have time to do much else but make snowflakes?"

"How does God have time to do . . . oh my," Rose struggled. "That's a hard one. Let me see. I should know the answer to that, shouldn't I? Let me see . . . Maybe snowflakes . . . Maybe snowflakes . . . Maybe God . . . I can't remember. I'm going to cry, Phoebe. I'm just going to cry."

"Don't cry, Rose. It's all right. Maybe they'll let you have a Coke for lunch."

Two women, curious and unlikely creatures, on their way to lunch as the snow falls in a curious and unlikely corner of the planet—The State Mental Hospital—where they are for curious and unlikely reasons, though perhaps no more curious and unlikely than any of us curious and unlikely creatures are, wherever it is that we are.

The last of the many jobs Phoebe did to support her invalid mother was selling hot dogs and soda as a street vendor. Her cart was mounted on a three-wheel bicycle she rode about town. When her mother died, Phoebe kept riding her cart, selling her hot dogs and listening to the voices she'd begun to hear about a year before.

One evening she'd ridden her cart to a corner near the Symphony Hall where stylishly dressed people had to walk around her while she hawked her wares. When a policeman told her to move, she argued that she wouldn't because stronger voices than his had told her to come to that particular corner on that particular night, and she wouldn't move.

"Thank you very much, get lost Buddy Boy!"

The argument got heated, the policeman threatened to arrest her, and Phoebe began throwing paper cups and hot-dog wrappers around on the sidewalk, followed by buns and hot dogs. A crowd gathered. When the embarrassed policeman took Phoebe by the arm to lead her away, she kicked him and threw soda on his uniform. He called a wagon and they picked her up bodily and carted her away.

After a night in jail, the court committed Phoebe to The State Mental Hospital for psychiatric tests. The tests were legally inconclusive, but since she had no family or outside advocate, her case got conveniently buried. So the women's geriatric ward became home for Phoebe.

Her friend Rose had been married. Her one child, a son, had run off to join the Merchant Marine at seventeen and had not been heard from again. Rose's heart was broken. After her husband died, she'd ended up living alone in a small apartment on his pension. At first she had a cat to talk to, but after a while she'd begun talking not only to the cat but to herself. Slowly she seemed to lose track of things, including the thread of her own conversations.

Then one winter evening a policeman had found her shivering on a street corner, talking rapidly in what seemed to him an irrational and incoherent way. They held her in the Women's Detention Center for several weeks, but tracing her through missing persons turned up nothing, and Rose simply couldn't remember where she lived or anyone she knew. So after much indecision, someone in the Welfare Department suggested The State Mental Hospital and, thus nudged into the bureaucratic maze, Rose found her way at last to the women's geriatric ward and the bed next to Phoebe's.

Two women, curious and unlikely creatures, side-by-side in a curious and unlikely corner of the planet. Though perhaps they are no more curious and unlikely than any of us curious and unlikely creatures are, side-by-side, wherever it is that we are in our corner of the planet.

* * *

Phoebe and Rose had become inseparable. One was round, the other bony. One shuffled along, the other swayed in a bow-legged way. One talked to herself, the other heard voices. Neither could put into words how they felt about the other, and it did not occur to them to try. They didn't even think about it. They were simply inseparable.

"Here's the dining room, Rose," said Phoebe. "Give me your arm for the steps."

"Orange is nice, all sticky and spice, icky as mice, ran up the clock, hickory dock, cat on the block, which one is right, right is nice, nice is bright, bright is nice, nice is . . .," Rose rambled on.

"Rose."

"Yes? Oh, Phoebe. It's you. I was listening, I certainly was. Certainly, yes, listening I was. I was, really, I . . ."

"Here is the dining room," instructed Phoebe. "Give me your arm for the steps."

"Oh yes! Good, good, good. Time for lunch. Thanks a bunch. Do you think I can have a Coke? Phoebe, do you think I can have a Coke? For lunch? Do you? Do you think I can, do you, do you, do you?"

"Maybe," replied Phoebe. "Maybe you can have a Coke, and I can get some gum. Got a quarter in my pocket. For the gum machine. Pull the lever; it says, 'Thank you!' Do you hear it say that, Rose? Pull the lever; it says, 'Thank you. Here comes the gum. Thank you! Thank you!' Do you hear it, Rose?"

One loved Coke, the other loved gum. Curious and unlikely! Though Phoebe didn't have many teeth left, she loved to chew gum, though chewing was only *one* thing she did with gum—perhaps the least of the things she did with it. She sucked on it, gummed it, rolled it around in her mouth, swallowed it, blew bubbles with it (if it was bubble gum, getting it all over her face), pulled it out of her mouth in long strings, put it behind her ear sometimes where it usually got stuck in her hair.

Worst of all, she would leave wads of chewed gum every place. Many of the places she left it, and forgot about it, were harmless enough. Often she would leave it on her little bed stand overnight and chew it again the next day, marveling at how hard it got during the night, and how she could see her tooth marks in it just as she'd left it when she'd gone to bed. But other places she left her gum were more troublesome.

Phoebe and Rose worked in the hospital laundry together, Rose folding towels, Phoebe folding sheets. Many times Phoebe had left her used gum next to a pile of just-washed sheets before they were rolled through the big mangle irons. Often her gum ended up sticking on the sheets when they rolled through the mangles, and the resulting mess caused furor after furor until, finally the laundry supervisor simply forbade her to chew gum, which, for the most part she didn't, while she worked.

Still, her gum also caused problems when she accidentally left it where people sat, or walked. To top everything, when Reverend Thurston came, once a month, to give Holy Communion in the chapel over the dining room in her building, Phoebe would invariably go forward with the others to receive the elements, only to remember her gum just as the bread was being passed. So, just as invariably, she would remove her gum and put it, only for a moment she thought, on the communion rail while she chewed the bread, thinking it would be terrible to mix her chewing gum with the "Body of Christ."

But, invariably, Phoebe forgot about her gum and left it behind when she returned to her pew. So, regularly, Reverend Thurston stopped by the ward on his way back to his church and gave her a little talk about good manners in worship, which meant, specifically, that she should not chew gum in the chapel. She was never sure exactly what he was saying, or why, but each time, she agreed not to chew during worship, only to forget her agreement by the time the next month's communion came around.

Recently, Reverend Thurston had approached her again about the gum she'd left on the rail during the Advent communion service.

"Phoebe," Reverend Thurston admonished, "you put your gum on the communion rail again. You simply must stop doing that. It is irreverent, it is offensive to God, and it desecrates a holy place."

"I'm sorry, Reverend," Phoebe answered. "I just forget. I don't mean no harm, really. What does 'desecrate' mean?"

"It means . . . well . . ." Thurston groped for words to explain what it never occurred to him needed explaining. "It means to take something clean and make it dirty. Phoebe, how would you like it if someone took your clean sheets and got them all dirty after you washed and folded them? Well, that's how God feels about gum on the communion rail."

"But, Reverend, ain't people supposed to get sheets dirty? If you use 'em, how can you keep from getting 'em dirty? That's why we wash 'em. I don't understand about desecrate."

"Well," stammered Thurston, feeling flustered, "desecrate is, well . . . it's . . . it's taking something that's supposed to be used one way, the right way, and using it another way, the wrong way. That's what desecrate means. Using something wrongly, for what it wasn't intended to be used for. You see what I mean, Phoebe?" He felt pleased with himself.

"I think so," Phoebe nodded, smiling. "It's like Jesus being born in a stable, like you read in the Bible to us. That's using the stable for another way than was meant, right? Jesus desecrated the stable. Is that sorta what you mean?"

"No, that is not at all what I mean." Thurston's face contorted between anger and foolishness. "Phoebe, you are deliberately refusing to see my point."

"I ain't trying to miss it, Reverend. Really. I'll . . . I'll remember next time not to chew gum. Don't worry, Reverend."

"Good." Thurston was relieved to leave the subject of desecration. "Just think how other people feel, seeing your gum on the rail when they come to the Lord's Table, Phoebe. Try to remember next time." He turned to leave.

"Excuse me, Reverend, but . . . I been wondering about them wise men, you know, the ones you read about? Why did they bring them gifts to baby Jesus?"

"To honor him as King and Deity," answered Reverend Thurston, turning back.

"But what is franka . . . franka . . ."

"Frankincense, Phoebe? It is like incense. It smells good. It's used to worship the Deity. It means Jesus is Lord."

"Oh. And what about the other stuff they brung? Not the gold. The other stuff. You know."

"Yes, myrrh. That is like a rare resin, Phoebe."

"Resin? What's that?"

"Well, it's like a kind of gummy substance," replied Reverend Thurston.

Phoebe brightened. "Gummy? Like gum?"

"Not *gum* gum, Phoebe. It's more like . . . well, they use it to make perfume and to make a liquid they used to bury people with in ancient times."

"Oh. Bury people? Ain't that a stupid thing to bring a little baby, Reverend?"

"It's symbolic, Phoebe. They brought it because they knew Jesus would die for the sins of the world. As it says in the Bible, in Revelation, 'Worthy is the Lamb who was slain, to receive power and wealth and wisdom and might and honor and glory and blessing.' It's symbolic, the myrrh."

"A lamb, Reverend? I don't get it."

"Well, Phoebe, that's symbolic, too. A lamb is a symbol of innocence, you see. A little lamb is innocent. And Jesus was innocent. An innocent sacrifice is acceptable to God. Because of it, God forgives our sins."

"Sort of like Jesus helps us and helps God," Phoebe mused.

"In a manner of speaking," Thurston replied.

"And that's what myrrh means?" she asked.

"That is what it means. Or close enough for you. Now, I have to go. Just remember, Phoebe, no more gum in the chapel." He sighed as he walked away.

Phoebe didn't understand what Reverend Thurston was saying, but probably he didn't either, though his departing sigh was as close as he'd ever come to admitting it, even to himself. So the difference was that she was troubled by not understanding and he wasn't. She struggled to understand because she knew she didn't; and he didn't struggle to understand because he thought he did.

And that is how messages get missed—curious and unlikely messages from curious and unlikely creatures hanging on for dear life to the reins of the Lord's chariot wheeling in curious and unlikely places.

* * *

Another curious thing about this curious place was that many of the buildings of The State Mental Hospital were connected by underground tunnels that were used for walkways as well as passages for plumbing and heating lines. It was an old building, built before electricity or inside plumbing or central heating. So when each of these conveniences was added, all sorts of conduits and pipes were attached to the walls. When you entered the building, you felt a little like Jonah in the belly of the whale, watching and listening to its vital juices pass through its tracts and ducts and glands. Rumor had it that the old building was to be torn down soon and another built to replace it.

In fact, much of the life of the hospital took place in those tunnels and in the veritable warren of storage rooms and closets running off them. The dining room of Phoebe's and Rose's unit was on the first floor in the center of a two-story building. The chapel was over the dining room on the second floor, so, "symbolically," God and the kitchen held together the women's geriatric ward in the east wing and the men's geriatric ward in the west wing.

It was into the belly of this whale that Rose and Phoebe made their way to lunch. They had just come to their table and sat down when Dr. Kaplan announced that the Trinity Church youth choir would be singing Christmas carols for them that noon, and the auxiliary of the local Rotary Club would pass out gifts. The gifts turned out to be a box of Kleenex and a bag of candy for everyone. Phoebe gladly noted that the bag of candy had a package of gum in it. Suddenly overwhelmed by the prospect, she began to cry.

And no sooner than the choir began to sing, Rose began to talk: "Trick or treat, kiss my feet. Wear your rubbers, oh yes, mother. Bundle up, you'll catch your death, look at there, you can see your breath. Johnny's all dead and gone. Everybody sing a song. Red is dead and so's the brain inside your head, and so is Fred with dirty feet . . ."

"Rose, shhh," whispered Phoebe, "they're singing . . ."

Rose blithely babbled on, "Freddy stinks and Mary winks and Daddy drinks. But I won't tell, so what the . . ."

"Rose, Rose, shhh, They're singing. SHHHHHHHHH. ROSE."

"Yes? Oh, Phoebe. It's you. I was listening. Really. I was . . . Oh, Phoebe, you're crying. Oh, don't cry. Please, don't cry. What's the matter? Oh, I'm going to cry, too. Oh, Phoebe, Phoebe."

"Shhh, Rose. I'm just feeling a little bad 'cause people give us things, and I ain't got nothing to give nobody. Not even you, Rose. Nothing to give for Christmas."

"Ahh, Phoebe, you're my friend. You give me you. Best thing anybody could have. You're my friend. Don't feel bad, please. You're the nicest friend anybody ever had. Don't cry, Phoebe, please don't."

"Shhh. Rose, be quiet. Listen to the music now. Stop talking and listen. Shhh."

Rose turned to listen, and Phoebe looked at her a long time, thinking about what she had said, until the choir finished and everyone was clapping. An idea had begun to form in her mind.

Since the snow continued to fall, Phoebe and Rose and most of the other patients used the tunnels to return to their afternoon activities. On their way back, the group stopped and gathered in a large storage room where several mattresses had been put on the floor and an old record player stood in one corner. At odd hours, especially at night, patients would sneak down to this room for little parties and social liaisons, all officially forbidden but unofficially sanctioned by the hospital authorities. Such activities obviously helped patient morale and so helped the hospital run more smoothly. And on this particular day, many in the little gathering were grumbling about the gift of Kleenex and wishing some group would give them some beer sometime, or something for a party.

But while they grumbled, Phoebe was busy trading her candy to women for their gum and giving kisses and other small favors, along with the promises of future considerations, for the men's gum. By the time she returned to the laundry, she had eighty-seven packages of gum and promises of at least twenty-three more. That night she also counted her little savings, slowly dividing it into little piles, each of which would buy one package of gum; she determined she'd be able to buy another thirty-four packages, maybe more.

During the following week, though no one really noticed, Phoebe left no wads of chewing gum anywhere. And every night, late into the night, Phoebe sat on the edge of her bed chewing stick after stick of gum until her jaws ached.

"Phoebe, what are you doing?" asked Rose sleepily on her midnight return from the bathroom.

"Chewing gum, can't you see?" Phoebe sighed. "Just go to sleep, Rose. Don't worry."

"Why are you chewing all your gum like that, Phoebe? Why don't you save it? You're using it all up. Why are you doing that?"

"I'm making something is why. For Christmas."

"What, Phoebe? What are you making? Something for me? For me, Phoebe? For me?"

"Not exactly for you, Rose. It's a . . . surprise. It's mainly for God."

"God? You're making something for God? Ain't that something. For God. That's something, Phoebe. It certainly is. It is, certainly. How did you know what God wants, Phoebe?"

"I don't know. I just . . . I don't know."

"Surprise. For God. Ain't that something. Phoebe, you said that God made snowflakes, but I forgot what else you said. About snowflakes. What'd you say?"

"That I heard 'em talking?" answered Phoebe.

"That's it. Good for you, Phoebe! You remembered. That's what you said, all right. You heard 'em talking. You certainly did. How come I don't hear 'em, Phoebe?"

"You're too busy talking," Phoebe replied.

"Oh. I never thought of that. What do they say, Phoebe? The snowflakes. What do they say?"

" 'God made us. God made us.' That's what they say, Rose. And Rose, no two snowflakes is alike, remember?"

"That's right," said Rose. "That's what you said. I remember now. And you said there was zillions and zillions of 'em. See, I was listening, Phoebe. I was. How many is a zillion, Phoebe?"

"A lot," Phoebe answered. "A very, very lot, as you say."

"Oh. Why was we talking about that, Phoebe?"

"'Cause I was wondering, if God made all them snowflakes, how does God have time to do anything else? Answer me that, Rose."

"Oh. OHHHHH. I forgot what you said. Let me see . . . I forgot. I . . . I think I'm going to cry. Phoebe. Yes, I am. I'm going to cry."

"It's all right, Rose. Don't ciy. I don't know either. God must be pretty busy. So . . . so I'm making God a little surprise. Now go to sleep."

During that week, Phoebe chewed one hundred thirty-seven packages of gum. She used all the money she had saved to buy more, and she begged from doctors and nurses and attendants, and traded with other patients, and even took some from the commissary when the clerk wasn't looking. And every night she chewed. By the week before Christmas she had asked Rose to help her.

"But I don't like to chew gum, Phoebe," said Rose. "I just ain't got no good teeth."

"You gotta help, Rose. Or I won't finish my surprise in time for Christmas."

"But I can't talk good when I chew gum. The gum sticks to my teeth. See, ah caahhn't tahhk gahhd."

"You don't have to talk," said Phoebe. "Just chew and chew and chew, Rose. Rose? Rose did you hear something just then?"

"Ahhh, naaw. Ahh dahhn't heaah nahhthin."

"Shhh. Listen. It's singing, Rose. Singing. You hear it?"

"Naaw, nahhthin. Ahh daahhn't heaah nahh sahhing."

"Chew, Rose. Chew faster. The angels is coming. Already. Listen. That's them singing. Oh, hurry up. Hurry."

So the night before Christmas Eve, Rose and Phoebe sat on their beds across from each other and chewed the last packages of Phoebe's hoard of gum. When they had finished, they gathered the fresh wads of chewed gum, snuck out past the night attendant who was asleep in the little glass-enclosed office, and went downstairs into the basement. They made their way along the dimly-lit tunnel to a small closet off one of the storage rooms. Phoebe lit a candle she had hidden there.

"See, Rose. That's what I been making," said Phoebe. "That's where the gum I been chewing went. See. What do you think?"

"Why, that's the biggest wad of chewed up gum I ever seen, Phoebe. Ain't that something. It certainly is. It certainly is something, ain't it? You been making that? It's something. What is it, Phoebe?"

"It's a statue, Rose, can't you tell? Here, I'll pick it up so you can see. See, the gum got all hard when I stuck it together. Now, what do you think?"

"Let me see," answered Rose, "I should know what that is. It's . . . it's chewing gum, that's a fact, ain't it? Chewing gum all chewed up, little clumps stuck together in a statue of . . . of . . . of . . . a cat? That's it. A cat! It's a cat is what it is. Like my cat. Emily cat. Nice cat. Orange cat. Orange peel, real meal, happy deal . . ."

"Rose. ROSE!"

"Yes, Phoebe?"

"It's not no cat," said Phoebe. "It's a lamb. Can't you see the wool? Curly all over it. Now, this gum we chewed tonight is for one ear and a little tail. Stick some on right there, and . . . there. Like that. Squeeze it a little. There. Good. That will be hard in the morning. And see there, his legs bent under him, 'cause he's lying down. And this here's the nose. Could of been a little longer, maybe, but I run outta gum. It's a lamb, Rose."

"Good for you, Phoebe! You knew right off it was a lamb. Of course. It certainly is. That's what it is. A lamb. Yes, that's what it is, all right. What are you going to do with it, Phoebe?"

"Put it on the altar. In the chapel. For God."

"Does God chew gum, Phoebe? How did you know that? I didn't know that. Now ain't that something. Certainly is. It certainly is something that you knew . . ."

"NOT TO CHEW, ROSE! It's like, how did Reverend say it, it's 'symbotic.' That's it. 'Symbotic.' Gum is what I love. So this lamb is symbotic of me, of my love. So it'll be like me, on the altar. You see, like Jesus was symbotic of the lamb. Or the lamb was symbotic. I ain't too clear on that. But I just thought, since God's got so much to do, with the snowflakes and everything, and . . . I ain't got much. But . . . to cheer God up and help out, I'd give this . . . symbotic . . . gum lamb . . . of my love . . . or something like that."

Befuddled, Rose returned to her own thoughts and conversation. "Coke is good. Are two small Cokes more than one big one? But too much ice is not too nice. Slip on ice, slide on snow. Go and blow and stop the show."

"Rose!"

"Phoebe? It is you. I was listening. I was. I certainly was. I just got thirsty is what happened. Can we get a Coke, please. Can we? Please?"

"Rose. Rose. Dear, Rose. Come on. I got a quarter. We'll sneak down to the dining room machine." Sneak? No! One shuffled, the other swayed through the tunnel of The State Mental Hospital to the Coke machine in the dining room, then back to the women's geriatric ward and bed. Curious unlikely creatures in a curious unlikely place for curious unlikely reasons.

* * *

Then it was Christmas Eve, that holiest of times. After the lights were out, Phoebe and Rose snuck out again. It was easier this time, since most of the attendants were off. Down they went to the basement, into the tunnel, on to the little closet where Phoebe picked up her chewing gum lamb which, crude though it was, bore a striking resemblance to a real lamb, since the wads of gum did look surprisingly like tufts of wool. Then slowly the two friends made their way to the dining room and on up to the chapel above.

The chapel was plain, the floor wooden and creaky. The big windows were of clear glass through which, this night, came the soft light of a full moon. The pulpit was on one side of the small platform, the lectern on the other, as Thurston had properly arranged them. The altar was on the wall to the rear, and on it were two candles and a cross. A dark curtain ran halfway up the wall, and a tiny window, much like a porthole, or a Cyclopean eye, was near the top. In front of the platform was the communion rail. The pews sagged, which gave them a tired look, and there was a musty smell about the place. And it was very warm, warmer even than it usually is in a state building for old people. The two women stood timidly at the back, near the door.

"Shhh," whispered Phoebe.

"Shhh?" asked Rose. "Why? Somebody sleeping in here?"

"No. Ain't no service now. Just don't want nobody to hear us."

"Why? What are you going to do, Phoebe?" asked Rose.

"I ain't exactly sure. Say something, Rose. Something religious. You know. Anything."

"Religious? Something religious. Let me see. I should know something. I . . . Oh, yes. The Lord is my shepherd. I shall not' . . . not . . . ahh . . . shall not . . ."

"Want, Rose. Want."

"Want what, Phoebe? What?"

"Nothing, Rose. Just, 'I shall not want.' 'Want' is what you couldn't think of. 'The Lord is my shepherd, I shall not want.' "

"Don't be cross, Phoebe. I just forgot. I forgot. I . . . I'm going to cry. I don't think I like it in here alone like this."

"You ain't alone, Rose. I'm here. Now come on! I'll just put my lamb on the altar and we'll go. Come on."

"Phoebe, I don't like sneaking around like this. Don't like sneaking. Don't like creaking. Yellow's bad but black is sad and green is seen beneath the dream . . ."

"Shhh, Rose! Do you hear something?"

". . . beyond the scheme, the trees are bare, there's no cat hair, the night is spare, there is nowhere . . ."

"Rose! ROSE!"

"Yes? Oh, Phoebe. Yes, I'm listening. I am. I certainly am."

"Do you hear something, Rose? Do you? High, like music?"

"Do I hear. . . music? Do you? What is it, Phoebe? Why can't I hear it?"

"Listen. Listen. Where is it? Voices. Where are they coming from? Where? Where? Come on, Rose. We got to follow 'em. Come on.

They left the chapel and stood in the hallway, listening. To their left were the big wooden doors leading to the women's ward, second floor, and to their right, the same kind of doors leading to the second floor of the men's ward. Those doors were kept locked and looked formidable. But from behind the doors on the men's side came the sound of voices, weak but panicked voices, moans and screams without much volume, as from old men, sick, tired, confused. What looked like smoke was coming from under the doors.

"Look, Phoebe. Look. Look," cried Rose.

"I see. I see. Come on. Quick, quick."

As fast as they could, they moved down the hall and began pushing on the doors.

"Push, Rose. Push. Push," yelled Phoebe. "As hard as you can. Push."

"I am. I am, Phoebe. As hard as I can."

Big as the doors looked, they were old and had been ignored for years.

Their locks were old-fashioned, too, and gave way rather easily. The women pushed into the men's ward. It was full of steam—hot, live steam that made it hard to see and harder to breathe. Side gates were up on most beds, and many men were unable to get out of them without help. They were gasping, coughing. Those closest to the leaking steam pipe were being scalded as the steam gushed out from the pipe where it ran along the wall two- or three-feet off the floor. The pipes were unusually large because they not only carried steam for the entire wing, but also went from the heating plant, through this building, down into the tunnel, and on to three more buildings,

"We got to help these men get out, Rose," shouted Phoebe. "Through the doors. Quick, quick."

Somehow Rose and Phoebe were rejuvenated rather than panicked by the crisis. Coughing, they edged into the room, reaching the first men.

"I can't . . . see too good . . . Phoebe," Rose sputtered, reaching to take one of the old men's hands, then saying to him, "Here, this way . . . this way. Come on . . . that's it. Climb out . . . over the end. Never mind those bars . . . Come on . . . Phoebe . . . Phoebe, where are you?"

Phoebe was crawling along, pushing her lamb ahead of her and toward the hissing sound, following it to its source. The steam hissed and roared, tore at her lungs, clawed at her face, scalded her flesh, and seared her eyes whenever she opened them. Finally, she stood, held her gum lamb in front of her, and pushed it with all of her strength at the hissing sound. Slowly the sound muffled. She pushed harder. The steam dissipated slightly. With her hands she could feel where the joint had pulled loose. The heat softened the gum. As best she could, she stuffed it around the leaking wound in the pipe. Then she turned to help the man in the nearest bed. He was moaning. She tried to push the bed down the aisle toward the door. She couldn't see *very* well. Her eyes were swollen nearly shut. The pain came with a roar and then a yawning silence. She fell into a merciful blackness.

The next thing she knew, she was lying on her back and someone was holding something to her face, telling her to breathe. It hurt to breathe. She squinted into the light. Rose was holding her hand and crying, "Oh, Phoebe. Oh, Phoebe."

Phoebe could hear something way off. Was it a siren? Or music? She lifted her head, listening. A voice spoke: "Easy. Just take it easy."

She peered as best she could through her swollen lids and could just make out that she was in the chapel, up near the altar. People were moving around. They were all in white, like angels. Other people were lying in the nearby pews.

She could see another person in white, bending over her, looking at her with a bright light, talking in a deep voice to someone she couldn't see: "Some pretty bad burns here. Luckily, everyone got out alive. This woman is the worst. She's burned pretty bad. The word is that she helped save the others. I don't know what she used, but apparently she managed to stop the steam long enough for everyone to get out."

Phoebe pushed the oxygen mask away. She spoke hoarsely, "It was my gum lamb."

"Take it easy, ma'am," the voice said tenderly. Then to the unseen person, it asked more loudly, "What did she say?"

Another voice replied, "I didn't catch it."

"Her gum lamb," replied Rose. "That's what she done. Put her gum lamb on that busted pipe. Ain't that something? Oh, Phoebe. You got to be all right. You got to be. You hear me? You will be, won't you?"

Phoebe smiled and nodded. She had given what was 'symbotic' of her love where it was needed. She didn't understand it all, but she was pretty sure God would. In spite of what the Reverend had said to her, she believed what she'd done was a desecration, sort of like the baby Jesus in the stable. Like it, but different. Like snowflakes are alike, but different. She'd helped a little. She lifted her head again, and listened.

"Do you hear something, Rose," she rasped. "That music, do you hear it?"

"Music? Well . . . maybe I do. Yes, I think I do, Phoebe. Ain't that something? I do. I certainly do. I hear it, Phoebe. Really I do. I do hear it."

Ah yes, that music, do you hear it? Before you answer, you will do well to remember who really asks. For when the chariots of the Lord roll out on shafts of light and through timeless darkness, and break rank to wheel around planets such as our own, finding their way to curious and unlikely corners of it, for curious and unlikely reasons, bearing curious and unlikely messages, embodied in curious and unlikely creatures such as . . . well, who knows? Things are wilder by far than we think and more wondrous than we may yet have dared to believe. Do you hear the music?

> *"For you shall go out in joy and be led forth in peace; the mountains and the hills before you shall break forth into singing, and all the trees of the field shall clap their hands."*[1]

* * *

1 *Isaiah 55:12, RSV*

A Personal Epilogue
"Christmas in the Ruins"

One way or another, I always seem to ruin Christmas before it arrives. In committing the ugly deed, I have the usual accomplices everyone recognizes—the relentless rush and commercialism of the season, the depressing idealization and impossible expectations that gild the holiday, the pernicious mix of adrenaline and exhaustion. But when it comes down to it, I also manage to put my own fingerprints on the ruining. Each year I swear it will be different and strain to make it so. And yet . . .

I recall the year my wife Jan and I scheduled a dinner for friends a week or so before Christmas. On the morning of the party, we admitted to each other that we were too tired and pre-oecupied to enjoy it, and we fleetingly considered canceling out, but didn't. When our guests arrived, they hinted at having similar feelings. Apparently we'd all "pressed on" out of a sense of social obligation.

Not surprisingly, during the course of the evening the conversation got a bit heated. It was on some topic so important I can't remember it now. Whatever it was, it was laced with a lot of "men *always*, women *never*" comments that tie everyone in a knot of irritation and frustration. The party limped to a close in a mode of sulky civility. No one wanted to prolong the evening by trying to repair the breach we all felt.

When the guests finally left, my accumulated anger hung around like a vampire looking for blood to suck wherever it could be found. "Up on the house top, carp, carp, carp . . . down through the chimney, blame, blame, blame." I picked fights with whoever approached, which happened to be Jan and Smidgeon, our dog. Not only was I angry, I was *righteously* angry. I was not one of those "men *never*" types I'd been lumped with.

Like most righteous anger, mine had disastrous consequences. I was helping to clean up the kitchen as I prosecuted my case to an imaginary jury who nodded their heads in agreement with my every word. In the process of ranting and raving, I broke the handle off an old, flower-gilded, gold-rimmed pitcher that had been given to Jan by her beloved, departed grandmother.

I don't know if it was rage or despair, or a misguided impulse of self-justification, or a fit of perversity, but rather than apologize or examine the pitcher to see if it could be repaired, I hurled it to the floor. It smashed into a thousand pieces, the shards and splinters skittering through the kitchen, into the two adjoining rooms and down the stairs to the basement.

Tears filled Jan's eyes as she picked up a piece of the pitcher and held it in her hand. Then she looked at me and whispered, "It's too bad." Without another word, she left the kitchen. I listened to her climb the stairs and walk slowly to our bedroom.

I stood in the ache of silence and felt tears trickle down my cheeks as I realized I'd blown it again. Now it was too late for Christmas to be different this year. And, until that night, I'd been trying so hard! It occurred to me that maybe trying so hard to make it different was part of my problem. I leaned against the kitchen counter and stared at the pieces of porcelain lying on the floor, casualties of some strange warfare in me. Why wasn't I as good as I wanted to be?

I don't know how long I stood there, but my self-examination was interrupted by the sound of Jan's footsteps coming back down the stairs to the kitchen. Without a sideward glance, she got out the broom and dustpan, and in silence we began to sweep up the broken pitcher. I could not find words for my shame. It seemed pitiful to say, "I'm sorry," but I did, and Jan said, "I know." For what seemed a very long time, the only other sounds were Smidgeon's sympathetic whimpering, the swish of the broom, and the clinking of the porcelain being swept, picked up, and dropped in a trash bag.

Regret and remorse kept me awake most of the night. In the morning, Jan assured me of her forgiveness, for which I was grateful. Yet I knew her grandmother's cherished pitcher was no more, and worse, something had been broken in her granddaughter's heart. I also knew the breaking was typical of me. I felt a dull, lingering ache.

For the remaining days leading up to Christmas, I kept finding fragments and splinters of that shattered pitcher in strange places. I kept finding them even though I thought I'd found them all several times. I kept finding them in out-of-the-way corners when the light hit them just so—between the counter and the stove, under a chair, in the fold of a jacket hanging on a hook near the door, in small cracks in the wooden floor, behind a rubber boot, under the base of the telephone, on different risers of the basement stairs.

Each time I found another piece of that pitcher, I thought about how much it had meant to Jan, how it had been filled not only with water but with many memories, and much love, and all the hopes that immigrant grandmother had for her granddaughter. I wondered if her grandmother had purchased it at a secondhand store for some of the few pennies she'd saved from her work as a seamstress making buttonholes for suits sold at a large department store in the city. Whatever its story, this vessel of a grandmother's love was an accurate, priceless gift to Jan. I often thought about the piece Jan put on her dresser that night when I broke it.

I found what may have been the last piece of that pitcher before going to bed early

Christmas morning, after coming home from the midnight Christmas Eve Communion Service. Maybe it had fallen out of the trash bag, but however it got there, the small piece was lying on the driveway just where it intersected with the back alley. I found it because the light of the moon, or the stars, or neighbors' window, hit it just so.

It came to me then that maybe Christmas is like finding those pieces in curious places after the shattering happens. Finding little pieces and slivers of what Christmas means, of what the gift is, in the corners of our lives, in the cracks of our failures and ruinations, down the steps of defeats, and yet, in friends' small expressions of love and forgiveness and trust, in the chances to begin again, and again. Alleys and starlight. God here and there and everywhere. The light penetrating the darkness and hitting just so, unexpectedly, off what is broken and somehow mysteriously reflecting hope.

I picked up the broken piece from the driveway and held it as I walked to the back door, somewhere between Christmas Eve and Christmas morn. I remembered again a grandmother, a granddaughter, and then another woman who long ago had been in painful labor on this night and a child born in an out-of-the-way place, an accurate gift. God there, here, working in a broken world amidst broken people who break things. For the first time, I realized that Christmas isn't about anyone *making* it different. It's about our being aware that it *really is* different, more different than we dare to hope.

I went into the house, through the kitchen, up the stairs and into the bedroom. I put the piece of the pitcher I'd found next to the piece Jan kept on her dresser. This little thing, this token, no matter where it had come from, was truly a gift, reminding me that I hadn't really ruined Christmas—I had found it. Or, more's the truth, Christmas had found me.

* * *

About the Author

The Rev. Dr. Theodore W. Loder was the senior minister of one of Philadelphia's most unusual churches, the First United Methodist Church of Germantown (FUMCOG), for almost thirty-eight years. With imagination and intensity, Loder led FUMCOG to the fore-front of artistic endeavors, political activism, and social justice. His congregation was a Public Sanctuary Church, a founding church of the Covenant Against Apartheid in South Africa, a Reconciling Congregation that advocates for the rights of homosexual persons.

Loder's own social action grew out of a long history of involvement in social causes, including marching with Dr. Martin Luther King Jr. in the sixties. Loder was cofounder of Metropolitan Career Center (a job-training program for high school dropouts); cofounder of Plowshares (a nonprofit housing renovation corporation); and cofounder of Urban Resource Development Corporation (an ecumenical effort to rehabilitate abandoned houses). He also served on the Philadelphia Mayor's Advisory Commission of Children and Families.

For many people who have "given up" on the church, Loder brought a breath of fresh air. His blend of scholarship (cum laude degree from Yale Divinity School, a university fellow of the Yale Graduate School, and two honorary doctorates) and creativity (named by the National Observer as "One of America's Outstanding Creative Preachers") stimulated his refreshing openness to hard questions, to change, to relevance, to justice, and to joy. Dr. Loder served on the National Advisory Board of the National Council of the Churches of Christ in the USA. Loder died in 2021 at the age of 90.

About the Artist

An internationally known painter, Ed Kerns is professor of Art Emeritus and was Chair of the Department at Lafayette College in Easton, Pennsylvania. He has mounted more than thirty one-person shows in galleries in New York, Philadelphia, and other major cities. He has also participated in more than 150 group exhibitions in the United States, France, Italy, Switzerland, and Mexico. His work is in numerous public and corporate collections, and has been reviewed in many journals, magazines, and newspapers. Kerns, whose interests include painting and digital imagery, was awarded the Clapp Professorship in 1988. Through scholar research projects, independent studies, and honors projects, he has mentored more than four hundred students.